ARIE SELINGER'S

POWER VOLLEY-BALL

ARIE SELINGER'S POWER VOLLEYBALL

St. Martin's Press
New York

All figures (with the exception of figures
6-3–6-11) were computer generated by Arie
Selinger.

Book design by Peter A. Davis

Library of Congress Cataloging in Publication
Data

Selinger, Arie.
  Arie Selinger's power volleyball.

  1. Volleyball.   I. Ackermann-Blount, Joan.
II. Title.   III. Title: Power volleyball.
GV1015.3.S45   1986   796.32′5   86-13816
ISBN 0-312-04916-1
ISBN 0-312-04915-3 (paperback)

First Edition

10 9 8 7 6 5 4 3 2 1

To my magnificent player,
my friend and teacher,
Flo Hyman.
Her remarkable contributions
to volleyball can never be forgotten.
A giant in stature and in spirit,
she will always live in my heart.

ACKNOWLEDGMENTS

Many thanks go to Marlon Sano, Jim Coleman, and Mario Treibitch for their helpful input, support, and suggestions on the contents of the book. Thanks also to Dr. Gideon Ariel and Danny Saar at the Coto Research Center for their biomechanical computerized data and insight of data analysis. And to Fifi Oscard, whose enthusiasm helped to initiate the project. A very special thanks goes to Jess Money for his invaluable contributions in editing and writing in the final stages of the book.

Co-author's Note: Because this book is written for both men and women and because both women and men play volleyball, we have taken the unusual step of alternating the "he" and "she" personal pronouns in each chapter.

—Joan Ackermann-Blount

CONTENTS

1   BASIC ELEMENTS

The Court ● Court Directions ● The Net ● The Ball ● The Team and Substitutes ● Player Position and Rotation Order ● The Game ● The Flow of the Game ● Phases and Skills of the Game ● Protocol ● The Most Common Fouls ● Roles of the Officials

2   TEAM COMPOSITION

Player Specialization ● Categories of Players ● Alignments and Arrangements ● Ranking Players ● Considerations for Court Alignment ● Alignment of Players ● The 4-2 Team Composition ● The 6-2 Team Composition ● The 5-1 Team Composition

3   THE SERVE

Types of Serves ● Serving Techniques ● The Ultimate Serve ● Preparation for Serving ● Time Element ● Serving Tactics

4   SERVE RECEPTION AND PASSING

The Pass ● Team Serve Reception

5   THE SET

Basic Setting Technique ● Setting for the Setter

6   THE ATTACK

Individual Attack ● Summary of Spiking Techniques ● Varying the Spike ● Team Attack—Formations ● Organizing the Attack ● Spiker Coverage

7   THE BLOCK

Basic Concepts of Blocking ● Individual Blocker's Technique ● Double Block ● Triple Block ● Blocking Strategy ● Blocking Adjustments

8   FLOOR DEFENSE

Basic Concepts of Defense ● Perimeter/See-and-Respond Defense ● Individual Defensive Skills ● Team Formations ● Man-Up Defense ● Man-Down Defense

*I*NTRODUCTION

This book is written for any coach, player, or fan interested in learning more about one of the fastest-growing sports in the country, *power* volleyball. The book aims to teach a detailed understanding of the game and to present principles that coaches or players can use as a foundation to create their own game. By presenting the "how" and the "why" behind basic skills, systems, and game strategy, I hope to stimulate thinking so that these principles become the basis for further exploration.

The ideas presented are a product of many years of experience, a careful and logical analysis of the game, and extensive biomechanical testing. They are primarily a result of the years I spent coaching the U.S. Women's National team from 1975 to 1984. During that period we developed a distinctive American style of play that has already become a standard for other teams. This style combines the quickness, skill, and finesse of the Asian style with the power of the Eastern European. As a result, the U.S. Women's team became one of the top three teams in the world and won a Silver Medal in the 1984 Olympics.

I see volleyball as a game of expectations, a game played primarily in emergency situations. Whereas many coaches tend to emphasize the most stable body positions for the execution of the fundamental skills, I emphasize the execution of skills in motion in the least stable body position. For me, the realization that volleyball is a geometrical game of angles led to the development of many unconventional techniques. Perfecting these basic techniques is a never-ending process for the player; basic volleyball skills demand continuous practice and repetition at any level of the game.

Because power volleyball is such a young sport, it is sorely lacking in adequate terminology. I have attempted in this book to introduce some terms to enrich the language of the game, to give players and coaches terms with which to communicate. Some of the terms I introduce here may catch on; others won't. I only know that volleyball will benefit enormously when it acquires a language that can fully convey its complexities and subtleties.

During the past decade volleyball has changed tremendously, not only in rules, techniques, and concepts, but also in the physical abilities of the players. Perhaps more than any other sport, power volleyball allows expression of the athlete's fullest capabilities. There is no reason to believe that the future will hold any less change and development. I hope that the ideas presented in this book will inspire players and coaches to do some creative thinking for themselves and come up with new ideas. I'm grateful for the opportunity to be a part in shaping a game possessed of such beauty, grace, and extraordinary inner logic—*American* volleyball.

—Arie Selinger
Laguna Niguel, California
September 1985

ARIE SELINGER'S
POWER VOLLEY-BALL

BASIC ELEMENTS

The purpose of this chapter is to acquaint the novice with the basic elements and terms of volleyball, and to present a broad view of the game. The sequence of events outlined in "Phases and Skills of the Game" provides the order for the remaining chapters: the serve, serve reception, the set, the attack, the block, and the floor defense. Once the reader has an overview of the game, he can proceed to the following chapters for a detailed analysis of each phase.

THE COURT

The court dimensions are 9m by 18m (29'6" by 59'). These measurements are made from the outside of the boundary lines; therefore, the sidelines and endlines are included in the playing area. The center line divides the entire playing court into two equal courts of 9m by 9m each. Each court is divided into two unequal zones, the front court and the back court, by the attack lines, which are located 3m (9'10") from the center line. Two service lines, each 15cm long, mark the service zone behind the right rear corner. All court lines are 5cm (2") in width. At least 2 meters of unobstructed space must surround the court, and the height of the ceiling must be at least 7m (27') (Figure 1–1).

The court dimensions create the nature of the game, making it a reaction game. Because of the limited court space, the fast unpredictable ball patterns require economical body movements to

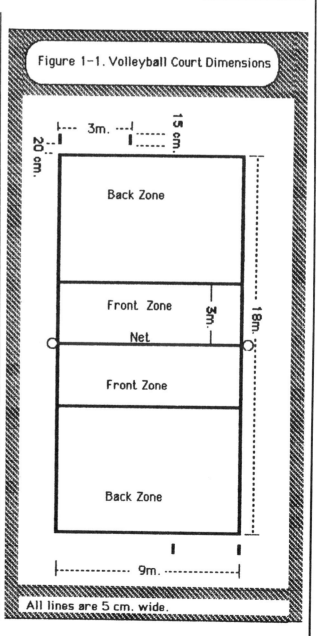

Figure 1-1. Volleyball Court Dimensions

Back Zone

Front Zone

Net

Front Zone

Back Zone

3m.

15 cm.

20 cm.

3m.

18m.

9m.

All lines are 5 cm. wide.

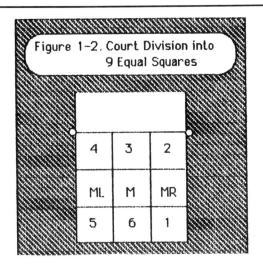

Figure 1–2. Court Division into 9 Equal Squares

4	3	2
ML	M	MR
5	6	1

react quickly over a short distance. The relationships between the court dimensions, the number of players, and the net height are directly responsible for player selection, specificity of training, movement mechanics, and game strategy. Most importantly, they demand carefully designed systems of play and well-defined traffic patterns to facilitate team coordination.

Even though the court appears to be small, it is very difficult for six players to cover all of it; the court dimensions require the utmost of human athletic performance (Figure 1–2). A well-trained athlete can only cover a distance of about 10 feet in a second in response to a cue. Therefore, if the court is divided into nine equal squares of 3m by 3m, it can be illustrated that with six players, it is only possible to cover six of the squares when there is less than one second to respond. As a result, a variety of defensive methods have been advanced over the years that attempt to protect one part of the court, but always at the expense of another.

Similarly, in designing attack, a coach can't ignore the relationships between the width of the court, the opponent's player distribution, and the time element. The width of the court can be covered easily given enough time, but if the time is greatly reduced, it becomes almost impossible for even three blockers to cover the net adequately. Therefore, a logical and effective attack should be quick and deceptive, using several spikers in combination attacks.

Court Directions

Volleyball is a three-dimensional game with three entities: the court, the ball, and the players. It can be a confusing task to describe the relationships between these three entities with regard to position and movement; terms for players' move-

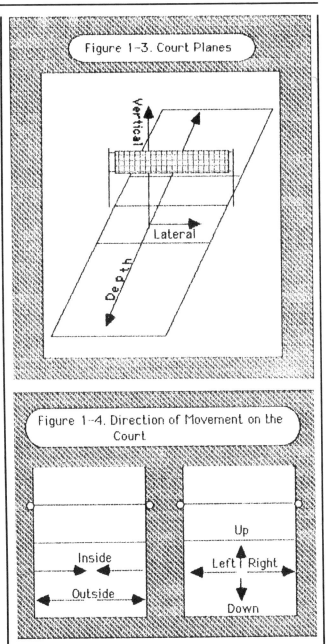

Figure 1–3. Court Planes

Figure 1–4. Direction of Movement on the Court

ments and court directions have to be clearly defined.

In Reference to the Court

The lateral plane is parallel to the net, and describes the width of the court. A player's movement on the lateral plane is to the right and to the left (Figure 1–3). When a player moves from a sideline toward the middle of the court, he is moving "inside"; when he moves from the middle of the court toward a sideline, he is moving "outside" (Figure 1–4). The *vertical* dimension is perpendicular to the floor and describes height. When a player moves up and down in this dimension, the terms "high" and "low" are used to describe his body position; these terms are also applicable to the ball's movement.

The *depth* dimension is parallel to the sidelines, and describes the longitudinal direction on the court. Movement toward the net is "up" and movement from the net toward the base line is "down." The closer to the base line a player is, the "deeper" he is. A ball that is served near the base line is a "deep" serve.

In Reference to the Players

Sideways movement is done along the body's *frontal plane,* which is described by the shoulder line. Forward and backward movement is done along the body's *sagital plane,* which is described by a line from front to back perpendicular to the frontal plane. A player's movement "high" and "low" (jumping and squatting) is done on the *vertical plane,* which is described by a line from head to toe; this vertical plane always coincides with the vertical plane of the court.

The term "horizontal" is reserved to describe the universal plane that is parallel to the court floor. Horizontal can, then, be used to describe ball movement or player movement in any given direction on that plane. A served ball, for instance, and a set ball can be said to travel horizontally, even though the served ball travels along the longitudinal plane and the set ball travels along the lateral plane.

THE NET

The net is 1m (39") wide and 9.5m (32') long. The mesh is composed of squares 10cm by 10cm (4" × 4"). Along the full length of the top of the net is a double thickness of white canvas within which is a cable. A cord runs along the bottom of the net to keep it tight. A strip of white tape, 5cm (2") wide and 1m (39") long, is positioned on each side of the net over the corresponding sidelines. These vertical tapes (side markers) are within bounds and are included in the playing area. An antenna is placed on the outside of each of the two tapes to mark the vertical side limits of the court; each antenna extends 80cm (32") above the height of the net, and the distance between the inside of both antennas should be 9m (26'6").

The net is placed over the middle of the center line. Although the height of the net is sometimes reduced for certain youth age-group competitions, in general the net height is 2.24m (7'4-⅛") for women and 2.43m (7'11-⅝") for men. The two ends of the net must be at the same height above the floor and can not vary more than 2cm (¾").

The net should be taken into consideration in the development of offensive and defensive skills and game strategies. It should not be looked upon as an obstacle, but rather as an integral and challenging part of the game. The team should learn to exert its presence and dominance through the net. Since players are not allowed to touch the net at any time, a player must learn to manipulate his body in such a way that he can react and exploit certain situations without committing any net violations. Players may block over the net, but they may not reach over it and contact the ball before the completion of the opponent's attack.

A player should learn to use the net as a reference point for three-dimensional orientation, for court position, and for gauging ball speed and direction. The presence of the net has to be so deeply rooted in the player's subconscious that he learns to control the net rather than be controlled by it.

THE BALL

The ball is made of twelve or more pieces of uniform material, usually leather or vinyl, and is light colored, preferably white. The specifications for the ball are:

Circumference	62–68cm	(25–27")
Weight	260–280g	(9–10 oz)
Inside pressure	.40–.45kg/cm	(5.5–6.5 lbs/sq in)

A unique characteristic of the game of volleyball is that at no time is the ball possessed; it is continuously redirected from one point to another by brief contacts. Thus, volleyball is a rebound game, so the physical laws and properties of the ball should be clearly understood and exploited.

Ironically, some players fail to understand that the ball is round, and actually treat it as if it were square. Indeed, the ball is round, and has special aerodynamic properties that should be taken advantage of. The ball can be given top, side, or underspin, depending on where it is hit relative to its center of gravity; or, it can be hit through its center of gravity to create what is called a "float," whose wobbling, unpredictable flight path is similar to that of a baseball knuckleball.

The volleyball will rebound off an object at a predictable angle that is equivalent to the angle of incidence. Because of its high coefficient of elasticity, a volleyball will rebound quickly with only slightly less velocity than its incoming speed prior to contact. The ball responds according to where the contact is made on its surface, how it is struck (with what force and in what direction), and the timing of the impact. To control the direction and the velocity of the ball, a player should learn to adjust his muscle tension to "cushion" the ball. Controlling the angle of rebound is accomplished by varying body postures. The amount of spin on the ball can be controlled by varying the point of contact with the ball. Even though the ball is fairly light, when it travels at a high velocity it generates a great momentum that delivers a hard, heavy impact; a player has to be physically and mentally ready to receive such a ball.

Since the human body and the ball are equally subject to the force of gravity, a player and a ball will fall to the floor from the same height at the same rate. This is a simple idea, but one of which every player should be keenly aware.

THE TEAM AND SUBSTITUTES

A team consists of twelve or fewer players. Only six players are allowed on the court at any given time. The starting six, called the starting lineup, is usually, but not necessarily, the strongest combination within the team. Prior to each game, the coach must submit a list of the starting lineup to the umpire. The remaining six players are called substitutes.

Substitution rules vary. Many high-school and college matches in this country are played with substitution rules that are more liberal than the international substitution rules. Under international rules, a team is allowed to make six substitutions during each game. Substitutions can be called at any time during the game, and any number of the six substitutions may be made at one time. Once one player substitutes for another, those two players are paired and may only substitute for each other during that particular game. A

starting player can be taken out and then returned to the game only once in each game. In U.S. high-school and women's college matches, each player, the starter and the substitute, may leave and re-enter the game up to three times.

The stricter international substitution rules require each player to be proficient in both front-row and back-court skills. The looser American NAGWS (National Association of Girls' and Women's Sports) rules encourage more specialization and offer greater tactical opportunities for the coach.

PLAYER POSITION AND ROTATION ORDER

The six starting players line up on the court in specific court positions numbered 1 through 6, starting at the serving zone and advancing clockwise (Figure 1–5). Players in positions 2, 3, and 4 are front-court or front-row players; RF stands for right front player, CF for center front, and LF for left front. Players in positions 1, 6, and 5 are back-court or back-row players; RB stands for right back player, CB for center back, and LB for left back (Figure 1–6).

At the moment the ball is hit by the server, all players on both teams must be in position according to rotation. At least a part of one foot of each front-line player must be closer to the court's cen-

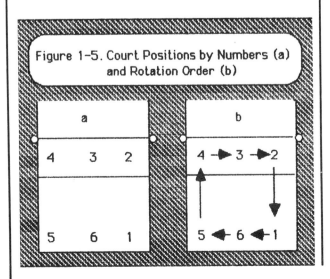

Figure 1–5. Court Positions by Numbers (a) and Rotation Order (b)

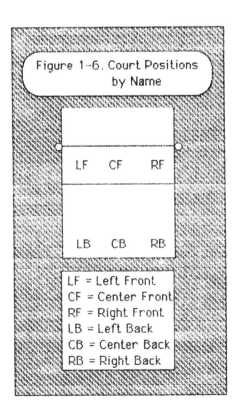

Figure 1-6. Court Positions by Name

LF = Left Front
CF = Center Front
RF = Right Front
LB = Left Back
CB = Center Back
RB = Right Back

ter line than either foot of his corresponding back-line player; the players in positions 2, 3, and 4 have to be in front of the players in positions 1, 6, and 5 respectively. A foot of the RF player, or the RB player must be closer to the right sideline than a foot of the CF or the CB player respectively. Similarly, a foot of the LF or the LB player must be closer to the left sideline than a foot of the CF or CB player respectively. If the players are not in their proper positions, the referee will penalize them for an "overlapping" violation.

However, as soon as the server has made contact with the ball, players may move to any court position with no restrictions, except that back-row players are not allowed to block or attack from within the front court. Although the rules governing rotation and player positions seem restrictive, they leave ample room to create deceptive serve-reception formations. They also allow for a high degree of player specialization. Both topics will be discussed in greater detail in the following chapters.

THE GAME

The object of the game is to send the ball over the net in such a way that the opponent is unable to return it without committing a fault. Each team is allowed three consecutive contacts with the ball. Since a player may not contact the ball two consecutive times, a team's allotted three hits will be performed by either two or three players. In some cases, as in blocking or digging a spiked ball, the ball may be returned to the opposition after only one or two contacts.

After the 1976 Olympics, the rules were amended so that if a ball touches the hands of front-line players who are blocking, that contact does not constitute one of the three hits. This rule change has contributed to longer rallies and added greatly to the excitement of the game.

Points are scored only by the serving team. If the team receiving serve fails to return the ball correctly over the net, the serving team scores a point and continues to serve. If the serving team makes an error on the serve, or fails to correctly play a ball returned by their opponent, then the opponent gains the right to serve, called a "side-out." Following a side-out, and just prior to the serve, each player on the serving team rotates one position clockwise (Figure 1–5).

The first team to score 15 points wins the game as long as there is at least a 2-point lead. If two teams are tied at 14–14, play continues until one team has a 2-point margin of victory. The first team

to win three out of five games wins the match. After each game, the teams change sides and alternate serves. If the match goes to the fifth game, a coin toss is used to determine which team gets the choice of serving or picking the court side. In a fifth game, the teams change sides as soon as one team scores 8 points.

THE FLOW OF THE GAME

In volleyball, there is a sequence of six distinct phases that repeats itself over and over, creating a rhythmical flow. These six phases are the serve; service reception; set; attack (service-reception attack or transition attack); block; and floor defense. Figure 1–7 illustrates this sequence, which begins with Team A serving. After the serve, Team B receives the serve, sets and executes a serve-reception attack. During Team B's attack, Team A blocks and plays floor defense behind the block.

This sequence can be disrupted and terminated at any time, or it can go into a cycle alternating between one team's attack and the other's defense. One such complete cycle is called a rally. At some point play will be halted, either by a fault or by the successful execution of a particular skill, usually blocking or spiking, by one team. Depend-

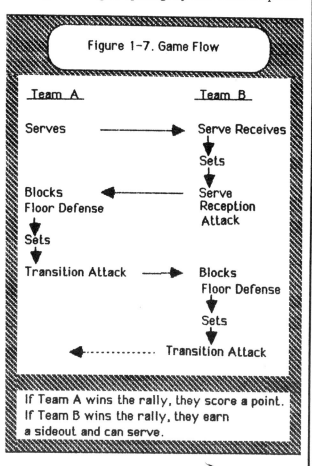

Figure 1-7. Game Flow

Team A		Team B
Serves	⟶	Serve Receives
		↓
		Sets
		↓
Blocks	⟵	Serve
Floor Defense		Reception
↓		Attack
Sets		
↓		
Transition Attack	⟶	Blocks
		Floor Defense
		↓
		Sets
		↓
⟵		Transition Attack

If Team A wins the rally, they score a point.
If Team B wins the rally, they earn
a sideout and can serve.

ing on which team wins the rally, the result is either a point or a side-out.

PHASES AND SKILLS OF THE GAME

The Serve

Play begins when the ball is served by the RB player. The serve must be executed from the serving zone, and the ball must be hit with one hand or any part of the arm. The distance behind the endline is limited only by tactical considerations or free space. The simple objective of serving is to put the ball into play by getting it over the net. At an advanced level of play, the serve becomes an important element of the team's attack and overall strategy, and is often a chance to gain a point.

The overhand and the roundhouse serving techniques are the most commonly used; these produce the float and the top spin, the most popular serves. Recently some men's teams have revived the spiking, or jump serve, with some success.

Serve Reception

Just prior to the serve, the serve-receiving team gets ready for serve reception by assuming certain positions on the court, positions that create serve-reception formations. There are a variety of serve-reception formations. The most commonly used are the *U* (semimoon) formation, using four players (Figure 1–8), and the *W* formations, using five players (Figure 1–9). Any formation can be used as long as the players remain in their proper positions by the rules of rotation. The two main considerations in choosing a formation are its effectiveness in serve reception, and the serve-reception attack that it leads into.

Otani of the Japanese National Team executes a roundhouse serve.

Flo Hyman of the 1984 USA Olympic Team executes an overhand serve.

The objective in receiving serve is to accurately redirect the served ball to a designated player, the setter, who stands in a designated target area.

The ball that is redirected to a setter is called a "pass," and the action of executing a pass is called "passing." The most commonly used passing technique is the forearm pass. On some occasions during rallies, certain balls may be passed to the setter with the overhand finger pass, a technique similar to setting.

The target area for each team can vary; some teams have more than one, a primary target and a secondary. Most teams position their setter at the net about 10 feet from the right sideline. Depending on where the setter is in the rotation, he either awaits the passed ball at the target area, or moves to it while the served ball is in the air.

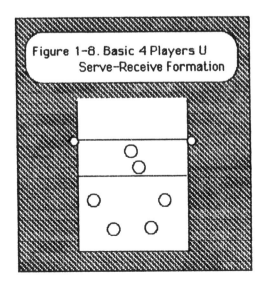

Figure 1–8. Basic 4 Players U Serve-Receive Formation

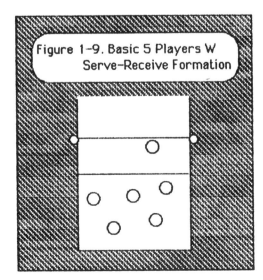

Figure 1–9. Basic 5 Players W Serve-Receive Formation

The passer should accurately deliver the ball to the setter to facilitate an effective serve-reception attack.

The Set

A set is a ball that is carefully propelled along a certain trajectory to a certain position so that a teammate can attack it comfortably. (Like the quarterback in football, the setter is the player who is responsible for directing a team's attack. When a properly executed pass has been directed to the setter in the target area, the setter will set the ball to a selected attacker.)

If the pass is off course and pulls the setter out of the target area, he will not have as many options and may be forced to set one particular hitter.

In a broad sense, a set can be defined as any ball that is followed by an attack (a spike, tip, etc.). A set is usually, but not necessarily, a team's second contact with the ball. In an organized game, setting is very refined and precise. It requires specific techniques and a great deal of skill. Setting is far more than just the mere placement of a ball in the air for an attacker; it is the key to an organized, well-timed, and well-coordinated offense.

The set is most commonly executed over the head with the fingertips of both hands; this technique is often referred to as the overhead pass. I simply call it a "set," and its execution "setting." An experienced setter can also execute a good set with the fingertips of one hand. During emergency situations, setters and other players must at times revert to a forearm set, a set executed with the forearms. Forearm setting is essentially the same as forearm passing.

Similarly, finger passing and finger setting both

Debbie Green, the setter for the 1984 USA Olympic Team, executes a jump set.

refer to essentially the same technique, but there are subtle differences in timing and touch. Through much practice, setters develop a special soft "touch," which is the ability to contact and control the ball with a smooth, gentle action. This soft setting touch prolongs the contact with the ball, providing more control.

The Attack

The attack is the culmination of all the team's efforts; more points are scored by the attack than by any other phase of the game. The term *attack* does not refer to any particular skill, but rather is a broad term that includes all the offensive skills and related maneuvers. Serve reception, defense, and the set all combine to determine the nature and quality of the attack.

The attack phase actually begins when the pass is delivered to the setter and the attackers jump. The pass (or dig) is the cue that sets the rhythm for the attack. The set determines the location and timing of the attack. The attack culminates when

the attacker contacts the ball, attempting to score a point or earn a side-out. The spike is the most conspicuous, glamorous, and powerful tool of the attack; more points are won with the spike than with any other technique.

There are two distinct attack phases: serve-reception attack and transition attack. Serve-reception attack is executed by the serve-receiving team immediately following serve reception; it can only earn a side-out. It is more sophisticated than the transition attack because it can be preplanned. For serve-reception attack, the setter and attackers communicate verbally or with finger signals prior to the serve.

Every other attack during the game is called "transition" attack; "transition" is used because the spike occurs at the conclusion of the transition from defense to attack. Depending on which team served, transition attack can earn a side-out or score a point. Usually it transpires spontaneously under extreme time pressure. Communication among players is accomplished primarily with eye contact and body language; over time, teammates develop a shared experience and common knowledge that further improve communication. Their reactions and executions of certain skills become instinctive and automatic.

The attack in volleyball has changed over the

Craig Buck of the 1984 USA Olympic Team executes a spike.

Terry Place Brandel of the 1980 USA Olympic Team executes a spike.

years more than any other phase of the game, and these changes have had a strong impact on the nature of the game. Volleyball players are taller, stronger, and more athletically capable. Attack tactics have changed as well, becoming more sophisticated and challenging. Most advanced volleyball teams execute quick, deceptive attack patterns called "multiple" or "combination" attack. In recent years, advanced teams have even incorporated back-court players into their attack formations.

All the efforts that have been made by the international volleyball federation to create more of a balance between offense and defense have been ineffective. The attack is still dominant. The answer to creating a more balanced game is not a simple one, and I don't think it lies in changing the rules. To create more balance there must be an improvement in defense, a time-consuming process requiring much dedication and a change in the attitudes of many coaches.

The Block

While one team attacks, the other team plays defense. The defense has two parts that are closely interrelated but still distinctly different: the block, and the floor defense. The first line of defense, *blocking* is the action of intercepting an attacked ball before, during, or immediately after it crosses the net.

The player's arms must be above the height of the net to constitute a block. Only the three front-court players are allowed to block, and the block can be formed by one, two, or three players, depending on the situation and the team strategy.

Blocking has several objectives:

1. to score a point or side-out by aggressively reaching over the net in an attempt to deflect a spiked ball downward into the opponent's court. This is called an "attack" block, or "kill" block.

Paula Weishoff (#1) and Carolyn Becker (#6) block Hirose during World Cup games in Japan, 1981.

2. to keep the ball in play by contacting it, reducing its velocity, and lifting it up to allow the back-line defense to receive it more easily. This is called a "soft" block.
3. to screen part of the court from the opponent's direct hard attack. This is called an "area" block.
4. to intimidate the opponent.

Blocking is a difficult skill that requires experience, timing, coordination, mastery of certain mechanics, and an understanding of the game.

Floor Defense

Players who do not participate in blocking assume assigned positions on the court, forming the floor defense. The main objective of the floor defense is to prevent a ball that penetrates the first line of defense, the block, from touching the floor. The distribution of the players on the court depends on the defensive strategy of the team, the location of the block, and on the particular situation.

The most common defensive formations are the "man-up" (Figure 1–10), and the "man-down" (Figure 1–11), or variations and combinations of the two. Some teams prefer to arrange their defensive players around the periphery of the court, and move from the outside to the inside. Other teams position their floor-defense players closer to the center of the court and have them move from in to out. Such differences are purely a matter of tactical consideration, and are often influenced by the agility and defensive capabilities of the players.

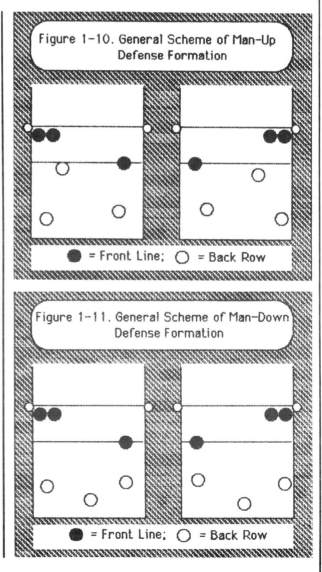

Figure 1–10. General Scheme of Man-Up Defense Formation

● = Front Line; ○ = Back Row

Figure 1–11. General Scheme of Man-Down Defense Formation

● = Front Line; ○ = Back Row

The forearm dig is the primary technique used in floor defense.

After the coin toss, both teams enter and line up on their respective sides. Players and coaches exchange gifts following the official presentation.

Most attacked balls are retrieved with the forearms in an underhand motion called "digging." A ball so retrieved is called a "dig." Actually, the forearm dig, the forearm pass, and the forearm set are essentially the same skill; each term is useful to designate a specific phase of the game.

Protocol

According to international protocol, it is customary for both teams to enter the playing court about twenty minutes prior to the official start of the competition. Just before entering, a coin toss is used to determine which team has the choice of court or service. The two teams enter the playing court and line up on their respective sides at which time presentation of the players, coaches, and officials is made. Following the presentation, the captains, coaches, and the teams exchange gifts.

At the end of the ceremony each team has either a three-minute separate warm-up or a five-minute joint warm-up. The team that wins the right to serve warms up first and the other team must clear the court.

Because Americans are used to having ball games and sporting events start right after player introductions, most high-school and college matches have a slightly different protocol. At these matches, the teams complete all warm-ups prior to introductions; they proceed to start the first game immediately after the handshake. Usually the gift exchange is omitted in these matches.

Since athletic events are also cultural events that exhibit good will as well as sportsmanship, it would be nice if all volleyball matches incorporated the international protocol to lend an air of formality and tradition to the event.

THE MOST COMMON FOULS

Of the many possible fouls in a game, the following are the most common. A team loses the serve or a point if:

1. A served ball touches the net or goes out of bounds without being touched by the opponent.
2. A player mishandles the ball by holding it.
3. The ball touches the ground or goes off the court and can not be saved by a teammate.
4. A player touches the net.
5. A team is out of rotation, overlapped, at the service.
6. A player makes two consecutive contacts with the ball. There are only two occasions when a player may legally touch the ball twice in a row. The first is when a player is passing or digging. Specifically, this means that a hard-hit ball can touch more than one part of the body when a player attempts to pass or dig it. The second is during blocking, when a player may block a ball and then play the rebound.
7. A back-court player jumps to spike the ball in front of the 3-meter line. It is permissible, how-ever, for a back-court player to jump behind the 3-meter line, spike the ball, and then land in front of the 3-meter line.
8. A team contacts the ball more than three times. A ball that bounces back off the hands of the block does not constitute a touch. After a ball hits the block, a team is still allowed three more contacts.

When a foul is committed, the referee blows a whistle and the game stops. The team that committed the foul either loses the right to serve or loses a point.

ROLES OF THE OFFICIALS

Volleyball is a judgment game. There are seven officials: the referee, who is aided by the umpire; the official scorer; and four linesmen.

The referee is the top man. His decision is final, and he is able to overrule any of the other officials. The referee is always elevated. The umpire stands on the floor and assists the referee. His responsibilities are to observe the net and the center line, to verify the lineups of both teams, to conduct the substitutions, and to observe the benches.

Each linesman is responsible for one of the two sidelines or one of the two back lines. A linesman watches to see if a ball lands within bounds or goes out of bounds; also, to see whether or not a player touches the ball before it goes out of bounds. The linesman also notes when a ball touches the block.

The scorer keeps a record of points, substitutions, and the serving order. If the serving order is violated, the scorer notifies the umpire, who signals the referee to stop the game.

At high levels of competition, such as in the Olympics or the Pan American Games, it is common to have a jury to oversee the match and make sure that all rules and regulations are followed. In case there is a dispute, the jury must make a decision. The jury has the power to dismiss the referee.

2

TEAM COMPOSITION

Simply described, team composition refers to the number of primary spikers and setters in the lineup. What I call "team composition" other coaches and books often refer to as "offensive system." The term "offensive system" is not, I feel, an accurate description of the concept it expresses. It limits itself only to attack. Indeed, team composition does affect the offensive system, but it also has far-reaching effects on other aspects of team function and performance.

There are three basic team compositions: the 4–2, the 6–2, and the 5–1. The first digit indicates the number of primary spikers on the team, and the second digit indicates the number of primary setters. A 4–2 team composition, for instance, indicates that there are four spikers, and two setters who are nonspikers. Each team composition has its tactical advantages and disadvantages. It is the coach's task to choose a team composition that meets her own game philosophy and maximizes her team's abilities. Choosing a team composition is an area where coaches often aim too low, underestimating their own players' abilities to understand and per-

form a more advanced form of team composition.

This chapter discusses the fundamental considerations a coach should take into account in choosing team composition.

PLAYER SPECIALIZATION

Specialization of players, in compliance with the rules of the game, is a prerequisite to a successful team. In simple terms, specialization means training each individual player for one or two particular tasks rather than training all the players for all the functions. Underlying the specialization concept is the assumption that the fewer functions an individual player has to learn, the greater the chance that she will become more proficient in performing those functions. It is the responsibility of the coach to identify the physical, technical, and mental potential of each individual player to perform certain tasks, and then train her for those particular functions. Specificity of training not only allows players to develop proper motor habits in the shortest possible time, but it also maximizes their potential. Once the performance of each individual player is maximized, then all players are combined into a harmonious team; the resulting performance is often better than the sum of its individual parts. This effect I often refer to as the "seventh dimension."

According to the rules, a player must play three rotations in the front court and three rotations in the back court. However, in either the front or back court, the player should specialize in only one position—left, right, or center. Each player should play only one front-court position (attack and defense) and one back-court position (defense and setting or back-row attack). To accomplish this, players must learn how to switch position in the front and back court during the flow of the game. Switching is done in three different phases of the game: after serving; during and after serve receiving; and during and after the attack. These switching maneuvers are specifically discussed later.

Besides specialization by position, there is also specialization by function. There are two distinct areas of players' functional specialization: setting and attacking. Because defense skills are vital to all players, specialization in defense is by position. Each player is either a setter or an attacker, and plays defense in two positions only; one in the front court, and one in the back court.

Reducing the number of tasks a player must learn maximizes practice time. The team can be divided into groups by function and court position. Each group can then be drilled according to the specific demands of their role in attack, and position in defense.

In addition to maximizing practice time, player specialization also promotes team coordination. Each player is always surrounded on the court by the same two players, allowing them to get used to each other and develop harmonious, intuitive reactions to fast-developing game situations.

CATEGORIES OF PLAYERS

Players are divided into two broad categories: hitters and setters. The hitters category is further divided into three subcategories by court position: left-side hitters, called "ace players" (A); center player, often referred to as "quick attackers" (C); right-side hitters, called "option players" (O).

Normally, there are two players for each subcategory who are positioned opposite each other in the rotation. In the 5–1 team composition, the player who plays opposite the setter is called a "utility player" (U). The utility player is considered to be the setter's pair, and usually plays right side.

The Setter

The setter is the playmaker and architect of the team's attack. During the game it is up to the setter to decide which spiker to set. She is probably the most important player on the team. The success of a team usually correlates with the quality of the setter, for no other player affects the team performance as much. Great attention must be given to selecting and developing the setter. It takes more time to develop a quality setter than any other position on the team.

The setter should have a natural sense and feel for the ball, plus extraordinary physical ability. She must be mentally tough and tenacious, a fierce competitor, yet cool under pressure. In addition, the setter must possess positive leadership qualities, an amiable personality, and a positive attitude toward the rest of the team. The setter must inspire cohesiveness and cooperation on the team, and should be willing to assume responsibility for an unsuccessful attack. The setter and the coach must have good communication and an understanding of each other, because during competition, while the coach sits on the bench, the setter directs the team.

The Center Player

Center players are often called quick attackers, or middle blockers. In the attack, the center players initiate a variety of quick and deceptive attacks instrumental in weakening the opponent's block. These maneuvers create better opportunities for the outside spikers to score. The center players participate in almost every blocking attempt and therefore their blocking ability greatly determines the overall blocking effectiveness of the team. Thus, the center players should be the best blockers on the team.

Center players are characterized by their physical and mental endurance. They should be endowed with great fighting spirit, hustle, be aggressive, and never give up. Center players do not have to excel in jumping (although jumping ability is a definite plus) but they must be tall so that they do not have to jump high and fully commit themselves to block potential quick-attack sets by the opposing team. If a center front player fully commits to blocking a fake quick set, the opposing setter can set an outside hitter who then has an opportunity to spike the ball before the center front player can land and move laterally to aid in blocking the outside hitter.

Because the center players play in the center of the court (most often front and back court) and are open to balls coming from every direction, they should have excellent court orientation and a thorough understanding of the mechanics of the game. In attacking, the center players rely upon speed and a variety of technical skills rather than sheer power.

The Ace Player

The ace attackers, or power hitters, play LF. They are most often the best jumpers on the team and possess exceptional power-spiking ability. When a left front power hitter rises for the kill, spectators hold their breath. A successful power spike is one of the most dramatic and glorious moments of the game. The ace players must be imposing and creative and must exhibit great self-confidence. Often in critical game situations, or when other options for the setter are not available, the setter is forced to set the LF power hitter. In these situations, the ace spiker must often combat the opponent's well-positioned two-player block. Such circumstances are the true test of the mental toughness and spiking ability of the ace player.

While the main role of the center player is in blocking and creating attack opportunities for the outside hitters, the main role of the ace spikers is to score points by attack. Therefore, the ace players usually hit more balls than other hitters, and should have the highest attack-kill ratio of all hitters.

The Utility Player

By definition, a utility player is the player who is opposite the setter in the 5–1 team composition. As the term implies, the utility player must be a well-rounded athlete who is proficient in all aspects of the game. Whenever the setter is unable to set, the utility player assumes the setting responsibility. This often happens when the setter is involved in digging the ball on defense, or when a dug ball arrives at the net so quickly that the setter cannot respond.

In the 5–1 team composition, the utility player, like the setter, plays RF and RB. Since she will often attack behind the setter, it is desirable that the utility player be left-handed. This helps speed up the attack, since the set does not have to cross the player's body before it is hit. On the other hand, there are many fine right-handed utility players. During my nine years as coach of the USA women's team, I never had a left-handed player, and we won the Silver Medal using two right-handed utility players, Sue Woodstra and Julie Vollertsen. Right-handed utility players should have a very good jump and explosive speed.

In attack, a utility player should be able to hit both quick and slow sets. Her abilities to serve-receive, serve, and attack from the back court are critical. In almost all serve-reception formations, the utility player is in position to receive a high number of serves. When the setter is front row, the utility player must serve very well, and attack with

great effectiveness from the back court in order to help offset the availability of only two front-row attackers.

The Option Player

The option player is an attacker who plays RF. Usually, option players are found in the 4–2 and 6–2 team compositions. If a team uses the 6–2 composition and has a short setter, an option player may be subbed into the game to play front row in place of the short setter.

In the 4–2 composition, the setters can play either RF or CF. If the setters play RF, there are no option players. If the setters play CF, then there are two option players who play RF.

Usually, there are no option players on a team that uses the 5–1. However, in some cases, a 5–1 setter plays CF, opposite another center player. When a 5–1 setter plays CF, there are two option players who play RF. Sometimes these option players are required to help set the ball in emergency situations.

It is important to understand the different situations and the different reasons involved in having a setter play CF. In the traditional 4–2 team composition, the setter plays in the middle in order to have two outside attackers at all times. This arrangement sacrifices quick attack possibilities for the sake of simplicity. (In the international 4–2 composition, the setter plays right side.)

In the 5–1 team composition, there are two reasons for using the setter in the middle. Obviously, if the setter is tall and a good blocker, positioning her in the middle helps strengthen the block. This often happens with high-school teams with a tall setter who is also a capable blocker. Another reason is to have at least two attackers in transition. Many times balls are dug to a position in the middle of the court, thus eliminating the middle blocker from the attack and forcing the setter to set to the LF ace player. But if the setter is playing CF, she still has another attacker behind her at RF.

It is desirable for option players to be left-handed. If the option player is left-handed, then her role becomes very similar to that of an ace player. A left-handed option player creates the effect of having two primary attackers, one on each side of the court. Of course, this permits more variations for the offense.

ALIGNMENTS AND ARRANGEMENTS

The term *alignment* refers to the players' positions in the rotational order. The term *arrange-*

ment denotes the players' roles, or actual playing positions. When each pair of players plays only two court positions (one in the front court and one in the back court), the players are said to be in a "balanced arrangement." Because they concur with the player-specialization concept, balanced arrangements are preferred.

In these arrangements, usually the ace players play LF and LB, while the center players play CF and CB. Setters and utility players or option players (whichever is on the court) play RF and RB. There is another common arrangement in which the ace players play LF and CB with the center players playing CF and LB. This is usually used when the ace players have superior range and defensive capabilities that can be best utilized in the CB position. Because the players still play only two positions, this is also considered a balanced arrangement.

An "unbalanced arrangement" results when the two players of a pair do not play similar court positions. This commonly occurs in a 5–1 composition when, for instance, the setter plays CF opposite another center player. The setter then plays CF and RB, but the other center player plays CF and CB. In this case, one of the four remaining players must play more than one back-court position. This unbalanced arrangement can be cured by having the other center player also play RB. Then the two option or utility players play RF and CB, resulting in a balanced arrangement.

When players of the same category (e.g., ace players) are positioned opposite each other in the rotational order, the result is called a "diagonally balanced alignment." A diagonally balanced

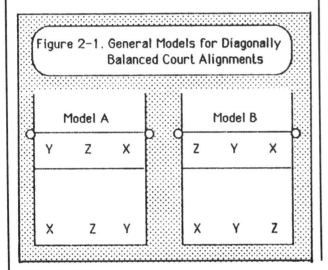

Figure 2-1. General Models for Diagonally Balanced Court Alignments

Model A

Y	Z	X

X	Z	Y

Model B

Z	Y	X

X	Y	Z

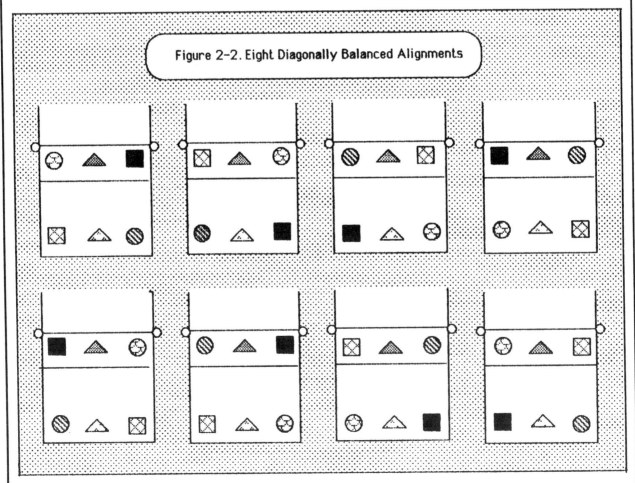

Figure 2-2. Eight Diagonally Balanced Alignments

alignment lends itself nicely to a balanced court arrangement. This, in turn, facilitates specialization, allowing players to learn only two court positions. Therefore, balanced alignments are preferred over nonbalanced alignments.

There are only two possible ways to place three pairs of players in a diagonally balanced alignment, as illustrated in Figure 2–1. However, when a distinction is made between each player in a pair, then *eight* diagonally balanced alignments are possible, as illustrated in Figure 2–2.

In order to distinguish between two players in a pair, they should be ranked.

RANKING PLAYERS

Players should be ranked within each category from one to four, one being the strongest. Ranking players is helpful for aligning players on the court in a balanced manner with regard to the skill level, height, quickness, and experience of each. In addition, ranking and grouping the players according to court positions helps in running practice more efficiently.

Normally, with twelve players on a team, there should be four players for each category. In a 5–1 composition, the left-side ace players would be ranked A1, A2, A3, and A4; and the center players C1, C2, C3, C4.

The setters and utility players are ranked in an integrated fashion, alternating S1, U1, S2, U2, as shown in the chart below. (Note that the bottom two rows of the chart comprise the starting lineup or first team, while the top two rows comprise the subs or second team.)

A4	C4	U2
A3	C3	S2
A2	C2	U1
A1	C1	S1

Players do not need to know their particular ranking, although they will soon realize their roles and position in the team hierarchy (starter, sub, bench warmer, etc.). In some situations, knowledge of their status may be useful, either in inspiring players to improve their position, or in getting a marginal player to accept a certain role.

CONSIDERATIONS FOR COURT ALIGNMENT

The coach must think through very carefully how to distribute players on the court, how to best position them in relationship to each other. This is probably one of the most critical decisions in maximizing a team's potential.

The coach must assess the qualities and abilities of each player carefully. The objective is to have at all times and in each rotation a *balanced* alignment. Such a balanced alignment takes into account the player's physical qualities, skill and experience levels, and intellectual capacity; also, tactical considerations. The coach should study statistics and score sheets to identify strong and weak rotations. Once the alignment is established and the team seems to be working well, then the coach should not do any further tampering with the alignment. It takes a long time for players to develop intuitive feelings for each other so that they can operate as a synchronized unit.

PHYSICAL CONSIDERATIONS The coach should evenly distribute players so that the average height in the front row is the same in all rotations. Players with a similar jumping reach should be aligned next to each other to facilitate an even block and a smoother attack. It is a good practice not to position players with equal speed and reflexes next to each other, because in defense they will respond to the ball at the same speed and hesitation or collision can easily occur.

SKILL CONSIDERATIONS Rotations should be balanced with regard to offensive, defensive, blocking, and serve-reception abilities. When a team gains or loses several points in cyclical streaks, the coach should look for an imbalance in the skill distribution.

MENTAL CONSIDERATIONS Experienced players with strong mental constitutions, which include both mental attitude and intellectual ability, should be distributed evenly on the court.

TACTICAL CONSIDERATIONS Special consideration should be given in a 5–1 team composition for back-row attack. Players who are better back-row attackers should be positioned farther away from the setter (see Figure 2–10).

At times, a player's weakness can be minimized and concealed by special court alignment. For example, if the setter in a 5–1 team composition is a short player and can not block very well, the three players who serve when the setter is in the front line should be especially strong servers who can take risks on the serve. The opponent's serve reception then becomes difficult and their attack more predictable. This allows the setter to drop away from the block and join the floor defense since the other two blockers should be able to adequately block the attack.

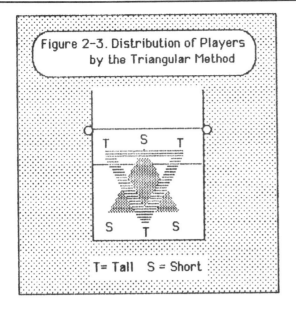

Figure 2-3. Distribution of Players by the Triangular Method

T= Tall   S = Short

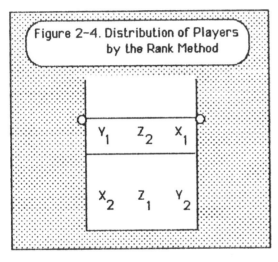

Figure 2-4. Distribution of Players by the Rank Method

Y_1 Z_2 X_1

X_2 Z_1 Y_2

ALIGNMENT OF PLAYERS

Many factors must be taken into account when establishing the rotational order of a team. There is no ready-made formula for aligning players on the court. There are, however, three basic methods that may be useful tools in determining the team's rotational order: the triangular method; distribution of players by their rank; trial and error.

The triangular method evenly distributes players on the court by alternating players who share similar qualities (Figure 2–3).

Figure 2–4 illustrates players' distribution by their rank. (Note that player distribution on the court by rank coincides with the triangular method.)

In distributing players into their proper align-ment, even the most logical and careful considera-tions will not always reveal some of the hidden factors that may affect the team's performance. To pinpoint these intangibles, the coach can resort to the trial-and-error method. Through continuous study of score sheets and statistics taken by rota-tion (see Appendix B), a coach can identify and correct certain alignment problems. This is a very time-consuming process, but it pays off in the long run.

THE 4–2 TEAM COMPOSITION

For many years the 4–2 team composition was considered to be the fundamental composition for beginning teams. The advocates of this team com-position stress its simplicity as its main asset. In-deed, the 4–2 team composition is simple to under-stand, but so are the other methods. From a negative standpoint, the 4–2 composition develops poor motor habits, offers little incentive for creativity, and provides limited opportunity for players' physical development. In my opinion, the 4–2 team composition should only be used when there is no other choice.

The 4–2 team composition consists of two set-ters (non-spikers) and four hitters, with two at-tackers and one setter in the front row at all times. There are two basic player arrangements of the 4–2 team composition: the "traditional arrange-ment" and the "international arrangement."

In the traditional arrangement the team consists of two setters, two ace players, and two option players (Figure 2–5). The setters play CF and RB (or behind the block in the man-up defense) and set to both sides over a wide horizontal spread. All too often the traditional 4–2 is synonymous with a high, wide, and slow attack. This method condi-tions the players to a type of attack where they see first and then respond. This timing is not only diffi-cult to retrain in later stages, but it is also far from being simple to execute, and definitely far from being effective. There are problems inherent in the traditional 4–2 team composition that make it less than attractive even for beginning players:

1. The setters must learn how to both pass and set if a "w" serve reception formation is used.
2. Most often, the setters are the weakest block-ers, yet they play in the most important block-ing position, CF.
3. The attack is very predictable because there are only two front-row attackers in each rota-tion and the attack patterns are limited.

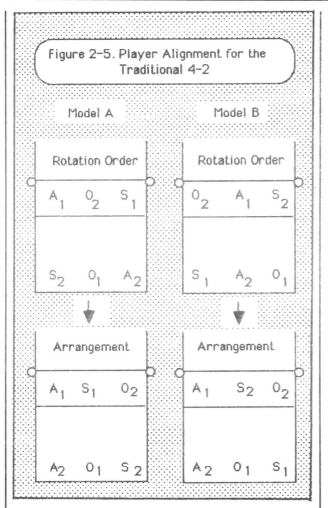

Figure 2-5. Player Alignment for the Traditional 4-2

Model A

Rotation Order

A_1	O_2	S_1
S_2	O_1	A_2

↓

Arrangement

A_1	S_1	O_2
A_2	O_1	S_2

Model B

Rotation Order

O_2	A_1	S_2
S_1	A_2	O_1

↓

Arrangement

A_1	S_2	O_2
A_2	O_1	S_1

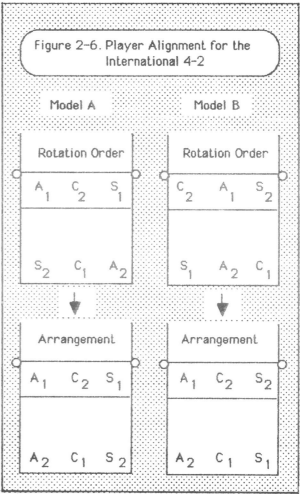

Figure 2-6. Player Alignment for the International 4-2

Model A

Rotation Order

A_1	C_2	S_1
S_2	C_1	A_2

↓

Arrangement

A_1	C_2	S_1
A_2	C_1	S_2

Model B

Rotation Order

C_2	A_1	S_2
S_1	A_2	C_1

↓

Arrangement

A_1	C_2	S_2
A_2	C_1	S_1

Because it places no emphasis on speed or anticipation, the traditional 4–2 arrangement also develops poor motor habits and is not conducive to proper physical development of the athlete.

In the international 4–2, the setters play RF and RB (or behind the block in the man-up defense). If this arrangement is chosen, the team composition is then two ace players, two center players, and two setters (Figure 2–6). I recommend this method over the traditional method for three reasons:

1. It allows for the development of two center players who are better blockers and attackers.
2. It offers possibilities for a certain amount of quick combination attack between the ace and center players.
3. It lays the groundwork for the transition to a 5–1 or 6–2 team composition as the team advances.

Whether playing a traditional or an international 4–2 team composition, it is advisable to arrange the team in a diagonally balanced alignment. If player ranking is considered, then there are only two ways to distribute the players on the court by the triangular method in a diagonally balanced alignment (Figures 2–5 and 2–6). Either the ace player precedes the center (or the option player), or the center player (or the option player) precedes the ace player. Both possibilities are valid and have merit.

THE 6–2 TEAM COMPOSITION

In the 6–2 team composition, there are six spikers, two of whom also act as setters. In each rotation, the back-row setter comes up to the net, a movement called "penetration," and the front-row setter is free to attack. Figure 2–7 shows two diagonally balanced alignments for a 6–2 team composition. These alignments are similar to those of the 4–2 team composition (Figures 2–5, 2–6). As with the 4–2, if players' rankings are considered, then there are only two possible diagonally balanced alignments. When the setter plays the center position while in the front row and RB in the back court, then there are two option players on the court who play RF and usually CB (Figure 2–5). It is a good policy to have players play the same side in both the front and back court. Setters usually play behind the block in the man-up defense. In the man-down defense, it is best to keep setters in the RB position.

Because there are always three spikers available for attack, many coaches view the 6–2 team composition as very attractive. In theory, the 6–2 may be the ultimate method, but in reality it is almost impossible to perfect. To develop two setters requires dividing the training time in half for each setter. Because there is direct correlation between quantity of training and quality of skill proficiency, neither setter can develop to full potential. Thus, the advantage to be gained by creating an extra attacker in three rotations is outweighed by the inevitable loss in the quality of setting. If the team does not have good setting, it really doesn't matter how many spikers there are, because the attack eventually becomes slow and loses all deceptiveness. The team might as well use the best spiker at all times. An excellent setter can do more with two attackers than a mediocre setter can with three.

Another disadvantage of the 6–2 is that both setters must also excel in spiking and occasionally in serve reception. In addition, the 6–2 makes it more difficult to achieve proper attack timing because the hitters must adapt to sets from two setters with different physical attributes, personalities, and setting styles.

To build an attack around two setters requires tremendous coordination and understanding. A certain amount of gray area and hesitation is inevitable. Often, the front-line setter hesitates slightly before backing off the net (after blocking) to get into comfortable spiking position; this hesitation often eliminates her from the transition attack so the team winds up with only two spikers anyway.

Among the top-ranked international teams, of both men and women, only a few employ the 6–2 team composition. For women it is a particularly poor choice because women can not jump as high and stay in the air as long as men can. Therefore, the margin of error in setting is very small, and the setter must be precise and skillful. The 6–2 team composition is a good choice when there are two talented players with the same setting rhythm and height, the coordination between the two seems natural, and there is *ample practice time* to give each setter enough time to develop fully.

THE 5–1 TEAM COMPOSITION

A 5–1 team composition uses five attackers and one setter who sets 85 to 90 percent of all balls. There are numerous advantages to the 5–1 system:

1. It requires only one good setter, rather than two as in the 4–2 and 6–2.
2. The setter does not have to master either spiking or serve-reception skills.
3. The setter does not have to share practice time with another setter. Combined with the fact that the setter does not have to learn spiking and passing, this allows the setter to specialize in setting, thus becoming more proficient.
4. In rallies and transition situations, the setter is in charge and does not have to worry about coordinating with another setter with regard to balls in gray areas. This eliminates hesitation and improves efficiency.

The 5–1 composition is simple to understand; even young players can learn it quickly. The 5–1 develops a high-quality setter, a prerequisite for executing a quick multiple attack. If a coach's philosophy is to use a quick multiple attack, she should choose the 5–1. Most top-ranked teams use the 5–1 method; among the top fifteen internationally ranked women's teams, only one uses the 6–2 composition.

Figure 2–8 illustrates two models of the most commonly used diagonally balanced alignments for a 5–1 team composition. Both models are balanced in accordance with players' ranking. In these alignments the setter and utility player play RF and RB, the center players play CF and CB, and the ace players play LF and LB. If the ace players are better defensive players than the center play-

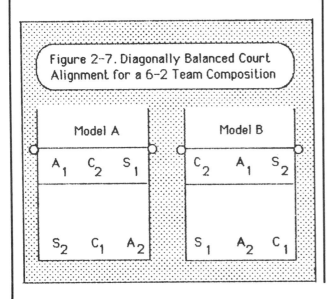

Figure 2–7. Diagonally Balanced Court Alignment for a 6–2 Team Composition

Model A

A$_1$	C$_2$	S$_1$

S$_2$	C$_1$	A$_2$

Model B

C$_2$	A$_1$	S$_2$

S$_1$	A$_2$	C$_1$

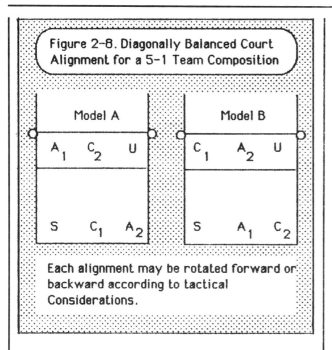

Figure 2-8. Diagonally Balanced Court Alignment for a 5-1 Team Composition

Model A

A₁	C₂	U
S	C₁	A₂

Model B

C₁	A₂	U
S	A₁	C₂

Each alignment may be rotated forward or backward according to tactical Considerations.

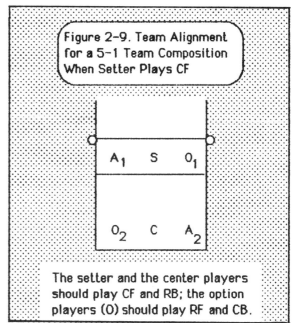

Figure 2-9. Team Alignment for a 5-1 Team Composition When Setter Plays CF

A₁	S	O₁
O₂	C	A₂

The setter and the center players should play CF and RB; the option players (O) should play RF and CB.

ers, it is possible to play them at CB and play the center players at LB. Such a switch may also facilitate back-row attack by the ace spikers from the RB position.

The basic difference between the A and B models is that in the A model, the quick attackers (C) precede the ace spikers in the rotation order. In the B model, the ace spikers precede the quick attackers. Most of the Asian women's teams use the A model, while the USA women's team used the B model. Each of these alignments has certain advantages, which should be considered before adopting either one.

The A model allows the A1 spiker to serve-receive twice in the LF position and once from CF (in the W serve-receive formation). The B model does the same for the A2 spiker. Since LF is the ace player's normal position, the question for the coach becomes, "Which player should have the most advantageous position two times?" Some coaches choose to exploit the talents of their best attacker, the A1 spiker. Other coaches favor making things as easy as possible on their weaker spiker, A2.

The A model also appears to be better suited to a single-tempo attack, whereas the B model is more effective for a multiple-tempo attack. Simply put, in a single-tempo attack, the ace players and quick attackers are each trained to hit certain sets of the same basic speed and height. In a multiple-tempo attack, all the hitters learn to hit sets of varying heights and speeds. The advantages, disadvantages, and underlying philosophies of the single-tempo and multiple-tempo attack concepts are explained in great detail in the chapters dealing with serve reception and attack.

The A model lends itself to the single-tempo attack where center players are quick attackers and the ace players attack slower, second-tempo sets. The B model is best suited to teams where all the attackers can attack both quick and slow sets.

Another advantage of the B model occurs in the W serve-receive formation when the setter is positioned at LB. In this rotation, the setter and the center player can move up closer to the net. This shields the center player from receiving serve and provides an easier penetration path for the setter from the back row.

Having the setter in the center (Figure 2–9) has its merits, in particular in transition attack, when one of the option hitters is a strong left-handed spiker. Quite often the center attackers are eliminated from the attack by digs that are not directed to the target area. When this happens during the three rotations that the setter is in the front line, then there is only one front-line spiker left to set to —the ace spiker. However, when the setter blocks in the middle, two setting options still remain: one to the left-side ace player, and a backset to the option hitter. In addition, when the setter plays CF, she is almost always eliminated from defense, making her available to set the second ball. The problem with this alignment presents itself when the setter, playing CF, has to block on the left side and then immediately race to the passing target to set.

In recent years back-row attack has become a very important consideration in the overall attack strategy in a 5–1 team composition. The back-row attacker serves to offset the lack of one spiker in

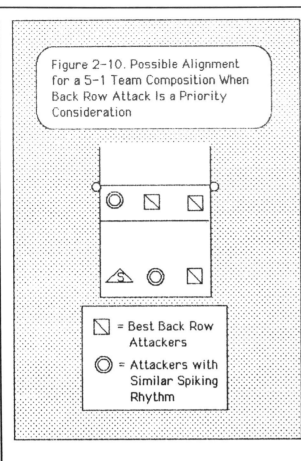

Figure 2-10. Possible Alignment for a 5-1 Team Composition When Back Row Attack Is a Priority Consideration

�****◻ = Best Back Row Attackers

◎ = Attackers with Similar Spiking Rhythm

the front line during those three rotations when the setter is front row. The possibilities for back-row attack should be given a lot of consideration in designing the court alignment. Figure 2–10 illustrates one such possible alignment.

In conclusion, each team composition not only affects the style and nature of play, but also affects the players' physical and mental development. Once motor habits and attitudes are shaped, it is very difficult to retrain them. A player who was initially taught to play slow and high will remain a slow player. Therefore, correct concepts should be taught from the beginning; this is the most direct route to success. A coach should never underestimate the abilities of players to understand, and execute, nor should she reduce her demands to a level where there is no challenge or incentive for the players to improve.

The 5–1 team composition is simple and eliminates most of the problems of the other two team compositions. It is a challenging system that offers the players the opportunity for proper physical, mental, and skill development.

THE SERVE

The serve is the team's first attack. It has two primary objectives: to hinder the opponent's serve-reception attack by slowing it down (thereby making it more predictable for the block), and to score a direct point. A point scored with a serve is called an "ace." Even at high level of play 2 to 4 points a game are scored directly by serving. At lower level of play, the number of aces may reach 6 or 7 points per game. This is because of the imbalance between the serving ability and the serve-receiving ability of young players. It is easier and takes less time to become an effective server than an effective passer. Therefore, in the initial stages, the coach should emphasize serving.

Adequate training time for serving should be allocated in every practice. Generally speaking, a player should serve at least fifty balls every practice session.

The serve can also be used effectively to regulate the rhythm of the game and disrupt the opponent's concentration. To speed up the pace of the game, players should get to the serving position as quickly as possible and serve immediately after the whistle is blown. To slow the game down, players can walk slowly to the serving area, and take their time serving (as long as they execute the serve within the alloted five seconds after the referee's whistle). Occasionally, in gyms with bright lights and very high ceilings, serving high into the lights may make it very difficult for the opposing players to see the ball and properly time the pass.

During no other phase of the game does a player have such complete control over the execution of a skill. The serve is the only time in volleyball when a player completely possesses the ball and can choose the moment to initiate the action.

Under these conditions, serving is a relatively easy skill to master; however, it requires a lot of experience and training to control the ball's speed, trajectory, and direction in a game situation under pressure. The serve is one of the most emotionally charged and difficult moments of the game, because while the server has complete possession of the ball, he is also the focal point of everyone's attention. Repeated training in gamelike situations, relaxation techniques, and proper serving routine can help reduce the anxiety level during serving, but ultimately, experience under competition conditions is the best teacher.

I recommend that, initially, each player master only one serving technique that best suits his physical abilities. Except for very young players, the overhand and roundhouse serving techniques should be taught. As the player gains experience and improves in ability, he should acquire additional serving styles.

TYPES OF SERVES

Serves are divided into two broad categories, according to the ball movement after it is struck: *float serves* and *spin serves*. Figure 3-1 illustrates the relationship between the point of contact with the ball and the flight pattern it creates.

The Float Serve

The float serve has little or no spin at all. Because a ball with no spin is very unstable, the float serve travels through the air with a wavering, breaking, sinking action, moving from side to side and up and down like a knuckleball. This unpredictable flight pattern makes it a very difficult serve to pass.

The fairly low risk involved in serving the floater, and its high effectiveness, have made float serves the most popular among top men's and women's teams.

To produce a float serve, the force of the impact must pass through the ball's center of gravity in the direction of the desired flight. The center of gravity in a symmetrically round object (a ball) is in its center.

It is generally considered that the ball's floating, wavering action is due to what is known as Bernoulli's effect. This theory states that when a flying stream of gas speeds up, its pressure decreases,

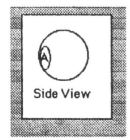

Side View

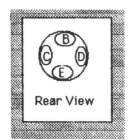

Rear View

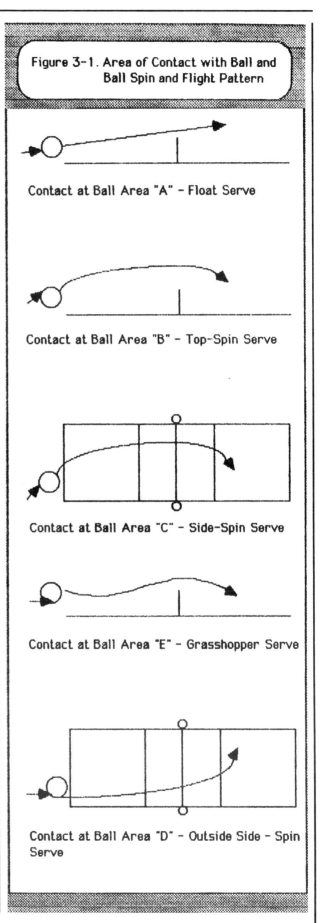

Figure 3-1. Area of Contact with Ball and Ball Spin and Flight Pattern

Contact at Ball Area "A" – Float Serve

Contact at Ball Area "B" – Top-Spin Serve

Contact at Ball Area "C" – Side-Spin Serve

Contact at Ball Area "E" – Grasshopper Serve

Contact at Ball Area "D" – Outside Side – Spin Serve

and vice versa. If an air foil (Figure 3–2) is made to move through air, the stream of air entering the region just above the air foil is forced to flow into a constricted area and its speed is increased; when the speed increases, the pressure decreases.

A ball has the shape of a three-dimensional foil and therefore, when traveling through the air, it creates a funnel, or a tunnel of low pressure, around it. If the low-pressure areas around the ball are exactly balanced, the ball will fly with no wobbling effect at all. However, because the friction at the face of the ball is not even, and because the ball has seams that break up its spherical surface, the air breaks around it in an unsymmetrical way. The air pressure in the tunnel is not perfectly balanced, and consequently the ball wobbles from one low pressure point into another. The turbulence behind the ball creates even more sinking and wobbling action.

The greater the horizontal velocity of the ball, the greater the wobbling effect. Therefore, it is recommended that the float serves be served from a relatively long distance behind the endline—twenty to thirty feet. Apparently, there is an optimum serving distance that produces a maximum floating effect. This distance needs to be found for each individual server, independently, by experimentation and observation. (Young players should learn to master the technique of the float serve first, and move progressively farther back in the serving zone as their strength and ball control increase.)

The Spin Serve

Up until the early sixties, serve-reception passing was done with the overhand finger-setting technique. Therefore, the spin serve was very effective and popular. However, when the rules were changed to require the use of the underhand forearm passing technique for serve reception, the spin serve immediately lost much of its effectiveness and appeal. This eventually led to widespread use of the float serve.

The most common type of spin serve is the top spin. Top spin creates a downward curved flight pattern that reduces the flight time of the ball to a minimum. While a float serve may stay in the air .95 to 1.3 seconds, a hard top-spin serve may take only .7 to .9 of a second. Recently, the jump-spike serve has brought a new dimension and effectiveness to the spin serve, especially in men's competition. A spiked jump serve may stay in the air for an even shorter time than a normal top-spin serve.

The relatively short flight time and rapid descent angle of a top-spin serve are its main virtues. It may beat the serve receiver to the spot.

The more spin a ball has, the more stable it becomes. A ball can have top spin, underspin, or sideways spin. Sideways spin can be used to make the ball curve inward into the court or outward toward the sideline. To create a spin it is necessary to hit the ball in such a way that the force line does not go through its center of gravity. The farther the force line is from the center of gravity, the more spin the ball will have.

Since some of the force of impact is consumed in creating the spin, only the remaining force is available to propel the ball forward. Therefore, a serve with much spin has to be hit very hard in order to get it over the net. In the case of a top-spin serve, its rapidly increasing downward trajectory must also be taken into consideration. In general, the top-spin serve is launched with a higher initial arc in order to clear the net. Because of these factors, spin serves are risky and many players do not use them.

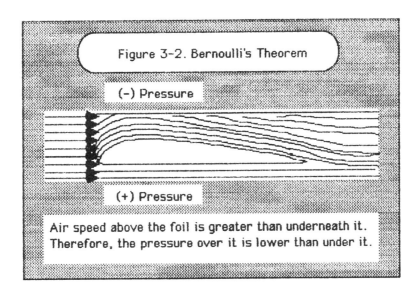

Figure 3-2. Bernoulli's Theorem

(−) Pressure

(+) Pressure

Air speed above the foil is greater than underneath it. Therefore, the pressure over it is lower than under it.

To understand why a spinning ball curves, it is helpful to turn to Bernoulli's theorem. According to Bernoulli, a clockwise spinning ball (reverse spin) has a layer of air that clings to it and is carried around with it. The velocity of the air at any point near the ball is made up of two components: wind, due to movement of the ball through the air; and the spinning of the ball. Above the ball these components move in the same direction, whereas below the ball they move in opposite directions (Figure 3–2).

It follows that the air velocity at the top of the ball is greater than at the bottom; according to Bernoulli's theory, the pressure increases at the bottom, and decreases at the top. The imbalance that occurs causes the ball to rise as it moves forward. This is why balls with reverse spin, such as a pass or a set, rise. If the ball has top spin, the pressure decreases at the bottom and increases at the top; therefore, the ball curves down. The same principle applies to a ball with side spin.

SERVING TECHNIQUES

There are four basic body actions that can be used in serving: underhand, overhand, round-house, and jump spike. These four basic serving techniques can produce a variety of serves: under-hand serve, overhand float serve, overhand whip serve, roundhouse float serve, overhand top-spin serve, roundhouse top-spin serve, side-spin serve, jump-spike serve, grasshopper.

The Underhand Serve

The underhand serve is easy to learn and execute, but it is very ineffective. The underhand serve is uncommon among top teams unless it is served to a great height with underspin, or as a floater. The high underspin serve is occasionally used when playing outdoors (beach players call it a "skyball") or in a facility with a very high ceiling and bright lights. Such tactics may irritate and disrupt the passer.

Beginning players who lack strength and coordination should be allowed to use the underhand

serving technique in its simple form. The server stands by the endline, facing the court, holding the ball at hip height with both hands. If the server is right-handed, the left foot is slightly in front of the right foot and the knees are slightly bent. The server should extend his right arm, but only slightly, behind the back. (Big backswings often result in missing the ball.) The serving action starts with a step forward and toward the court with the left foot. Body weight is transferred onto the left leg. The ball is carried forward in the left hand with a slightly bent arm. The right arm swings forward in a synchronized action with the left arm. The ball is released and immediately hit by the right hand. Emphasis should be placed on the synchronization of the forward swing of both arms, as a pendulum in motion, and a very low toss. Carrying the ball forward while still holding it gives the ball an initial velocity toward the target, and reduces the amount of effort needed to deliver it over the net. The contact with the ball is underneath the ball, with both the palm and the fingers. The striking hand should be held fairly loose.

The Overhand Float Serve

The overhand float serve is the most popular serving technique in North and South America, and in Europe. Recently it has been gaining popularity in Asia, which has been the home of the roundhouse float serve. The main drawback of the overhand float serve is that it requires more shoulder strength than other types of serves and at times may result in a shoulder injury. Nonetheless, this serving technique provides for an easy concentration of the body's forces into the direction of the serve, and it is fairly easy to learn and control. Since the basic motion is similar to spiking, there is also a residual muscle memory from spiking that helps in learning and perfecting this service technique.

READY POSITION The server stands in a relaxed position behind the endline, facing the court, with feet shoulder-width apart and the left foot slightly in front. The front foot points toward the net, while the back foot is at a 45-degree angle to

Rita Crockett of the 1984 USA Olympic Team demonstrates the underhand serve.

Rita Crockett demonstrates an overhand float serve. Contact with the ball should be abrupt, with the elbow slightly bent.

the net; the knees are relaxed and slightly bent. The ball is held waist or chest high with the lifting hand underneath the ball and the hitting hand placed gently on top. Just prior to the tossing action, the server should make eye contact with the target. The serving distance behind the endline varies according to individual preference, tactical consideration, and the confines of the playing area.

THE TOSS As the server strides forward on the left foot, he lifts the ball with the left hand, crossing the midline of the body toward the side of the hitting arm. The tossing arm remains almost straight as it lifts the ball in a smooth, continuous motion. The ball is released when the hand reaches shoulder height. It is tossed in front of the server, and no more than 2 to 3 feet above the head, in line with the serving target. It should have as little spin on it as possible.

SERVING ACTION The serving arm is drawn back to a cocked position, with the elbow slightly below shoulder height. The palm should be rotated slightly outward to enable the server to pull the arm farther back without undue stress. As the body weight shifts forward to the left foot, there is a slight rotational movement of the whole body, and the serving arm rotates around the shoulder. Just prior to contact, the arm decelerates rapidly and the hand contacts the ball with an aggressive,

abrupt punch like a karate chop. This deceleration allows the server to transfer the momentum of the arm into the ball and produce a fast ball with relative ease.

CONTACT The ball is struck at its center, or "sweet spot," with the heel and the palm of the hand. The hand and the wrist are held in a rigid position with the fingers together and the palm flat. The wrist must always be fairly stiff to reduce the elasticity coefficient of the hand and prevent it from absorbing any of the force imparted to the ball. To avoid creating top spin at the time of contact, the arm is slightly bent at the elbow. To produce a flat trajectory, the ball should be contacted in front of the server. After a short abrupt contact, the arm stops quickly and there is no follow-through with the fingers (to prevent top spin).

The Overhand Whip Serve

Players who do not possess enough shoulder or arm strength to execute the overhand float serve can gain extra arm velocity by doing the overhand whip (float) serve. The overhand whip serve is similar to the overhand float serve in every way except for the arm swing.

In the overhand float serve, the hitting arm is first raised to a cocked position and then brought forward; in the overhand whip float serve the arm rotates in one continuous smooth motion. When

a. The overhand whip serve. Extra arm velocity can be gained by a whipping action with a very loose arm and wrist.

b. Front view of the overhand whip serve.

the toss is completed, the shoulder pulls the arm down and around in a tight circular motion similar to that in a spike or throwing action. The contact with the ball is made in the same manner as in the overhand float serve, with the wrist stiff, and no snap.

I recommend the whip float serve because it is a very natural motion. Mechanically sound, it prevents injury and undue stress to the shoulder. With practice, a player can achieve an equal, or better, floating effect than with the overhand float serve.

The Roundhouse Float Serve

The roundhouse float serve, often called the "Asian" serve, became very popular in the sixties. There were two main reasons for its popularity: the whole body is involved in producing the power needed for the serve and it therefore does not demand as much shoulder strength as the overhand float serve; and contact with the ball can be made at maximum reach height.

Recently, however, the popularity of the roundhouse serve, even among Asian teams, has declined in favor of both the overhand float and the overhand whip float serves. The probable reasons are:

- The roundhouse serving action is not as natural a body action as are those of the overhand and the whip float serves (it is therefore more difficult to learn and to control).
- The roundhouse serving style does not provide as much eye contact with the opponent's court and target area as the overhand and whip float styles do.
- The timing of the roundhouse serve is difficult, particularly for long-distance serves.

- Directing the roundhouse serve to a particular target area is considerably more difficult than by use of the other two serves.
- Today's volleyball players are bigger and stronger than ever before; therefore, shoulder strength for serving is no longer a problem, and maximum reach height is not a critical factor.
- The sudden deceleration of the arm in the overhand whip serves transfers all the body's momentum into the ball. In the roundhouse serve, the arm does not decelerate prior to contact with the ball, making the roundhouse serve possibly less powerful than the other two serves.
- The whip float serve demands very little shoulder-muscle strength, and resembles a natural throwing action that makes it very easy for even beginners to learn.

READY POSITION The server stands erect, comfortably balanced, with the shoulders just about perpendicular to the net. The feet are placed side by side and the foot closer to the net is placed slightly behind the back foot. The bottom of the ball is held evenly with both hands at waist height.

THE TOSS Three simultaneous body actions are involved in producing the toss. First, the ball is transferred to the tossing hand, which initially sinks slightly after receiving the ball and then lifts the ball up with a straight arm. Then the hitting arm is drawn back. Finally, the server takes a step with the front leg toward the endline as the body weight shifts back onto the back foot, with slight hip and shoulder rotation along the body's vertical axis. The higher the lifting arm goes, the farther back the hitting arm goes; the two arms always work in conjunction with each other. The ball is released about head height (toward the shoulder of the nonhitting arm) with the tossing arm at a 45-degree angle to the sideline. If the tossed ball were to drop, it would land just in front of the front foot. The ball should be tossed to no more than two feet above the head. A higher toss makes it more difficult to time the contact with the ball and gives

The roundhouse float serve.

Ready position.

Serving action.

Contact with the ball.

the opponent more time to key on the server's body action and anticipate his intention.

SERVING ACTION The entire serving action should be one smooth, synchronized body movement, with the power generated from the back leg, transferred into the hips and finally into the shoulder that leads the hitting arm.

Just before the ball reaches its peak, the server pushes off from the back leg, transferring body weight and momentum onto the front leg; the longer the step, the more power is generated. The direction of the toes of the front foot dictate the direction of the serve. As the body weight shifts forward onto the front foot, the hips rotate forward, followed by the shoulder, which pulls the hitting arm through in a circular windmill motion. Just prior to contact with the ball, the hitting arm is behind the shoulder and the hips thrust around the vertical axis of the body.

CONTACT Just before contact with the ball, the hips and then the shoulders decelerate quickly, while the hitting arm, which lags behind the shoulders, accelerates through the contact with the ball. The contact with the ball is made in front of the left shoulder at an angle of about 30 degrees from the vertical line. The ball is struck directly through its center with either the palm of the hand or with the distal part of the forearm next to the wrist joint. The hand can be open, or the fingers can be bent in a loose fist, and the wrist slightly extended.

FOLLOW-THROUGH The hitting arm follows through and the back leg may or may not cross over in front of the front leg.

The Overhand Top-Spin Serve

A quality overhand top-spin serve is risky, but the rapid descent of its trajectory makes it a worthwhile addition to a team's serving repertoire. Initially, the ball rises, but once it begins its descent it drops suddenly.

Because of its abrupt downward curve, the top-spin serve is not in the air very long, cutting down the serve-receiver's response time. A low trajectory enhances the sudden sinking motion. The forward top-spin serve is difficult to execute and requires much strength.

READY POSITION The ready position for the overhand top spin is almost identical to the ready position for the forward float serve. The angle of the feet to the endline can be slightly more oblique, depending on individual preference.

THE TOSS The toss is similar to that in the overhand float except that the ball can be tossed a little bit higher—three to four feet above the head.

SERVING ACTION Unless the player is exceptionally strong, a relatively deep knee bend is used to generate the power required to create the spin. The body leans back over the bent knee and the power is generated from straightening the back leg. The force passes through the hips, creating a forward hip rotation that squares the server's shoulders in relation to the target. The arm swing of the forward top-spin serve is very similar to a spiking motion.

Sue Woodstra of the 1984 USA Olympic Team demonstrates the overhand top-spin serve.

Side view of the overhand top-spin serve.

The roundhouse top-spin serve with the optional approach step. Note the cross-behind step.

At the completion of the toss, the hitting arm is about shoulder height slightly bent at the elbow. The hitting arm winds back down and around in a slight circular motion with the elbow leading, and then suddenly thrusts forward in an aggressive spiking motion. The left arm naturally counterbalances the movement of the right arm.

CONTACT Contact is made with an open, slightly cupped palm on the lower midsection of the ball (Figure 3–1). The heel of the palm contacts the ball first, and then the fingers come over the top and turn the ball forward with top spin. The heel supplies the power and the fingers supply the top spin. It takes a strong deliberate snapping wrist action to set the ball turning forward. At the time of contact with the ball, the arm must be fully extended.

The amount of spin on the ball depends on how close to its center of gravity the ball is hit. The farther away the contact is from the ball's sweet spot, the more spin is imparted to the ball. Because some part of the force is consumed to produce the spin, the ball must be hit very hard to generate enough velocity to travel over the net. The relationship between the horizontal velocity and the spin determines the arc of the curve; the higher the rate of spin to horizontal velocity, the greater the curve and the sinking motion.

The Roundhouse Top-Spin Serve

The roundhouse top-spin serve combines the arm and body movement of the roundhouse side-arm float with the contact action of the forward top-spin serve. The powerful contact with the ball causes it to arrive in the opponent's court quickly and then drop drastically, giving the serve-receiver little time to react.

This serve was very popular and effective in the late fifties and early sixties among top male players (particularly, Eastern European players) when serve reception was executed exclusively with the overhead finger-passing technique. In the mid-sixties, when most international teams adopted the forearm passing technique, the relatively predictable trajectory of the roundhouse top-spin serve rendered it ineffective; thereafter, the serve was seldom used. In my opinion, the time limitation that this serve imposes on the opponent's serve reception is so severe that it has merit, especially when used in a sequence with other serves. Time measurements show that there is very little flight-time difference between this serve and the jump-spike serve.

READY POSITION The server stands approximately two meters behind the endline, facing the right sideline, with the line of the shoulders perpendicular to the endline. The feet are placed shoulder-width apart and side by side with the left foot slightly in front. Prior to the toss, the server makes eye contact with the serving target.

THE TOSS The tossing arm should be fully extended at the time of release. The ball is tossed about 4 feet high in the direction of the court just in front of the left shoulder. As the ball is tossed, the left foot steps toward the court. The hitting arm swings down and around behind the back, and the player leans back over the right leg with a slight rotation of the hips. The back knee bends, the right shoulder drops, and the whole body winds back like a spring, ready to uncoil.

SERVING ACTION Just before the ball reaches the apex of the toss, the arm action begins. The body pushes off from the back leg and the hips rotate forward, bringing the shoulders square to the net; the degree of rotation of the hips controls the direction of the serve. The shoulder leads the arm up and around in a circular motion as the body weight shifts forward. The hitting arm trails the shoulder.

CONTACT Contact is made over and slightly in front of the hitting shoulder (slightly higher than in the roundhouse float) with the hitting arm fully extended. The ball is struck with an open cupped palm. The top-spin is created by hitting the ball on

its lower midsection with the heel of the palm and then abruptly snapping the wrist forward. The arm continues in a pronounced follow-through movement with the body following the arm and the back leg crossing in front of the left.

AN OPTIONAL APPROACH STEP Some roundhouse serving specialists implement an approach step. The approach is similar to that used in the javelin throw. The initial position is, again, sideways to the net, approximately 7 to 8 feet behind the endline to allow space for the approach. The ball is tossed slightly higher and toward the endline. The server starts the approach with the left foot, crosses behind with the right, opens with the left, hits the ball, and then follows through with the right foot in front of the left.

The Side-Spin Serve

The side-spin serve has both side spin and top spin. The side spin causes the ball to curve laterally; the top spin causes the ball to curve downward. The curve of the ball largely depends on the ratio between the two spins.

Side spin is created when the ball is hit on its side tangent to its diameter line. With strong side spin, a ball can curve almost outside the court and veer back into it. This technique requires a lot of power to create such a strong spin and yet impart enough force to propel the ball forward very fast and over the net.

The greatest advantage of this serve is its unpredictable deflection off the passer's arms. The side spin causes the ball to go in a circular motion that is very difficult to redirect to the passing target because the ball crosses the shoulder line of the passer. The top spin poses additional problems in controlling the vertical rebound of the ball. Because the passing target is on the right side of the court, the crosscourt side-spin serve is more effective for right-handed servers. Another advantage of the serve is its speed: flight time is about one

second, which gives the opponent a relatively short reaction time.

The server stands close behind the endline and close to the inside line of the serving zone. This allows room for the ball to curve drastically to the outside without hitting the antenna. The server stands at a 45-degree angle to the net, the feet parallel. The serve is similar to the top-spin serve in all respects except that the contact with the ball is different. The heel of the palm contacts the ball on the lower midsection off to its right side. The heel delivers the power and the fingers impart top spin; the whole hitting action is a slicing clockwise motion.

The effectiveness of this serve was demonstrated by Flo Hyman during the 1977 USVBA national championships and the 1984 Olympic Games. I highly recommend the side-spin serve, particularly for tall female athletes.

The Jump-Spike Serve

The first time I was introduced to the jump-spike serve was in Poland, in 1955. Recently, this serve has become popular with several international men's teams. During the 1984 Olympics, the Brazilian men's team reached second place due partially to their excellent use of the jump-spike serve.

It has the shortest flight time of any serve, making it difficult to respond to, especially for teams that pass with fewer than three people. Recently I measured the flight time of some jump-spike serves executed by European men. The time varied between .7 and .9 of a second, which doesn't give the serve-receiver much time, considering that the human reaction time is .3 of a second. If the jump-spike serve continues to be successful, adjustments in serve-reception formations will be necessary. Some men's teams may be forced to abandon their two-man serve-receive formations in favor of formations with at least three players in a more linear pattern.

The jump (spike) serve. Note the slow one-two takeoff. After jumping from behind the endline, the server is permitted to land inside the court.

READY POSITION The server stands behind the endline, facing the net, leaving enough room for two run-up steps and a hop approach.

THE TOSS The server tosses the ball forward (toward the endline) and fairly high to allow enough time for the approach. The toss is made during the second approach step, to a height the individual server can jump-reach. The ball is tossed inside the court; as long as the server takes off behind the endline, he may land inside the court after contacting the ball.

For a right-handed server, the approach would begin with the right foot, followed by a longer step with the left, then a long hop off the left foot into a one-two (right-left) sequence takeoff. The one-two sequence covers a wide distance, about three feet, to facilitate a broad jump. (For a more elaborate explanation, see spiking technique in Chapter 6 "The Attack.")

Each server should measure his own approach distance from the base line. This will ensure consistency and decrease the chances of foot-fault violations.

CONTACT The arm swing is very similar to the spiking action, and the contact with the ball is similar to that in the overhand top-spin serve. Obviously, the higher the contact point, the more advantageous the serve, because it more nearly simulates a direct spike. Since no server can jump-reach fifteen feet or more off the floor, it is impossible to hit a ball at an angle that is straight down over the net. Therefore, the greater the top spin, the greater the curve and the shorter the flight.

Recently, some women players have attempted to implement the jump-spike serve. Its potential success with women is very similar to the success of a down ball attack. It would be very interesting to see if the top-spin jump-spike serve could develop also into a floater. I wonder what would happen if the toss for the serve was made by another player; the rules make no provisions against it.

The Overhand Reverse-Spin Whip Serve—Grasshopper

The overhand reverse-spin whip serve is similar to the overhand whip float; however, the ball is hit slightly underneath its center of gravity to create a mild reverse spin on the ball. Initially, the ball will sink, and then suddenly gain height as if it were jumping over the net like a grasshopper (Figure 3–1). The serve should be done from a short distance behind the line; otherwise the ball might sink into the net. The ball movement created is deceptive and unnatural. Because of its reverse spin, it will deflect from the arms of the serve-receiver with a top spin and be likely to go over the net.

THE ULTIMATE SERVE

The ultimate serve, one with the highest probability of acing a team with perfect passing skill, would possess the following qualities: short flight time; short distance; high horizontal velocity; unpredictable angle of deflection due to unpredictable flight pattern.

The two serves with the greatest potential for having these qualities would be a jump-spike float, and a side-spin serve. Each of these balls could be hit with great horizontal velocity. I have not seen either of these serves executed, but I predict that serves will develop in this direction.

The jump-spike float serve could become the most effective serve of all. I do not ignore the fact that it is impossible to hit the ball straight down over the net, because it takes a jump reach of at least fifteen feet or more, which no one, at this point, is capable of doing. Nevertheless, with the correct balance between horizontal and vertical velocities and the right longitudinal distance behind the endline, such a serve could be more effective than any of the existing float serves. I would recommend that players attempt to learn the jump-spike float; please give me a call when you've mastered it.

PREPARATION FOR SERVING

Every play begins with a serve, and serving should be thought of as a weapon. Here are some handy guidelines that will help eliminate or reduce costly serving errors:

1. Each player should mark out the same distance from the endline to ensure that he always serves from the same spot. (Some players will move up or back depending on how deep they wish to serve into the opponent's court.)
2. Each player has to develop a serving ritual that gradually eases him into the actual execution of the serve. Some players like to bounce the ball a few times. This should generally be discouraged because it is often done at the expense of other more beneficial actions, like making eye contact with the target.
3. The server should be occupied with thoughts that relate to his purpose, such as where and to whom to serve. This is preferable to thinking about how to serve.
4. The server should make eye contact with the target so the brain can send the proper signals to the muscles that will execute the serve. Visual contact with the target gives the body a sense of collective purpose and direction. The brain receives a clear picture of the amount of muscle power needed to deliver the ball in a certain manner to the target location.
5. A player should be in control of the serving situation. In general, players—especially beginning players—should not run to the serving area. They should walk to position, turn around, make their mental preparations, aim well, and then serve.
6. On teams that favor a quick-tempo game, experienced players may sometimes try to increase the pressure on their opponents by serving as quickly as possible after the referee's

Prior to serving, the player should relax, concentrate, and make eye contact with the target.

signal. But in these cases the players rush to the serving area as quickly as possible, usually while the other team is getting into serve-reception formation. This allows them time to perform their mental preparations prior to the referee's signal.

7. Players who experience emotional problems under pressure, or who find it difficult to calm down, should take a few deep breaths and even count them. This has a tranquilizing effect.

8. If the toss doesn't feel comfortable, the server should let the ball drop and try again. This shouldn't become a habit, but it is better to let the ball drop than to miss the serve.

TIME ELEMENT

Every ball travels through the air in almost a perfect parabola. The peak height of the ball depends on the ball's vertical velocity and the horizontal distance depends on its horizontal velocity. The greater the vertical velocity, the higher the ball will go; the greater the horizontal velocity, the farther it will travel. Long-distance serves require a greater horizontal velocity than short-distance serves.

Many coaches mistakenly believe that a short-distance serve gives the opponent less time to react to the ball. This is not true. What determines the flight time of a ball is the height of its peak, not its horizontal distance. Gravity acts with the same force on a ball with a short trajectory as it does on a ball with a long trajectory. A ball that travels 200 yards will land at the same time as a ball that travels 50 yards, if they are hit at the same time and if the peak of their flight—say 20 feet off the ground—is the same. A shorter serve is not necessarily a quicker serve.

SERVING TACTICS

Serving ability must be taken into the alignment considerations, particularly for teams using a 5–1 team composition. The best servers should be positioned farthest from the setter in the rotational order. In the three rotations when the setter is front row with only two attackers, and the opponent has three attackers in the front line, it is very important to serve tough. It is desirable that players with different serving styles alternate in the rotational order. To add diversity to a team's serving rhythm, each player on the team should serve from different longitudinal and lateral distances behind the endline. Varying the rhythm, the distance, and the type of serve forces the opposing team to continuously adjust its serve-reception formation.

Players should always serve to score a point, especially when the opponent is quite a bit ahead or far behind; also, near the end of a game or a match. One of the worst mistakes a team can make is to ease up on the serve near the end of a match. This can be particularly disconcerting when the team has the lead and the players become nervous. They want to win so badly that they become afraid to take the amount of risk necessary to win. Easy serving can drain a team's momentum and change a winning situation into a defeat. A positive serving ratio is 50 percent, which means that for each serving error there should be one ace or an indirect point scored. An *indirect serving point* is a point scored by the block or transition attack due to an opponent's passing difficulty. On many occasions there is a negative correlation between the number of serving errors and winning. This is particularly true at a very advanced level of play where the serve-reception attack is operating at 50 percent efficiency or better.

Powerful, and at times risky, serving becomes a very important weapon against skillful teams that employ a quick combination attack. There are, however, certain moments during a game when it is especially imperative that a player avoid making a serving error, even at the expense of easing up and being cautious. A player should not miss a serve when:

• the player is the first server;
• the opponent has just taken a time-out;
• the preceding server missed the serve;
• after a long hard rally;
• the opponent gained a few points in a row;
• the player is a fresh substitute.

The serve is a very important weapon in regulating game pace. The rules of the game do not dictate at what pace the server should go to the serving position. He may run quickly, or walk very slowly. The serving team should stall a) when playing against an anxious opponent; b) when playing against a team that likes to play at a fast pace and makes every attempt to speed up the game; c) after a few unusual errors of the serving team; or d) after losing a long rally.

Slowing down the pace against a stronger opponent that does not show particular enthusiasm may prove to be, at the time, a good strategy. The serving team should speed up the serving a) when the opponent shows signs of confusion and fatigue; b) after scoring a few consecutive points; and c) in particular, when the opponent does not have either time-outs or substitutions left.

Beginning players should concentrate on serving their best serves into the court, without regard to a specific target. As soon as players are capable of controlling their serves, they can be directed to specific areas. (Trying to force beginning players to serve specific areas may result in too many easy serves and errors.)

At the international level, coaches are prohibited from coaching while on the bench. But at all other levels, coaches may communicate serving instructions to their players using finger signals to indicate a prenumbered position on the court. Here is a list of the areas and options to be considered in directing serving tactics:

• to deep-court areas;
• to the right back corner. (A serve to this area forces the setter to break eye contact with the spikers.)
• a weak passer;
• a substitute player. (Beware of teams that have a back-row specialist who is an excellent passer.)
• seams between two passers;
• an open area, such as the short middle of a four-man or two-man serve-reception formation;
• a front-row quick attacker. (Receiving serve can slow down a quick attacker. If your opponent uses a 5–1 team composition and has the setter in the front row, then taking a quick attacker out of the attack by forcing him to receive serve will make it much easier for your block and floor defense to defend against the ace spiker.)
• a player who has just committed an error;
• a key player. Forcing the other team's key player to receive a high number of serves can wear him down. Often, fatigue leads to serve-reception errors, which builds frustration, which in turn can lead to spiking errors.

SERVE RECEPTION & PASSING

Serve reception refers to that particular phase of the game when a team receives a serve. The term *serve reception* encompasses passing, which is the individual skill used in serve receiving, as well as the arrangements of players on the court, arrangements called "serve-reception formations."

This chapter is divided into two main parts: The Pass and Team Serve Reception.

THE PASS

The pass is the first contact with the ball after the serve. The main objective of the pass is to direct the ball to the setter in a specific, predetermined target area. The ability of a team to execute an effective attack following serve reception depends largely on the accuracy and quality of the pass. If the pass is not precise, then the setter's options are reduced, creating an attack that is slow and predictable.

Usually the pass is done with the forearms; however, it is legal, and occasionally more effective with slow serves, to pass the ball with the fingers overhand, a motion that is similar to setting and is called "finger passing." In emergency situations, a player can even pass with one arm (see the explanation of the one-hand dig technique in Chapter 8, "Floor Defense").

Although the passing technique is one of the easiest skills in volleyball, it is perceived as being one of the most difficult. There are three main rea-

sons for this: 1) coaches tend to talk about passing as a difficult skill; 2) players are given inadequate instruction that ignores the proper mechanical and geometric principles; and 3) the mental aspect of passing is, indeed, challenging. Awaiting the serve is an emotionally charged moment, perhaps even more so than the moment of the serve itself.

The Target

The target is not a person, but rather a specific fixed location along the net where the setter expects to receive the pass (Figure 4–1). Actually, a team can have two target areas: primary and secondary. The primary target is 3m (about 10′) from the right sideline, and is 1m (3′3″) long and about 1.20m (3′11″) wide. (It can be slightly wider for men.) The secondary target has the same dimensions as the primary target. It is located just to the

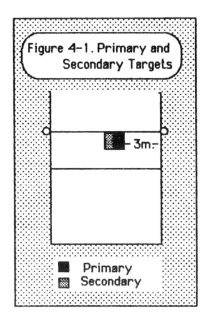

Figure 4-1. Primary and Secondary Targets

■ Primary
▩ Secondary

left, toward the center of the court from the primary target.

Unless there is an emergency situation, the passer usually tries to pass the ball to the primary target. On occasion it is tactically beneficial to run the attack from the secondary target. In emergency situations, when it is risky or impossible to pass the ball to the primary target, the passer should pass the ball to the secondary target. In such cases, the setter should recognize the situation, anticipate the pass, and move immediately toward the center.

Ready Body Posture

The ready body posture is the posture assumed by each player in her initial position just as soon as the server is ready to toss the ball.

The ready body posture should be relaxed, but conducive to quick movement. The posture described here facilitates the quick movements required to respond to fast and short serves in front of the passer.

The feet should be slightly wider than shoulder-width apart with the right foot slightly in front of the left foot. The toes of both feet should be pointed inward slightly. The weight distribution should be mainly forward, on the inside of the balls of both feet; there should be no weight back on the heels.

To ensure that the weight is sufficiently forward, the ankles should be bent forward at an angle of about 70 degrees, bringing the knees forward in front of the toes. The greater the flexibility at the ankle, the less strenuous this position is for the knees.

The knees are bent slightly, and the trunk is bent so that a straight line formed by the back, if continued, would intersect the floor at about a 45-degree angle. The back of the head is in line with the line of the back. Shoulders should be relaxed and slightly forward of the knees; arms hang freely, shoulder-width apart, palms facing inward, elbows slightly bent at about a 45-degree angle.

Once in the ready body posture, the passer should focus on the server and look for cues that might betray her serving intentions—her feet position, distance behind the endline, eye direction, and technique. As the server progresses through the serving movement, the passer should focus more and more on the server's hand. The passer's eyes follow the movement of the served ball, using the net as a reference point, attempting to look at the bottom of the ball as the passer brings her body underneath the serve to receive it.

Forming the Platform

Passing is usually done with both forearms together in an underhand manner. The ball is contacted simultaneously by both forearms, about 2 inches above the wrist. To achieve consistency in passing, the forearms should be as close together as possible. The distance between the elbows should be no more than ½-inch for women, and an inch for men. To be able to get the elbows this close together, the player has to elevate the shoulders and shrug them forward, creating a hollow chest; at the same time, the arms must be rotated outward slightly (supination). This posture is easier to achieve if the action starts with the shoulders, in this sequence: elevate the shoulders, shrug them forward, make a hollow chest, bring the arms together, rotate them outward, and form the grip.

The passing platform should be created toward the end of the adjustment movement to the ball. If

The ready body posture is assumed by each player to receive serve. Arms are loosely held straight down or can be slightly bent at the elbow.

Contact with the ball is made about two inches above the wrists.

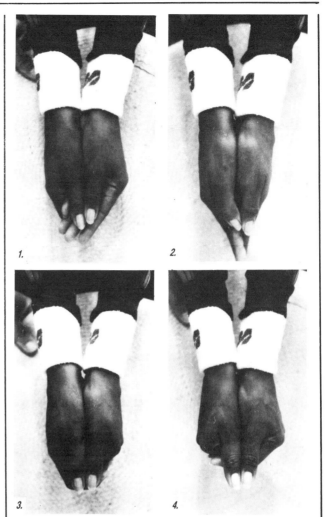

There are several possible grips to use for passing and digging: 1. The hand-overlap grip. 2. The finger-interlock grip. (Front view.) 3. The fist grip. 4. The fist grip with index finger tucked under the thumbs.

the player puts her arms together too soon, her body adjustment to the ball will be slowed down considerably and she may lose balance and coordination. When the serve is slow and there is no movement needed at all, then the player should form the platform fairly early and concentrate on body alignment with the ball. After forming the platform, the player should form the grip. Experienced players form the platform and the grip simultaneously.

The Grip

There are three basic grips that I recommend: the hand-overlap grip, the finger-interlock grip, and the fist grip.

To form the hand-overlap grip, bring the hands together at their sides, palms up. A right-handed player should then slide the left fingers over onto the right fingers, keeping the sides of the hands joined; a left-handed player should slide the right fingers over onto the left fingers. Close the hands up until the thumbs are touching and parallel on top. There should be a slight pressure at the heel of the palms where the hands touch, not between the thumbs.

To form the finger-interlock grip, bring the palms together and then, starting with the little fingers, cross the fingers at the first joint until all are crossed and the thumbs are touching parallel on top. The fingers should remain straight and the center of the palms can pull apart slightly to widen the grip as long as the heels stay together. Again, pressure should be felt at the bottom side where the hands meet, not between the thumbs.

To form the fist grip, a right-handed player should make a fist with the left hand and wrap the right hand around the fist; a left-handed player should make a fist with the right hand and wrap the left hand around the fist. The thumbs should be parallel and touching. To strengthen this particular grip, a player can straighten the index finger of the hand in a fist and tuck the finger under the thumbs.

One of the main functions of the grip is to help the player create a consistent passing platform, with the forearms always kept at the same rotation and the same distance apart. A second function is to prevent the arms from splitting apart upon contact with a hard hit ball. Third, the grip draws the elbows as close together as possible and exposes the forearms to receive the pass.

Make sure that the grip is not too tight. Once the grip is formed, rotate the wrists down. By rotating the wrists down, the forearms are straightened even more and the elbows are brought into a locked position. The arms now act as one unit with the hinge at the shoulders. If the wrists are not rotated down, the elbows do not lock and the platform created by the forearms is unstable. If the arms are brought together properly, they will create a V-shaped platform with the inner part of the forearms exposed and close together.

An advantage of the finger-interlock grip is that it never varies and always creates the same relationship between the forearms. The disadvantage of this grip is that when a player has to go for a ball that is very close to the floor, the two little fingers are vulnerable to injury. To protect the little fingers, a player can learn how to open up the grip at the bottom and smoothly cushion herself on the floor with her hands.

A disadvantage of the fist grip is that it abbreviates the arm length to some degree and does not always create a consistent, even platform; nevertheless, it is a popular grip.

Angle Considerations

The serve can travel in a wide range of directions: crosscourt, to the center, and down the line. Regardless of the direction of the serve, the passer must always redirect the ball to the same target. Thus, the angle of deflection varies with each passer's position on the court. Because the ball rebounds off the arms in both the lateral and vertical planes, the passer has to be prepared to adjust the vertical and the lateral positioning of the arms (passing platform) to create the required angle of deflection. Determining how to angle the arms for passing is really a question of geometry and common sense.

To illustrate, let us assume that player X stands in the left back position, with shoulders perpendicular to the line of the served ball (line A, Figure 4–2). The passer must now angle the ball laterally along line B, with an angle C. In general, there are three basic methods of redirecting or passing the ball toward the target:

1. Rotating the shoulders right or left, which allows the platform to face the target, contacting the ball in front of the body.
2. Stepping around the ball, facing the target, and contacting the ball in front of the body.
3. Dropping the right or left shoulder and lifting the platform to the side (left or right respec-

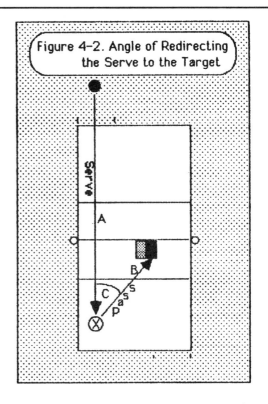

Figure 4-2. Angle of Redirecting the Serve to the Target

tively), and passing across the body. When the ball is to the left of the passer, the right shoulder is dropped and the platform is raised to the left of the body to the proper height. The passing action is from left-to-right across the body. When the ball comes to the right of the player, the situation is reversed. As opposed to the first two methods, in this method neither the platform nor the player are facing the target upon contact with the ball. The first two methods involve direct deflection of the ball to the target. In the third method, the ball is being redirected to the target by manipulating the angle of the platform; the angle of incidence coincides with the direction of the target. This method of passing allows a quicker response over a greater range and offers better adaptability for emergency situations.

Until recently, coaches taught only the first two methods and were very strict about forcing players to pass only in front of the body, keeping the arms perpendicular to the floor and facing the target. Actually, passing in front of the body is the most difficult position for controlling the ball, in particular when passing a serve that is moving across the body from left to right (or vice versa). Nevertheless, this method is acceptable when passing high balls having substantial vertical velocity. High balls with much vertical velocity do not pose any particular demand for passing laterally; the only consideration is the angle between

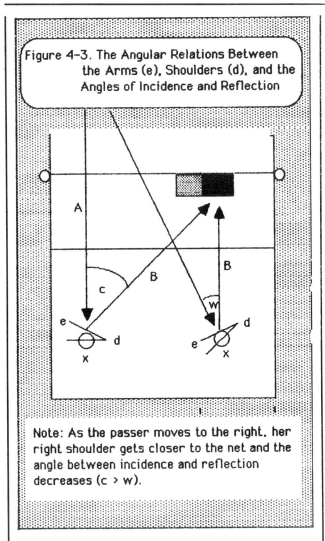

Figure 4-3. The Angular Relations Between the Arms (e), Shoulders (d), and the Angles of Incidence and Reflection

A

c

B

B

w

e

d

d

x

e

d

x

Note: As the passer moves to the right, her right shoulder gets closer to the net and the angle between incidence and reflection decreases (c > w).

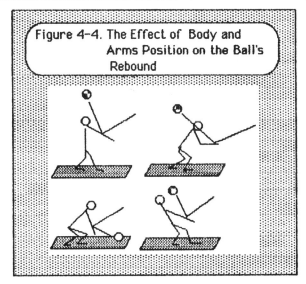

Figure 4-4. The Effect of Body and Arms Position on the Ball's Rebound

the arms and the floor, to create proper deflection in the vertical plane.

Any of the three methods can be used to direct the ball sideways. However, a serve with much horizontal velocity is more difficult to direct in the lateral dimension. There is no margin for error. If the platform is not perfect, or if the contact with the serve is not timed exactly right, the pass will not be properly directed to the target.

An attempt by the X passer (Figure 4–2) to pass balls with great horizontal velocity to the target along line B by either of the first two methods would be very risky. Angling the arms to the right in the vertical plane, by shoulder rotation, and passing in front of the body leaves a very narrow area of the arms exposed to the incoming ball in the lateral dimension. If the arms are not placed in the exact angle, the ball may ricochet and not deflect to the desired target. At times, the ball may even hit only one arm. It is also very risky and difficult to step outside, around the ball, face the target, and pass along line B. There is very little margin for timing error. If the ball is hit too soon, it goes to the left side of the court, away from the target, and if it is hit too late then the ball goes wide to the right or off the court.

To minimize timing and contact errors, coaches should teach the third method. The player starts with the right foot slightly in front of the left, keeps her hips open to the ball, and drops the right shoulder, which will elevate the arms (platform) to the left. The ball is contacted with a left-to-right arm action. With this method, timing and contact area

From the LB court position, the player here passes with a left-to-right arm action.

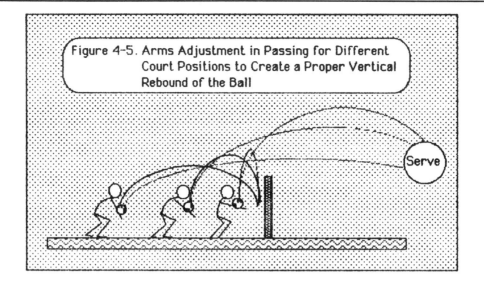

Figure 4-5. Arms Adjustment in Passing for Different Court Positions to Create a Proper Vertical Rebound of the Ball

Serve

are not as critical, because the ball can hit any-where along the length of the arm, not just in one particular spot, and still be directed accurately to the target. It is just a simple matter of angles.

For those who are interested, it is possible to determine the angle between the line of the shoulders and the platform necessary to pass the ball from a given court location to the target. In Figure 4–3, the shoulder line of the passer (line d) is perpendicular to the line of the incoming ball (line A). To pass the ball to the target along line B, the arms of the passer (e) should be placed in relationship to the shoulder line (line d) at an angle that equals half of the angle (C) formed by lines A and B.

Obviously, a player can not stop and do mathematical calculations on the court during a game, but a conceptual understanding of the geometry involved can enhance her passing and defensive play. In essence, the game of volleyball is a game of angles.

The vertical rebound of the ball is determined by the angle of the passing platform to the floor (Figure 4–4). To illustrate the point: on a fast flat serve, if the arms are parallel to the floor, the ball will rebound and go backward. If the arms are perpendicular to the floor, the ball will rebound downward in front. The angle between the arms and the upper body on the vertical plane is critical in controlling the vertical rebound of the ball. In general, to develop consistency, the arms should be kept at a consistent angle with the upper body. Then, by bending or straightening the knees, the player can adjust the vertical height of the arms to contact the ball. Obviously, some minor arm adjustments are needed as the player comes closer to, or goes farther away from, the net. The closer the player is to the net, the more parallel with the floor the arms should be (Figure 4–5).

Passing Zones

The rules of the game dictate that serving must be done from the designated serving zone, an area of limited width. The passing target area is a fixed location by the net. Consequently, the court can be divided into three distinct passing zones as shown in Figure 4–6.

In Zone 1, the largest area, the passing should be done cross-body with a left-to-right arm action while dropping the right shoulder down. The closer the passer is to the net, the more acute the angle of the arms.

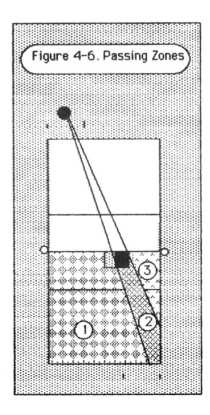

Figure 4-6. Passing Zones

The player can pass with either a parallel or a staggered foot position without affecting the angle of the pass; however, the shoulders must always be perpendicular to the incoming ball.

In Zone 2, which is much narrower than Zone 1, the passing should be executed in front of the body, "face on" to the target. This is because the direction of the served ball and the deflection angle to the target coincide.

In Zone 3, there are two options. From a purely geometric perspective, passing in this zone should use body mechanics the exact opposite of those used in Zone 1. That is, the left shoulder should be dropped and the passing action should be right-to-left across the body. However, in addition to the pure geometry, there is a practical consideration that must be taken into account for passing in Zone 3: most of the balls arriving in this area are high serves with relatively little horizontal velocity. This allows the player ample time to adjust to the location and flight path of the ball. Therefore, I recommend passing in Zone 3 with the same left-to-right mechanics used in Zone 1. The use of this same form in both Zones 1 and 3 will lead to more consistent passing.

When passing in Zone 3, the player must make sure that the vertical elevation of the arms creates the proper rebound to the target without "over-passing" (passing the ball over the net).

Alignment with the Serve

In the ready position, the *players should face the server straight on* in all court positions. Thus, players who are closer to the right sideline will be at more of an angle to the net, with the right shoulder closer to the net. The right foot should be in front of the left, in all court positions. Once the player identifies the direction of the serve, she must immediately make any necessary lateral or up-and-down adjustments, all the while maintaining eye contact with the ball. She should move with short steps toward the ball, always keeping one foot on the floor to allow for refined adjustments. In every passing attempt, and in all court positions, the player should align herself behind the ball in such a way that the *shoulder line is perpendicular to the direction of the served ball* (Figure 4–7).

All players face the server straight on in the ready position, keeping the right shoulder a bit closer to the net than the left shoulder.

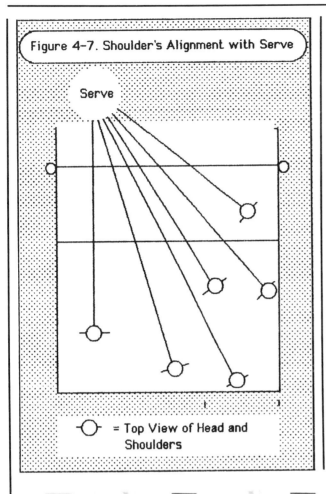

Figure 4-7. Shoulder's Alignment with Serve

Serve

-○- = Top View of Head and Shoulders

The speed with which the player travels is determined by the speed of the ball. If it is a slow serve, the player should not move too quickly to position, because she might overrun the ball, in particular a float serve. Also, the faster a person moves, the poorer her eyesight is; at high speeds (100m dash), we are practically blind. And the faster a player moves, the less capable she is of clear thinking. Generally, *a player should always move at the slowest speed the situation allows.*

Footwork to the Ball

When moving toward a served ball, a player can use shuffle steps, running steps, or crossover steps. All steps should be short, quick and smooth, and done on the toes. During all movements, eye contact with the ball must be maintained.

The shuffle is a smooth, gliding movement that allows the player to keep her head level so eye contact with the ball is undisturbed; it is the best footwork to cover short distances. To shuffle to the right, the right foot leads and the left closes in while the right foot continues sideways; the feet never cross and the distance between the feet is maintained. To shuffle to the left, the left foot leads and the right foot follows. To shuffle forward, the right foot leads and the left foot follows; backward, the left foot leads, right foot follows. It is

Sue Woodstra side-shuffles to her left. The body maintains its initial ready posture, and one foot is always in contact with the floor.

Rita Crockett shuffles at a forward diagonal into a knee drop. Right foot leads; left follows. Note the shoulder alignment behind the ball and the left-to-right arm action.

To receive a serve that is a medium or long distance away, a forward running step into a knee drop can be used. A low body posture must be maintained, particularly during the first step with the left foot.

important to shuffle on the toes, because a flat-footed shuffle is too slow. While shuffling, the body maintains its ready body posture so that the center of gravity moves at a level height and the eyes can focus clearly on the ball.

Running is effective when covering a long distance in emergency situations. A passer can turn in any direction to run forward, backward, or sideways. After running forward, if there is time, the player should try to stop, square off, and then push through the ball. After running sideways, the passer should try to square off with a crossover step and continue moving through the flight path of the ball during and after contacting it. When running backward, the passer should pivot and run, keeping the head turned back toward the ball all the time. The player should then turn around, try to square off with the ball, execute the pass, and continue moving backward if the momentum carries the player back.

A crossover step is a transition step that can be used at the end of running to square the body off with the incoming ball. When there is no time, the pass can be made during the crossover step and the player continues "running through" the ball. I don't recommend starting a shuffle movement with a crossover step because it raises the hips. The consequent up-and-down motion causes the eyes to lose their reference point, creating the illusion that the ball is moving up and down.

Passing Action

The passing action is a smooth and rhythmical action of the whole body. It begins by pushing off the left leg. The force that is generated passes through the knees, the hips, the shoulders, and, eventually, the arms. The arm action begins from the shoulder muscles; the arms should be held straight with the elbows locked. Very little arm movement is required to pass a fast, hard-hit ball, whereas a slow lob ball might require more of a lifting arm action. Contact with the ball is made about two inches above the wrist, with the soft part of the inside of the forearms. Except for passing from Zone 2, the passing action should be left-to-right and across the body. The contact should

A crossover step in preparation for or during passing allows the player to pass in an off-balanced body position, providing for a wider range to serve receive.

be a fairly short and controlled push, elevating the ball rather than banging it.

Upon contact, the feet should be substantially wider than shoulder-width apart, and the toes of the left foot should be in line with, or slightly in front of, the heel of the right foot. The knee of the left leg should point toward the passing target but the foot should be rotated slightly outward. In situations when the player must extend her arms outside the body and to the left, then the left foot can swing forward in front of the right foot and the player must go through the ball while contacting it. These situations are quite common for the LB passer when the serve comes to her left. The arm action is still left-to-right. Having the left foot in front of the right will help the passer get to the ball faster and deflect it in a sharper angle to the target.

At contact with the ball, the hips should be slightly below the height of the ball. A float serve should be contacted at a higher point than a top-spin serve, which should be contacted close to the floor with a scooping action going underneath and through the ball. This scooping action reverses the top spin into a backspin that slows down the forward movement of the ball and prevents it from going over the net. The backspin also makes the ball "hang" in the air for an extra split second, giving the setter more time to get under it.

In general, the body should be (and usually is) in some sort of motion during passing. This body motion could be in response to the ball, or in actual pursuit of it. Movement through the ball promotes better ball control. It is particularly important when the passer must pursue the ball and reach outside of her body. Moving through the pass imparts spin to the ball, which in turn helps redirect the ball to the target at a sharper angle. The following is a description of some common nonemergency passing situations and the mechanics of the correct passing technique.

1. If the ball is in front of the passer, then the passer should go forward and underneath the ball toward the target. The right foot should step forward in front of the left foot in the direction of the target.

2. If the ball is on either side of the passer, then the player must drop either the right or the left shoulder, extend the arms, and make contact while going through the ball. This movement will help to deflect the ball to the target and facilitate better ball control.

3. If the ball comes directly at a passer so quickly that she cannot take the time to move backward, she should raise her back to a more erect position and shift body weight onto her back leg. In passing Zone 1, the player should drop her right shoulder, lean back and to the right, and pass the ball with a left-to-right arm action. By shifting the body weight onto the right foot, contact with the ball is made to the left of the midline of the body. In Zone 2, the passer just leans back and contacts the ball in front of her body. If a hard ball comes at the passer, then she should lean back and rebound backward while passing.

If the ball is in front of the passer, he should move forward and through the ball underneath to impart underspin. A follow-through step with the left foot toward the target is helpful.

If the ball comes to either side of the passer, he must drop the right or left shoulder, extend his arms, and make contact while moving through the ball. Note that if the ball comes too quickly for the player to move backwards, he should assume a more erect position and shift his body weight back; if the ball is chest high, the player may need to pass the ball while stepping back with one leg or while jumping backward.

For a low ball to the left, a player should step toward the ball with his left foot, drop his right knee to the floor, and pass. For low balls to the right, he should drop his left knee.

Emergency Passing

For years, coaches taught their players to always pass directly in front of the body in a stationary position. Actually, in real game situations, passing often takes place while in motion, on either side of the body in a nonconventional manner. The following are some of the common emergency situations:

CHEST-HIGH BALLS If there is enough time, the passer should step back with both feet. Backing up makes the point of contact lower and affords more of a chance to effectively cushion the ball. If there is only enough time to step back with one foot, a passer should step back with the left foot and shift her weight back onto it. If the ball is so fast there isn't enough time to take any normal steps, the passer must jump up and backward, or rotate and elevate on one leg, contacting the ball while in the air.

BALLS OVER THE HEAD The passer should quickly turn sideways, run, do a crossover step, square off, make contact, and keep retreating backward.

FAST, MEDIUM-HIGH BALLS TO EITHER SIDE For a ball on the left, the passer should take off on the left foot and pursue the ball with a short run; for a ball on the right, take off on the right foot. If there is time, the passer should use a crossover step, square off, contact the ball, and follow through. Following through creates a side spin on the ball and deflects it at a sharper angle to the target. In addition, it allows the player to align herself better with the ball even though she is still in motion.

If the player doesn't have time to do the crossover step and square off with the net, she should simply pass during the crossover step or on the run, following through in both cases. This technique is much better than trying to stop and reach out. In most cases, when a player reaches out, she loses control and the ball deflects wildly off her hands.

FAST LOW BALLS TO EITHER SIDE For a low ball to the left, a passer should step toward the ball with the left foot, let the right knee drop to the floor, and pass. For balls to the right, the passer drops the left knee. This technique is called "knee drop" and is described in Chapter 8, "Floor Defense." In addition, the knee drop, passing fast low balls on the side, requires the passer to rotate and drop the inside shoulder smoothly and quickly.

FAST LOW BALLS IN FRONT If there isn't enough time to step toward the ball and get into an ideal serve-reception posture, the passer can make one long step forward with the right foot, lower the body, and drag the left foot behind in a forward knee drop. For an even faster ball, she can go through the same motions and continue pushing through the ball into a forward extension roll. In this situation, contact with the ball might be as much as 2 feet in front of the body. (For further details, see Chapter 8, "Floor Defense.")

Cushioning the Ball

A ball that strikes a solid object, a wall, for instance, will rebound with only slightly less than its incoming speed. A ball that strikes a soft object will impart some of its force and speed to the object and rebound at a slower rate. In addition, unless there is a spin on a ball, the angle of reflection, rebounding off an object, is always equal to the angle of incidence with the object. In passing and digging, it is very important to be able to control the rebound of the ball directly to the passing target. In digging, the task of controlling the ball is even more difficult than in passing, because usually the speed of the spike is greater than the speed of a served ball. Nevertheless, there are some basic techniques by which the rebound of the ball can be controlled.

The average speed of a float serve at contact with the passer's arms is about 55 kmh (34 mph). This speed does not allow enough time for the passer to create a cushioning action through a voluntary response. Because of the time limitations, all the cushioning of the ball during passing contact is an unconscious response, an inherent result of how the pass is executed. There are four ways by which the rebound of the ball can be controlled:

1. *By relaxing the tension in the muscles of the* forearms. Thus, the surface of the passing platform is softer and more prone to absorb some of the ball's speed.
2. *By loosening the shoulder muscles* and allowing the arms to give on contact with the ball. With experience, a player will acquire a feel for how subtle changes in shoulder-muscle tension affect the rebound of the ball.
3. *By imparting underspin or sidespin* to the ball. To prevent a fast ball that drops in front of the passer from rebounding forward and over the net, the player should drive underneath and through the ball, reversing its top spin into backspin. Fast balls that come to either side of the passer can be kept from going over the net by passing while moving at an angle through the ball, thus imparting side spin that helps di-

rect the ball to the passing target.

4. *By rebounding back* while passing. This method is effective when passing fast balls that are coming directly at the passer.

Mental Preparations

Coaches sometimes make the mistake of stressing the difficulties of passing. In so doing, they create undue anxiety in their players. In fact, from a purely physical standpoint, passing is a relatively easy skill. It is the *emotional* aspect of passing that is challenging. Fear of the unknown, self-doubts, and a great sense of responsibility may cause anxieties that interfere with the physical execution of the skill. Many players exhibit good passing technique in practice but under pressure in a game situation they can not perform up to their abilities. To prepare players to pass well under pressure, the coach should allocate an ample amount of practice time for passing.

At least 20 percent of every practice session must be dedicated to passing drills of one form or another. Quantity of training may help improve a player's self-confidence and make passing second nature. In addition, the coach should utilize a variety of drills that simulate game situations. These drills can be in a form of quotas that must be achieved, either by each player individually or by the team as a whole. For example: the team must make ten sets of five consecutive good passes. The count starts over from the beginning every time the pass is not to the target. These passing quotas can be adapted to the particular level of the players. This kind of drill creates an environment of dependency among the players, and forces each individual to do her best at all times.

Passing statistics in practice games must be kept, and passing norms must be established. The players must be made aware of both.

Passers must be taught to concentrate on thoughts regarding the server's strategy rather than on doubts about their own techniques. If a player is eager to pass, instead of dreading it, she can respond to a serve with zest and perform to her fullest capabilities. An attempt by the coach to correct the passing technique of a player during competition may make the player even more doubtful and insecure. A player awaiting the serve should not think about success or failure, but should concentrate on the server and the ball.

Players who have emotional difficulties in passing should take a few deep breaths and count their breathing. The deep breaths have a tranquilizing effect on the body, and counting the number of breaths will help to take the player's mind off any doubts, fears, and insecurities.

TEAM SERVE RECEPTION

Serve-Reception Formations

The rules of the game allow for a great variety of serve-reception formations. Since the setter does not participate in receiving the serve, that leaves the other five players as possible receivers. In some formations, all five players are positioned in such a way that any one of them might receive the serve. Other formations deploy four, three, or two players in the area to which the opposing team is most likely to direct their serves. Almost all formations can be adjusted to create different patterns.

When considering which particular serve-reception formation to use, the coach should evaluate: 1) whether the formation maximizes the team's potential for serve reception, and 2) whether the formation allows for a smooth transition into an effective reception attack. Because the serve reception is, in essence, the beginning of serve-reception attack, one can not be considered without the other.

The coach must evaluate her players' passing abilities and place the players in a formation that exploits their talent and yet also conforms to her overall attack philosophy.

Team Preparation for Serve Receive

It is important that all players get to their initial positions in the formation as quickly as possible after the previous play has ended. This gives them more time to regroup, to concentrate, and to organize their attack. In the initial position, the team prepares itself in three ways:

1. Each player checks to see if she is in the proper position in relation to other players, as dictated by the serve-reception formation.
2. The setter and the hitters communicate, by whatever system the team uses, regarding the attack.
3. Mental preparations for receiving the serve begin as each player starts to focus on the server.

As the initial preparations are completed, the players assume the ready body posture.

Some teams get into the ready posture upon ver-

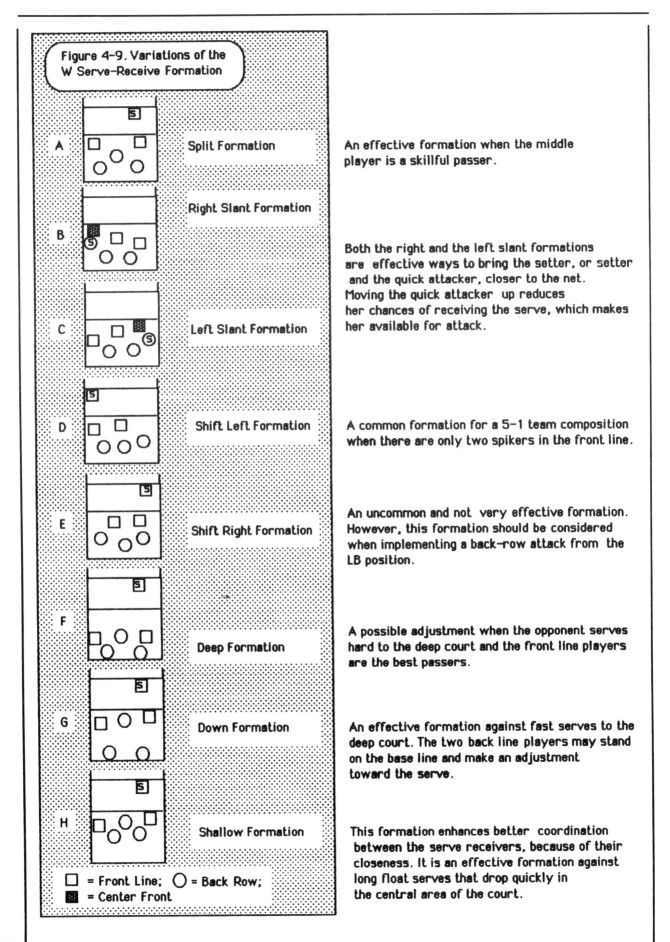

Figure 4-9. Variations of the W Serve-Receive Formation

A — Split Formation
An effective formation when the middle player is a skillful passer.

B — Right Slant Formation

C — Left Slant Formation
Both the right and the left slant formations are effective ways to bring the setter, or setter and the quick attacker, closer to the net. Moving the quick attacker up reduces her chances of receiving the serve, which makes her available for attack.

D — Shift Left Formation
A common formation for a 5-1 team composition when there are only two spikers in the front line.

E — Shift Right Formation
An uncommon and not very effective formation. However, this formation should be considered when implementing a back-row attack from the LB position.

F — Deep Formation
A possible adjustment when the opponent serves hard to the deep court and the front line players are the best passers.

G — Down Formation
An effective formation against fast serves to the deep court. The two back line players may stand on the base line and make an adjustment toward the serve.

H — Shallow Formation
This formation enhances better coordination between the serve receivers, because of their closeness. It is an effective formation against long float serves that drop quickly in the central area of the court.

☐ = Front Line; ◯ = Back Row; ▨ = Center Front

bal signal from one of the teammates; others take the cue from a particular movement of the server. To avoid excessive physical and mental strain, the player should not get into the ready posture too quickly before the server is ready to serve. On the other hand, the player should *focus her eyes on the server as soon as possible.* This will allow more time for her eyes to adjust to the serving distance and the background, thus improving depth perception.

The W Formation

The *W* formation is sometimes called "five-player serve reception," because all five players are potential passers. This formation is very popular among women's teams; through the 1984 Olympics, eight of the ten top teams in the world, including China, Japan, and the USA, used this formation.

With proper training and the right personnel, the *W* formation is the most effective serve-receive formation. In addition, the *W* formation is a very adjustable formation that lends itself quite nicely to attack, especially multiple attack. Players can be mobilized easily from one side of the court to another, so a spiker can attack at any given point along the net.

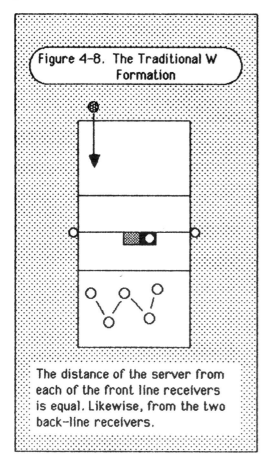

Figure 4-8. The Traditional W Formation

The distance of the server from each of the front line receivers is equal. Likewise, from the two back-line receivers.

The *W* formation does demand, however, that everyone on the team be a good passer. It also requires that the players be disciplined in executing their specific passing assignments in each court position. Because of the number of passers involved more gray areas are created. To prevent hesitation or collisions between players, passing lanes and areas of responsibilities must be clearly defined.

Figure 4–8 illustrates the traditional *W* serve-reception formation in which the three front-line passers stand at equal distances from the server on an arc; the two back-row passers are also positioned on an arc, each one an equal distance from the server.

The traditional *W* formation is a classic formation that can be varied either by adjusting the inner relationship between the players or by relocating the whole formation up or down the court. Figure 4–9 shows some of the most common adjustments of the *W* formation. The main reasons for modifying the basic *W* formation are:

1. To position a back-row setter in a better location, one enabling her to get to the passing target faster.
2. To position a quick attacker closer to the net. This reduces her chances of serve receiving and brings her closer to the attack position. Receiving a serve often eliminates a quick attacker from the attack, or slows her down considerably. Moving the quick attacker under the shadow of the net frees her to concentrate solely on attacking.
3. To position the team's best passers in the most likely area for serve reception so that they will receive more serves than the weaker passers.
4. To move the whole formation up or down on the court, adjusting to opponent's serving tendencies.

The W Diagonal Slide Method

The diagonal slide *W* formation is a modification of the standard *W* formation. The 1984 USA Women's Olympic team developed and successfully used the slide *W* for many years. This method was developed to complement the team's particular style of passing, which was discussed in the first section of this chapter. Figure 4–10 illustrates the basic player arrangement, area of responsibility, and the traffic lanes for each passing position.

In all positions, the player stands facing toward the server. The right foot is in front of the left foot, and the right shoulder is closer to the net than the

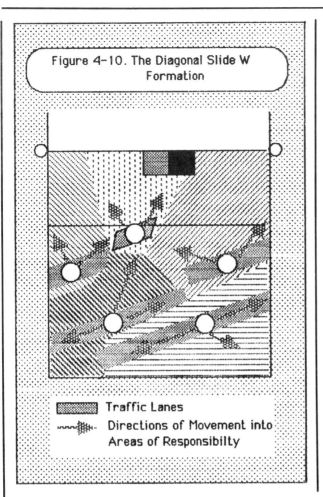

Figure 4-10. The Diagonal Slide W Formation

Traffic Lanes

Directions of Movement into Areas of Responsibilty

left shoulder (see "Ready Body Posture" in previous section). In this way, players on the right side of the court (RF and RB) are more at an angle to the net than players on the left (LF and LB). The center front player stands about 1 to 3 feet behind the 10-foot line and about 3 feet to the left of the center court. The right front player is positioned about 7 feet from the 10-foot line and also 7 feet from the right sideline. The left front player stands about 6 feet from the 10-foot line and 3 to 4 feet from the left sideline. The left back is positioned 8 feet from the left sideline and 7 feet from the endline. The right back stands 6 feet from the endline and 9 feet from the right sideline.

Each player has a specific area of responsibility that can be covered in designated movement lanes. These traffic lanes cut across the court at a diagonal and are designed in such a way that the players can move across the court and align themselves perpendicularly to the ball without colliding with each other. These diagonal lanes proceed naturally from the player's orientation in the ready posture. If the players were to move along their respective lanes, keying off the center front player, they would stack up in a straight line behind the CF. The order would be as follows: CF, LF, RF, LB, and RB.

When executing a pass, the arm action should always be left-to-right across the body, except from passing Zone 2 (Figure 4–6). The center front

The ready position in a W serve-receive formation. Note that all players face the server, keeping the right foot slightly forward.

is responsible for balls that come in front of her and those that can be reached with one step to the left. The left front is responsible for balls in front of her and short balls that come at an angle to either side. The right front is responsible for balls falling directly in front of her and also short balls slightly to the left or right.

The left back player has the heaviest passing responsibilities. She picks up balls falling short behind LF and CF, as well as any ball between the two. In her traffic lane, LB has the responsibility to cover from the left back corner to center court. High balls that go over her head are the responsibility of the right back player.

After LB, RB is the second primary passer on the court. She covers from behind right front diagonally across and deep behind LB. RB also has the responsibility to receive deep balls to the right back corner. In general, the forward movement of the right back passer is limited to one step.

Movement and areas of passing responsibilities for the W diagonal slide formation.

1.

1. Initial W formation. 2. LB passes a short ball from center court. (RF not seen.) 3. LF passes a short ball; LB covers behind. (RF not seen.) 4. RB covers behind LB and passes a long ball. (RF and LF not seen.) 5. LB passes a ball; RB covers behind. LF stepped to the sideline. (RF not seen.)

Considering the LB player's court position and the location of the target, it seems at first glance that RB, rather than LB, should pass balls that are coming to the center of the court. The USA team tried this option, but it did not work too well. The problem involved crosscourt serves that go over the center. These balls might drop short or go long to the right back corner. Having LB responsible for passing balls that are coming to the middle of the court frees RB from making decisions about whether the ball is long or short. When LB sees the ball on the right side, she simply slides to the right. If the ball is short, LB passes it. If the ball is long, then RB passes.

When passing balls in the center court, the left back player should make every attempt to get her body into position so that she can pass the ball with a left-to-right arm action. At times the ball will be too fast and the left back passer will have no choice but to extend her arms to the right side. In this case, she should not attempt to pass to the primary target (Figure 4–1) because the ball could be easily deflected to the right side. Instead, LB should drop her left shoulder and pass the ball to the secondary target.

Passing is the collective responsibility of the team. All team members must see and respond as a unit to the flight of the serve. This includes the setter, who should make a conscious effort not to interfere with the passer's sight lines and eye contact with the ball. Players who are not involved in the actual pass must maintain visual contact with the passer and follow the trajectory of the ball to the target.

If a player does not see the pass, her timing will be off and she will be out of sync with the delicate

machinery of the attack. Eye contact with the pass is maintained by always turning to the direction of the serve. Thus, when the ball comes on the right side, the player should turn right, and when the ball comes on the left side, the player should turn left. At times the player will find herself in the direct path of the ball. When this occurs, the player must open what is called the "passing lane." If, for instance, the ball is served between the right front player and the sideline, RF should not move toward the sideline but rather turn right, taking a step backward with her right foot toward the center of the court. In this way, RF avoids crossing the passing lane of the right back player, allowing RB to maintain visual contact with the ball. Consequently, as a rule, when a ball passes a player on the right, she opens to that direction, taking a step back to clear the zone. Similarly, when the ball is on the left, the player opens to the left.

Players should learn to call their own balls by saying, "Mine!" and they also must learn to call the ball "In!" or "Out!" RB should make the call for the right front and left back passers; LB should make the call for the right back and left front. All players should be involved in calling.

The principles described for this particular *W* formation can be easily applied to other five-player serve-reception formations, as well as to formations with fewer players.

Application of the W Formation to Team Composition

Figure 4–11 illustrates the slide *W* formation for six rotations for a team with a 5–1 team composition. Note the setter's position and penetration path from the back row. From behind LB and RB, the setter should penetrate by taking an outside path to the target near the sidelines, rather than between front-row passers (CF and LF, or CF and RF). These outside patterns eliminate the possibility of the setter interfering with the serve reception of the back-court passers by running across their sight lines.

In addition, in rotations 2, 3, and 4, the team is arranged in a "shift left" pattern (Figure 4–9). A split formation, or the "shift right" formation are possible options for these rotations, and should be considered when correlating serve reception and attack. The split formation should be considered whenever the player at right back in the rotation (U, C2, A1) is either a very good or a very weak passer. When the player at right back is a good passer, she can remain at right back, as shown in Figure 4–9a. Note that if the split formation were not employed, the player at RB in the rotational

In the W serve-reception formation, RF and LF should open the passing lanes for RB and LB respectively. If the serve comes over the outside shoulder, they should step toward the inside of the court; if the serve comes over the inside shoulder, they should step toward the sidelines.

1. Initial formation. 2. RF opens the passing lane by stepping toward the inside of the court. RB passes the ball. 3. LF opens the passing lane for LB by stepping toward the inside of the court.

order would be positioned at RF in the serve-reception formation.

If the player at RB in the rotational order is a weak passer, the team has two choices. One, obviously, is to go to the shift left formation. But if the team wishes to remain in the split formation for tactical reasons (such as attacking quickly behind the setter), the weak RB passer can be hidden to some degree by moving her closer to the 10-foot line and bringing the CB serve receiver back deeper into the court. Generally, when the player at RB in the *rotation* is not a good passer, the team is better off using the shift left formation which moves this weak passer up into Zone 3, a difficult area to serve to effectively.

Aside from serve-reception considerations, the coach should also determine whether a split for-

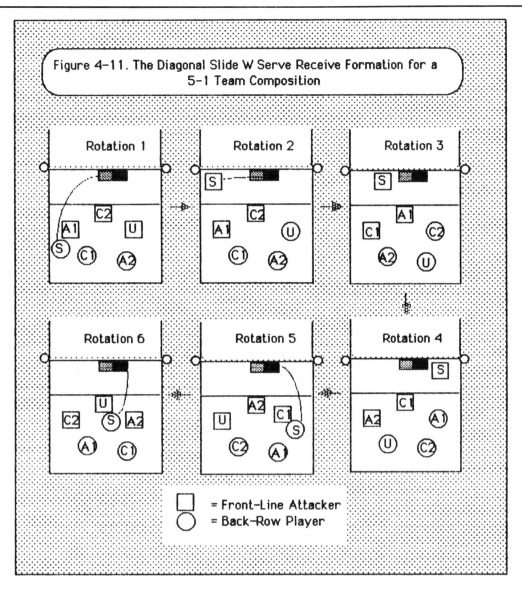

Figure 4-11. The Diagonal Slide W Serve Receive Formation for a 5-1 Team Composition

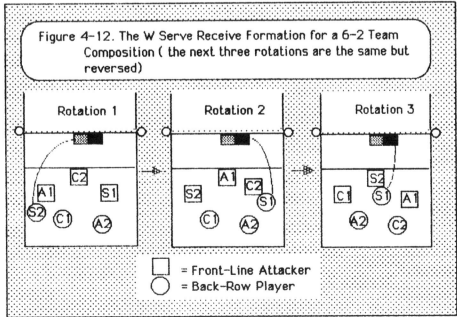

Figure 4-12. The W Serve Receive Formation for a 6-2 Team Composition (the next three rotations are the same but reversed)

mation is conducive to her attack scheme. A shift right pattern should be considered only when LB is a skilled back-row attacker. The shift left formation is generally the most popular formation.

Careful observation of all six rotations shown in Figure 4–11 reveals that in all rotations the serve-reception pattern is exactly the same. The importance of this observation will be discussed in "Attack Priority vs. Serve-Reception Priority formations").

Figure 4–12 illustrates the setter's position and penetration pattern from the back row to the passing target in three rotations for the 6–2 team composition. Because there are two setters in the 6–2 composition, the other three rotations are the same, only with the other setter penetrating. As mentioned before, in the 6–2 team composition, the setter should always penetrate from the back row so that the front-row setter can be used in attack.

Four-Player Serve-Receive Formations

When the players are highly skilled or large in size, a four-player serve-reception formation may be used. Because large players occupy more physical space, they have the effect of reducing the "open" areas into which the other team may serve. They also generally cover more area quicker than small players.

Four-player serve-reception formations are often used by men's teams. Men are usually quicker than women and, because they play on a higher net, a typical men's serve has a slower velocity and higher arc than women's serves.

Four-player serve-reception formations can be of a variety of shapes:

- the U-shape formation (Figure 4–13a);
- the semimoon formation (Figure 4–13b);
- the staggered left or staggered right formations (Figure 4–13c,d).

The advantages of four-player serve-reception formations include:

- eliminating one poor passer from serve-reception responsibilities;
- shielding a spiker from the serve;
- overloading one side of the court with two or three spikers (called a "stack" or "overload" pattern); and
- bringing the setter closer to the net for an easier path to the passing target.

The U formation (or any other four-player for-

mation) can be used in conjunction with the W formation in the one rotation when the setter is in the LB position (Figure 4–13a, and Figure 4–11, rotation 1) and has difficulty getting to the passing target on time. Moving both the A1 attacker and the setter (S1) closer to the net should help the setter get to the passing target more quickly.

Figure 4–14 shows two possible models for the allocation of court responsibilities among four primary passers organized in a U-shape serve-receive formation. Note the similarity of traffic lanes for this formation and the slide W formation (Figure 4–10).

Three- and Two-Player Formations

Only the three best passers are used in the three-player formation (Figure 4–15), hiding the setter and two other players who could be weak passers or quick attackers. Using only three passers offers more freedom to manipulate the serve-reception formation, and there is less gray area between passers. But two difficulties arise: each passer has more court space to cover; and often the setter has to be placed far away from the net (Figure 4–16). (This happens when the same three players pass in all six rotations.)

This formation is not as popular among women's teams as it is among men's. Because the women's net is lower, the serve is usually much faster, and women, in general, are not as quick as men (although they can be more skillful). Up until the 1976

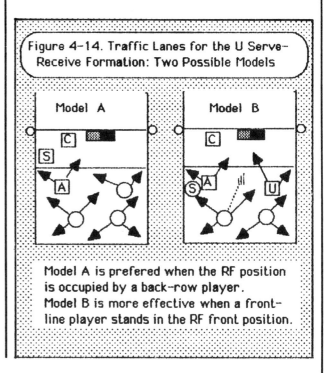

Figure 4–14. Traffic Lanes for the U Serve-Receive Formation: Two Possible Models

Model A   Model B

Model A is prefered when the RF position is occupied by a back-row player.
Model B is more effective when a front-line player stands in the RF front position.

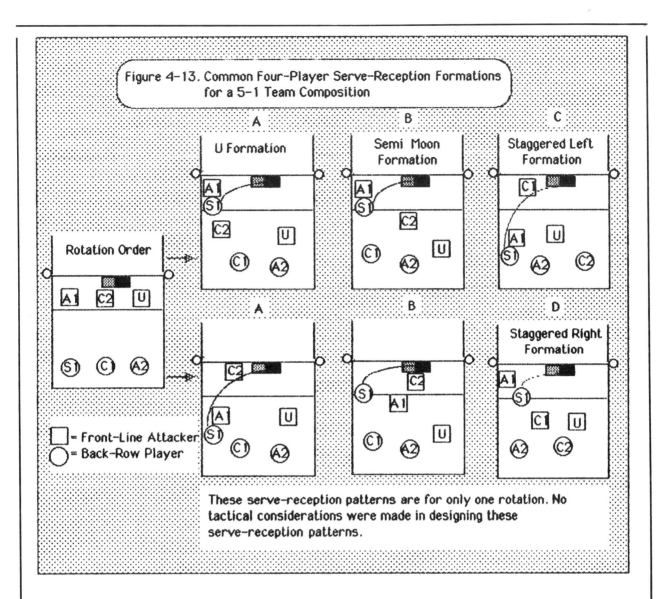

Figure 4-13. Common Four-Player Serve-Reception Formations for a 5-1 Team Composition

A — U Formation

B — Semi Moon Formation

C — Staggered Left Formation

Rotation Order

D — Staggered Right Formation

□ = Front-Line Attacker
○ = Back-Row Player

These serve-reception patterns are for only one rotation. No tactical considerations were made in designing these serve-reception patterns.

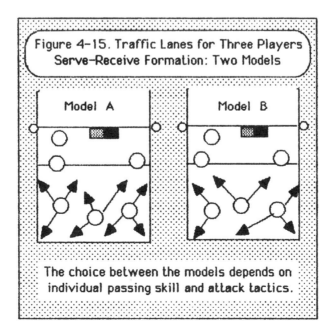

Figure 4-15. Traffic Lanes for Three Players Serve-Receive Formation: Two Models

Model A

Model B

The choice between the models depends on individual passing skill and attack tactics.

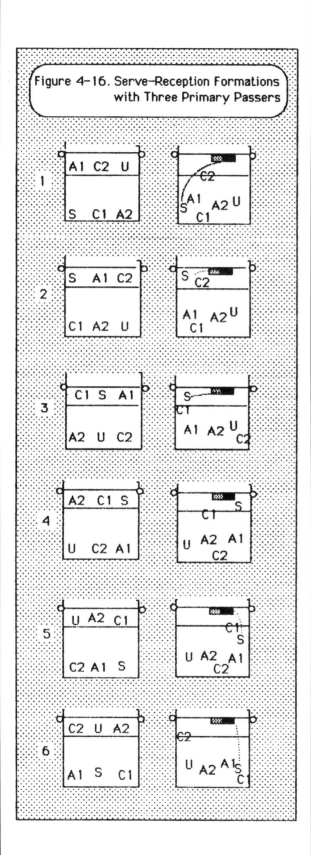

Figure 4-16. Serve-Reception Formations with Three Primary Passers

Olympic Games, the women's team of the USSR implemented the three-player serve-receive formation with relative success. Figure 4–16 shows how to arrange a three-player serve-reception formation in such a manner that the first three rotations are the same and the last three are the same.

The two-player serve-reception formation (Figure 4–17) has been attempted periodically by Eastern European teams. In the 1984 Olympic Games, the USA men's team was very successful with it. This formation is particularly effective when the same two players do all the passing in all six rotations. In order not to hinder any of the quick attackers, either the ace players, or an ace player and the utility player, should be the two primary passers (see Chapter 6, Figure 6 45). Now, however, with the recent rule change that prohibits blocking the serve, and with the increased popularity of the jump-spike serve, this formation may become very vulnerable. It simply might not provide enough reaction time for the two passers to cover their large area of responsibility.

Attack Priority vs. Serve-Reception Priority Formations

Serve reception and the serve-reception attack are deeply interrelated, each shaping the other. Consequently, only a careful design of the serve reception and the attack can maximize both.

There are two general approaches in designing the serve-receive patterns of a W formation: "serve-reception priority" pattern, and "attack priority" pattern. The serve-reception priority pattern places emphasis on strengthening the team's serve-reception abilities. The attack priority pat-

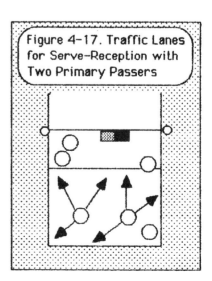

Figure 4-17. Traffic Lanes for Serve-Reception with Two Primary Passers

tern emphasizes the team's attack goals. To create harmony between serve reception and the serve-reception attack, each of the serve-reception strategies must be matched with a complementary attack philosophy.

There are two basic attack concepts: the single-tempo strategy, and the multitempo strategy. In the single-tempo attack strategy, each attacker is trained primarily to attack at only one tempo, either slow high sets, or low quick sets. Hence, center hitters, or quick attackers, only attack at first tempo (quick and relatively low sets), whereas the ace players only attack at a second tempo (higher sets). In the multitempo strategy, every player on the team can attack at both tempos.

Teams using the single-tempo attack strategy must give priority to the attack-formation serve-receive patterns. With the single-tempo attack strategy, the serve-reception formation must be adjusted so that the quick attackers are placed close to the net, near the passing target. This reduces their chance of receiving the serve and places them in position for the quickest possible attack. Figure 4–18 illustrates variations of the *W* serve-receive formation as adjusted for the quick attackers (compare Figures 4–11 and 4–18).

Teams that use the multitempo strategy can afford to stress formations maximizing their serve-reception capabilities. Under these circumstances, the coach designs a *W* pattern that appears to yield best passing results, and this pattern is maintained in all six rotations with no special adjustments for quick attackers (Figure 4–11). The USA women's team used the serve-reception priority *W* formation coupled with the multitempo attack strategy.

Unless a coach carefully selects and consistently emphasizes one approach, there is a danger that she will end up with a compromise system that does not maximize either service reception or attack.

Men's teams often use serve-reception forma-

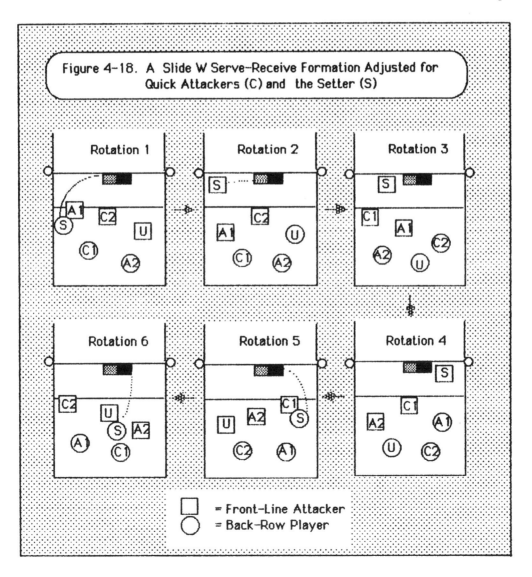

Figure 4–18. A Slide W Serve–Receive Formation Adjusted for Quick Attackers (C) and the Setter (S)

□ = Front-Line Attacker
○ = Back-Row Player

tions with four, three, and even two primary receivers. When the serve reception is good (that is, when the primary passers perform at a high level of consistency and efficiency), these formations allow the team to adopt the single-tempo attack concept, and yet maintain the same serve-receive pattern in all rotations. In these formations, the front-row quick attacker or a back court attacker can always be released from serve-reception responsibilities; yet there is no need to adjust the serve-receive pattern. In serve-receive formations with less than four players, the main passing burden should fall on the ace players and the utility player. The main difficulty of these formations is that they often position the setter and one or more front-row attackers far away from the net (see Figure 4–16, rotations 1 and 6).

Concealed Serve-Reception Formations

In a concealed serve-reception formation, front-line attackers are put in passing positions to create the illusion that they are actually back-row players (Figure 4–19). If an opponent does not carefully monitor the order of the rotation, they can get confused and neglect to block the concealed attacker. This kind of formation can not be executed on a continuous basis because the opponent will soon wise up to it.

A concealed formation can also be used to switch a good passer from the front row to the back row to replace a poor passer. A back-row passer who stands in the front line should participate in the attack pattern as a fake; in this way, four people drive for attack instead of the usual three, and the opposing block can become confused.

In designing and implementing concealed serve-reception attack formations, the coach should take into consideration the risk of actually losing one spiker, who could get involved in an emergency passing situation by standing in a high-probability passing zone. The coach should also consider that when four players drive for attack, spiker coverage becomes more complicated and less effective.

The fewer the number of passers involved, the greater the variety of possible concealed forma-

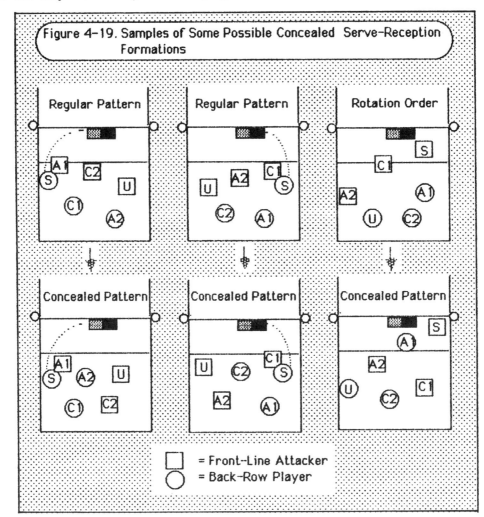

Figure 4-19. Samples of Some Possible Concealed Serve-Reception Formations

Regular Pattern   Regular Pattern   Rotation Order

Concealed Pattern   Concealed Pattern   Concealed Pattern

☐ = Front-Line Attacker
○ = Back-Row Player

tions. Each team should have in its repertoire some concealed formations to be used sporadically during the game.

Whenever concealed serve-reception formations are discussed, some coaches and players become confused because they do not clearly understand the overlap rules that govern the rotational order. Simply stated, here are the rules to remember:

1. CF must be between LF and RF.
2. CF must be in front of CB.
3. CB must be between LB and RB, and behind CF.
4. LB and RB must be behind LF and RF respectively.

Do not get mixed up with regard to the players' positions opposite (diagonal to) each other in the rotational order. Sometimes it is perfectly legal to put a back-row player in front of her "pair" partner. This is the case in the third example shown in Figure 4–19 where A1 is ahead of A2 even though A2 is the front-row (attacking) player. Notice that A1 is still to the right of the CB player (C2) and is still behind the player at RF who is the setter. Conversely, A2 is still positioned to the left of C1 and ahead of the LB utility player.

At lower levels of play, especially high-school and junior-club competition, it is often a good idea to alert the officials to the arrangement of your concealed formations prior to the match. Otherwise, they may not correctly recognize the formation and mistakenly call an overlap or rotational violation. Even if the referee immediately realizes her mistake and corrects the call, the element of surprise is lost.

Adjusting the Formation for Different Types of Serves

Different types of serves may require slight adjustments in both the passing technique and in the serve-reception formation.

A float serve can be passed from around hip height. Top-spin serves should be contacted lower to the floor, around knee height. With float serves the feet should be slightly wider apart than with spin serves so the passer can adjust to the unpredictable lateral movement of the ball.

An outside side-spin serve (ball rotates counterclockwise) should be contacted on the right side of the body with the left shoulder slightly lower than the right; an inside side-spin serve (ball rotates clockwise) should be contacted on the left side of the body.

Responding to a float serve served from the base

line or about 6 feet behind the base line, the serve-reception formation should adjust to a down formation (Figure 4–9g). Responding to a float serve served far behind the base line, the formation should move up and become more shallow and centered (Figure 4–9h).

For top-spin serves, which are usually served near the base line, the two back passers should be 6 feet from the base line and the formation should be quite shallow. For outside spin serves, the whole formation should move slightly to the right. A jump-spike serve may require three passers in the deep court.

Time Considerations

When designing a serve-reception formation, a coach should understand the difficulty involved in covering an area of 81 square meters under severe time limitations.

Computerized measurements made at the Coto Research Center during the 1981 World Cup women's competition in Japan show that the average peak height of a served ball was about 365 centimeters (12'), and the average speed of the ball was about 15.5 meters per second, or 36 miles per hour. The average maximum speed of the players on the serve-receiving team was about 360 centimeters (11'10") per second. The average elapsed time between the release of the served ball and contact by the passer was about 1.2 seconds.

Using this data, Figure 4–20 illustrates how much court area five players can cover. The five triangles represent the positions of the players on the court in a *W* formation. The circles represent the area each player is capable of covering. The range was calculated with the assumption that the average flight time of the serve was one second, and the average forward speed of each player was 250 centimeters and the average backward speed was 220 centimeters.

The figure shows that the right and left corners of the court, the deep center of the court, and the zone within the 10-foot line are especially vulnerable. However, the arc required to clear the net makes it very difficult to serve a high-velocity ball into the area in front of the 10-foot line.

Observations made during men's competition show that the speed of a top roundhouse serve, and a jump-spike serve, gives the passer no more than .85 of a second to respond. Taken together with the recent rule change prohibiting serve blocking, the awesome speed of these types of serves may necessitate that men's teams return to serve-reception formations with more than two passers.

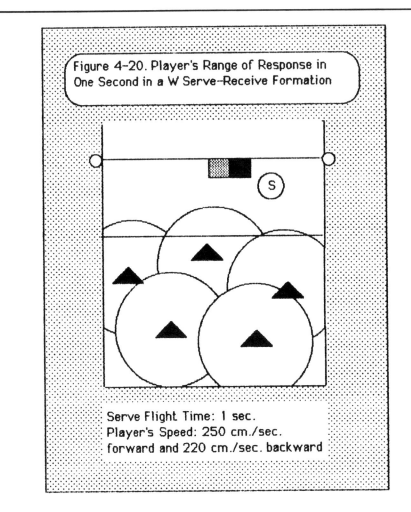

Figure 4-20. Player's Range of Response in One Second in a W Serve-Receive Formation

Serve Flight Time: 1 sec.
Player's Speed: 250 cm./sec.
forward and 220 cm./sec. backward

THE SET

The *set* is a ball that is directed with a precise trajectory and speed to a particular hitter so that he can effectively attack it. The set is usually, but not necessarily, the second contact with the ball by a player, following a pass or a dig. The action of delivering a set is *setting,* and *setters* are players who specialize in setting.

Setting is usually done with the fingers of both hands over the head, a technique that allows for sensitive ball handling. The set can be executed from high, medium, and low body postures. In each posture the actual hand movement and timing are the same; what varies is the extent to which the knees are bent. In emergency situations, setting can be done with the forearms in a motion similar to passing or digging, but the setter will not be able to control the height and location as well with this "bump" setting technique. What defines a ball as a set is the function it serves, not the technique.

Every player on a team should master the basic setting techniques, because there will be times when the setter is un-able to reach a ball and someone else will be forced to set it. In high-level competition, the ability of all players to set competently is a prerequisite. Currently, the overall level of setting skill in the U.S. is the poorest of all skills. This is partly because inexperienced and poorly trained referees, especially at the high-school level, are too harsh in calling fouls (double contacts, or carrying) on young players using the overhand setting technique. This discourages players from aggressively using the overhand set and often leads them to use the forearm set.

For the team's setter, setting encompasses strategic considerations far more complex than just the setting technique. Setting is a very refined skill that implies the specific timing and coordination of a preplanned offense.

This chapter is divided into two parts: part one describes the basic setting technique to be used by all players, and part two describes more advanced setting skills and strategy specifically for the setter.

BASIC SETTING TECHNIQUE

The basic setting technique can be executed from the normal standing, low, roll, or jump body positions. In this part we will discuss only the basic posture.

BASIC SETTING POSTURE In the basic setting posture the player assumes a position directly underneath the ball with his shoulders facing the spiker square on. The feet should be placed shoulder-width apart with the right foot half a step in front of the other (Figure 5–1). The knees should be slightly bent and the trunk almost vertically upright. The posture is similar to sitting, only without the chair. It is very important that the hips be underneath the ball to enable the setter to set forward or backward equally well. If the hips are too far back, then it is impossible to set backward.

The arms hang loose with the elbows bent at about a 100-degree angle and the hands in front of the body. As the ball nears the player, he should elevate his arms maintaining the same angle at the elbows. The elbows should be comfortably spread above and in front of the shoulders. There is no need to forcefully draw the elbows together. The angle between the forearm and the upper arm should be about 100 degrees, and the angle between the inside of the upper arm and the shoulder line should be about 145 degrees.

The arms are raised until the hands are about 6 inches above the head and slightly in front of it. The hands are held in a straight line with the forearms with no lateral (in or out) flexion at the wrist, but with *slight* backward flexion. The palms are slightly cupped in the shape of the ball.

The fingers should be comfortably spread with the thumbs pointing toward each other, not toward the nose or away from it. The amount of stiffness in the fingers depends on the height of the descending ball and the distance it must travel for the set. Beginners should hold the fingers a little bit stiffer than is actually necessary. As their setting skills improve, they'll learn to loosen their fingers. The shape formed by the fingers and the thumbs is similar to the shape of a spade in a deck of cards. The index fingers should be about 1½ to 2 inches apart, and the thumbs should be about 1 inch apart.

CONTACT WITH THE BALL Contact with the ball should be made about 6 inches above the head and just slightly in front of it, over the center of the body. (If the player were to let the ball drop, it

Figure 5-1. Foot Position for Setting in the Ready Body Posture

would fall on his forehead.) The lateral position of the hands can vary slightly as long as one hand is in front of and over the head. If contact is made with both hands outside the shoulders or behind the back, it will probably be considered a mishandled ball by the official. The contact is not made just with the fingertips, but rather with the whole length of the fingers and the thumbs, although the little fingers may touch the ball only with the fingertips. The palm should not touch the ball. The more contact with the ball, the better the control. It is important that the thumbs contact the ball; otherwise ball control is reduced and backsetting is very difficult.

SETTING ACTION As the ball arrives, the player elevates his arms, counts one, then pushes through the ball. The player should push through with a smooth action that resembles a very quick catch and throwing motion. He should not poke at the ball abruptly. Just prior to contact, the angle at the elbows can decrease slightly. Once the hands contact the ball, the angle at the elbows must continuously increase. If the angle decreases, it's a held ball.

The propulsive force behind the set begins in the back leg as both knees straighten. Then it builds, passing through the hips as they rotate toward the target, through the elbows as they straighten, and finally through the wrists that push through the ball. The fingers act as a springboard, prolonging contact with the ball as long as possible. The hands push through the ball in four simultaneous directions: underneath, forward, up, and out. At the completion of the contact with the ball, the thumbs should point away from the body toward the direction of the set. The arms, however, should remain parallel with each other. The cumulative forces generated by the body should pass at an angle slightly beneath the center of the ball, creating a very slight reverse spin on the ball.

When setting balls a long distance toward the net, the player should bend his elbows and knees more than usual. He can then act as a spring by straightening first the legs and then the elbows to generate more power. At times when the spring action is done quickly and forcefully, it lifts the player off the ground. This jump imparts the extra thrust the ball needs to cover the distance.

After contact, the arms follow through to complete extension and then drop, relaxed. The ball should have very little or no spin. If there is any, it should be reverse spin, an indication of a proper wrist action.

The precise timing involved in setting is critical and depends largely on eye-hand coordination. As a player's timing improves, his touch becomes softer and softer, and he gains more and more control over the ball. This soft touch is something that the player acquires with experience as his hand and body movements become smooth and synchronized.

SETTING FORWARD AND BACKWARD A forward or backward set can be delivered equally well from the same basic body posture, as long as the body is underneath the ball. Too often players overlook this fundamental fact and limit their setting potential to only a forward or backward direction. When setting from deep in the court, this is not critical. Setting forward and backward from along the net is usually done by the setter and will be discussed in "Setting for the Setter."

When setting from the deep court forward, the player should face the target square on. If the target is to the left of the player, the right foot should be closer to the net and in front of the left foot. If the target is to the right of the player, the left foot should be closer to the net and in front of the right foot. This positioning allows the force that comes from the back leg to rotate the hips toward the target and push the ball toward the net. It's critical that before setting the ball, the player make eye contact with his target. Eye contact helps orient the player and cues the brain to summon the appropriate amount of force needed to propel the ball the required distance.

When setting from the deep court backward, the player must stand with his back and shoulders square to the target. The right foot should always be forward as there is no hip rotation. The back may be arched backward slightly. The player should make brief eye contact with the target, looking back over his shoulder if it's at all possible.

The main difference between frontsetting and backsetting lies in the wrist action. In backsetting there is a pronounced backward flip of the wrists and a push in the backward direction. The thumbs are critical in helping to direct and support the ball. If the thumbs are not in contact with the ball, much ball control is lost and setting is almost impossible unless the ball is behind the head (a very awkward position). After backsetting, the player follows through by moving forward. In frontsetting, the wrist action is forward, underneath, and through the ball.

MOVEMENT TO THE BALL Forward movement for short distances (one or two steps away) should be done with a forward slide, the right foot leading and the left foot closing. Running should be used for longer distances. To stop forward body momentum, the second-to-last step should be a very short step with a heel-toe action; this last step should get the body into the proper basic position.

Backward movement for short distances should be done with a sliding step starting with the left foot, and closing with the right. For longer distances, the player should turn, take a crossover step, run, turn back, and face the target. During movement, the player should not lose eye contact with the ball. If the player doesn't have the time to turn back and face the target, he must use a backset.

Lateral adjustments are made using three or four short sliding steps to the right or the left. Sliding to the side should be on a slight curve. At the end of the movement, the right foot should be in front of the left when setting to the left side. When setting to the right side, the left foot should be in front of the right. For distances more than three or four steps away, the player should simply run on a curve and swing around to align himself with the ball, using a crossover step for the second-to-last step.

During movement to the ball, the arms should be held down and used naturally by the body for movement. Only when the player is in position to set should the arms be elevated. Just before getting into position, the player should make eye contact with the target.

Usually, players who are not setters and who must set a ball from the back row have time to come to a standstill and get in a balanced position. But sometimes the player has to set the ball on the move. Therefore, coaches must design drills in which players practice setting to different targets on the move from different court positions.

BALL TRAJECTORY FROM THE DEEP COURT Balls set from deep court must have a high trajectory and a fairly substantial reverse spin so they'll drop as vertically as possible. The longer the distance, the higher the trajectory should be. Balls with a low trajectory are very difficult for the spiker to time, and if set with too much force stand a risk of going over the net. The balls should drop about 3 to 4 feet off the net and about 4 feet inside from the antenna.

Balls from right back should usually be set to the left front, and balls from the left back should be set to the right front. When players become more skillful and experienced, LB can often set LF, especially if he is the best spiker, or if RB is the setter (or a weak spiker). If the player has difficulties or is not strong enough to set from the deep court to the net, he can lean forward into the ball or even jump into it while setting, imparting extra power to the ball.

Spikers receiving deep-court sets have to be particularly crafty because the opponent's block has time to be ready in the blocking position. Because of the angle the set is coming from, the spiker can not see both the set and the block at the same time.

SETTING FOR THE SETTER

The Setter

The setter is probably the most important player on the court. His role is similar to that of a quarterback in football. He is the playmaker, the architect of the team's attack. The spikers present opportunities, making themselves available for attack, but the setter makes the decisions, choosing which attack plan to implement and which spiker to set. Good spikers with a mediocre setter can not make a good team, but a good setter with mediocre spikers can make a relatively good team.

The setter must work in close cooperation with his players and with the coach. He is the direct extension of the coach, and the two must have a close understanding. The number-one priority of the coach is to identify the setter and make sure that the team will always have good setting over the years. Too many coaches ignore this fact and concentrate mainly on recruiting top spikers, forgetting to recruit the setter.

A good setter should be perceptive and have great physical and mental stamina. He should be capable of setting the ball from all court positions with great accuracy and timing from all kinds of body postures—high, low, balanced, and unbalanced. For too long coaches have perpetuated

the idea that sets need to be made in a perfectly balanced position. This may be true for non-setters, but for setters, most sets are made from unbalanced body postures.

The personality of the setter is almost as important as his technical abilities, because he plays such a critical role in fusing the team together, making the players work as a tight cohesive unit. The setter must be a leader. He should be hardworking, creative, disciplined, and crafty, always aware of opportunities to catch the opposing team out of position and exploit their weaknesses. He must be well liked by his teammates and inspire trust and confidence. A spiker needs to feel that his setter is supporting him, not challenging him.

The role of the setter is critical not only because he touches 90 percent of the balls, but also because the quality of his setting directly affects the quality and efficiency of his team's attack. A team's attack is only as good and as ingenious as its setter.

Setter's Penetration to the Target

PENETRATION DURING SERVE RECEPTION
In the 5–1 team composition, the setter needs to come from the back row to the target in three rotations (Figure 5–2). In the 6–2 team composition, one of the two setters comes from the back row in each rotation in the same manner. Obviously, the distance that the setter needs to travel depends on the specific serve-reception formation used and his position in that formation. The principles of penetration described for the *W* formation apply to other similar situations.

The speed of the setter in getting to the target should be synchronized with the speed of the ball. There's no need to move faster than necessary and sacrifice good vision. However, the setter should get to the target area before the pass is made. The setter must maintain continuous eye contact with both the serve and the pass.

Penetration from Position #1 (RB): When the setter penetrates from RB, he should stand behind the right shoulder of RF, with his toes slightly behind the toes of the right front player. When the server contacts the ball, the setter should run to the net on a path with a slight outward curve.

Penetration from Position #6 (CB): When the setter penetrates from CB, he should stand behind the right shoulder of CF with his toes slightly behind the toes of CF. As soon as the serve is struck, the setter goes directly up to the net, turns counterclockwise with his back to the net so that he is facing the court. He looks at the ball over his left shoulder while backpedaling along the net to the target.

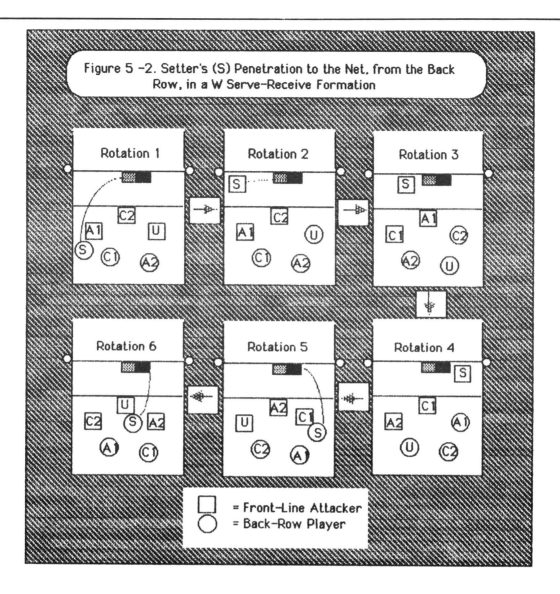

Figure 5 –2. Setter's (S) Penetration to the Net, from the Back Row, in a W Serve-Receive Formation

□ = Front-Line Attacker
○ = Back-Row Player

Penetration from Position #5 (LB): When the setter penetrates from LB, he should stand behind the left shoulder of the left front player (in particular when LF stands deep in the *W* formation). If the serve goes crosscourt, the setter should run straight up to the net and along the net facing the right sideline. Once he arrives at the target, he simply turns *clockwise.* If the ball is served down the line, the setter must run on an angle to the target, maintaining eye contact with the ball. When he arrives at the target, he turns *counterclockwise.*

If the serve is very fast, or if the setter is not quick enough, then the serve-reception formation can be adjusted to shorten his route from LB to the target:

1. The *W* formation can be adjusted to slant to the right by moving the left front player closer to the net (Figure 4–9b and Figure 4–18, rotation 1).
2. The left front player and the setter can move all the way up to the net and the serve reception is done with only four players (Figure 4–13a).
3. The setter can stand behind the right shoulder of LF, and penetrate along a direct angle to the target. The disadvantage is that the setter might cross through the passer's line of vision with the serve.

PENETRATION AFTER THE OPPONENT'S ATTACK The first responsibility of the setter is to participate in the floor defense, but as soon as the setter is sure that the ball is not coming in his direction, he must move to the target area as quickly as possible.

The setter's movement to the target must be carefully synchronized with the position and movement of RF, usually the utility player. After the blocking, the utility player should back off the net, moving toward the center of the court to a spot about 5 or 6 feet from the sideline. Therefore, the setter should penetrate to the net by going outside and around the utility player. It is the setter's responsibility to find the quickest route to the net without colliding with the utility player. This is because the setter can always see the right front player while at times RF can have his back to the setter. Verbal communication by the setter is sometimes needed to prevent collisions.

MOVEMENT TO THE TARGET FROM THE FRONT ROW DURING SERVE RECEPTION

Movement from Position #4 (LF): When the setter is at LF (whether by rotation or by arrangement), he should run to the target, maintaining eye contact with the serve. If the setter arrives at the target before the served ball crosses the net, he must turn counterclockwise to maintain eye contact with the ball. If the serve is very fast and crosses the net before the setter reaches the target, the setter should turn clockwise if the serve is crosscourt, and counterclockwise if the serve is down the line.

Movement from Position #3 (CF): Because the distance from CF to the target is very short, the setter should always reach the target before the ball crosses the net. Therefore, he should always turn counterclockwise to face the court.

Movement from Position #2 (RF): Moving from RF does not pose any problems. The setter can maintain eye contact with the serve and the pass just by turning his head as he steps to the target.

MOVEMENT TO THE TARGET FROM THE FRONT ROW AFTER THE OPPONENT'S ATTACK

When the setter is in the front row he usually plays on the right side. When the opponent

The setter's body in relation to the net.

attacks, he either participates in the block with the center front player or he participates in the floor defense as the off-block digger.

After coming off a block on the right side, the setter must move to the target in coordination with the center front player, who is between him and the target area. Most often, the center front blocker will back off the net first, and the setter will move to the target between the net and the center front. Occasionally, when CF is late for a jump or comes down off balance, the setter may need to go behind him to reach the target or chase a dig.

When the setter acts as the off-blocker, he usually plays back on the 10-foot line about 3 or 4 feet away from the right sideline. If he does not dig the ball, with a few steps he should be able to reach the target without any difficulty.

SETTER'S POSITION ON TARGET The setter should stand in the center of the primary target (Figure 4–1, Figure 6–17) as close as possible to the net, because it's always better to move away from the net than toward it. His back should be at a diagonal to the net with his right foot closer to the net than his left; a line between his feet would create about a 45-degree angle to the net. When the setter is in the front line in a 5–1 team composition, he can stand a little bit farther away from the net, giving himself room for a short hop approach for a spike or jump set.

This optimum body position allows the setter to see the whole court without having to move his head. It also allows him to see the blockers in front of him in his peripheral vision. To see the opponent's left front blocker, he can simply glance over his left shoulder.

The setter should not stand with his right arm elevated, as some coaches recommend, because as much as his hand might provide a target for passing, it is also an excellent cue for the opponent's block. This raised hand also hinders the setter's maneuvers. The passer, who is looking at the ball anyway, should know where the target is. To reinforce the passer's orientation to the target, the setter can make an audible call such as "I'm in" or "Right here."

BASIC SETTING ACTION FOR THE SETTER The basic setting action for the setter is similar to that for other players (see "Basic Setting Technique"), but the setter has to have more versatility and deception in his setting. Other team players usually set from deep court while the setter usually sets from along the net, handling balls that come to him with a variety of speeds and trajectories. These factors demand certain adaptations of the setting skills.

Nakada of Japan, one of most outstanding setters in the world, sets from a high point by keeping her elbows only slightly bent.

As described, the setter stands near the net with his shoulders at a 45-degree angle to the net. His arms hang loosely by his sides with the elbows slightly bent at about a 100-degree angle. As the pass or dig approaches, the setter quickly elevates his arms up over his head toward the incoming ball (maintaining the same angle at the elbows), and immediately sets the ball.

There are eight basic differences between the setter's technique and the setting technique of the other players:

1. *Rhythm*—The setter elevates his arms and sets the ball immediately on the same count all in one motion. The other players elevate their arms and then set on the second or third count. Using the swift nonstop movement allows the setter to be more deceptive and provides less of a cue for the opponent's block.

2. *Contact Point*—The setter should contact the ball at a higher point than other players and therefore should not bend his elbows as much. This higher contact hastens the setting action and creates a shorter set trajectory. To manipulate the timing of the set, or if he is required to set a very long distance from the deep court, the setter can bend his elbows more.

3. *Position Under Ball*—The setter must always be underneath the ball to give himself the option of setting either forward or backward, and to conceal his intentions.

4. *Foot Position*—Unlike the other players, the setter should always keep his right foot forward unless he's setting from deep court facing the net.

5. *Wrist Action*—Refined setting demands active wrist action. Other players create most of their thrust from extending the elbows, whereas the setter derives most of his power and control from his wrist action. The setter's elbow extension is followed by a nice smooth wrist action forward, underneath, up and through the ball.

6. *Soft Touch*—The setter has to develop a soft touch, a delicate feel for the ball that yields great control. Keeping the fingers loose, the setter lets the ball come deep into the hands (mak-

The set should be released with a rhythmical and delicate soft touch.

ing contact with the full length of the fingers, not with the palms) and sets with a timely wrist action, imparting a slight reverse spin. This reverse spin is particularly necessary for shoot sets, and for high outside sets to LF.

7. *Facing the Target*—Unlike other players, the setter does not always have to face the target. (This will be explained in the next section.)

8. *Backsetting*—The setter should be able to set forward and backward with the same ease from basically the same body posture. Nonsetters often arch their back when they intend to backset. The setter should avoid arching when he sets, because the arch can reveal his intention to opposing blockers. Obviously, this is not a problem if he arches all the time, but overarching can injure the back.

To be able to frontset and backset with equal efficiency, the setter must be positioned so that: 1) his hips are directly underneath the ball at the point of contact with one foot in front of the ball and the other behind, and 2) his thumbs always have complete contact with the ball.

Backsetting should start the same way as the action for frontsetting, but toward the end of the arm extension, the setter pushes his hips forward underneath the ball. Stepping forward, the setter flips his wrists, and the thumbs, supporting the ball, roll forward and up.

To avoid giving cues, the body posture should be the same for front- and back sets. The delivery is accomplished primarily with wrist action. 1. Anticipation for the ball. 2. Just prior to contact, the setter positions himself underneath the ball. 3. Frontset. 4. Backset.

A long, fast backset may require a substantial amount of back arch. Note the head rotation toward the net as it follows the ball; also note the forward thrust of the hips.

EYE CONTACT SEQUENCE As the setter stands at the target or moves toward it, he must maintain eye contact with the serve (or the spiked ball), and then with the pass (or the dig). Once the direction of the ball is obvious and it is clear that there is no emergency situation, the setter takes his eyes off the ball momentarily, looks at the block, and makes eye contact with the spikers. Then the setter looks back at the ball as he sets it. Good setters see the block in their peripheral vision as they set the ball.

Most beginning setters don't realize how much time they have between the pass and the set—1.5 seconds or more—and they look only at the ball. A coach must design special drills that force the setter to make eye contact with his setting target (spiker) prior to every set. For example, in practice the spiker can make finger signals just prior to the set and the setter must call out the number of fingers the spiker displayed. The coach also has to design drills that increase the setter's awareness of the block's position and movement. For example, in a spiking drill against the block, the block should shift positions after the pass is completed, and the setter's objective is to set in the opposite direction, away from the block.

The setter's ability to see both his spikers and the opposing block greatly determines his success. Audible communications between the setter and the spikers should be used to enhance visual communication, or to take its place in emergency situations when the setter is too busy to look at the spiker.

SETTING PASSES WITH HORIZONTAL VS. VERTICAL VELOCITY The setter's technique has to adjust to the particular trajectory and speed of the ball coming toward him. The ball can have either a) substantial horizontal velocity (if not stopped, these balls would cross over the net into the opponent's deep court), or b) substantial vertical velocity (balls that drop downward at a sharp angle). Each type requires a slightly different method of ball handling.

Balls with great horizontal velocity should be set with the setter standing at a 45-degree angle to the net with his right foot forward and his right shoulder closer to the net. The setter should place his right hand directly against the force line of the incoming ball to stop it from going over the net, setting sideways over his right shoulder. The direction of the force applied by the setter to the ball is away from the net, but the ball travels along a vector resulting from the two forces acting upon it —the horizontal force with which the ball travels toward the net, and the force applied by the setter

Ogawa, of the Japanese National Team, jump-sets a ball that approaches the net with great horizontal velocity. Keeping her right shoulder closer to the net allows her to stop the ball from going over the net and to set it along and parallel to the net.

(Figure 5–3). If the player were to set this ball with his shoulders perpendicular to the net, the force applied by the setter to the ball would add to the force and direction of the pass and the ball would carry over to the other side of the net.

Since it's desirable that a pass be delivered with a low trajectory, passes that come to the setter with substantial horizontal velocity are common. This is one reason the setter must maintain his body position at a diagonal to the net at almost all times, with his right foot in front of the left and his right shoulder closer to the net. By keeping his right hand closer to the net, the setter can position his hands on the ball in such a way that it is easily redirected toward the spiker's point of attack.

For high passes or digs that come to the setter with great vertical velocity, the setter should square himself off with his target attack zone by pushing off from his initial position on his back (left) leg, and rotating his hips toward the target. He then sets the ball along the net.

MOVEMENT TO THE BALL Seldom is the dig or pass delivered directly to the setter. More often than not, especially in transition attack, the setter has to move to the ball as efficiently as possible with short economical steps. Setters often move around too much, taking too many steps or overrunning the pass. Coaches must realize that setting

When setting balls with great vertical velocity, the setter can keep his shoulders perpendicular to the net and face the target.

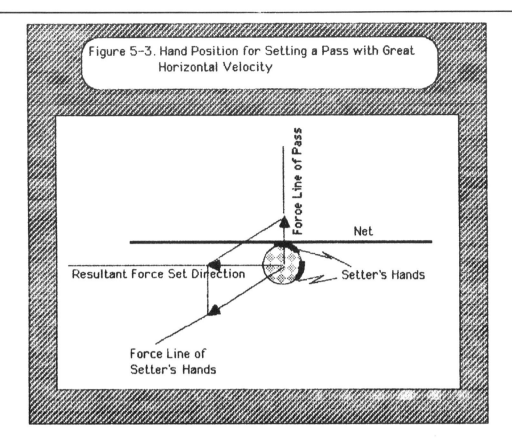

Figure 5-3. Hand Position for Setting a Pass with Great Horizontal Velocity

after moving to the ball is different from setting from a standstill. Just because a player can set from a standstill does not mean he'll be able to function in a game. Not only does the setter have to move to the ball, he often has to set while in motion. Therefore, special drills have to be designed to train the setter to set while standing still; after movement to a variety of court positions; and while in motion.

When moving a short distance forward, the setter should use shuffle steps leading with the right foot. When moving a short distance backward, he should use shuffle steps leading with the left foot. For distances longer than two or three steps, the setter should simply run to the ball. After running, if there is time, the setter can stop to set. In this case, the second-to-last step should be a short, stopping step. If there is no time to stop, obviously the setter must make the set while in motion.

The setter should always attempt to contact the ball at the highest possible point in order to speed up the attack. Therefore, if the pass is falling too much along its trajectory, the setter should move off the net toward the ball, and set it back toward the net, rather than waiting by the net and setting it from a lower point.

The following are some common adjustments and setting positions illustrating principles that can be applied to other situations. While the setter is making these adjustments, he must first look at the ball, then the block, then the spiker, and finally back to the ball.

Case 1: If the ball drops short to the left of the target at just about the 10-foot line, the setter should use two quick shuffle steps toward the ball, leading with his left foot. Or, he can step out with his left foot, cross over with his right foot, and then swing his left foot back around.

If the ball is fairly low, the setter should keep his body at a diagonal with his back to the net, his right foot closer to the net than the left, and set sideways to LF, or backward to RF. If the ball is relatively high, giving him sufficient time, the setter can step around the ball, facing LF with his body open to the net. He can then set straight to LF or sideways to RF. This is a preferred orientation because the setter can see the net and the opposing blocker better, and make a better set selection.

Case 2: If the ball drops far in front of the setter near the 10-foot line, he should run to the ball and perhaps execute a one-foot jump set (see section on the jump set), or he can position himself in the same ways described for Case 1.

Case 3: If the ball comes behind the setter's back, near the net and the right sideline, the setter must step sideways with the left foot, cross over in front with the right foot, bring around the left foot and jump-set, if possible. At times, when the ball

When the ball drops short of the target near the ten-foot line, the setter should keep his body underneath the ball and at a diagonal to the net, setting sideways to LF and backward to RF. 1a, b. Sideways set to LF. 2a, b. Backset to RF.

arrives relatively quickly to this position, it is necessary to set and keep retreating away from the ball along the net, without jump-setting or stopping.

Case 4: If the ball is dropping near the 10-foot line on the right sideline or outside the court, the setter should run along a curved path behind the ball, with his back to the net, keeping eye contact with the ball. He should come around the ball in a clockwise fashion to position himself behind the ball and set it while facing LF. If it's a fairly fast ball, the setter must drop his left shoulder down, get behind the ball, and set it while going through the ball. After setting the ball forward, the setter should continue moving backward away from the ball.

Emergency Setting

It would be nice if every ball came to the setter at the proper trajectory, height, and distance. But this is not the case. Because the setter has to be able to set every ball to a very specific target, he must learn certain emergency techniques that allow him to manipulate his body around the ball and yet set with accuracy. The following are some of the most common emergency setting techniques:

BASIC LOW BODY POSTURE In the low body posture the knees are almost completely bent. The feet should be wide apart with the front (right) foot flat on the floor and the back foot up on the toes. The butt should be low, close to the heel of the back foot. This wide base gives the setter more stability and a wider setting range around his base of support. His upper body must be vertically upright with his hips directly underneath the ball.

The setting action begins by pushing off from the left leg, raising the body slightly as the arms extend toward the ball.

SIDE SQUAT When a low ball comes to either

Setting from a low body posture.

side of the setter, he should take a long sideways step toward the ball, bending his knees, lowering his body, and shifting his weight over that foot. The upper body should be straight and the hips directly underneath the ball. The amount of leg push used to set from this position is determined by the height and distance that has to be covered to set the ball to the desired hitter.

KNEE DROP When the setter squats as low as he can and it is still not enough, he should drop a knee to the floor. When the ball is on his right, he should drop his left knee; when it's on his left, he should drop his right knee. There should always be a 90-degree angle between the two thighs. The body weight should be poised mainly over the foot of the raised knee, with the butt close to the heel of that foot. Most of the power for the set comes from pushing up and through with the raised leg.

Some setters prefer to get under a low ball by dropping both knees to the floor and leaning backward slightly. This technique can be particularly useful in retrieving balls that bounce off the net, or balls that drop low in front of the setter. The setter

When the ball comes on either side of the setter, he should take a long sideways step toward the ball, aligning the center of his body with the ball.

Debbie Green demonstrates the knee drop, a common technique for setting low balls or for retrieving balls that bounce off the net.

When the ball drops just behind the setter's back, the back roll allows the setter to get underneath a very low ball and set it either forward or backward.

runs quickly to the ball, bending his knees more and more as he leans backward and drives both knees to the floor under the ball. Leaning backward will lower his knees to the floor in a soft, cushioned way, and put him in a better position underneath the ball to set equally well forward or backward.

As you can see, all the bending that is required of a setter means that he must have great leg strength and stamina. For this reason, setters should do extra bending, stretching, and jumping exercises, both during practice and on their own.

Roll Set

To avoid being called for a ball-handling violation, the setter must always position his body in such a way that the ball will come to him between his shoulders. In some emergency situations, the setter does not have enough time to get in this position just by footwork alone. In these instances, he usually ends up setting in an off-balance position while falling to the floor. To prevent injury, and also to get into the most comfortable position while setting, the setter must learn to cushion his fall by doing a roll. There are four distinct rolls: to either side, backward, and (not frequently used) forward. Variations of the roll can be applied to any diagonal body movement.

THE BACK ROLL The back roll is used for setting very low balls from a low body position. Unlike the defensive rolling maneuvers in which the player goes completely over on his shoulder or back before coming up, the setting roll is only a half-roll, actually more of a rocking action, with the back curved like the rails of a rocking chair.

As the setter moves to the ball, he tilts his body slightly backward, letting his hips and feet lead him into a low squat position. One leg should be slightly in front with the feet shoulder-width apart. He should position himself so that the approaching ball aims for his forehead. If no contact were

To recover from any roll, the setter rolls backward, keeping one leg straight and the other bent. The straight leg acts as a leverage, enabling the setter to roll forward and get quickly back up on his feet.

made, the ball would drop behind his back, or just behind one shoulder.

The setter should allow himself to fall backward, bringing his butt as close as possible to the heel of his back leg. This will curve his back and prevent injury to it. The setter should contact the ball while falling, just before his shoulder blades hit the floor. At the time of contact his back is slightly curved but almost parallel to the floor. From this position he can set the ball with elbow extension and wrist action either forward or backward.

In order to recover quickly after setting the ball, the setter rocks back with his butt coming off the floor. He should keep the front leg straight and the back leg bent, using the straight leg for leverage to rock forward onto the foot of the bent leg. If this move is done properly and smoothly, the combination of forward momentum and power from the muscles of the bent leg should bring the setter back on his feet with little effort.

THE SIDE ROLL The side roll is executed from a side squat position. If the ball is outside his left shoulder, then the setter should roll to the left. If it is outside his right shoulder, then he should roll to the right. Because of his position on the right side of the court, most of the time a setter will use the left roll.

The forward roll is an advanced setting technique. The side roll is done in a similar manner but with less pivoting and more side movement.

To execute the left-side roll, the setter should take a long step into a side squat, straightening out the right leg as the body weight shifts onto the heel of the left foot. If this side squat is sufficient to bring the setter's shoulders under the ball, he can set from that position, using a slight pivot movement that aligns the setting motion with the target.

However, if this long stride does not bring the body over far enough, then the setter must allow himself to fall to the left. While falling, he should pivot slightly to the right so that he can set the ball in the correct direction. After setting, he should fall smoothly back onto the floor, up to his shoulder blades, and right himself as explained for the back roll.

To execute the right-side roll, the same procedure is used in reverse as the setter steps to the right.

THE FORWARD ROLL When a setter has attempted to get to a low ball but it is still in front of him, he can lunge forward and use a forearm set. A very skillful setter will do a forward roll. The forward roll is very difficult and requires much practice to learn.

If the ball is in front of the setter between him and LF, for instance, the setter should take a long squatting step toward the ball with his right foot. He should then pivot counterclockwise, turning on the ball of his right foot with his left leg extended forward along the net until he ends up with his back to the target. Now he can backset to LF or frontset to RF. It is also possible to set other directions, using the same technique. From this position the setter can now set the ball while falling backward, recovering in the same manner used for the back roll.

The Forearm Set

A setter should avoid using the forearm "bump" set if possible. It does not allow the setter to control location and height nearly as well as the overhand setting technique does. At times, however, a forearm set is the only way to handle very low balls that travel parallel to the floor and drop short of the target.

The forearm set (Rita's flip) allows the setter to handle very low balls coming far in front of him between court positions 3 and 4. Note how the setter goes in a left shoulder roll from the right foot.

For example, when a ball drops in front of the setter around the 10-foot line between court positions 3 and 4, the setter should step with his left foot on a diagonal toward the ball. Then he should take a longer step with his right foot toward the ball. Bending his right knee and reaching with his arms under the ball, the setter gets his body into an off-balance position. The body pivots around the right foot clockwise (to the left), which brings the left leg around. The setter makes contact with the ball and continues falling forward onto the side of his left thigh and on up to his left shoulder blade (reverse roll). Once the body contacts the floor the player should allow the momentum to carry his body in a follow-through.

The Jump Set

A jump set is executed while the setter is suspended at the peak of a jump. It has three main purposes:

1. to fake the opposing blocker, forcing him to jump with the setter;
2. to speed up the attack and make it easier to hit first-tempo sets by decreasing the trajectory of the ball; and
3. to save a pass or dig that is headed over the net.

The setter should always try to jump-set the ball. Jump-setting should become the preferred technique for the setter.

Jump-setting is an important skill that should be taught to every player on the team. Many times a ball will be near the net and high enough to spike. If the team still has two contacts left, the ball can be hit or jump-set. A spiker can fake the block by jumping as if to spike, almost completing his arm swing, then turning in midair and setting the ball to another spiker. (Obviously, he can only do this if the ball is passed to him directly.) The block must consider the attack threat posed by the

The jump set should be done whenever possible.

player who jump-set. This will make it more difficult for the block to properly reassemble on the opposite side of the court against the spiker who was set.

The jump set can be done with a one-leg or a two-leg takeoff.

TWO-LEG TAKEOFF The setter should take off either exactly underneath the ball or from such a distance that when contact is made the body is underneath the ball. The setting action should take

The two-leg approach takeoff for a jump set is similar to one for a left hand spike: left foot-right foot takeoff into a jump.

The one-leg takeoff (from either foot) allows the setter to jump set distant balls when he is forced to run and jump in a hurry.

place at the peak of a jump. At times, the set can be executed just prior to reaching the apex of the jump. The set should *not* be executed during the descent, because too much ball control is lost.

The jump set can be executed from a standstill, making it similar to a jump shot in basketball, or it can be executed with an approach. When the setter leads into the jump set with an approach, he should use the same approach that a left-handed attacker uses to spike (see Chapter 6, "The Attack"—"Individual Attack"). The left foot leads into a short hop and contacts the floor first. The right foot comes around and is placed closer to the net, slightly in front of the left foot. Coming off the hop, both feet contact the floor almost simultaneously. After the hop, the shoulder line is at an angle to the net with the right shoulder forward and closer to the net than the left.

Usually, the setter can not afford to broad-jump into a jump set because he will probably get in the spiker's way. Also, the height of the contact is lowered. Nevertheless, at times the setter has no choice but to broad-jump into a jump set.

ONE-LEG TAKEOFF A one-leg takeoff should be used when the ball is far from the setter and he must run to it and jump without slowing down. The transition into the one-leg takeoff is much quicker than into the two-leg takeoff. The setter should be able to jump from either foot to avoid having to switch legs at the last second, a time-consuming process.

The takeoff for a one-leg jump is similar to the takeoff for a lay-up in basketball. At takeoff, the knee opposite the takeoff leg is raised. The setter should learn to frontset and backset from a one-leg takeoff. Actually, it's very comfortable to backset from a one-leg takeoff, because the setter has substantial horizontal velocity that allows him to go through the ball comfortably. With proper timing, the setter can be well underneath the ball upon contact.

During the jump set, it really doesn't matter what the legs are doing at the time of contact as long as the hands and the upper body are in a relatively comfortable position to handle the ball. The legs only serve to balance the upper body. A good setter can set the ball from different body postures while suspended. Debbie Green, from the 1984 USA Olympic team, has a great variety of body postures she uses when jump-setting.

The One-Hand Set

Balls that seem likely to go over the net can be rescued and set with the one-hand setting technique. The setter can use a one-hand finger set or a one-hand bump set.

To execute a one-hand finger set, the setter should stiffen his fingers, drawing them close together but not touching. Upon contact, the hand should be positioned underneath the ball and against the force line of the ball, with the elbow slightly bent. The setter should then push the ball by straightening the elbow and using a slight wrist action.

This setting technique is very deceptive because the opponent has the impression that the ball will cross the net. At the last second the setter steals the ball from the opposing blocker or spiker. At times it can be advantageous for a front-row setter to use the one-hand set instead of spiking or tipping the ball. At many levels of play, setters use the one-hand set only for short sets, but an advanced setter is capable of setting all kinds of quick attacks, including forward and backward shoot sets, using the one-hand setting technique.

At times when a ball is about to drop on the other side of the net, the setter can save it by bumping the ball with the heel of his palm, directing it outside for a high set. The one-hand bump set is basically an emergency rescue set that affords little control.

The one-hand set, best used for close, quick sets, allows for a higher point of contact and rescues balls that seem likely to go over the net.

Debbie Green (#10) delivers a one-hand set.

The side set can be executed facing the net or with the back to the net. The hands must be placed evenly and simultaneously on the ball.

The Side Set

Setting to the side over one shoulder is useful for handling balls that drop into the net or directly over it, or when the setter is late getting into position. When a ball coming from the opponent's side drops almost on top of the net, the setter should side-set instead of spiking the ball, because the opponent's block is usually in a ready position in anticipation of a spike. The side set can also be useful when the setter is in the back row and has to race to the net for the ball during the transition from defense to attack. In cases where the dug ball has a quick, flat trajectory, the setter is actually racing the ball to the net and often does not have time to assume his normal body posture.

To side-set, the setter keeps his shoulders square to the net, either facing it or with his back to it. He contacts the ball evenly with both hands. When the setter is directly underneath the ball, he'll be able to set to the left or right just by tilting his shoulders while maintaining even hands and hips. If the ball is on either side of him, the setter must drop the respective shoulder and bend his knee to adjust his hands in such a way that they both contact the ball evenly. In this posture the setter can then set only in that direction.

The side set can be executed in any body posture—low, normal, or during a jump.

Set Quality and Spin

A setter should deliver a ball that is comfortable for each individual spiker to hit. Since different spikers don't have the same reaction time, height, or jumping ability, the setter must learn each spiker's tendencies and preferences in order to accommodate his needs; a good setter is one who maximizes his spikers' abilities.

A well-set ball should have very little spin on it. What spin it does have should be reverse spin. The reverse spin will allow the setter to deliver a shoot set with good horizontal velocity that will peak at the point of contact by the spiker. A shoot set with top spin requires greater horizontal velocity to travel the same distance as a set with reverse spin on it, and instead of peaking, the ball can suddenly drop short. A shoot set ball is prone to floating, or wobbling, and can be too fast for a spiker to respond to effectively.

Because it has less horizontal velocity, a ball set with reverse spin improves the timing of the spiker with the ball. This point is critical, particularly in regard to executing very long shoot sets; if there is no reverse spin on the ball, the horizontal velocity in such a long low trajectory set will be beyond the reaction time of the spiker, and he can completely miss the ball or hit it out of bounds. The longer the shoot set, the more critical it is to impart some reverse spin. For short distances, it is less critical. On high sets it's desirable to create a reverse spin so that when the ball descends, it will come down in as close to a vertical line as possible.

Recovering Balls That Rebound Off the Net

Many balls that are dug or saved during defensive plays go into the net, and it's usually the setter who must recover these balls. A good setter should be able to recover and set 90 percent of them. During competition the setter should be aware of the tension of that particular net. He should note whether there is a rope or cable at the bottom. To avoid surprises, he'd be wise to explore the net before the beginning of the match. Some setters toss a few balls into the net to test the rebound at various points.

When the setter stands at the target area and sees a ball coming to the net, he should pay careful attention to the angle and speed of the ball so that he can estimate the rebound angle. A ball that hits the top of the net will tend to drop down along the net and have little rebound action off the bottom. A ball that comes to the bottom of a good tight net will rebound up and arc farther away from the net.

If the setter sees that the ball will hit the top of the net, he should stand closer; if he thinks that it will hit the bottom, he should stand farther away. It's important that the setter stand perpendicular to the net, not facing it. He should be far enough back from the point of contact so that he can play the ball out in front.

At times the setter will have to use a forearm set, or a knee drop, or set from a low squat, or use a roll. The technique will depend on the amount of time he has and the height of the rebound of the ball. If there is a poor rebound, the setter should attempt to set the ball to anybody he can. If the ball has a higher rebound, the setter might be able to make the most advantageous set.

If a setter can competently recover balls off the net, the team can use the net to its advantage. It is always better for a defensive player to hit the ball into the net and let the setter play the rebound than it is to give the opponent a free ball. The ball should be aimed at the bottom of the net to yield a better rebound trajectory.

A team should learn to appreciate the net as an integral part of the game rather than see it as an obstacle. The net will always be there, so the team might as well use it to its advantage.

Avoid Giving Cues

The setter must be very deceptive. The fewer cues he gives to convey the direction of his set, the more chance he has to deceive the opponent's block and create a one-on-one situation for his spiker. With the proper quick-setting arm action, a setter should be able to conceal his intentions.

Setters who don't pay attention to their body posture usually give away the backset by arching back too much every time they want to backset. A setter should always stand with his hips underneath the ball. A backset can be accomplished with minimum arching by leaning on the back leg and flipping the ball back with the wrists and the thumbs. A setter must position himself in such a way that he always has more than one spiker to select without exposing his intentions.

When players other than the setter execute the finger pass (the overhand setting motion) they normally elevate their hands toward the descending ball a little sooner than an experienced setter does. They will set with a slow one-two count—arms up, wait, then set. The setter cannot afford to take this time. His arm action has to be swift. If he is too slow, the block will use the extra time to study his hands and determine the direction of the set.

Setter as Attacker

When the setter is in the front row in a 5–1 team composition, he must continually pose a threat to the opponent's block and floor defense. If the blockers can disregard the setter, they are free to concentrate on only two spikers, which gives them a strong advantage.

Quite often the setter in a 5–1 team composition is not a powerful spiker. Sometimes this is due to a physical limitation since setters often tend to be players too short to be effective spikers. Also, because they spend so much time practicing setting, it's hard for setters to get enough practice spiking;

The setter should disguise his intention to tip until the last possible moment.

during the course of a game, a setter usually doesn't have enough time to make a strong approach.

For all of these reasons, a setter should learn the hard and soft tipping techniques (see Chapter 6, "The Attack"—"Individual Attack"). The tip should achieve two things: keep the opposing blockers spread along the net; and keep the opponent's floor-defense players up higher and closer to the net to guard against the tips.

A setter should be able to tip effectively with both his left and right hands. With the right hand, the setter should only attempt to tip balls that are over the net. Usually they should be tipped behind his back toward the opponent's sideline near LF. The setter should place his palm at a 45-degree angle underneath the ball with his forearm rotated clockwise so that the palm faces his head. He contacts the ball over the top of the net, bending his elbow past his right ear and flipping his wrist. This is a "soft" tip. Very tall setters can almost master a hard right-handed tip for use on high passes. With his hands in the normal setting position, he suddenly turns his right wrist and pushes the ball down past the blockers. This is the quickest of all tips, but it is recommended only for tall, skilled setters.

With his left hand, the setter should learn how to do both soft and hard tips. The soft tip is ex-

1. Soft tip with the left hand.

2. Soft tip behind the back with the right hand.

3. Hard crosscourt tip with the left hand.

ecuted by placing the hand underneath the ball, pushing it up and over the net by straightening the elbow and propelling the ball with a slight wrist action. The "hard" tip is done by placing the hand on top of the ball and pushing downward with a quick wrist action. With the left hand, tips toward the center of the court or crosscourt behind the opponent's right front blocker are very effective.

The setter should use tips as a surprise weapon in both serve-reception attack and transition attack, taking care not to reveal his tipping intention. He should bring his arms up as if to set and then tip the ball at the last possible instant. This can be very effective because the opponent's block and defense are both preparing for the third contact by one of the spikers. Tips often catch the opponent by surprise when they are done in coordination with a quick attack from the outside or in conjunction with a quick attack in the middle. This is especially true when the opponent uses see-and-respond blocking tactics where the blocker jumps against quick attack only after the release of the set. If the opponent uses commit blocking tactics, tipping by the setter is more difficult because the blocker who jumps with the quick attacker is often close enough to reach over and block the setter's tip attempt.

In addition to tipping, the setter and the utility player should be taught to spike balls from a standing takeoff using no approach. Balls that are tight to the net can be hit in this manner, usually crosscourt with the right hand. With some experience a setter can also hit these balls down the line.

Timing Manipulation

In a multiple attack the spikers usually come to the net at a variety of tempos. For a first-tempo (quick) set, it is the spiker's responsibility to establish the correct spatial relationship to the setter, but it is the setter's responsibility to create the correct timing. For the slower second- and third-tempo sets, the setter must set the most comfortable set to the spiker's position, but it is the spiker who controls the timing.

For first-tempo sets, if a spiker is delayed or jumps too soon, the setter can adjust the timing of the set to compensate.

To *delay* the set, the setter can:

- bend his wrists backward and absorb the ball a little more into his hands;
- bend his elbows more to whatever extent is required;
- bend his knees to set from a lower point;
- any combination of the above;
- set the ball a little higher.

To *speed up* the set, the setter can:

- jump to the ball with arms fully extended, rush the contact with the ball and have a quicker release;
- set with one hand at a higher point, especially for quick middle attack;
- set a ball with a lower trajectory.

For second-tempo sets, the setter is responsible for putting the ball in the most comfortable position for the spiker to hit it. The setter must be sensitive to the spiker's situation and his particular position on the court. For instance, if the spiker is delayed getting to his position after digging, the setter must take this into account by setting the ball a little higher, slightly more inside the court so the spiker will not have to circle out as far on his approach.

To be able to make these fine adjustments, the setter must always maintain eye contact with his spikers and be aware of each spiker's situation.

THE ATTACK

Attack is a general term that encompasses the collective offensive efforts of a team as well as the individual offensive efforts of a player to score a point or earn a side-out.

Volleyball is a continuous struggle between defense and attack. The attack continuously fights the opponent's block and floor defense, attempting to overcome them with power or to outwit them by deception. The success of a team's attack reflects the quality of the team's technical and tactical abilities. A smooth attack, created by precise movements of the players, embodies the grace and beauty of volleyball.

The USA team implemented a powerful and well-coordinated attack to beat the Chinese team 3–0 in the 1981 World Championship in Peru.

Attack correlates closely with winning or losing. A team without a strong attack can not be successful, but, a team with a strong attack can win (even with a mediocre defense). The Cuban women's team won the 1978 world championship by relying primarily on its aggressive powerful attack. Over the years many rules have been changed to strike a better balance between attack and defense, yet the attack continues to dominate the game.

INDIVIDUAL ATTACK

The Spike

Usually the spike follows a set and is the team's last contact with the ball before the opponent gains possession of it. *Spiking* is the explosive and dynamic action of hitting the ball hard and downward over the net into the opponent's court at a sharp angle. The spike is possibly the most dramatic and crowd-pleasing skill of the game. It is a team's most lethal offensive weapon for scoring

The spike is the most powerful attack technique, scoring the most points in a game.

points, earning side-outs, and exerting control over an opponent. About 60 percent of total points and 90 percent of side-outs are made by spikes. A team's spiking efficiency is a good indicator of its chances for winning or losing.

The spike can be executed using a variety of arm swings and a variety of quick and slower tempos. The ball can be given top spin, side spin, or underspin. It can be hit at a sharp downward angle or at a less-oblique angle deeper into the court. A good spiker can hit the ball down the sideline, crosscourt, and at a variety of angles in between.

Basic Spiking Technique

For instructional purposes, basic spiking skill can be divided into six phases: the approach, the takeoff, flight, contact with the ball, follow-through, and the landing. The following description of spiking technique is geared for a right-handed spiker approaching the net from the left front, position #4. The same description in reverse should fit a left-handed player approaching from right front, position #2. Later in the chapter the footwork and approach pattern for a right-handed player at right side is covered. Again, the opposite of this would apply to a left-hander at left side.

THE APPROACH The approach leads the attacker into the takeoff for the jump, which precedes the actual arm swing and contact with the ball. The approach has to generate horizontal velocity that can be converted upon takeoff into vertical velocity. An efficient approach can add from 5 to 8 inches to a spiker's jump and give the spiker greater maneuverability in the air. The more efficient the approach, the more height is added to the jump. In addition, a forceful, quick, and well-coordinated approach generates greater body energy that can then be imparted to the ball, intensifying the power behind the spike.

The approach has two phases: the run-up steps and the hop.

Run-Up Steps: The number of run-up steps required is determined by the distance the spiker needs to travel. The steps can be done in a straight line or in a curve or in a combination of the two, depending on the spiker's intention and starting location on the court.

The spiker should practice a variety of approaches from different distances at different angles. Because the hop always starts off the left foot, if an odd number of steps is required to cover the distance, then the spiker should begin with the left foot; if an even number of steps is required, begin with the right foot.

Rita Crockett demonstrates the six phases of the spike.

Flo Hyman demonstrates a spike.

Foot position at takeoff.

The most common approach uses two run-up steps plus a hop. The first step is a short step that shifts the body weight forward onto the toes of the right foot. The second step with the left foot is quicker and longer, about 2 to 3 feet long. The left foot lands almost flat as the body leans forward. The arm movement during the run-up steps is similar to the natural arm movement in running but slightly more restricted, not as broad.

The run-up steps should be smooth, light, and rhythmical, harnessing about 85 percent to 90 percent of a player's maximum running speed. Run-up steps at full speed can interfere with the body control and timing essential for a successful spike. Each player has a certain speed that maximizes her jump without affecting control. This speed depends largely on the strength of her leg muscles and her intrinsic muscle speed.

The timing and speed of the approach are critical. The cue to begin the approach can be the height of the pass, the dig, or the set. When the pass is high, the spiker should start her approach a little later. To be effective, once the player begins her approach, she *must* continue at a consistent speed—the optimum speed she should always use for every approach. Ignoring this rule leads to inconsistent approach speed, and therefore inconsistent timing with the setter. It also causes poor jumping and reduced power. At no time should the spiker lose eye contact with the ball.

The Hop: The hop follows the run-up steps in the approach for the jump. It is an explosive and relatively long low jump that takes about .25 seconds (Table 6–1). For female athletes, the length of the hop may vary between 4 to 8 feet, depending on the player's intention, takeoff style, run-up speed, size, and leg strength. The greater the run-up speed, the longer the hop should be. During the hop, the body's center of gravity is raised only slightly or not at all.

The purpose of the hop is to increase horizontal velocity and to allow the feet to get out in front of the body's center of gravity. It also helps take advantage of the muscle's elastic rebound quality for a quick takeoff. The neuromuscular action-stretch reflex facilitates the elastic rebound off the floor. Extension of the legs in front of the body's center of gravity provides for an abrupt absorption of the horizontal momentum (generated by the approach) and its subsequent efficient conversion into vertical momentum.

The hop begins off the left foot, and the point where the left foot touches the floor is called the "hop point." As the right leg shoots forward, both arms come up sideways and extend backward slightly bent at the elbows. Backward extension of the arms occurs naturally to counterbalance the forward leg movement. Once the body is suspended in the air, the left leg should quickly swing forward to catch up with the right leg, as in gymnastic vaulting. In the same way that the backward arm swing is synchronized with the forward action of the right leg, the forward arm swing is synchronized with the forward action of the left leg.

As the left leg moves forward, the arms come down and the elbows bend more and more, shortening the leverage of the total arm so that all the momentum is transferred into the forearms. This allows the forearms to move at a high velocity at

Table 6-1. Measurements of the Hop and Takeoff

Name	Horizontal Velocity Leading into Hop	Length of Hop from Left to Right Foot	Distance Between Feet at Takeoff	Time from Beginning to End of Takeoff	Peak Vertical Velocity at Takeoff	Horizontal Velocity at Takeoff	Peak Vertical Acceleration at Takeoff
	Cm./sec.	cm.	cm	sec.	cm./sec.	cm./sec.	cm./sec.^{2}
Flo H.	280	155	69.0	.31	255	210	1750
Rita C.	516	258	17.3	.10	390	-10	4700
Julie V.	415	207	57.5	.27	315	110	3500
Sue W.	285	167	52.0	.32	240	-60	1500
Jurie Y.	280	155	64.0	.31	255	200	1575
Average	355	188	52	.26	291	90	2605

Table 6-2. Measurements of Joint and Body Angles at Takeoff for Spiking
(Measurements were taken in actual competition.)

Name	Angle Beween Right Shank and Floor	Angle Between Right Thigh and Trunk	Angle at the Right Knee	Height of Jump	
	Degrees	Degrees	egrees	cm.	(In.)
Jurie Y.	57	164	140	78	30.7
Flo H.	81	150	145	79	31.1
Rita C.	99	148	145	98	38.6
Sue W.	72	146	130	74	29.1
Julie V.	81	121	124	81	31.9
Average	78	146	137	82	32.3

the instant of takeoff, bringing the arms more quickly into the spiking position. In addition, the high velocity of the forearms has the effect of increasing the body weight at takeoff. This, in turn, increases the body's force against the ground and results in an increased upward thrust for an improved jump.

Landing from the jump, the right foot contacts the floor first, followed by the left. When the left foot comes in contact with the floor, the hands should be on either side of the body or slightly in front but not behind. This is critical to help preserve the horizontal momentum at takeoff. With a fast efficient approach, the force generated against the floor during takeoff can reach as high as 1900 pounds.

Peak Horizontal Acceleration at Takeoff	Horizontal Distance from Takeoff to Ball	Height of Jump
cm./sec.^{2}	cm.	cm.
-250	93	79.4
-2995	43	98.0
-2500	44	81.0
-1950	19	74.0
-490	· 78	78.0
1637	55	82.1

THE TAKEOFF The faster the horizontal velocity generated by the run-up speed and the hop, the more the feet need to be extended in front of the body and the more the body leans backward. A conventional takeoff begins as soon as both feet contact the floor after the hop. (The one-foot "slide approach" takeoff will be discussed in "The Slide.")

There are two distinct rhythms for placing the feet: a quick one-two takeoff, and a slow one-two takeoff. The technique for both rhythms is essentially the same.

The landing from the hop starts with the right foot, which is placed on the floor with a slight heel-toe action at an angle of about 45 degrees to the direction of the body momentum created by the approach. The left foot lands forward of the right, closer to the net. Thus, the left foot and left shoulder are closer to the net than the right.

The left foot lands only on the toes, perpendicular to the direction of the approach. (The toe landing is done at a very slight angle, with the heel barely elevated.) This allows the calf muscles to absorb the shock and avoid strain on the lateral ligaments of the ankle joint.

At the time that both feet have made contact with the floor, the angle of the right knee may vary among individual players from 124 to 145 degrees (Table 6-2). During takeoff, this angle should not decrease.

In principle, the feet should be positioned at an angle of 45 degrees to each other (Figure 6-1). However, the position of the feet relative to the court varies with different angles of approach (Figure 6-2). The feet should always be placed on either side of the body's line of momentum. The toes of the *left* foot are placed *against* the direction and on the line of momentum. The *heel* of the right foot is also on the line of momentum (Figure 6–1).

Placing the feet at an angle rather than square to the net produces four major benefits:

1. It gives the hitter good continuous eye contact with both the ball and the opponent's court. This is particularly important for hitting quick sets.
2. A quicker, more efficient conversion of horizontal momentum into vertical momentum.
3. Less stress on the knees and less demand on the quad muscles of the thigh. Because the knees are at an angle to the direction of the approach and can not bend in this direction, the horizontal force generated by the approach is absorbed primarily by the feet and in the bone structure, without taxing the knees and the quadricep muscles. All muscle power can then be directed toward lifting the body up rather than stopping its horizontal momentum.
4. A more controlled and powerful spike. Because the hitting shoulder is farther away from the net, the spiker can develop a more powerful arm swing through rotation of the upper body. This eliminates most of the need to arch the back. Generating the spiking power by trunk rotation (rather than by arching the back) is not only quicker, but it also reduces the possibility of suffering a back injury.

In the quick one-two takeoff, the feet come in contact with the floor almost simultaneously and are slightly wider than shoulder-width apart. In

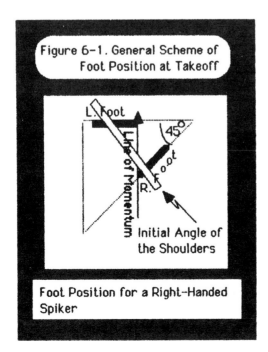

Figure 6-1. General Scheme of Foot Position at Takeoff

Foot Position for a Right-Handed Spiker

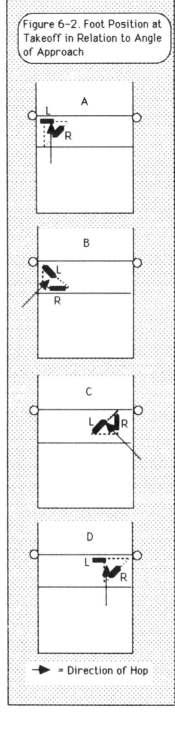

Figure 6-2. Foot Position at Takeoff in Relation to Angle of Approach

→ = Direction of Hop

A.
The angle of approach is 90 degrees to the net. The right foot is placed 45 degrees to the direction of the approach and the left foot is placed perpendicular to it (body's momentum).

B.
The angle of approach is 45 degrees to the net. The right foot is placed 45 degrees to the direction of the approach and parallel to the net. The left foot is placed perpendicular to the direction of the hop and 45 degrees to the net. Placing the left foot too far in front of the right foot may limit the possibility of hitting down the line.

C.
The angle of approach is 45 degrees to the net. The right foot is perpendicular to the net (45 degrees to the hop) whereas the left foot is 45 degrees to the net and perpendicular to the direction of the body's momentum.

D.
Similar to "A." However, to provide for longer eye contact with the ball, one may place the left foot slightly wider.

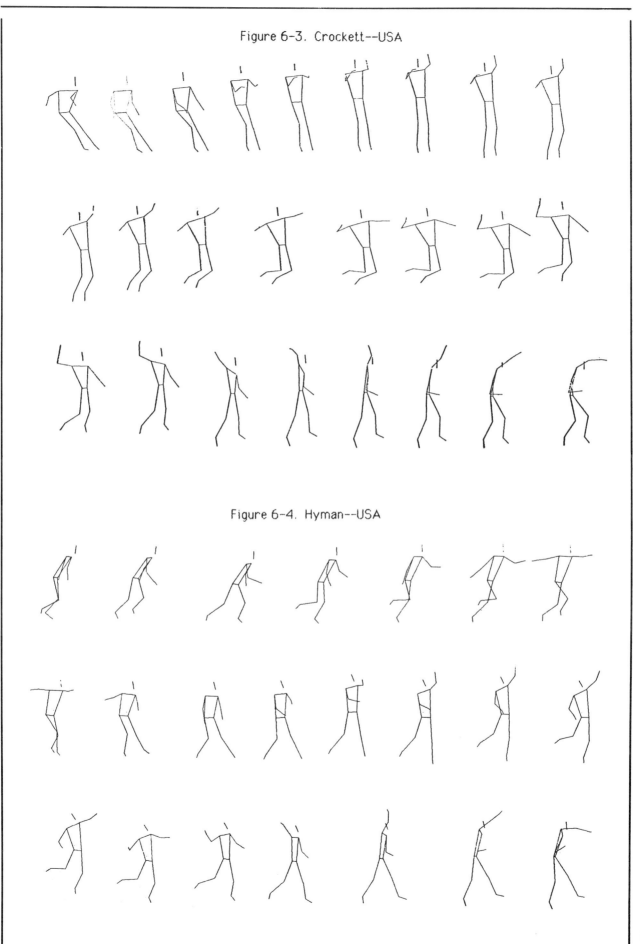

Figure 6-3. Crockett--USA

Figure 6-4. Hyman--USA

91

quick takeoffs, the body's center of gravity is behind the feet.

In Figure 6–3, Rita Crockett demonstrates a quick one-two takeoff. The time interval between the landing of the right foot and the left foot is only .03 seconds. The total time between contact with the floor and the jump is no more than .10 seconds. The distance between the feet is 17.3cm (6.8") (Table 6–1).

In the slow one-two takeoff, the feet are placed wider apart in a more prolonged action, and the body's center of gravity is between the feet. In Figure 6–4, Flo Hyman demonstrates the slow one-two takeoff. Flo's takeoff lasts .31 seconds, and the time between the placing of the right and left feet is .14 of a second. The distance between Flo's feet is 69cm (27"). Measurements for other American and Japanese national team players are presented in Table 6–1.

While the quick takeoff is well suited for quick attackers, a slow takeoff is often used by ace spikers. A slow one-two takeoff is also a required technique for a back-row attacker and should be used for executing the jump-spike serve.

POSITION OF TAKEOFF The location of the takeoff must be far enough behind the set that the spiker does not end up underneath the ball. The ball should be at least an arm's length or more in front of the spiker at a lateral position somewhere between the spiker's hitting shoulder and the elbow of the hitting arm when extended sideways.

This position allows the spiker to hit the ball in any direction. If the ball is too far inside the court (to the right of the right shoulder), then a power hit can only be hit to the right. If the ball is to the left of the midsection, a power hit can only be hit to the left (See Figure 6–13).

Obviously, individual adjustments have to be made for a slow and a quick one-two takeoff. At times the spiker may even want to jump for quick attack in an off-position. This decoys the blockers by lifting them at an incorrect point along the net. The setter then delivers a ball that is slightly short or long in relation to the hitter's shoulder.

Flight (Hitting Arm Motion)

After takeoff, the body rises and both arms swing up together, bending at the elbows. What the arms do next depends on the choice of arm swing. The arm swing should yield good ball control, the highest possible reach, and maximum power, but without injuring the hitting arm or shoulder. Over the years, different schools of volleyball have advocated different arm swings. The five most common arm swings are: the straight arm, the bow-and-arrow, the snap, the circular, and the roundhouse. The circular arm swing can be further divided into the wide circular and the limited (restricted) circular. I advocate the wide circular arm swing for power hitters, and the snap or the limited circular arm swing for quick attackers. The wide circular arm swing is not recommended for quick attackers. It limits the variety of shots they can execute, and it is often too slow for the time constraints imposed by certain quick sets. On the other hand, the limited circular arm swing can be used by power hitters as well as by quick attackers.

THE STRAIGHT-ARM SWING For years, many coaches taught players to spike by raising the arm straight back up above the head, believing that this technique maximized the highest possible contact with the ball. In fact this high contact point can be reached by other methods; the only limiting factor is time. If a player had the time, she could execute a somersault and then contact the ball at her maximum reach.

The straight-arm swing demands tremendous power at the shoulders because the muscle has to mobilize a relatively long leverage. People who use this technique are susceptible to shoulder injuries. For any given shoulder strength, this technique is not the most efficient way to optimize the speed of the arm. Because they operate over a shorter range, short leverages generate faster speeds than long leverages. In addition, spiking with the arm raised straight up limits the spiker's ability to control a variety of sets. If the ball is set to a point lower than the spiker's palm, she has no choice but to hit the ball downward, often right into the block.

Left front power hitters with superior shoulder strength might find this technique useful at times; however, I definitely do not recommend it to quick attackers who encounter many different types of sets and who must be quite versatile in overcoming the block.

THE BOW-AND-ARROW ARM SWING An arm swing that resembles shooting an arrow from a bow is quite popular (Figure 6–5). After takeoff, the left arm continues going up, while the elbow of the right arm is drawn back and slightly above shoulder height. The forearm is almost horizontal to the floor and is then flipped back until it is almost perpendicular to the floor, facing forward. The arm then extends upward to contact the ball.

This technique allows for good ball control and power. However, the ballistic action of drawing the elbow back quickly and above shoulder height puts a tremendous strain on the frontal head of the

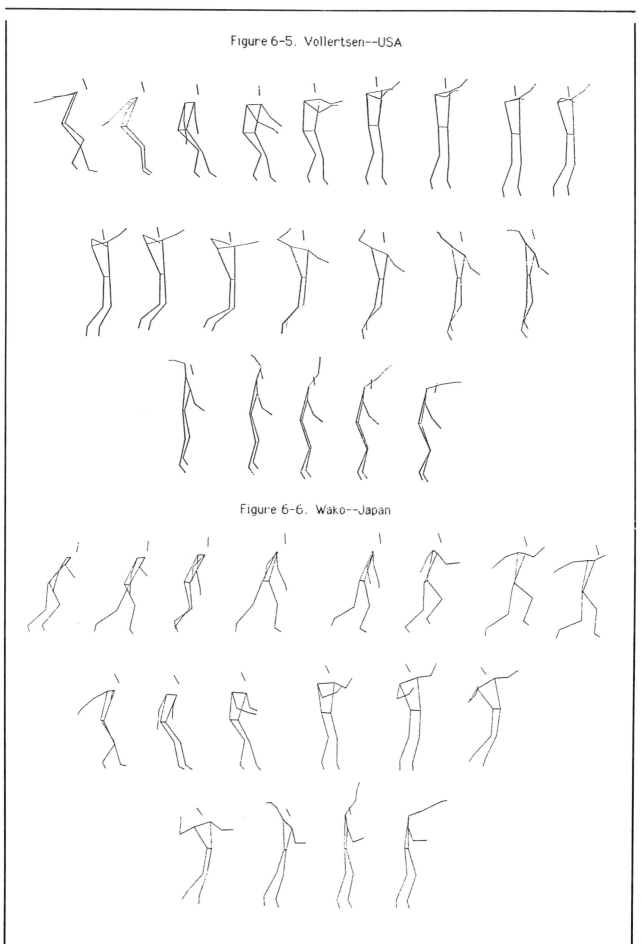

Figure 6-5. Vollertsen--USA

Figure 6-6. Wako--Japan

deltoid muscles. Also, the hitting arm is drawn back to a complete rest from which it has to quickly accelerate forward over a relatively short distance. After some years, players who use such a technique often experience shoulder problems.

THE SNAP ARM SWING The snap arm swing (Figure 6–6) is similar to the bow-and-arrow but does not create as much stress on the shoulder joint as the bow-and-arrow does. The arm is raised, bent at the elbow about 90 degrees, and brought around sideways at shoulder height with the elbow slightly below the shoulder and the forearm perpendicular to the floor. From here the arm swings upward toward the ball. This movement can be abbreviated by not drawing the elbow completely back, a useful adjustment when attacking balls with considerable horizontal velocity.

Mechanically, the snap arm swing is sound and offers great versatility in spiking and good ball control. However, as with the bow-and-arrow technique, the arm comes to a complete rest and has to move forward from zero velocity. A player must be able to generate a lot of power in the shoulder to hit the ball hard. I would recommend this arm swing primarily to quick attackers for whom ball control and speed are more important than power. The spiker should rely heavily upon a fast wrist snap and develop an ability to direct the ball anywhere on the court.

THE CIRCULAR ARM SWING The circular arm swing is similar to the snap arm swing except that when the arm comes sideways, the elbow continues to move downward and around the shoulder, never coming to a complete stop. There are two ranges of circular arm motion: the limited, as demonstrated by Rita Crockett in Figure 6–3, and the wide, as demonstrated by Flo Hyman in Figure 6–4.

In the limited circular arm swing, the right hand comes up slightly above head height and then rotates downward and around, maintaining an angle of about 90 degrees between upper arm and forearm, with the forearm parallel to the floor. Toward the end of the arm swing, the arm extends toward the ball.

This circular arm motion works the joint in its natural way. It allows the arm to accelerate continuously with very little stress in a circle toward the direction of the spike. The motion resembles the natural throwing motion of a baseball. For some unexplained reason, coaches have long tried to ignore this obvious natural arm swing. The arm can adjust easily to different ball heights, which allows complete control of sets that arrive at unexpected locations. At all arm heights, the circular

motion produces substantial power. This technique is recommended for both quick attackers and left-side hitters.

In the wide circular arm swing, during takeoff the right arm swings forward only to waist height. Then the arm starts its downward motion around the shoulder joint and up to the ball. The radius of the swing is much wider than for the limited circular arm swing. When pure power is needed, this is the technique to use.

THE ROUNDHOUSE ARM SWING In addition to the snap, the bow-and-arrow, and the circular arm swings, there is the roundhouse arm swing, which has the similar windmill arm motion of the roundhouse serve. This technique has recently gained some popularity, in particular for fast-tipping a ball, or in emergency situations when the spiker ends up underneath the ball.

Another situation where the roundhouse swing can be useful is when a short pass pulls the setter 6 to 8 feet off the net. Often the setter will set a fast set to a quick attacker that moves toward the net and diagonally across the attacker's body. In this situation, the roundhouse swing can be easier to execute than a conventional swing; it often gives the hitter a greater selection of hitting angles.

I recommend that all spikers become familiar with this emergency technique.

Flight (Nonhitting Arm Motion)

For all hitting techniques except the straight arm and the wide circular arm swings, both arms are raised simultaneously to roughly about head height. The right arm then draws back or around into its arm swing, while the left arm continues to rise slightly. In the straight arm swing, the right arm simply goes straight up while the left arm usually stays somewhere between waist and shoulder height, depending on the style and mechanics of the individual hitter. In the wide circular arm swing, the left arm comes up as for other arm swings, but the hitting hand and arm only come to waist height before starting to rotate around the shoulder joint.

The nonhitting arm effectively counterbalances the movement of the hitting arm. Once the body is airborne it derives power and balance through the muscles that work one part of the body against another. As the right arm pulls back, the stretch reflex in the chest muscles is activated; the subsequent contraction of these muscles contributes to the forward speed and power of the arm swing. Once the hitting arm begins its upward stroke toward the ball, the left arm drops down to about stomach height. Just prior to contact, the elbow of the left arm bends and stabilizes, working against the right arm.

Usually there is no need to teach a player what to do with the nonhitting arm because the movement occurs naturally. Sometimes a coach can observe what the left hand is doing to find a problem for a player who is very uncoordinated or who is naturally left-handed and spikes incorrectly with the right hand. Since the nonhitting arm acts as a natural counterweight to keep the body in balance, an apparent problem with the movement of the nonhitting arm may actually be a clue to another problem, probably having to do with footwork on the approach, or the takeoff position relative to the ball.

Body and Leg Movement During Flight

After takeoff, the degree to which the knees bend depends on the power applied to the ground during takeoff; the more power, the more the knees will bend. Also, the bending of the knees is a natural response to the drawing back of the arm and the rotation/lean of the upper body. When the hitting arm swings backward, the upper body rotates with a pronounced clockwise hip movement (for right-handed players). A player should not arch the back too much because arching can cause injury to the lower trunk, and the spiker needs to learn to derive power from trunk rotation rather than from arching.

There is a definite correlation between the action of the knees and the arm swing. During flight, both knees should bend with the heels coming up toward the thighs. As the arm swings forward to contact the ball, the left knee should come forward and up in front of the body. This hastens the action of the hitting arm. If the left leg remains straight, then the leverage arc becomes too long and the arm action is slowed down.

When a player's knees don't bend and the heels don't come up during flight, it signals that one or more of the following things did not happen:

- the hitting arm was not drawn back far enough;
- there was not enough rotation of the hips; or
- the takeoff was not explosive enough. The player did not push off with her calf muscles.

If a spiker has a slow arm swing, the coach should study the action of the left knee. By bring-

When the hitting arm moves across the body, the non-hitting arm responds naturally, moving across the body as well. When the hitting arm moves straight forward and down, the non-hitting arm, bent at the elbow, moves up until it stabilizes at about chest height upon contact with the ball.

ing up the left knee, the leverage arc is reduced, enabling the spiker to swing as fast as her own individual musculature allows. A fast arm swing will be slowed down if the left leg stays straight. Getting the correct knee lift with the left leg can hasten, to some degree, a naturally slow swing.

Once the body is suspended, the limbs act against each other with short leverages while the stomach muscles contract, acting as a stabilizer to help generate the power needed to hit the ball forcefully.

Contact with the Ball

Done properly, the actual arm swing involves coordinated movement of five body parts: the trunk, shoulder, upper arm, forearm, and hitting hand. The action begins as the trunk of the body rotates forward, supplying great initial power. As the knee opposite the hitting arm bends upward, the shoulder comes forward. The trunk, shoulder, and upper arm accelerate and then, almost in unison, decelerate, transferring the momentum into the hand, which whips forward as a separate unit.

Contact with the ball is made first with the heel of the palm and then with the fingers. The heel of the palm supplies the power and the fingers supply the direction and the top spin. The palm should be fairly loose so it can conform to the shape of the ball. The timing of the contact is very important. It is desirable to hit the ball at the peak of the jump to give maximum reach and the most ball control.

A good spiker should be able to hit any ball to any court position. Spikers should develop the ability to hit hard balls to the parameters of the court, in particular to the corners. Too often spikers hit the ball straight down, a satisfactory and sometimes glamorous motion, but most points are made by long hard spikes. Hitting at a more oblique angle allows a player to hit the ball sooner, a plus for quick attackers because the palm does not have to go on top of the ball as it does when hitting straight down. It also adds height to the reach because the ball can be hit on the side; the spiker doesn't have to wait for the ball to drop. The angle gives the spiker a better chance to go over the block.

Power is mainly a function of the speed of the arm. The ball will travel at the speed of the hand. The faster the speed of the arm, the faster the spike. A woman can hit the ball with enough power to produce a ball speed of about 100 miles per hour.

The physical mass (size) of the arm plays a minor role in generating power. When an athlete is very tall or has a very high jump, the point of

contact with the ball is not critical. In this situation it is possible to increase the power of the spike by hitting the ball on the way down. This places the player's body weight on top of the ball and can increase the speed by about 5 to 7 percent. Obviously, this is done at the expense of some height and ball control.

Follow-Through

After contact with the ball, the arm should follow through by continuing its swing. The follow-through does not increase the power of the hit, but it does help direct the ball with more control and it helps the arm clear the net. After contact, the arm should loosely continue its path, clearing the net in whichever way it can as the body descends.

Landing

The most important objective in landing is to come down softly with as little shock to the joints as possible. The toes should contact the floor first and then the knees should bend, absorbing the force of the body's descent. In extreme situations, a player might even need to drop all the way down to the floor. (This occurs sometimes with a back-row attacker who has generated tremendous momentum with her approach.)

There is no advantage in landing on two feet as

Lang Ping (Chinese Olympic team) and Flo Hyman, the two most outstanding Ace players of the 1984 Olympic games, in action. Note the follow-through arm movement.

Forcing the spiker to land on both legs may prevent her from assuming an off-balance position in the air, restricting her spiking options. Paula Weishoff of the 1984 USA Olympic Team lands on one foot after a one-leg slide spike.

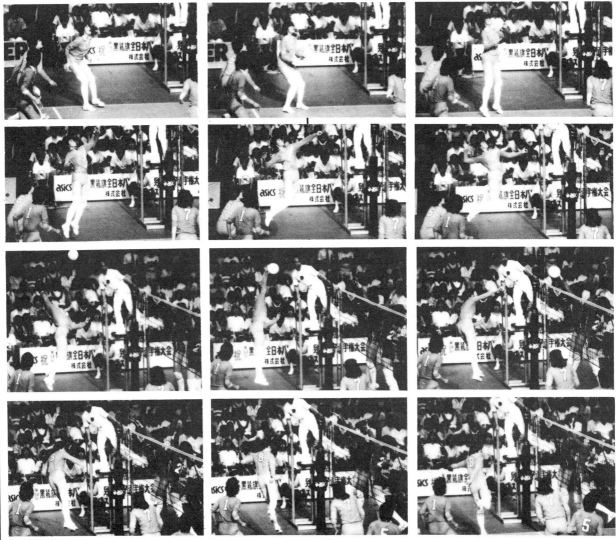

Note how this excellent shot would be impossible if the player had to land on both feet.

recommended by some coaches. It is not whether the hitter lands on one leg or two that determines the quality of cushioning, but rather the manner in which it is done. Actually, because one leg is weaker, it can give more. Forcing the hitter to come down on both legs can prevent her from getting into an off-balance position in the air, which is sometimes necessary for attack sets not timed or positioned perfectly.

It is definitely important to teach proper landing from all body postures. This gives the player confidence. Dr. Jim Coleman, the 1968 Men's Olympic coach, has developed the following equation to evaluate the force of impact of a spiker hitting the floor:

$$\text{force} = \text{body weight} \frac{\text{falling distance}}{\text{cushioning distance}} \text{ (any units)}$$

This formula shows that the more a player drops during cushioning, the less shock there is to the body.

Biomechanical Analysis of the Two-Foot Takeoff for the Jump

Jumping is a very complex body maneuver. Because of the critical role jumping plays in spiking, we have taken time here to review some pertinent biomechanical data.

The data presented here, obtained in actual game situations and analyzed at the Coto Research Center, was extracted from figures similar to Figures 6–7 and 6–8, and Figures 6–9 and 6–10. It represents cumulative analyses of five of the world's top players: Flo Hyman, Rita Crockett, Julie Vollertsen, and Sue Woodstra of the USA, and Juri Yokohama of Japan. It is summarized in Table 6–2.

The data may be considered suggestive rather than conclusive. It suggests the following:

1. The average horizontal velocity of a player after the run-up steps is 234cm/sec (7'8"/sec). At the completion of the push-off into the hop,

Figure 6-7. Velocity Curves for Components of Center of Gravity--Hyman (USA)

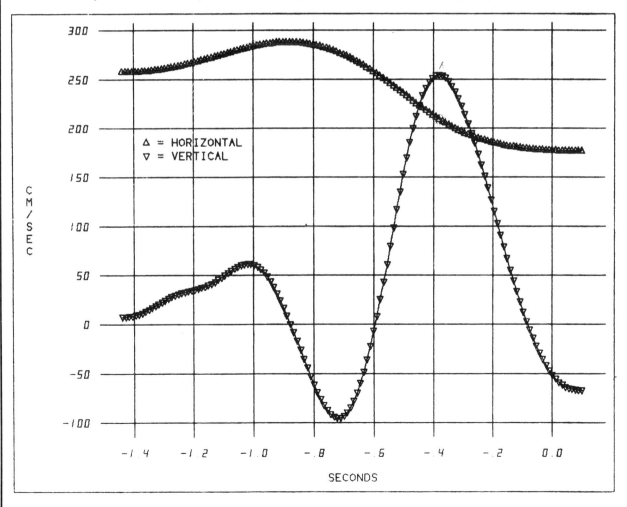

Figure 6-8. Acceleration Curves for Components of Center of Gravity--Hyman (USA)

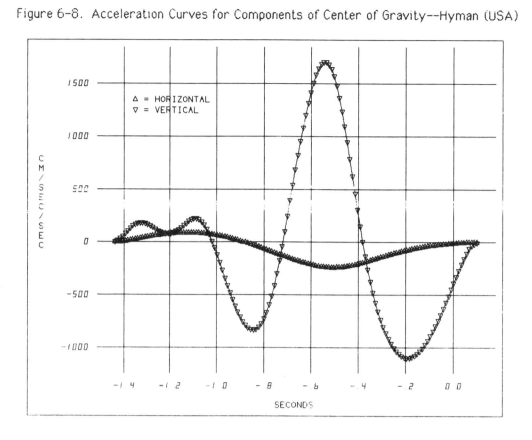

Figure 6-9. Velocity Curves for Components of Center of Gravity--Crockett (USA)

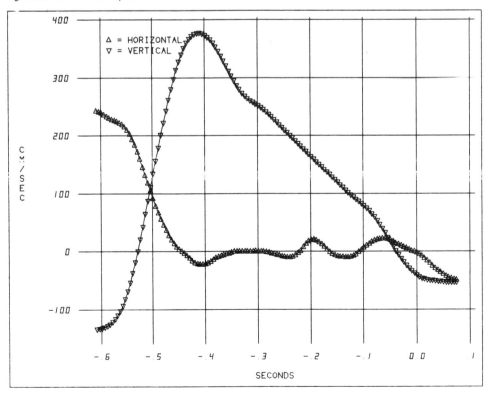

Figure 6-10. Acceleration Curves for Components of Center of Gravity--Crockett (USA)

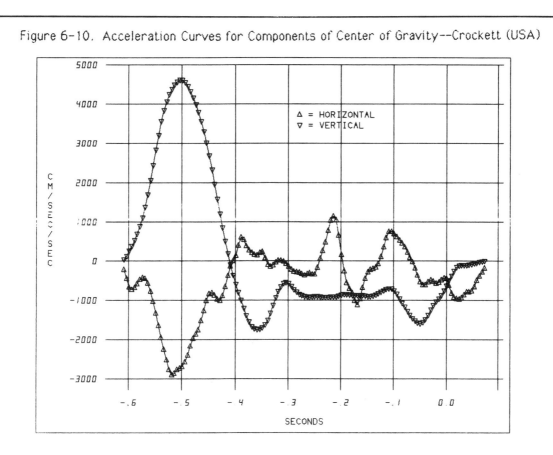

the horizontal velocity increases to an average of 355cm/sec (10′2″/sec).

2. It appears that a greater horizontal velocity during the hop is directly related to a longer hop and a higher jump.

3. The shorter the time of contact with the floor by both feet, the higher the jump.

4. The greater the vertical velocity at takeoff, the greater the jump. Rita Crockett achieved the highest vertical velocity at takeoff of 390 cm/sec with the highest vertical jump of 98cm (38.6″).

5. The greater the horizontal deceleration and vertical acceleration at takeoff, the higher the jump. Rita's acceleration was 4700cm/sec², and her deceleration was −2995cm/sec².

6. The greater the horizontal velocity at takeoff, the broader the jump.

7. It is not evident from this data that a player who broad-jumps is detracting from the height of the jump. Nevertheless, the data does suggest that for a player who has a given amount of leg power, dividing the power into a vertical component and a horizontal component may reduce the height of her jump.

As shown by the velocity and acceleration curves for Rita Crockett in the quick one-two takeoff, the peak vertical and horizontal velocities are far apart. Actually, as Rita's feet are placed on the floor coming off the hop, her horizontal velocity drops to zero, and her horizontal acceleration dropped to −3000cm/sec² (Figure 6–10).

In contrast to the quick one-two takeoff, Flo Hyman's slow one-two takeoff shows that the peak vertical and horizontal velocities are very close. Only a small loss in horizontal velocity takes place during takeoff. There is substantial horizontal velocity during contact with the ball. Hence, the body's deceleration during takeoff is not as abrupt as in the quick one-two takeoff.

Explained another way, Flo Hyman was still going forward as she rose to hit the ball, while Rita Crockett decelerated almost completely and converted her forward momentum into impetus for a nearly vertical jump. At present there is no conclusive data as to which takeoff, the quick or the slow one-two, is superior. The data seems to suggest that the quick one-two maximizes the height of the jump. But conversely, there is no evidence that the slow one-two takeoff detracts from the jump.

While the quick one-two is recommended for quick attackers, there is no generalization that can be drawn about which takeoff works best for ace spikers. Nor does the height of the player seem to matter. Rita Crockett of the USA and Yuri Yokayama of Japan are both international-caliber ace spikers. They are the same size (5′8″), yet Rita

Figure 6-11. Vector Analysis of Takeoff--Crockett (USA)

uses the quick one-two and Yuri the slow one-two. If the spiker uses the wide circular arm swing, the slow one-two takeoff may be required in order to properly synchronize the placement of the feet with the movements of the arm swing.

The average length of the hop measured from left foot to right foot is about 188 centimeters (6'2"). The average elapsed time between placing the right foot and the left foot is .11 seconds, and the average distance between the feet is 52 centimeters (20.5"). The average time for takeoff is .26 seconds. The conclusion we can make is that the quicker the one-two takeoff, the shorter the distance between the feet and the quicker the takeoff.

Figure 6–11 shows a vector analysis of takeoff as demonstrated by Rita Crockett. It shows that initially the horizontal velocity is absorbed by the heel-toe action of the right foot (frame D) and as the body progresses (frame F), the right foot pushes upward while the left foot pushes away from the net. Just before takeoff (frame G), all body forces, including the legs, trunk, and arms, coincide to lift the body vertically.

SUMMARY OF SPIKING TECHNIQUES

Here is a brief description of the specific spiking techniques that should be used by attackers playing various roles or positions.

Ace Spikers

An ace spiker should master an approach that uses one to three steps followed by a slow one-two takeoff, and either a limited or a wide circular arm swing. The slow one-two takeoff enables the spiker to adjust to a greater range of outside sets: short, long, tight, or deep.

Quick Attackers

The key to a successful quick attack, especially by CF, is quickness and timing. Power is only a secondary consideration. Therefore, the quick attacker should use only one or two run-up steps and a short hop followed by a quick one-two takeoff. The approach begins 12 feet behind the net. At times, a CF quick attacker may use only a hop without any run-up steps. The snap and the limited circular arm swing are recommended for quick attackers. In addition, quick attackers should employ an abbreviated backward arm swing. The arms should not be fully extended backward, but rather the elbows should be kept bent. At times, even the follow-through may be cut short in order to avoid contacting the net. In these situations, the arm stops forward movement immediately upon contact with the set.

The CF quick attacker must master a variety of quick spikes with complete control.

Utility Spiker

The utility spiker often attacks in a variety of tempos and from a number of different court positions. Therefore, she should master both the quick and the slow one-two takeoffs, using two run-up steps. The limited circular arm swing is the preferred spiking technique for utility players, since it can be used effectively to hit both quick- and slower-tempo sets at any position along the net.

Back-Row Attackers

Depending on the organization of the team's offense, ace players and/or utility players may be required to attack from the back row. Occasionally, tall middle blockers are also employed as back-row attackers. When attacking from the back row, the spiker should use the slow one-two takeoff. Since it does not matter if the spiker lands in front of the 10-foot line, broad jumping is desirable when hitting out of the back row. This enables the spiker to contact the set closer to the net, sometimes as close as 5 feet for men. The number of run-up steps will vary according to the starting position of the back-row attacker, the height and location of the set, the time available, and the spiker's personal preference. As a general rule, the spiker should build up as much momentum as she can without losing body control. Hitting from the back row is a very demanding assignment and a player cannot afford to sacrifice body control, because this will lead to a decrease in accuracy and spiking efficiency.

One-Leg Takeoff

The one-leg takeoff was the standard takeoff until the fifties; with the introduction of the two-leg takeoff, the one-leg takeoff became obsolete. In 1977, I began to wonder what the potential might be for incorporating the one-leg takeoff into the attack under special circumstances. Patty Dowdell, one of the greatest U.S. players of all time, and I experimented with it. It didn't take long to discover that the one-leg takeoff can be an effective attack weapon.

Paula Weishoff executes a one-leg takeoff slide spike in a match against the Chinese team.

1. The one-leg takeoff "slide spike" for a right-handed player.

2. For a left-handed player.

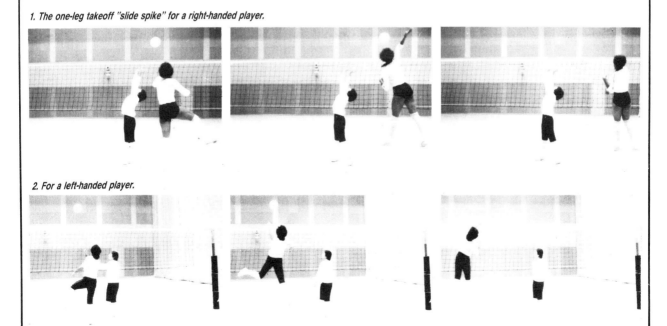

The one-leg takeoff is mostly used for a slide spike behind the setter's back (for a right-handed player). It can, however, be used for quick attack in front of the setter as shown here.

The one-leg takeoff allows a player to quickly mobilize the body from a fast run into a vertical jump while broad-jumping. It also allows the player to move along the net and then hit a fast set at different points of its trajectory with good ball control, either straight down the line or at an angle. A right-handed player should implement this technique when moving from left to right; a left-handed player, when moving from right to left.

The technique resembles the basic footwork in a lay-up shot in basketball. The right-handed spiker runs along the net or at a slight angle to it and takes off from the left foot with the right leg and arm leading upward. Actually, this kind of jump can yield a higher reach than a 2-foot takeoff. In a game situation the one-leg takeoff can be incorporated in combination plays for quick attack in the slide spike (See Figure 6–40).

VARYING THE SPIKE

For a spiker to be effective she must be deceptive, concealing her intentions as long as possible, and she must have a variety of different shots in her spiking arsenal. The spiker should be able to hit the ball to any court position at any speed regardless of her position at takeoff. The following are some of the most frequently used attack techniques in addition to the spike: spin spike, off-speed shots, the tip, the shove, the wipe-off, and hits off the block.

Spin Spike

For techniques on how to impart different spins to the ball, see Chapter 3, "The Serve"—"The Spin Serve."

The player should learn to spike the ball with top spin, side spin, underspin, and no spin (float) to all points of the court. The top spin is useful for going over the block and for hitting sharp angles. The more top spin, the sharper the angle. A ball with less top spin is effective for hitting perimeter areas of the court, particularly the sidelines and corners.

Side-spin shots are useful in hitting the ball into the block. Side spin makes the ball rebound outside the court and toward the antenna. Also, side spin is very useful for a sharp-angle crosscourt hit,

Hitting around the block to the perimeters of the court, particularly to the sidelines and corners, does not require much top spin on the ball.

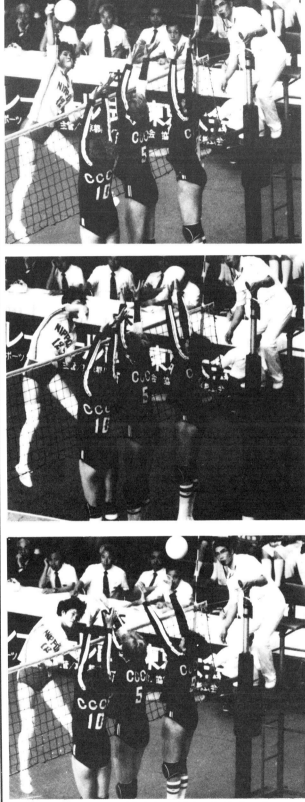

The inside spin from the LF and the outside spin from the RF are very useful for sharply angled crosscourt hits.

When the spiker is trapped underneath the block, she should hit the ball upwards with underspin to deflect the ball off the block.

Hitting the ball with side spin (clockwise spin) into the block can be very useful to beat the block. Side spin makes the ball rebound toward the antenna and outside the court.

squeezing the ball in between the net and the 10-foot line. On this shot, inside spin should be used from the left side and outside spin from the right side. Balls with side spin are more difficult for the defense to dig accurately.

Underspin on a spike can be used to deflect the ball upward off the block. This is useful when the set is tight to the net, trapping the spiker underneath the block.

The float spike (no spin) is used to hit balls very hard with great velocity into the center of the court and the corners in particular. It is also used against a nonpenetrating block in an attempt to deflect the ball off the block as far back as possible out of bounds. A primary advantage of the float is that the ball can be hit quickly on its side at the top of the spiker's reach. Since the spiker doesn't have to wait for the ball to descend, this speeds up the attack.

Off-Speed Shots

An off-speed shot is a spike, but with something less than full force. It is a controlled placement shot that the spiker directs exactly to a specific location. The approach and takeoff are identical to a normal spike, but the arm swing is slower and less power is exerted. Most of the power and direction control come from wrist action. The object of the off-speed shot is to catch the opponent unprepared. It is effective when there is an opening and probability for a hard spike. The defense expects a powerful hit. When the spiker eases up on the shot, the ball drops short and the defenders are caught off balance, unable to react quickly enough.

The Tip

The tip is a ball that is pushed gently upward or downward. There are two types of tip, the soft tip and the hard tip. For both, the spiker should ap-

proach the tip with the same intensity and manner as for a real spike. To execute the "soft" tip, the player should go through the normal arm swing and then at the last second decelerate very quickly, putting his arm up underneath the ball with the elbows slightly bent. The hand is placed so that the length of the fingers and the tip of the thumb are in full contact with the ball. With a soft wrist motion, the ball is pushed slightly up and over the net or the block.

A soft tip is often very effective if it is done towards an opening for a hard spike.

Rose Magers of the 1984 USA Olympic Team executes a soft tip in the semi-final match against Peru.

Karch Kiraly of the 1984 USA Olympic Team executes a hard tip, pushing the ball down by the block.

A hard tip executed with a roundhouse arm swing is a deceptive, quick attack, increasing the attacking range of the spiker. Center players, in particular, should master this technique.

The soft tip can be done at the top of the jump or just at the beginning of the descent. The spiker should be able to tip short or long. Short balls go to the left, to the right, and up over the block. Long-range tips are directed to the center of the court and to the corners. It is very effective to create the impression that one is going to tip to one side, and then suddenly flip the hand and tip to the other side.

For the "hard" tip, the fingers should come on top of the ball after the arm decelerates, and push it down with an abrupt wrist action. The hard tip should be done at the peak of the jump.

Recently the hard tip has become a very potent weapon, especially among setters, because it can place the ball very accurately. When the ball is passed close to the net, the setter jumps as if for a regular jump set. Then at the last second, the setter twists whichever wrist is closer to the net, places her hand on top of the ball, and forces it down in front of the opponent's 10-foot line. Al-

A roundhouse fast tip is executed with a tight, sideways, circular arm swing.

A Korean player attempts to wipe-off the ball out of the hands of Cuba's Mercedes Perez.

though the speed of the ball is slower than for the spike, because of its proximity to the net the hard tip is very difficult to defense.

The hard tip, executed either by the setter or an attacker, is particularly effective at the end of long transition rallies where the opponent's defense is out of sync and expecting only hard spikes.

In addition, it's effective in a very fast attack, even faster than first tempo. (My team called it "minus tempo.") The quick attacker approaches from the left with the intention to hard-tip. The setter delivers a ball with a greater horizontal velocity and a lower trajectory than usual. The ball can be pushed downward in any direction, but in most cases a tight, sideways, circular arm swing is used to push the ball down across the body to the left (a similar arm swing to the roundhouse arm swing).

The Shove

The shove is very similar to the tip but instead of placing the hand under or on top of the ball, the hand is placed on the side of the ball and behind it. With the hand behind the ball and the elbow fairly bent, the hitter has good control of the ball, and can generate a great deal of force from the tricep muscle in the upper arm. This technique is useful in shoving balls to the deep end of the court or in pushing balls into and through the block.

The Wipe-Off

The wipe-off is an effective technique used to overcome a strong block, especially in situations when the block camps on a spiker who is in a disadvantageous position. The spiker simply puts her hand slightly on the inside of the ball and, with a fairly prolonged arm action, pushes the ball into the block and out of bounds. This is often done when the set is tight to the net and the block penetrates. The spiker should hesitate slightly, let the block descend, and then sweep the ball over the blocker's hand, pushing through and out.

Hits Off the Block—Spiker vs. Blocker

Often there are two or three blockers confronting the spiker and she finds that she can not go over or around the block on either side with a hard spike. In this situation, the spiker can make use of these tactical shots:

- hitting into the seam of the block,
- hitting on either outside hand of the block,
- hitting a ball with side spin or underspin upward off the block,
- wiping the ball off the block, or
- shoving the ball through the block.

A short player trying to beat an imposing block should aim for the outside forearms or elbows of the blockers, or into the face between the forearms. If the block does not penetrate but keeps the palms straight up, the spiker should hit a level ball into the fingers of the block so that the ball will be deflected back into her own court. If deflected back, the ball will usually travel in a smooth arc, easily played by the players covering the hitter.

If everything seems hopeless, the spiker should hit a controlled shot into the block, and then be ready to immediately recover the ball. This should be done after a slight hesitation, so that the ball will be deflected as the block is descending.

Often the seam of the block is vulnerable to quick attack; therefore, the attack should be done quickly before the block closes the seam.

When hitting off the block, the spiker should aim at the outside forearm of the outside blocker, imparting side spin to deflect the ball out of the court.

Direction and Angle of a Power Spike

Contrary to popular belief, the direction of the approach should not limit the direction of the spike. In fact, players must learn to hit the ball to different court directions from a variety of approach patterns (Figure 6–12). The lateral direction of a power spike is determined by the location of the ball in relation to the shoulder of the hitting arm (Figure 6–13). For a right-handed spiker, if the ball is too far out to the right side, she will only be able to hit the ball hard in a crosscourt angle because the ball is in line with her arm swing. However, trying to hit the ball toward the inside of her swing will result in a loss of power, altitude, and ball control.

If the set ball is in front of the spiker, between the hitting shoulder and the body's midline, then the ball can be hit with full power straight forward or to the left of the spiker. To hit the ball to the right, the spiker must lean to the left, slow down her arm swing and hit an off-speed shot with a forceful wrist action. If the ball is past the midline of the spiker's body to her left, then a hard hit can only be directed to the left with an arm action that travels right-to-left across her body.

It is very important that a spiker line up with the ball in a way that leaves as many options for power and off-speed hits as possible so that the opponent's defense can not anticipate either the

The spiker must learn to vary the directions of her shots from the same approach by manipulating her body around the ball and mastering different arm actions. Proper alignment with the ball at takeoff is imperative for spiking versatility.

Spiking down the line.

Cross-court spike.

Cross-body spike.

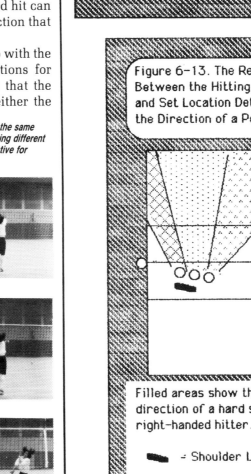

Figure 6-12. A Spiker (x) Must Learn to Hit Cross-Court or Line from Either a Straight or an Angle Approach

Figure 6-13. The Relationship Between the Hitting Shoulder and Set Location Determines the Direction of a Power Hit.

Filled areas show the possible direction of a hard spike for a right-handed hitter.

▬ = Shoulder Line

○ = Ball Locations

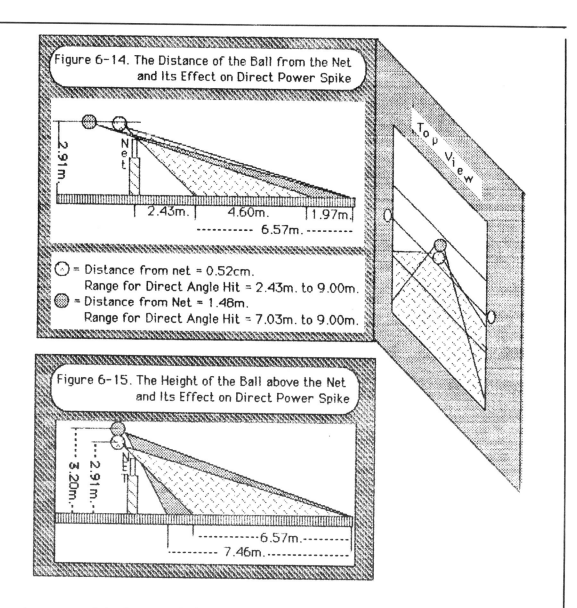

Figure 6-14. The Distance of the Ball from the Net and Its Effect on Direct Power Spike

2.91 m.
Net
2.43m. 4.60m. 1.97m.
6.57m.

◔ = Distance from net = 0.52cm.
Range for Direct Angle Hit = 2.43m. to 9.00m.
◕ = Distance from Net = 1.48m.
Range for Direct Angle Hit = 7.03m. to 9.00m.

Top View

Figure 6-15. The Height of the Ball above the Net and Its Effect on Direct Power Spike

3.20m. 2.91m.
Net
6.57m.
7.46m.

direction or the power of the hit. A right-handed spiker must jump behind the ball and about a foot to the left of the desired contact point on the lateral plane. This position yields the most options for power hits.

The height of the set and its distance from the net dictate the vertical angle of a direct power spike (Figures 6–14 and 6–15). Therefore, the height of the ball and its distance from the net dictate to which court position the ball can be hit. A ball that is poised directly over the net can be hit to any point on the court. The farther back the set is from the net, the more limited the range of possible hits. As a result, the farther away the ball is from the net, the more imperative it is to contact the ball at the highest point of its trajectory to increase the shot options. Hitting the ball with top spin also adds variety.

When a ball is close to the net, a spiker who is tall or who can jump well has more chance to go over the block, but less lateral range to hit to either side of the block. Farther away from the net the vertical range is reduced, but the lateral range is increased. A team must gauge what the optimum height and depth of sets should be for different opponents. When a tall team plays against a short team, it is beneficial to set balls tight to the net so the tall spikers can go over the short blockers. When a short team plays against a tall team, it is better to set deeper off the net so the spikers can attempt to hit to either side of the block. A deep set can be attacked more quickly with a flat hit, a ball contacted on its side instead of on top.

When the other team has a good block, it is sometimes advisable to have the setter vary the depth of the sets. This makes it more difficult for the blockers to establish a rhythm and properly time their jumps. Naturally, varying the set depth takes considerable practice and communication between the setter and the attackers.

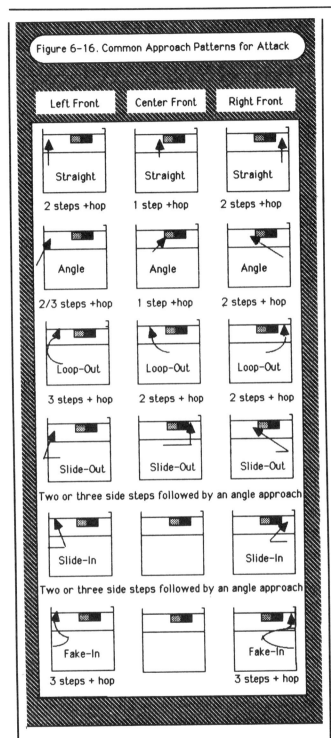

Figure 6-16. Common Approach Patterns for Attack

| Left Front | Center Front | Right Front |

Straight — 2 steps +hop | Straight — 1 step +hop | Straight — 2 steps +hop

Angle — 2/3 steps +hop | Angle — 1 step +hop | Angle — 2 steps + hop

Loop-Out — 3 steps + hop | Loop-Out — 2 steps + hop | Loop-Out — 2 steps + hop

Slide-Out | Slide-Out | Slide-Out

Two or three side steps followed by an angle approach

Slide-In | | Slide-In

Two or three side steps followed by an angle approach

Fake-In — 3 steps + hop | | Fake-In — 3 steps + hop

Straight Approach

Basic approach for all spikers. Commonly used by the RF and CF. Following the straight approach, spikers tend to hit down the line, so crosscourt hitting from this approach should be emphasized in training.

Angle Approach

Most commonly used approach by the LF and CF. The RF often uses this approach for X plays.

Loop Approach

The loop-out approach is a continuous movement along an arch which helps improve eye contact with the ball and block at the same time. The LF often uses this approach for high outside sets. It is also used to attack on the sidelines after passing in center front position. The CF player often uses this approach for shoot sets in front of the setter. A loop-in approach is done toward the inside of the court. A wide-loop is a movement from one side of the court to the other. It is usually done during serve reception attack in order to switch players' positions.

Slide Approach

The slide-out and the slide-in are very common footwork for spiking, divided into two phases: lateral adjustment usually done with two or three shuffle steps parallel to the net, and then an approach that could be straight or at an angle done with one or two run-up steps.
The slide-out is commonly used by the LF in serve reception and transition attacks adjusting for a poor pass or a poor dig, respectively.
The RF may use the slide foot work in adjusting position for an X attack.

Fake Approach

The fake-in and the fake-out (opposite direction to the fake in) are continous movements. Usually used by the concealed attacker (LF and RF) in combination attack to deceive the opponent block by a quick change of direction. The LF starts the fake-in approach with the left foot followed by 2 run-up steps and a hop. The RF may use the fake-in approach as a lead for a slide spike.

Timing the Spike

After the player takes off, her center of gravity travels in a parabola as she rises for the spike and then descends. This flight path is determined by the pull of gravity and can not be changed no matter what the spiker does. To maximize ball control and reach, the spiker should contact the ball at the peak of her jump, timing her arm swing so it is completed at just that instant. Occasionally, tall spikers and very good jumpers can hit the ball just as they begin to descend to increase the power behind the hit.

Sensing the Block

The spiker must develop an intuitive feeling for the block's movement and response tendencies. She should pay attention to the initial position of the block before serve reception and immediately after a dig. The instant a ball begins traveling to the setter, the spiker should again glance at the opponent's court. An experienced player can even see the position of the block in her peripheral vision during the approach. Just prior to contact, the hitter should see the block again in her peripheral vision.

The coach should use different drills to train the spiker to see the block. One rather elaborate but useful system I devised was placing six lamps on the court (with metal guards) that I could turn on and off from a control box off the court. A light would go on after the spiker took off and her task was to aim at the light.

A simpler drill is varying a two-player block. One time blockers will set up for the crosscourt shot and the spiker has to hit down the line. Another time the block will provide a hole and the spiker has to hit into the hole. Drills should be designed to provide the experience a spiker needs to anticipate and see the movement of the block.

In addition, the spiker needs to develop a sense for a block's response to combination attacks and to learn what openings are created by different attacks. There is no real substitute for seeing the block, a skill that comes with experience.

Approach Patterns

In advanced volleyball, players use a variety of approach patterns to get to the net for their attack. Some of these are fake patterns designed to confuse the opponent's block. The players must have a keen understanding of the relationship that footwork has with distance and the tempo of the attack. Correct footwork is always crucial. It is important to remember that for a right-handed attacker, the hop is always done off the left foot; for a left-handed attacker it is always done off the right foot. The takeoff is similar for all approach patterns. Figure 6–16 illustrates some of the more common approaches and footwork used in attacking.

Play-Set System

As a team's level of attack becomes more sophisticated, the players need to have a language system to designate different kinds of sets. With this language, a spiker and setter can communicate quickly with each other regarding the height and placement of a set. The ability to communicate this information quickly is crucial for organizing an attack. Using finger signals and/or calling out numbers, letters, or words, can quickly convey a complete offensive pattern, accurately indicating who goes where and does what. Different teams have different methods of communication to suit their needs.

Language System Used by the 1984 U.S. Women's Olympic Team

In 1973 Dr. Jim Coleman proposed a numbering system for describing the height and location of each type of set. I modified Coleman's system and used this version for the USA women's national team. Here is an explanation of the modified system. Later you will see how it is implemented during a game. Two digits are combined to convey: where the spiker should go; and how high the set should be.

To specify location, the net is divided into nine equal parts, or slots (Figure 6–17). Each slot is 1-meter wide and extends from the midline back to the 10-foot line. The slots are identified as follows: 5 designates the outermost left slot, and then, moving from left to right, 4, 3, 2, 1, 0, A, B, C. The 0 slot, where the setter stands, coincides with the primary target.

The second digit signifies height and tempo. "Tempo" is the word used to describe the timing or speed of the set. When the second digit is 1, the set is a first-tempo set and the ball should peak about 1 to 2 feet (30 to 60cm) above the net. When the second number is a 2, it's a second-tempo set and the ball should peak about 2 to 4 feet (60 to 120 cm) above the net. A 3 is a third-tempo set, one that peaks 5 feet or higher above the net.

If a spiker wants a second-tempo set in slot 1, she would ask or signal for a 12. A B1 indicates a first-tempo set, delivered about 1 to 2 feet above

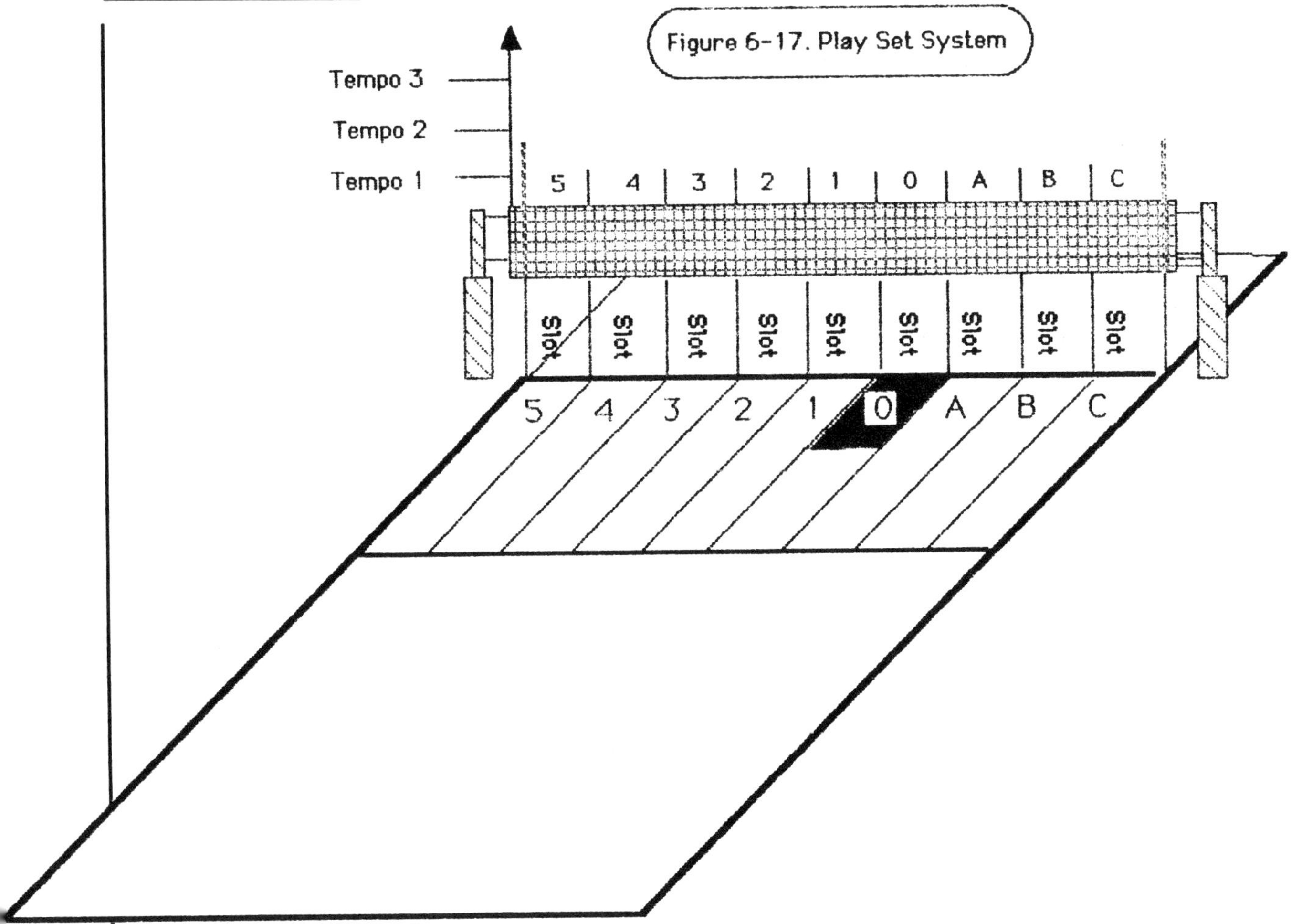

Figure 6-17. Play Set System

the net in slot B. A 53 indicates slot 5 with a third-tempo set that peaks 5 feet or higher above the net.

Generally, there are eight play sets in each tempo:

First tempo: 51, 41, 31, 21, 11, A1, B1, C1
Second tempo: 52, 42, 32, 22, 12, A2, B2, C2
Third tempo: 53, 43, 33, 23, 13, A3, B3, C3

In all of these tempos, the spiker should jump as high as she can and hit the ball at her maximum reach. With first-tempo sets, the spiker may occasionally hit the ball at a point slightly lower than her maximum reach, sacrificing some altitude for quickness. But coaches should be very careful and watchful about this. Too many times the setter will set first-tempo sets too low, sometimes just barely over the top of the net. If the attacker can reach much higher, setting the ball too low just pulls the hitter's arm down and makes the ball easier to block. This can often prevent the hitter from getting a good swing at the ball, subtracting from its power and velocity. If the quick attacker can reach high, then the setter should jump-set or use other techniques to deliver the set very quickly to the hitter's maximum reach.

In the second and third tempos, the spiker should always hit at her uppermost reach. Spiking at the highest point improves the hitting angle and increases the chance of going over the block.

After a team has become familiar with the basic system, further abbreviation can be used to simplify communication during a game. For example, if a player signals just one number instead of two, the implication is that the set is a first-tempo set; only the slot position is called. This simplification should come only after a team is thoroughly familiar with the system.

If a coach or player wants to be even more descriptive about the set, conveying how far off the net the set is, she can describe the set as tight, normal, and deep. "Tight" describes a ball that is set right over the net. "Normal" indicates a ball set about arm's length (50cm/20″) back from the net. "Deep" describes a ball set a meter (3 to 4 feet) or more back. As an alternative, a numbering system can be used: 1 for tight, 2 for normal, and 3 for deep. Communicating three numbers during a game is impractical, but using this third number during practice can sometimes prove useful.

It should be noted that since the slots extend

from the midline back to the 10-foot line, back-row attackers also communicate with this system. The setter simply adjusts the depth of the set back to the 10-foot line. When attempting to hit from the back row, the spiker should attack as quickly as possible, first or second tempo. The depth of the set should be adjusted for the back court spiker.

Floating vs. Fixed Systems

There is a complication that often arises during the attack with the play-set system outlined above. This complication has to do with the positioning of the setter and the spikers. Assume that a spiker asks for an 11 set (slot 1 and 1 to 3 ft. above the net). The spiker expects to be just to the left of the setter who should be in the target area, slot 0. But suppose the pass pulls the setter over to slot 3. Now, if the spiker remains in slot 1, she is to the right of the setter, and from the setter's position, an 11 set has now become a backset.

The question is: should the spiker remain in the slot she initially indicated, slot 1, or should she adjust and position herself in front of the setter so that she achieves the same relationship to the setter that she initially requested? To make this adjustment, the spiker would go one slot to the left of the setter, into slot 4. The first solution illustrates the fixed system; the second, the floating system.

In the *fixed-play set system,* no matter where the setter is, *the spiker always goes to the slots she initially communicated.* The slot number indicates a fixed position on the net, one that doesn't move. The distance and direction of the set can change depending upon the position of the setter. The fixed concept can be advantageous if a team wants to attack at a specific area of the net regardless of the position of the setter.

In the *float system,* the location of the attack slot varies in relation to the setter's position (Figure 6–18). The slot-numbering system always starts from the setter. The only two slots that never change position are slots 5 and C.

The hitter's slot number indicates her relationship to the setter; that is, how far away from the setter she wants to be, and whether she is to the right or the left of the setter. That relationship is mobile; it can "float" along the net, adjusting to the location of the pass.

The fixed system is more difficult for the setter, because she must make all the adjustments. The floating play-set system puts the strain on the spikers, for they are the ones who must adjust to the location of the pass.

With my team, certain rules were outlined for the right front player in certain situations. For example, if the right front player had called an A1 (behind the setter's back) and the pass didn't go to the target, the right front had the obligation to follow the setter until the setter crossed the midline of the court. Once the setter crossed the midline, the A1 automatically became a C-1.

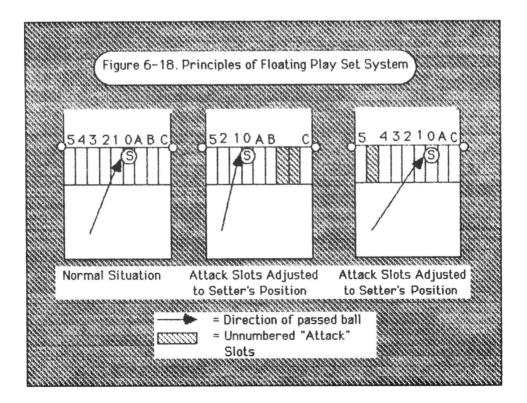

Figure 6–18. Principles of Floating Play Set System

| 5 4 3 2 1 0 A B C | 5 2 1 0 A B C | 5 4 3 2 1 0 A C |
| Normal Situation | Attack Slots Adjusted to Setter's Position | Attack Slots Adjusted to Setter's Position |

⟶▶ = Direction of passed ball

▨ = Unnumbered "Attack" Slots

Both the fixed and floating systems have merit, and both are used at high-level competitions. A coach, in choosing one of these two systems, must understand the implications of each. With the 1984 U.S. women's Olympic team, I implemented the floating play-set system. I feel it is a better approach because it is less complicated. Even though we used it at the Olympic level, it is also easier for beginning volleyball players to master.

First-Tempo Sets

Generally, a first-tempo set is attacked very quickly after the release of the ball by the setter. The hitter is already up in the air, ready to swing, when the set is released. Coaches and players should remember that "tempo" refers to the elapsed time between the release of the set and contact by the spiker. Tempo does not mean low and does not automatically indicate the speed of the ball. The longer shoot sets, such as the 31, 41, and (particularly) 51, have fairly fast horizontal velocity, while the 11 and the A1 may be virtually motionless at the peak of their trajectory when hit by the spiker.

The height of a first-tempo set is about 1 to 2 feet above the net. It will vary slightly according to:

- the height and maximum jump reach of the spiker. The higher the spiker reaches, the higher the set should be.
- the timing of the spiker. If she is delayed, the set should be higher. If she is early and jumps too soon, the set should be lower.
- the spiker's position in relationship to the setter. First-tempo sets to the outside zones (51, 41, and sometimes C1) should be a bit higher than the short-distance first-tempo sets such as the 11 and the A1.

First-tempo sets can actually be subdivided into three timings or rhythms:

- *Regular rhythm:* The spiker jumps first, and then the set is delivered.
- *Slower rhythm:* The spiker jumps just as the set is released. This rhythm is used for the long first-tempo attacks like the 51 and C1, and when the spiker does not possess good jumping ability. The set is at least 2 feet above the net.
- *Minus rhythm:* This is actually called "minus tempo." A minus-tempo set is usually faster and lower than a regular first-tempo set. The attacker does not spike the ball but instead shoves it or hard-tips it. In the minus tempo, which is effective for players who don't have a fast arm swing, the jump comes a bit sooner than for reg-

ular first tempo. Minus-tempo sets are often used by advanced teams during transition when the dig comes to the setter so fast that the quick attacker does not have enough time to make a full approach and complete either her jump or her arm swing.

If for some reason the spiker is delayed or can't assume the proper position in relation to the setter, or if the setter is not in position to make a first-tempo set, then the spiker should attack in the same position (slot), but at a slower tempo. This adjustment should be audibly communicated by the spiker and/or the setter.

THE 11 SET The first-tempo 11 set is sometimes called a "jap" because the Japanese perfected it. A key function of the 11 set is to freeze the center front blocker or force her to jump with the spiker (who jumps before the set is released).

In a multiple-tempo attack system, from serve reception a team has two choices: any front-row player can approach for the 11 set, or the CF

Flo Hyman about to takeoff for an 11 set.

quicker attacker can attack an 11 set from any starting position in the serve-reception formation. In a single-tempo attack system only the quicker attacker, CF, would attack an 11 set.

In transition attack (after a dig or free ball) it is usually the center player who goes for the 11. Because it is by far the most common first-tempo set, the eleven is often abbreviated and called a one set.

To attack the 11 set, the spiker normally starts about 12 feet off the net and close to the setter. After the setter assumes position and is about to contact the ball, the spiker jumps close in front of the setter, starting the initial phase of her arm swing. The setter then delivers the ball, 1 or 2 feet above the net depending on the reach of the spiker, and the spiker hits the ball as it is rising or just at its peak. The set should be parallel to, or slightly off, the net. It should not be too tight, trapping the hitter.

It is the spiker's responsibility to create the correct distance between herself and the setter. It is the setter's responsibility to observe the spiker

An airborne Rita Crockett waits for an 11 set.

and deliver a consistent trajectory in the set. For first- and second-tempo attacks, the setter should always try to jump-set. This means that the spiker must get into position promptly and be on time to attack the jump set. If the spiker is late, the setter does not jump-set, but instead bends her elbows before contact a little to create more time for the spiker to jump. If even more time is needed, the setter can bend her knees and go down to a low position. Setting an 11 set from a low position is not very effective because the long travel interval between the release of the set and contact by the spiker allows too much time for the block to react.

Because the spiker is airborne when the setter contacts the ball, the opposing blocker has one of two choices: jump with the spiker, or jump after the release of the set. If the blocker jumps with the spiker, the setter should deliver the ball to another hitter. If the blocker does not jump, the setter should set the 11 set, which normally should go straight up to the spiker's hand. Against a tall middle blocker, it is advisable to set the 11 slightly off the net so that the spiker can hit it deep. As the setter and her hitters become more proficient, the setter can learn to move the 11 set a few inches laterally to either side to give the hitter a better angle around the block.

If the pass or dig is short, the setter should make every attempt to move toward the ball and jump-set it back toward the net. In principle, whenever the setter is off the net, the spiker has to adjust over to a higher number slot to her left. She should take off in front of an imaginary line. If the pass is relatively low and the setter is side-setting, the line is drawn through the setter's shoulders (not her feet) to the net (Figure 6–19a). If the pass is higher and the setter has time to pivot around toward left front, then the imaginary line for the quick attacker is drawn diagonally between the setter's shoulders to the net (Figure 6–19b). The farther the setter is off the net the greater the distance between the setter and spiker should be. For a hard tip, the hitter can come inside the imaginary line and execute the tip with a restricted windmill (roundhouse) arm action.

A spiker who does not possess very good jumping ability can not afford to take off ahead of the ball because the margin of error for the set becomes too limited. If she does get the set, it may be so low that a tall opponent can block it simply by going up on her toes. The spiker needs to jump with the release of the ball for a slow 11 set. As the ball goes up, the spiker goes up. This adjustment in tempo increases the height of the spiker's contact with the ball and provides a good opportunity for the spiker to manipulate the shot options.

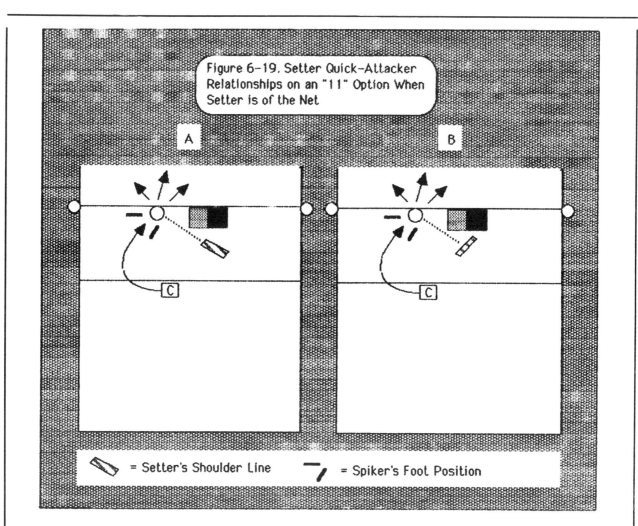

Figure 6-19. Setter Quick-Attacker Relationships on an "11" Option When Setter is of the Net

A

B

[C]

[C]

⬛ = Setter's Shoulder Line   ➖ = Spiker's Foot Position

For a quick 11, the spiker jumps ahead of the set. For a slow 11, the spiker jumps upon release of the set; as the ball goes up, the spiker goes up. This adjustment in tempo increases the height of the spiker's contact with the ball, providing the spiker with more shot options.

Umi Egami, the 1984 Japan Olympic Team captain, executes a slow tempo 31 spike with an angle approach from the LF court position. Because the ball is delivered with relatively great horizontal velocity, the 31 set is often spiked with cross body arm action into the seam of the block. A 31 attack from the LF imposes great difficulties on the opponent's block.

Another method to offset a relatively low jump is to implement the minus-tempo attack. In the minus-tempo attack, the spiker jumps early, ahead of when she would jump for a first tempo. She has no intention of spiking but instead hard-tips the ball. Many women's teams implement this technique successfully because it speeds up the attack.

The success of the quick 11 set rests mostly in the hands of the setter and hinges on her decision making. For the slow 11 set, the responsibility shifts to the spiker. Both timings can be effective, but implementing the slow 11 set requires high-quality deceptive setting and quicker delivery of sets to the outside.

A 21 SET Spiking the 21 set is similar to spiking the 11 set, except that the spike takes place one slot over to the left. The height of the set for the 21 is similar to that for the 11, but because the ball has to travel a greater horizontal distance, the set must have slightly greater horizontal velocity. The 21 can work with the three possible timings: regular, slow, and a minus for hard tips.

The 21 can be incorporated into the total attack scheme as an independent play, substituting for the 11 when the opposing center blocker has a tendency to line up opposite the 1 slot rather than taking her cue from the movement pattern of the quick attacker. The 21 is also useful in a 5–1 team composition during those rotations where there are only two front-row spikers and RB (usually the utility player) is attacking from the back row. Because the 21 forces the opposing middle blocker to move to her right, it cuts down the time available for her to move back to her left into position to block the RB attacker.

The 21 can also be built into a double quick combination where one player goes for the 11 and another for the 21. I like to call this a "tight double quick." In addition, as mentioned earlier, the 21 becomes an automatic replacement option for the 11 in emergency situations when the setter is pulled off the net by the dig or pass.

In serve-reception attack, any player who is positioned in LF, CF, or RF may go for a 21 set (in a multitempo attack system). The approach patterns are the same as for an 11 set (Figure 6–19). In transition attack, usually only the center quick attacker goes for the 21.

A 31 SET The 31 set, sometimes called the "shoot-in," is spiked in the third attack zone about 8½ feet in front of the setter. The 31 goes between the seam of the opponent's right side and center front blockers. The 31 is like an extended 11 set in that it can be attacked at a regular, slow, or minus tempo. In the minus tempo, the horizontal velocity is so great that the spiker usually has to tip across her body to the left.

During serve-reception attack it is usually the player in the CF or LF position who approaches for the 31. When CF attacks for a 31, she often pulls the opposing middle blocker over so that the right side player is left in a one-on-one situation with the opponent's LF blocker. A 31 attack coming from LF in coordination with an attack by the two remaining attackers behind the setter's back is very difficult to stop. It is very difficult for the opposing middle blocker to guard against the 31 or shoot-in attacker coming from the left side, because her eyes are focused primarily on the setter and the movement patterns developing behind the setter.

During transition attack most often CF attacks the 31. But very experienced teams that use the multiple-tempo attack concept can also use the 31 as an option play for the ace player coming from LF.

If the setter is off the net or has to set from a low position, the spiker may need to delay her jump. Unlike the 11, the 31 usually does not require the spiker to adjust laterally or change the slot, as long as she maintains a distance of about 8 feet from the setter. The angle of the spiker's approach should be about 90 degrees to the setter's shoulder line. I reiterate that in the floating concept, it is up to the spiker to position herself at the proper distance in relation to the setter.

A 41 SET A 41 set is wider than a 31 and can become an option play for the 31 when the opponent's blocker stands in front of the 3 slot. The 41 is usually attacked from the left side of the court and can be effectively hit down the line outside of the end blocker. Players with a good jump or superior height can effectively spike a 41, which requires an extra sense of timing and a very fast arm swing because the ball travels with great horizontal velocity. Once mastered, it becomes a very effective play as demonstrated in the last Olympics by Rose Magers of the USA women's Olympic team. It can also be useful when two spikers attack in a split double quick, with one spiker behind the setter's back and the other in front of the setter.

A 51 SET A 51 set, sometimes called a "shoot-out" set, is very difficult to execute. Because of the length of the set, gravity and the natural resistance of the air have a chance to work against the ball, pulling it down below the desired height. There are two ways to overcome this problem. The first method is called "direct delivery," which calls for the setter to push the ball with great horizontal velocity on a straight line to the desired point of contact by the spiker. This becomes a very fast and difficult set to hit, with crucial timing and very little room for error by the spiker.

The other method is called "indirect delivery" and simply involves setting the ball with a slight lob in the trajectory. The ball still shoots out to the hitter, arriving much quicker than the blocker, but the lob compensates for the pull of gravity and allows the set to have far less horizontal velocity. Thus, it is easier for the spiker to hit. The lob will generally put the highest part of the set about 3 feet above the net, and the elapsed time between the release of the set and contact by the hitter will be about one second. If it's faster, the hitter may miss the ball, and if it's slower, the block will have time to react. With the indirect method, the hitter jumps just after the set is released.

Setting the ball 1 meter (3′) back off the net can help the attacker by shortening the distances she has to travel to get to the ball. If the block assembles successfully, she'll have a wider lateral range to hit around the side of the block.

The 51 can be useful as part of a triple quick attack where each spiker attacks straight on. It is also effective when two spikers overload the right side, leaving the left front player in a one-on-one blocking situation. In this case, either the cross-court shot or the line shot opens up. The 51 can be used in a split-attack play where one player charges behind the setter for a quick attack. It is also effective where two spikers work a double quick in front of the setter and a back-court attacker comes from the right side (usually for a second-tempo set).

It is difficult for the opponent's center blocker to move outside fast enough to block a 51. If the opponent's right side blocker is positioned close to the center of the court, she also might have difficulty moving back to the outside. Even if she does get there, she may well be off balance, unable to penetrate properly and vulnerable to being hit off by the spiker. A 51 set should be used only when there is a middle quick attacker to hold the opponent's CF blocker. Otherwise the 51 may become a trap set for the spiker.

AN A1 SET The A1 is the equivalent of the 11 set. It is a first-tempo set located in the zone behind the setter's back. For a left-handed spiker the A1 will have the exact same tempo and timing as an 11 set has for a right-handed attacker. For a right-handed spiker, the A1 will be slightly wider and a bit higher. The extra width allows the ball to cross the hitter's body to her hitting arm. The extra height provides an additional split second of time for the hitter to drive the ball either left or right. If an A1 set is too low, two negative things may happen: either the block may trap the ball, or the hitter may be forced to hit a predictable crosscourt shot to the left.

The A1 is often used on X combination plays where one player leads for an A1 and another player comes as a concealed attacker for a second-tempo set. In addition, the A1 is an option for a spiker who asks for an 11 but then finds that the pass has pulled the setter laterally down the net to zone 2 or 3. The A1 is also useful in transition plays when either RF or CF leads for an A1 and the other player follows for a second-tempo set.

A B1 SET The B1 set is similar to the 21 but done behind the setter's back. For a right-handed spiker, the B1 should be set slightly higher than the 21 set. The B1 is often used with a one-leg takeoff when the spiker starts in front of the setter and then angles behind her, cutting off the set at the B slot. Occasionally, the B1 can be used for a back double quick attack. Actually the B1 is seldom used because the opposing blocker's starting position is usually opposite the B slot.

A C1 SET The C1 set is the backset equivalent of the 31. However, there are two subtle differences between the 31 and the C1. Since there are only three zones behind the setter, the C1 is the widest possible first-tempo backset. Also, where the 31 splits the block by cutting inside, the C1 splits the block by spreading it, drawing it as far as possible to the right side. A consistently effective C1 attack puts great pressure on the opponent's middle blocker and makes it more difficult for her to assist in blocking on the other side against the LF attacker.

For a right-handed spiker, the C1 is often done in slightly slower tempo (almost like a C2) where the spiker jumps with or just after the setter's ball release. The height of the set may reach 3 feet. The execution of the C1 attack is often helped by the use of the one-leg "slide approach" takeoff, where the attacker comes from the midline of the court, moving parallel or at a slight angle to the net. During the 1984 Olympics, Paula Weishoff demonstrated this particular shot often with a high degree of efficiency.

Setting for First-Tempo Attacks

It is important when a setter sets first tempo that she jump-set; if she can't, she should at least elevate herself on the toes of her right foot. Her arms should be almost totally extended straight up with the elbows bent very slightly.

The 11 set should be done with a delicate wrist action coming underneath the ball. For shoot sets, the fingers should be placed on the side of the ball about the horizontal midline; a slight forward movement of the arms pushes the thumbs forward underneath the ball, imparting a slight reverse spin.

In setting the long first-tempo sets such as the 31, 41, and 51, the setter must remember that the attack zone is where the hitter will contact the ball, not where the ball would normally fall. If the hitter missed a 51 shoot set completely, the ball would continue on its flight and fall somewhere outside the court. The greater the distance of the shoot, the more important it is to impart reverse

A C1 set and spike for a right-handed hitter. In principle, the C1 set is the backset equivalent of the 31.

A C1 attack by a left-handed spiker. A left-handed spiker would normally execute a quicker C1 spike than a right-handed spiker.

Common foot positions at takeoff for a C2 or C1 set for a right-handed spiker

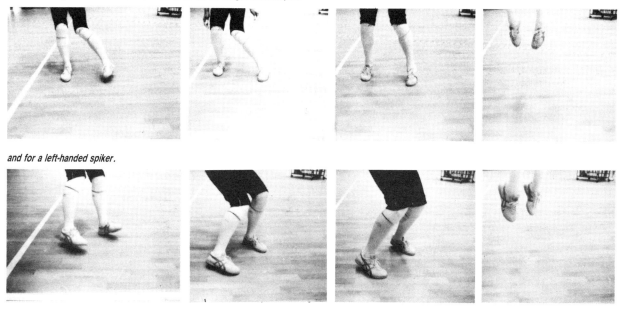

and for a left-handed spiker.

spin. The back shoots, which are slightly higher than the front shoots, should be done with a flip of the wrist backward.

A setter must learn to deliver quick attack first-tempo sets from a low body posture as well as from positions off the net. In the low body posture, the setter must be choosy about setting first tempo because the ball has a longer distance to travel, giving the block more time to react to the set. Setting quick attacks from a low body posture is usually most effective when the setter is in an awkward position and the fast set is unexpected. Also first-tempo sets delivered by a setter who is off the net often catch the block by surprise.

Second-Tempo Sets

A second-tempo set ranges in height from 2 to 4 feet above the net. The spiker jumps after the set is delivered. With short-distance second-tempo sets (12, 22, B2) the spiker normally jumps just before the set reaches its peak and contacts the ball at her maximum reach. For longer-distance second-tempo sets (32, 42, 52, and C2) the spiker contacts the ball at the beginning of its descent. In principle, the longer the set, the later the spiker should take off.

Even teams that do not implement a quick multiple attack should not use sets that are much higher than second tempo if the pass or dig is directed accurately to the setter. A higher set just creates more time for the block to assemble. It is also more difficult for the spiker to properly time contact with a high set. Bad passes and digs short of the target area often force the setter to set high trajectory balls, usually to the ace spikers at LF.

The second tempo is very useful when the setter is unable to set first tempo, or when first tempo becomes tactically inappropriate (for example, when the hitter is too late for first tempo). At times when the spiker has a considerable height or jumping advantage over the opposing blockers, a second-tempo set can be used to take advantage of the difference. In addition, when the passing is poor, there is often no choice but to use second-tempo outside sets.

THE 22 SET The spiker jumps just before the ball reaches its peak and contacts the ball at her peak reach. In most cases, if the set is delivered with the proper trajectory, the peak of the set and the peak reach of the hitter will be the same or very close. The 22 is most commonly used in X and sequential

The execution of the C1 attack is often helped by the use of the one-leg slide approach takeoff.

combination attacks where the attacker comes from left or right side. The height of the 22 is greatly determined by the timing of the lead hitter in the combination. If the lead player is late and goes for a slow first tempo, then the concealed player should get a slightly higher second-tempo set. If the lead attacker comes for a minus-tempo set, then the 22 set should be a little quicker and lower. Both of these adjustments are required to maintain the proper timing of combination plays. If the lead attacker is late but the 22 set is not set a little higher to compensate, the concealed attacker may not have enough time to get around the lead hitter, jump, and effectively attack the ball. Likewise, if the lead spiker is early but the 22 is set to normal height, the block will have too much time to adjust against the concealed attacker.

THE 32 SET The spiker jumps after the set has been released and contacts the ball at the beginning of its descent. The 32 set is used for wide right-side X combinations, and also in sequential combinations with a quick 21 set. The USA women's team used the 32 as an optional transition play for the left front spiker. During transition, LF should audibly call and visibly signal for a 32 set.

THE 42 SET The 42 set is often used in sequential and X combinations on the left side of the court in coordination with a 31 set. The spiker jumps after the set is released and contacts the ball on its descent. The USA women's team used the 42 as an optional transition play for the LF ace players.

THE 52 SET The 52 is basically a lob set to the outside. It is a safe set, yet it is fast enough to somewhat split the opponent's block. The timing of the 52 is fairly easy for both setter and spiker, and teams with tall spikers do not need to use outside sets faster than the 52. A well-executed 52 set should give the block no more than 1.1 seconds to respond. The risk factor for a 52 is much less than for a 51. If the block does assemble, the height of the 52 set gives the hitter more time to select her shot and manipulate the block. Therefore, the hitter is not nearly as much at the mercy of the setter's decision as she is with a 51. The 52 is also the most common set for transition and back-row attack. When delivered to back-row attackers, the height of the set and its distance from the 10-foot line should be adjusted according to the individual ability of the spiker. It should be as fast a set as possible under the circumstances of the situation.

THE B2 SET The B2 set is useful in combination attacks on the right side, either from serve reception or during transition. The timing of the B2 is

The setter should be able to set for a first tempo attack from every conceivable body posture, whether from a standstill or while in motion.

very similar to that used for the 22 set. (The B2 is not as common as some other sets, mainly because there is usually an opposing blocker stationed directly in the B slot.)

THE C2 SET The C2 is the most frequently used backset, especially for right-handed players. If executed properly, the elapsed time between the release of the set by the setter and contact by the hitter should only be .6 to .7 of a second, fast enough to force a one-on-one blocking situation. The C2 is also the most commonly used set for a back-row attacker. It should be about 5 to 6 feet from the net for men and 7 to 8 feet for women with slightly more height (about 4 feet) than a normal C2 set close to the net.

Setting for Second-Tempo Attacks

To set for second tempo, the setter has to be very sensitive to the location and speed of the approaching spiker. The setter must see the spiker at her initial stage of movement so she can gauge what height to set the ball. For a first-tempo set, the setter can focus on the spiker because she's closer or suspended, providing a target. But in the second tempo, the spiker has not yet jumped so the setter sets to an empty space. She has to learn not to rush the ball and to give it just enough height, but no more than is needed. Second-tempo sets should also be jump-set whenever possible.

Second-tempo sets are done with a soft touch and a slightly more prolonged contact with the ball. The hands are placed mostly underneath the ball, to create the proper vertical elevation and angle. The wrists push through slightly underneath the ball. Most second-tempo sets have no spin at all. It is nice, however, to create a reverse spin for the 42 and 52 sets so that the balls will drop in a more vertical line (see Chapter 5, "The Set"). For longer second-tempo sets, the setter may bend her elbows slightly more. If a first-tempo attacker is late and delays the whole combination, the setter can first bend her elbows substantially, and then bend her knees to delay the set.

Third-Tempo Sets

A third-tempo set is a set higher than 5 feet above the net that everybody on the team should be able to execute. It is often used in emergency situations, after a bad pass or dig, or when the setter is unable to set. A third-tempo set gets the ball safely to the net from any court position. The deeper the court position, the higher the set should be.

It is important to deliver the third-tempo set with reverse spin so the ball will drop as vertically as possible. Most often, the third-tempo set should be aimed toward the sideline, for LF or RF. However, a tall spiker in the center can very effectively hit a third-tempo set, particularly to the corners, and an attack from the center is difficult to defend against. In a situation when a tall block opposes a short spiker, the high set should be delivered from 1 to 1½ meters (3 to 5′) off the net. This increases the lateral range so a spiker can hit around the side of the block.

For third-tempo sets coming from deep in the court, the spiker should always attempt to position herself at a 90-degree angle to the set (Figure 6–20). By approaching at a 90-degree angle to the set, the spiker can maintain continuous eye contact with the set and also have a better view of the opponent's block. Because of the great height of third-tempo sets, the spiker starts her approach when the ball is at its peak. She contacts the ball on its descent. Naturally, slower players should start approaching sooner than quick players.

Left front attackers should master spiking high third-tempo sets because it is still a fairly common set in transition attack. The poorer a team's passing, and the worse its ability to control the ball on defense, the higher the frequency of third-tempo sets.

Additional Attack Techniques

In recent years the increased height of volleyball players has strengthened the block. In response, new attack techniques have been developed to outwit or confuse the block. The most common of these techniques, which use fake approaches and time manipulation, are the trick play, the pump, and the slide.

THE TRICK (T) For the trick play, the spiker approaches the net sooner than for a first-tempo set, using one or two run-up steps and a short hop, and lands on the toes of both feet. She then swings her arms as if for a takeoff. But instead of taking off she jumps sideways, then takes off and spikes the ball. To jump to the right or left, the player should lead with the right foot (for a right-handed spiker).

The main purpose of the trick play is to create the impression of taking off at one point for a first-tempo attack and then suddenly shifting 3 to 4 feet to either side and taking off for a second-tempo set. The ball should be set about 60cm (2') above the net. The spiker has to be careful not to land too close to the net on her initial hop. The idea is to leave enough room so that the spiker can retain some of her horizontal velocity and use it in her final takeoff by jumping at an angle to the net.

The trick play can be done at any court position. For example, a player could fake for a 31 and jump sideways for a 12, or fake for an 11 and jump sideways, going around the setter, for an A2. The spiker has to communicate to the setter where she is approaching so the setter will know where to deliver the ball.

To communicate the spiker can call out "trick" (T), plus a two-digit number. The first digit specifies the slot where the spiker will fake, and the second digit (or letter) specifies where the spiker will actually go and where the set should be. For example, Trick (T) 31 means the spiker will approach the third slot, fake, and jump sideways to the first slot.

The most common trick plays are the Trick 31, 35, 1A, and the Trick AC. Trick plays can be done in parallel by two players; for example, LF goes for a Trick 42 while the center front goes for a Trick 31. It is also possible to use a long extended trick play; for example, a Trick 4A. In this case, the spiker fakes a takeoff in slot 4 and then runs to make a real approach in slot A. This can be a very effective trick play and can be used from right to left or from left to right.

The trick play requires good height and good jumping ability; it is definitely a nifty devise to thwart the block. The trick play can also be executed as an option fake maneuver (for details see "The X Combination").

THE PUMP (P) To execute a pump, the spiker approaches for a first-tempo attack, using one or two run-up steps and a small hop to the toes of both feet. The spiker fakes a takeoff with the appropriate leg and arm movements, rocks back, and then swoops up again into her real takeoff. Unlike most other deceptive maneuvers that seek to get the block out of position laterally, the objective of the pump is to disrupt the vertical timing of the block.

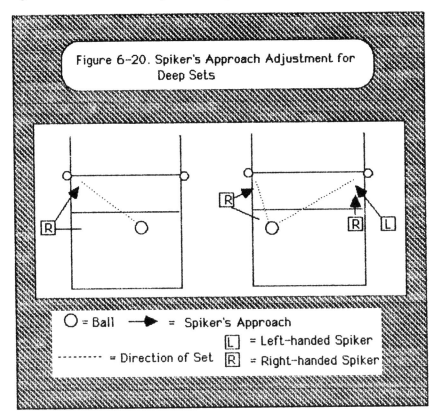

Figure 6-20. Spiker's Approach Adjustment for Deep Sets

○ = Ball   ➡ = Spiker's Approach

[L] = Left-handed Spiker

-------- = Direction of Set   [R] = Right-handed Spiker

Therefore, the key to a successful pump is to create the impression that the spiker is going to jump for the first tempo. If the block responds, it will already be coming down when the hitter actually takes off and contacts the ball.

The pump not only fools the block, but it also frequently throws the floor defense out of sync, making it more difficult for the back-row players to respond to the spike. Because of the time delay involved in the pump, the setter delivers a slightly higher set than for normal first-tempo attack.

The pump is a very effective play in transition situations when the blockers don't have much time to gather their wits and just respond spontaneously to the body language of the attacker. It is particularly effective when executed by CF, who comes off a block on the left side and executes a pump fake at either slot 3 or slot 2.

THE SLIDE (S) The slide is a slow first-tempo attack with two key elements. The first element is the approach pattern. The spiker approaches toward the net, then veers off and continues her approach along the net. The second key element is that the takeoff point and the attack point (contact with the set) are not the same. After takeoff, the attacker broad-jumps either parallel to the net or at a slight angle. The set is then hit at a different lateral point from the takeoff. For example, the takeoff may occur in slot A while the ball is actually hit in slot C.

The slide can be done with a conventional takeoff using both feet, but it is often easier and more effective to use the one-foot takeoff. Thus, the one-leg takeoff has become known in some circles as the "slide approach."

The set for a slide play is low and as parallel as possible with the net. This allows the spiker to attack the ball at as many points as possible along its trajectory. Often the slide gives the spiker the opportunity to hit off the block as it attempts to adjust sideways to the path of the spiker's jump.

To communicate with the setter, a spiker calls "slide" plus a number or a letter to specify where the set should go. For example: Slide C indicates that the setter should set to the C slot. The setter has to watch the spiker and adjust the speed, distance, and height of the set according to the spiker's position. It is very important that the spiker follow closely behind the ball.

There is a slight time difference between a slide with a two-leg takeoff and a slide with a one-leg takeoff. The spiker and setter have to work out the specific timing. With a two-leg takeoff, the spiker has to employ a slow one-two takeoff with fairly substantial run-up speed. Usually, the one-leg takeoff will allow the spiker to cover a greater horizontal distance and hit the ball from a slightly higher point. For a one-leg takeoff, a right-handed spiker will approach the slide from the left side of the court toward the right, and vice versa for the left-handed spiker. It is possible to combine the

This sequence illustrates the last step (the hop) and takeoff for a Trick 31 (T-31) play. The spiker fakes for a 31 and then jumps sideways for a 12. For speed, the entire maneuver should be done on the toes.

The pump is an effective form of attack, in particular against teams which implement commit-blocking tactics in which the blocker takes off at the same time as the quick attacker. (See chapter on blocking.)

trick maneuver and a slide spike, in particular with a one-leg takeoff.

The slide can be executed independently or in combination with a first-tempo attack in which the spiker goes behind the first attacker.

TEAM ATTACK— FORMATIONS

Slow Attack vs. Quick Attack

The attack in volleyball has evolved from a simple, slow, high outside attack executed by one spiker at a time, to a very complex quick attack in which several spikers drive simultaneously for the ball in multiple-attack formations. The high and simple game was played for years by the Eastern European teams who had a great impact on world volleyball into the sixties. The multiple-attack game was developed by the Asian teams. But is the multiple-attack concept, in fact, more effective?

If a spiker could overcome the block and floor defense by herself at least 55 percent of the time, there would be no need for a multiple-attack offense. But today the block is so strong and the defense so effective that in a confrontation between one attacker and two or three blockers, the attacker does not stand much chance. It is up to the attack to mobilize the ball quickly along the net in patterns that are too quick and confusing for the opponent's block. In modern volleyball, the trend is toward even more complex attack patterns incorporating quick *back-row* attack.

During the learning stages, a multiple-attack offense is somewhat risky because it demands much coordination. It is not mastered quickly or easily. Nevertheless, I feel it should be taught to young beginning players, because it makes the game so much more enjoyable and develops better all-around athletic ability.

In deciding between teaching a slow or a quick attack, many coaches make a common mistake; they misunderstand the degree of difficulty involved in hitting first- and second-tempo sets. Since volleyball started with the high, slow attack, these coaches assume that it is easier to hit high sets than low sets. Actually, the opposite is true.

A high set is difficult for a young or inexperienced setter to execute, because it requires great strength. From a hitter's perspective, a high set is harder to hit than slow first- and second-tempo sets, because high sets drop with considerable vertical acceleration. Second-tempo sets, especially the 12 and 22, are easier to set and hit than any other. Among first-tempo sets the 11 and the A1, if set to the maximum reach of the hitter, often appear to hang in front of the attacker, waiting for the powerful contact by the hitting hand.

It really is not logical in a game like volleyball when the time element is so crucial to set balls much higher than the spiker's reach. The extra time just gives the opponent more time to set up the block and adjust the floor defense.

Multiple Attack

The goal of multiple attack is to create openings for the spiker by confusing and outwitting the opponent's block and floor defense. This is accomplished with different attack formations using a variety of set heights and speeds. The multiple-attack formation's goal is to freeze the opponent's middle blocker so that she has difficulty in assisting either of the outside blockers on outside sets.

The four main strategies by which the multiple attack attempts to confuse or beat the block are:

By spreading the block out laterally along the width of the net. This is accomplished by first isolating the middle blocker with a quick attacker. and then mobilizing the ball along the net at a rapid speed that prevents the middle blocker from forming a double block with either of the outside blockers.

Manipulating the block's timing with the use of sequential or X plays. Two attackers attack the

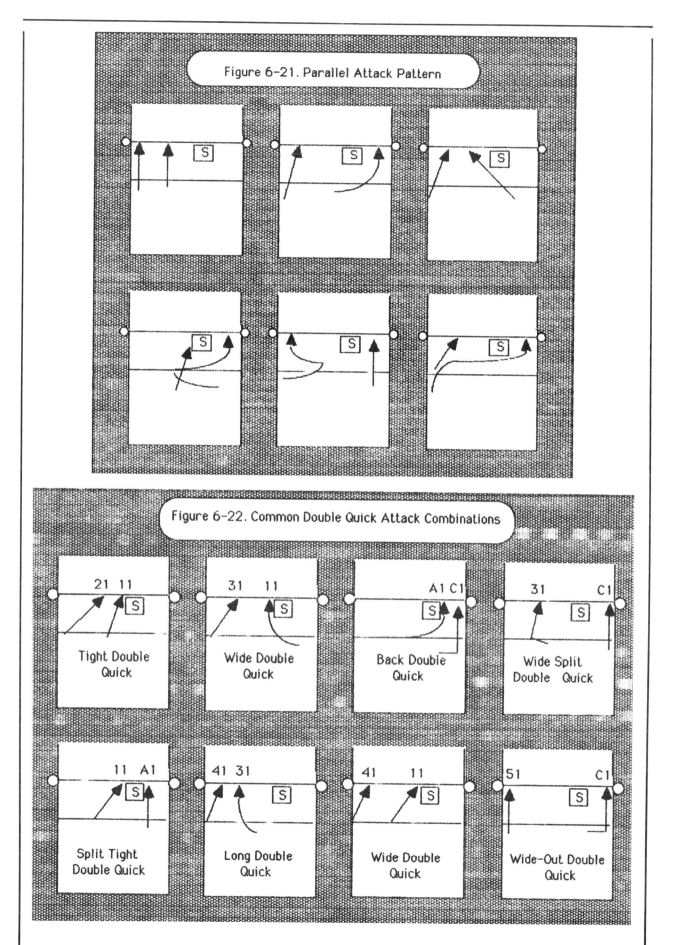

Figure 6-21. Parallel Attack Pattern

Figure 6-22. Common Double Quick Attack Combinations

21 11	Tight Double Quick
31 11	Wide Double Quick
A1 C1	Back Double Quick
31 C1	Wide Split Double Quick
11 A1	Split Tight Double Quick
41 31	Long Double Quick
41 11	Wide Double Quick
51 C1	Wide-Out Double Quick

129

same or adjacent zones at different tempos in an attempt to force the block to jump too early or too late. If successful, this creates at least a one-on-one blocking situation.

Deceptive approach patterns that, when executed with deceptive footwork, force the opposing blockers to continuously adjust their blocking responsibilities as they try to cover shifting spikers. If combined effectively with a very quick attack, the block will not have enough time to assemble.

Incorporating a back-row attacker to present an even further threat to the opponent. A back-row attacker can force the block to spread out or become hesitant about committing to a jump. She can complicate the blocker's responsibilities by creating a four-on-three situation. The multiple attack creates spiking opportunities for the attackers by confusing the blockers or by beating them to an opening. The key is that the opponent does not know which particular spiker will be set, or when and where. The blockers, therefore, have no choice but to guard all spikers at all times.

The setter plays a crucial role in any multiple offense. She must be capable of setting a variety of balls at different heights and speeds and she must be very sensitive to the court movement of both teams. The spikers present the opportunities, but the setter makes the final choice of whom to set. If the setter does not make the correct set selection, she should be substituted out of the game and advised by the coach before returning to the battle.

Attack Combinations with Two Spikers

The number of attack formations that three attackers can create is almost unlimited. Therefore, before attempting to describe these more complex attack formations, it is necessary to name and become familiar with the more simple attack combinations that use only two attackers. Actually, two-spiker attack combinations are the cornerstone of any attack formation. The third spiker in the formation usually acts as a safety, as a third choice for the setter if the play does not develop as planned.

DOUBLE QUICK COMBINATIONS In the double quick combination, both spikers attack at the same time at first tempo in a *parallel pattern*. A parallel pattern is one in which the relationship between the spikers in the final attack location is the same as in their initial positions, either in serve reception or defense. In the parallel patterns, the paths of the spikers never cross completely; fake approaches are not considered as a cross (Figure 6–21). In the double quick combinations, the two spikers can come from two adjacent court positions or from two positions farther apart. They can *overload* a particular net area by attacking two adjacent net slots or they can form a wider formation. Figure 6–22 illustrates common double quick attack combinations.

I like to call a double quick in attack zones 1 and

A wide double quick. Variations of the double quick attack formations are the fundamentals of a multiple quick attack.

A well executed double quick puts a tremendous strain on the block. To stop a double quick attack, the blocking team usually implements man-to-man blocking tactics.

A split tight double quick.   *A tight double quick.*

2, a "tight" double quick; and a double quick in zones A and B behind the setter, a "back" double quick. If one player goes behind the setter for an A and the other goes in front for a 11, it is a "split" tight double quick. If one comes behind the setter and the other in front of the setter more than two zones apart, it is called a "wide" split double quick. If the attackers come for 31 and 41, it is a "long" double quick, and if they are several zones apart, it is a "wide" double quick. When the spikers attack on both sidelines, it is a "wide-out" double quick.

SEQUENTIAL COMBINATIONS There are five basic attack combinations in which two players come for consecutive attacks at first and second tempos. Except for the *tandem* combination, the sequential combinations are divided into parallel and cross-sequential combinations. The parallel combinations are the parallel *sequence* (simply called "sequence") and the parallel *sting* (simply called "sting"). The cross-combinations are the *cross* sequence (simply called "cross") and the *cross-sting*. The player who comes to the net first for first tempo is the *lead attacker*. The player who follows for second tempo is the *concealed attacker*.

The sequential formations can be done with *parallel approach* patterns or with *cross-approach* patterns. In a cross, the approach paths of the lead spiker and the concealed spiker cross each other (Figure 6–23). Most often, the lead player in the combination uses an angle approach. However, the concealed player may use an angle approach or fake approaches: the *fake-out,* the *fake-in* (see Figure 6–16) and the *fake option* approach (Figure 6–24). The fake option approach is mostly used for the X combination.

In order to make the sequential combinations effective, they need to be executed with consistent timing and deceptive footwork while alternating the combination sequence in a logical order.

The following terms are used to name the sequence combinations: "wide" signifies that the two spikers are more than two attack zones *apart.* "Long" signifies that both spikers are more than two zones *away* in front of the setter. "Tight" signifies that the two spikers are very *close* to each other *and near* the setter. A "split tight" denotes that one spiker is directly in front of the setter and the other is directly behind her. "Back" refers to formations that occur behind the setter's back. "Cross" implies that the paths of the lead and concealed players are crossed, and "reverse" means

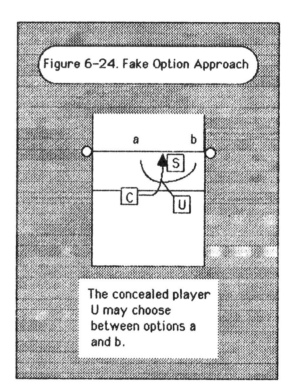

Figure 6-24. Fake Option Approach

The concealed player U may choose between options a and b.

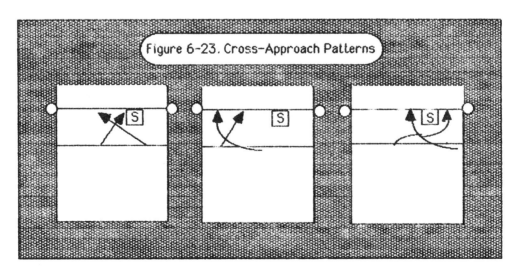

Figure 6-23. Cross-Approach Patterns

that a spiker other than the CF attacks for a first tempo.

When the name of the combination does not state who goes first, it always means that CF leads the combination. For example: a tight sequence means that the CF goes for 11 and the LF comes for a 22. In this case there is no need to specify that the left front comes for a 22 because this is the only possibility if parallel relations between the two spikers are to be maintained. Since it is a tight play, LF must come to Zone 2. Since it is a sequential play, LF must hit a second-tempo set.

When the name of the sequence starts with "reverse," usually there will be no mention of whether it is done with the left-side or the right-side player, because the name of the combination itself implies the only possibility that exists. For example, a "reverse long cross" means that the left-side player goes for 31 (or 41) whereas the center player crosses behind for a 42 (or 52). This can be the only interpretation of the name, considering that "reverse" indicates CF is not the lead attacker, while "long" and "cross" signify the attack slots and the hitter's path. Sometimes it is necessary to identify combinations in which only LF and RF participate. If the name of the combination is "left-right long cross," it means that LF attacks as the lead attacker for a first-tempo set. RF crosses behind as the concealed spiker. With the reverse combinations, and the left-right player combinations, since they are sequential plays, the concealed attacker must be in the second tempo.

THE TANDEM A tandem play is a combination of two spikers who attack at the *exact same zone* one behind the other at two different tempos. The following combinations are tandems: 11 and 12; A1 and A2; 21 and 22; 31 and 32; 41 and 42; B1 and B2; C1 and C2 (Figure 6–25). A tandem combination can also be done with one front-row and one back-row attacker.

The tandem combination accomplishes two things at the same time: it screens the concealed player from the blocker, and it overloads one narrow attack zone with two spikers against one blocker. If the timing of the lead spiker is correct and if the setter sees whether the opposing blocker jumps or not, the tandem should create a no-block situation for one of the spikers. If the opponent blocker jumps with the lead player, the setter should deliver the ball to the concealed player. If the blocker does not commit in response to the lead attacker's jump, the setter should set the lead spiker.

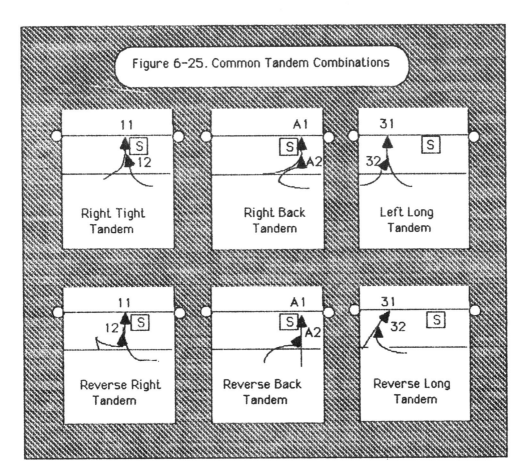

Figure 6-25. Common Tandem Combinations

The setter should deliver the ball to the concealed player after the lead player has already jumped, and just prior to the concealed player's takeoff. The set is a deep set, about 2m (5') off the net and behind the lead attacker's back. The concealed player lifts off when the lead player starts coming down and hits the ball through the same attack zone that the lead player would have used. The concealed player can use a loop or a fake approach if so desired, but the takeoff must be behind the screen formed by the setter and the lead attacker.

THE PARALLEL SEQUENCE In a parallel sequence play, the lead and the concealed spikers attack side by side at first and second tempo (Figure 6–26). They do not cross paths as they approach the net. The lead player is always closer to the setter than the concealed player. Usually, the concealed player's takeoff is slightly farther off the net than the lead attacker's. The set for the concealed attack should be placed on the outside shoulder of the lead spiker and about 1.5m (4' 11") off the net. The timing of the two attackers is the same as for the tandem combination. At times, a team may want to speed up the sequence play by

having the two spikers come at the net at a shorter time interval. In this situation, the concealed player must jump closer to the net and the set should be only 1m (3') deep off the net.

Any two attackers can create a sequence from any court position, but their approach paths must be parallel. Fake approaches do not count as crosses.

THE STING COMBINATION (PARALLEL) The sting combination is similar to the sequence combination except that in the sting, the concealed attacker approaches *between* the lead player and the setter (Figure 6–27). Having the quick attacker farther away from the setter has some advantages and some disadvantages. The setter has better eye contact with the concealed spiker and the set to her does not need to go over the lead player; therefore, it can be shallower. However, setting to the lead player may become riskier and more difficult. In general, the sting combination can be executed a little bit faster than the sequence combination.

THE CROSS-SEQUENCE The cross-sequence is similar to the sequence combination except that

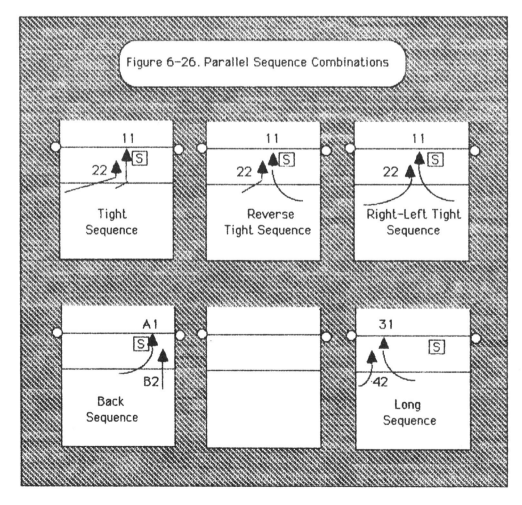

Figure 6-26. Parallel Sequence Combinations

Tight Sequence

Reverse Tight Sequence

Right-Left Tight Sequence

Back Sequence

Long Sequence

Figure 6-27. Common Parallel Sting Combinations

31 — **Reverse Sting** — [S] 22

31 — **Sting** — [S] 22

C1 — **Reverse Back Sting** — [S] A2

31 — **Left-Right Sting** — [S] 22

Note: Unless the word "back" is mentioned, all parallel stings are done in front of the setter. In addition, usually the stings in front of the setter are done in attack zones 3 and 2 and, therefore, there is no need to mention the distance of the combination from the setter, although it is possible.

A tight cross is a basic sequence attack. Note that the concealed player is left-handed. Also note that at certain points both spikers are airborne.

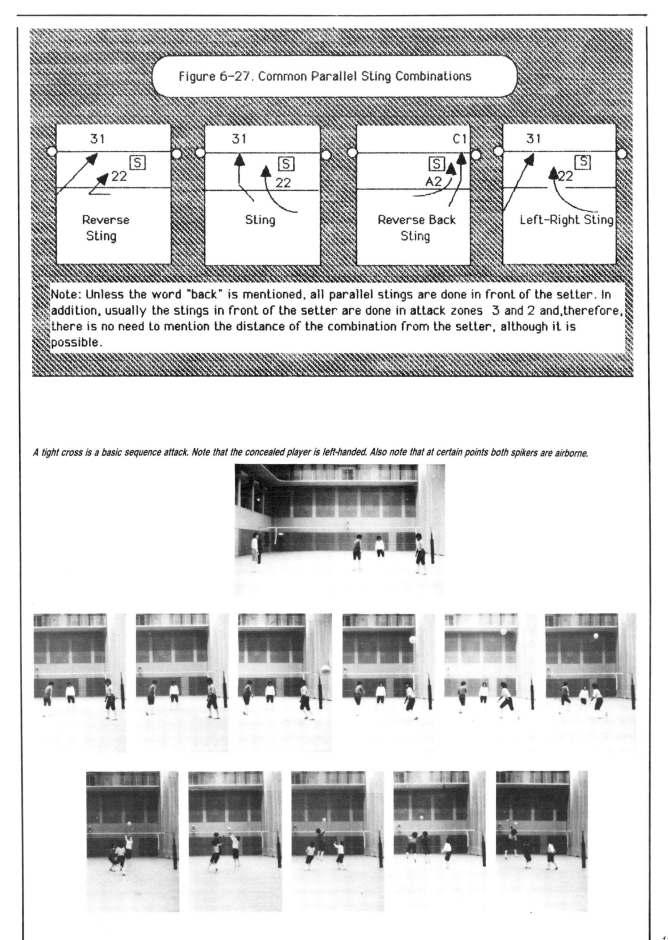

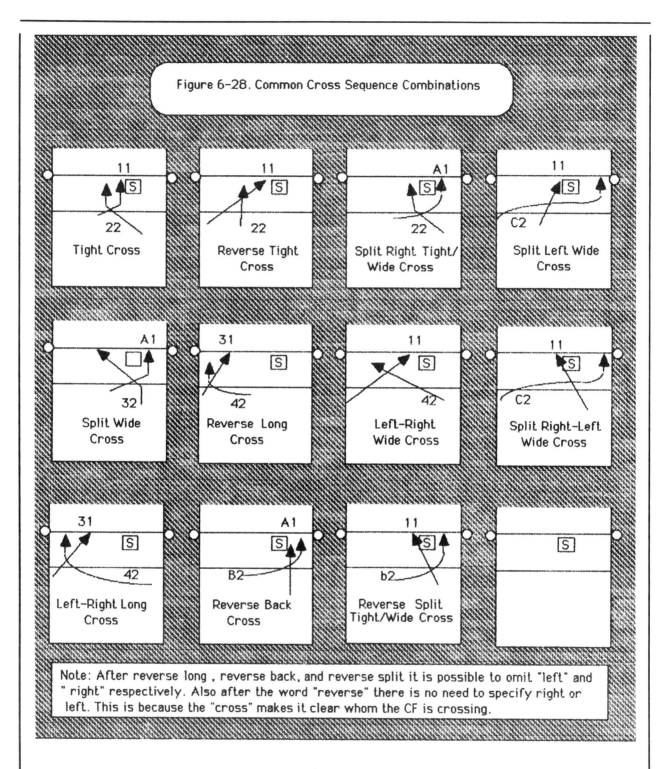

Figure 6-28. Common Cross Sequence Combinations

11 — Tight Cross	11 — Reverse Tight Cross	A1 — Split Right Tight/Wide Cross	11 — Split Left Wide Cross
A1 — Split Wide Cross	31 — Reverse Long Cross	11 — Left-Right Wide Cross	11 — Split Right-Left Wide Cross
31 — Left-Right Long Cross	A1 — Reverse Back Cross	11 — Reverse Split Tight/Wide Cross	

Note: After reverse long , reverse back, and reverse split it is possible to omit "left" and " right" respectively. Also after the word "reverse" there is no need to specify right or left. This is because the "cross" makes it clear whom the CF is crossing.

the paths of the spikers do cross each other (Figure 6–28). Because of this, cross-sequence plays are often slower than sequence combinations and also more difficult to perfect.

THE CROSS-STING In cross-sting combinations, the paths of the spikers cross (Figure 6–29). The cross-sting play is a very effective maneuver to draw the CF blocker out of position with the lead attacker. Then the concealed player comes in and strikes at the opening at the last instant, often with a delayed approach or, possibly, fake-approach footwork. The lead player often uses a slide approach in the back cross-sting or left-right back cross-sting. For many years, the USA women's team successfully employed the left cross-sting as a free-ball play. With the control opportunities that a free ball gives, the sting can be executed with perfect timing and speed. The left cross-sting play should also be considered as a possible tran-

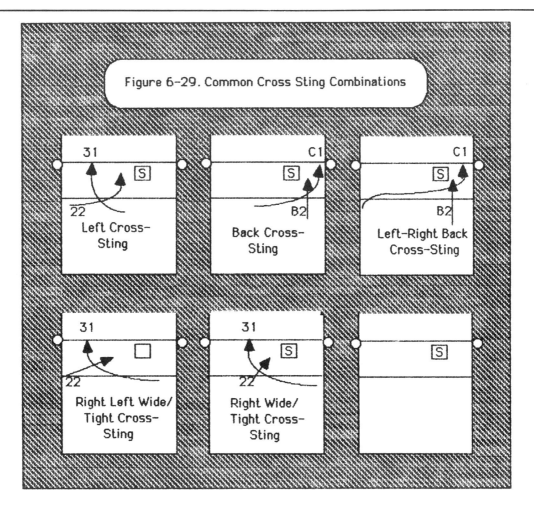

Figure 6-29. Common Cross Sting Combinations

31	Left Cross-Sting
C1	Back Cross-Sting
C1	Left-Right Back Cross-Sting
31	Right Left Wide/Tight Cross-Sting
31	Right Wide/Tight Cross-Sting

sition attack pattern, especially when the dig pulls the setter far off the net on the right side of the court.

The X Combination

In essence, the X plays incorporate all the various sequential plays. The only difference between the sequential combinations and the X is that the sequences are predetermined plays, while the X is an option play. In the X play, the concealed spiker may choose one of three options during the execution of the attack. As in sequence combinations, in X plays the lead attacker comes one tempo ahead of the concealed player and her task is to hold or lift one of the opposing blockers. The concealed player, following one tempo behind, attacks to the open area created by the blocker who jumped. If the outside blocker committed herself, then the concealed player attacks to the outside (option b, Figure 6-24); if the inside blocker jumped, the concealed spiker attacks the inside (option a, Figure 6-24). The decision where to go is made by the concealed player and is verbally communicated to the setter. The setter must maintain as much eye

contact as possible with the concealed attacker and be aware of her direction and speed.

In the 1976 Olympic Games, the Polish men's team perfected the X play on the right side of the court to such a degree that it got the nickname "the Polish cross." Since then, most men's teams have relied heavily on the X play as a main attack weapon. Women's teams, on the other hand, resort mainly to the sequence attack. This is because women do not jump as high as men, and therefore the concealed player does not have as much time to decide where the opening is in the block. In general, women's attack is not an option attack, but rather a predetermined attack pattern that relies heavily on the ability of the setter to outsmart the opponent.

The approach for an X play, whether from the *W* serve-reception formation or from a stack pattern, must be a fake option approach. Figure 6–30 illustrates two fake option approach patterns from the *W* serve-reception formation or a similar situation. The fake option approach can be executed in two configurations: a streamline pattern or an angle pattern. In either configuration, the hop point for the concealed attacker should be about 8 feet

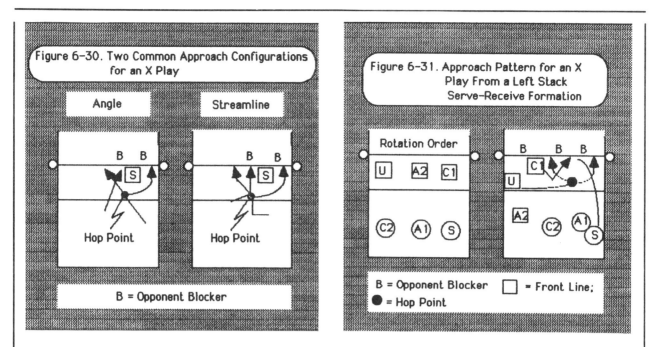

Figure 6-30. Two Common Approach Configurations for an X Play

Angle	Streamline
B B	B B
S	S
Hop Point	Hop Point

B = Opponent Blocker

Figure 6-31. Approach Pattern for an X Play From a Left Stack Serve-Receive Formation

Rotation Order	
U A2 C1	B B B / C1 / U
C2 A1 S	A2 C2 A1 / S

B = Opponent Blocker   ☐ = Front Line;
● = Hop Point

The Cuban team executes an X play against the Swedish team. The concealed player could break to the right or to the left (options a or b) at the hop point, hopping off the left foot. Note the footwork of the CF player.

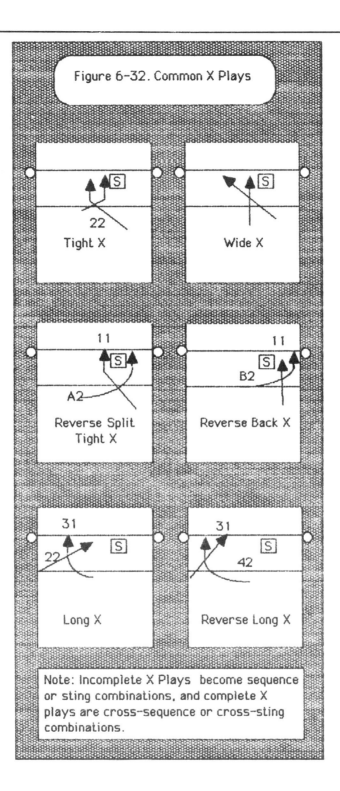

Figure 6-32. Common X Plays

22
Tight X

Wide X

11
A2
Reverse Split
Tight X

11
B2
Reverse Back X

31
22
Long X

31
42
Reverse Long X

Note: Incomplete X Plays become sequence or sting combinations, and complete X plays are cross-sequence or cross-sting combinations.

off the net and at a point on the court in line with the setter and the opponent's outside blocker. Figure 6–31 illustrates a possible fake option pattern for a stack left serve-receive arrangement. Stack patterns are created when receiving serve with four, three, or two primary passers, and are very popular with men's teams.

The concealed spiker usually uses two run-up steps and a hop. The hop begins after the setter has released the ball. At the hop point the spiker may break to the right or the left, depending on where the opening is in the block.

The streamline configuration makes it easy to sustain the horizontal velocity when breaking to the right. It is more difficult to break to the left with this configuration. The angle approach allows the player to sustain momentum forward toward the center of the net, but it hinders breaking to the right. Therefore, the angle approach is more effective for a wide X play.

Figure 6–32 illustrates some of the more common X plays and their descriptive names. The names of the X plays are actually the same as those of the sequence combinations.

Three-Spiker Attack Combinations

The number of combinations that three attackers can execute in three tempos to nine attack zones is almost unlimited. Generally, three-player attack patterns can be divided into three categories:

1. *Parallel attack patterns,* including the straight series, the double quick series, the sequence series, and the sting series;
2. *Cross-attack patterns,* including the following series: the cross-sequence, the cross-sting, the double cross, the slide, and the trick;
3. *X patterns,* a series in itself that actually encompasses all the sequence plays.

The Parallel Formations

The parallel formations are the fundamental formations of attack, in particular for transition attack. A parallel attack is one in which the paths of the spikers do not cross. Parallel attack is simple, orderly, and quick. Actually, the parallel attack is the quickest of all attack formations. All attackers can attack at first tempo, whether using angle, loop, or fake-approach patterns.

If a team implements a *W* serve-receive formation and exclusively uses the parallel-attack for-

The "flood right," (left in) is a classic parallel attack formation. All three attackers are prepared to attack at first tempo.

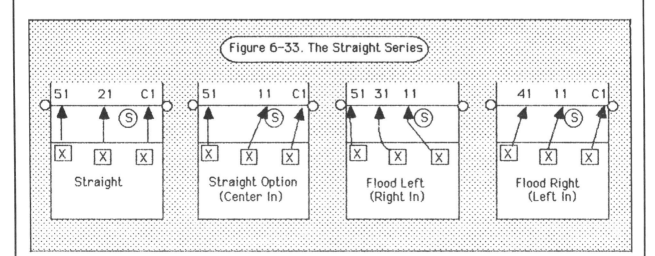

Figure 6–33. The Straight Series

| 51 | 21 | C1 |
Straight

| 51 | 11 | C1 |
Straight Option (Center In)

| 51 | 31 | 11 |
Flood Left (Right In)

| 41 | 11 | C1 |
Flood Right (Left In)

mations, then all players must learn how to hit second- and third-tempo outside sets as well as quick sets to the middle. Serve-reception formations with less than five passers, in particular formations with three and two passers, provide the flexibility necessary to adjust the formation in such a way that the quick attackers always hit the quick middle sets and the ace and utility players always hit the outside sets with no crossing patterns.

This is very important with regard to player specialization. The coach must decide whether she wants to maximize attack or serve reception. Occasionally, both can be emphasized.

THE STRAIGHT SERIES A straight is a classic parallel formation (Figure 6–33). All three attackers attack at first tempo. The straight formation has all the ingredients for a successful attack and is probably the fastest attack combination. Usually, the CF attacks for 11, RF for a C1, and LF for a 51. If successful, the straight attack will isolate the blockers and create either three one-on-one blocking situations or a very loose double block. It is a typical transition attack.

One difficulty with straight attack when using a *W* serve-receive formation is that every player on the team must learn to attack high outside as well as quick in the middle. In addition, from serve reception it does not lead the attackers to their specialized front-row positions. Players have to wait and switch at the completion of the serve-reception attack. In serve-reception formations with less than five passers, some of these difficulties may be resolved by adjusting the passing formation. To use the straight attack exclusively requires excellent setting and great jumping ability by the spikers. If the setting is poor and blockers

can read the direction of the set, the attack becomes too predictable and easy for the block to anticipate.

For straight attack, the outside set to the LF should be about 3 to 4 feet off the net. If the setter has difficulty setting a 51, then a 52 set should be used. One team that has used the straight formation exclusively and effectively is Cuba's national women's team, a team with extraordinary jumping ability.

THE DOUBLE QUICK SERIES In many ways the double quick is very similar to the straight attack. The major difference is that the double quick makes it possible to overload one net area with two attackers while the third attacker acts as a safety spiker (Figure 6–34). The safety spiker gets second-tempo sets and acts as an outlet in case of emergency. As the team becomes more skillful there is less need for a safety attacker. The safety attacker may then assume a role of an option attacker, hitting faster outside sets. The success of a double quick attack depends largely on the accuracy of the pass and the setter's ability to be deceptive.

The two quick attackers must always drive toward the seams of the block. The setter must be aware of the direction and the speed of the quick attackers, and then decide whether to set them or deliver the ball to the safety spiker. If the opponent's middle blocker does not shift to either side with the CF quick attacker, then either one of the quick attackers should be set. If, however, the middle blocker follows the CF quick attacker, then the outside safety spiker should be set.

Unless the setter is capable of seeing or sensing the movement of the opponent's block, the double quick becomes a guessing game. Any hesitation by

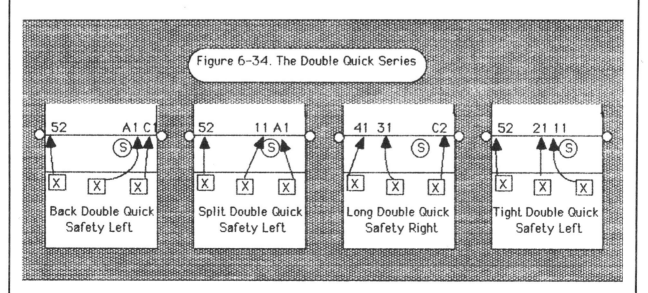

Figure 6–34. The Double Quick Series

| 52 | A1 C1 | 52 | 11 A1 | 41 31 | C2 | 52 | 21 11 |

Back Double Quick Safety Left   Split Double Quick Safety Left   Long Double Quick Safety Right   Tight Double Quick Safety Left

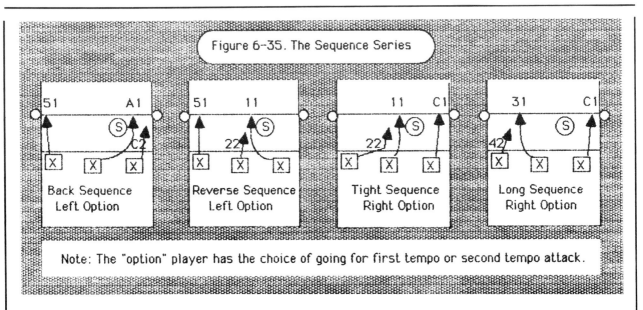

Figure 6-35. The Sequence Series

| Back Sequence Left Option | Reverse Sequence Left Option | Tight Sequence Right Option | Long Sequence Right Option |

Note: The "option" player has the choice of going for first tempo or second tempo attack.

a quick attacker before beginning the approach or during the approach, may result in a busted play. Therefore, the spikers must be consistent in their approach. Once they have started moving, they should continue to move at a consistent pace.

In essence, the double quick is a basic attack formation common to all attack patterns using two or three attackers, whether they are parallel, cross-sequence combinations, or X plays. The common tactic in all of these formations is that two attackers freeze two blockers while the third spiker attempts to find the opening.

THE SEQUENCE SERIES The sequence series overloads a particular net area with two spikers using both first- and second-tempo sets (Figure 6–35). While the double quick attempts to beat the opponent by the speed of the set, the sequence combinations attempt to manipulate the up-and-down timing of the blockers. In order to prevent the opponent's third blocker from coming to help against the sequence combination, the option attacker not participating in the sequence combination must attack fast outside. If 51 sets to the option attacker are not effective, then 41 or even 42 sets should be considered.

In a sense, in this series the concealed player acts as the safety player. Therefore, the outside spiker can afford to go for a quick set, creating a wide or wide-out–double quick with the lead spiker (Figure 6–22). Sequence combinations are effective if the timing between the lead player and concealed player is such that either one can be set. Sequence combinations also work well in conjunction with cross-sequence combinations, sting formations, and/or X plays. As always, deceptive footwork is instrumental in creating the proper effect.

THE STING SERIES The three-attacker sting series often combines a wide-out–double quick with a second-tempo set to the middle attacker coming between the two quick attackers. (Figure 6–36). When a team uses the *W* serve-reception formation, a chance for a sting combination is sometimes created when the CF player is forced to pass the serve and is therefore delayed in her approach. If the two outside spikers execute a quick straight attack, then CF becomes the safety spiker. The set for the sting play should be fairly deep off the net, and the spiker must be directly behind the ball in order to be able to hit it to any court position.

The Cross Formations

In cross formations the paths of two or three players cross. In these formations the attack attempts to freeze two blockers so that the third attacker can move to the opening. These formations force the opponent's block to make lateral adjustments and also to switch blocking responsibilities. If the opposing blockers have a poor communication system, often the cross attack may yield a no-block situation for the concealed spiker. In addition, the cross patterns allow the spikers to move to their specialized front-row positions directly from serve reception. Therefore, a coach who prefers the *W* service-receive formation should consider some of the cross- and the double-cross attack formations in designing her team's attack.

THE CROSS-SEQUENCE SERIES Figure 6–37 illustrates some of the more common cross-combinations. Right-side crosses are easier to execute than crosses on the left side of the court. However, just as the Polish X play helped the Polish men's

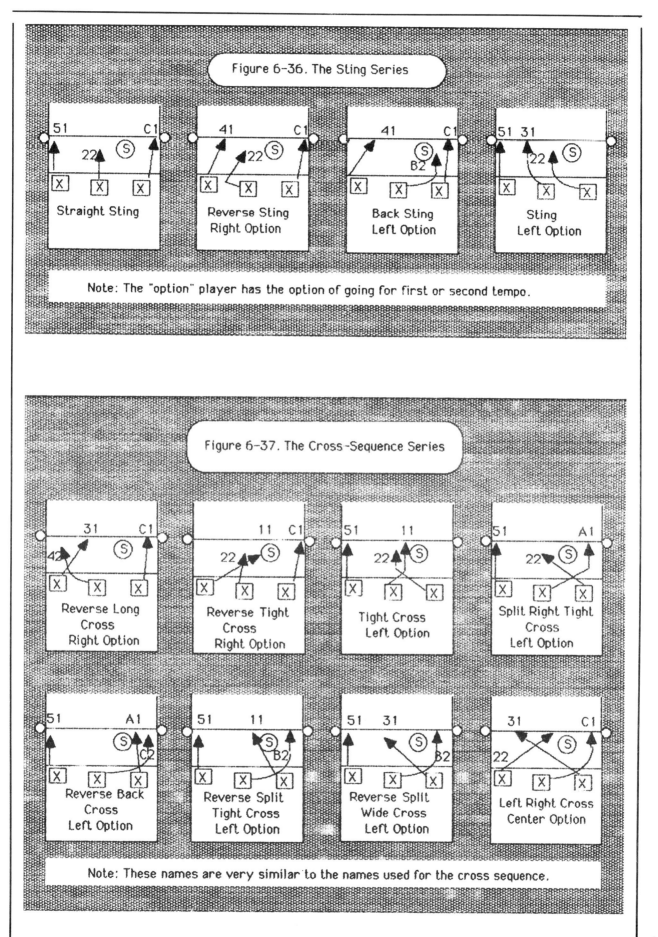

Figure 6-36. The Sting Series

Straight Sting

Reverse Sting
Right Option

Back Sting
Left Option

Sting
Left Option

Note: The "option" player has the option of going for first or second tempo.

Figure 6-37. The Cross-Sequence Series

Reverse Long
Cross
Right Option

Reverse Tight
Cross
Right Option

Tight Cross
Left Option

Split Right Tight
Cross
Left Option

Reverse Back
Cross
Left Option

Reverse Split
Tight Cross
Left Option

Reverse Split
Wide Cross
Left Option

Left Right Cross
Center Option

Note: These names are very similar to the names used for the cross sequence.

team win the Gold Medal in the 1976 Olympics, long crosses were an integral and effective part of the attack for the Japanese women's team, which also won a Gold Medal in the 1976 Olympic Games.

Long crosses are particularly effective when the opponent's setter is short. Since short setters are more common than short ace players, the long cross is therefore a good weapon for any serious team. In the cross-series, the concealed attacker assumes the dual role of safety spiker. Therefore, the third spiker in the combination should attack for first tempo to assist in freezing two blockers simultaneously.

THE CROSS-STING The cross-sting is part of the sequence combinations (Figure 6–38). While two players execute a wide double quick, the third spiker starts a fake approach and then changes direction, coming toward the center of the court between the other two attackers. Hitting from the center of the court provides a wide spiking range for the sting player. Because there is no other spiker between the sting player and the setter, the timing and placement of the set are easy. As mentioned before, the left cross-sting should be considered as a possible play for transition attack when the dig is off and to the right side of the net.

Figure 6–38. The Cross-Sting Series

Figure 6–39. Double-Cross Series

THE DOUBLE-CROSS SERIES From the W serve-reception formation, the double-cross series is very effective in switching players from one side of the court to the other. Essentially, the double-cross combination is a double quick formation with the third spiker going around both quick attackers (Figure 6–39). In the initial learning stages, the third spiker acts almost independently, apart from the other two attackers. But with training and experience, the third spiker becomes an integral part of the combination.

THE SLIDE SERIES The slide series combines some cross-, some double-cross, and some straight-attack combinations (Figure 6–40). The unique aspect of these combinations is the slide approach utilized by one of the attackers. While two spikers overload one net area, the slide attacker moves quickly and surprisingly into the open zone. When the slide attacker has to cross behind another spiker, she uses a wide second-tempo set. In a straight formation (double quick slide C1), the slide attacker should attack at first tempo after a fake movement or a slide adjustment to the opposite direction of the attack. Right-handed spikers should execute the slide to the right of the net, and left-handed spikers should approach from right to left. Actually, almost any attack combination can become a slide combination if one or more attackers execute the slide (one-leg) takeoff.

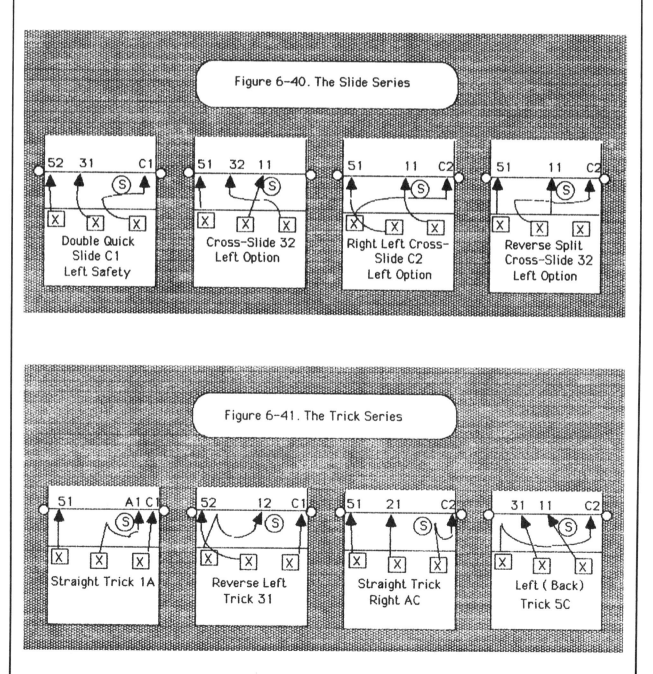

Figure 6-40. The Slide Series

Double Quick Slide C1 Left Safety

Cross-Slide 32 Left Option

Right Left Cross-Slide C2 Left Option

Reverse Split Cross-Slide 32 Left Option

Figure 6-41. The Trick Series

Straight Trick 1A

Reverse Left Trick 31

Straight Trick Right AC

Left (Back) Trick 5C

THE TRICK SERIES Figure 6–41 shows some of the more common trick plays. Like the slide plays, the trick plays are individual maneuvers that can be incorporated into any combination. Each player should have the latitude to call a trick play for a C1, 11 or 31 set, as long as it does not interfere with other players. The trick play is effective in isolating one blocker. It is very similar to a one-on-one fake in basketball, where the shooter (attacker) shakes off her defender (blocker) with a quick lateral movement after faking a jump. Because it steals some of the momentum from the spiker's approach, a trick play can reduce the attacker's jump reach. Therefore, the better jumpers on the team should use the trick play. For many years the USA women's team used the left back trick play very effectively. In addition, the team also frequently and successfully used the split left wide cross (Figure 6–28) in the form of a trick play in rotations with only two front-line attackers.

The X Play Series

The X play series can include all the sequential combinations, together with the slide and the trick

A tight X left option (or tight cross left option) attack formation, very common among men's teams. Note the stream-line approach configuration of the lead and concealed attackers, allowing the concealed spiker to momentarily disappear from the block and then reappear on either side of the setter for a 22 or C2.

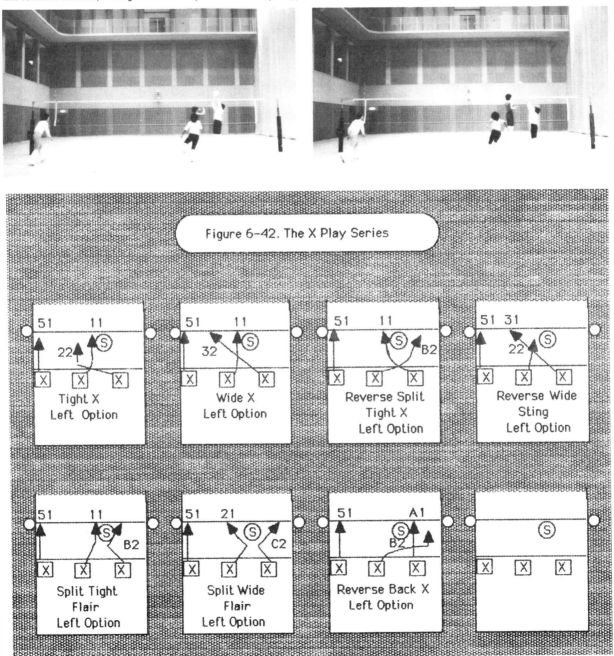

Figure 6–42. The X Play Series

Tight X
Left Option

Wide X
Left Option

Reverse Split
Tight X
Left Option

Reverse Wide
Sting
Left Option

Split Tight
Flair
Left Option

Split Wide
Flair
Left Option

Reverse Back X
Left Option

plays. Like most other three-spiker attack formations, the X play is a double quick combination with one player acting as a concealed spiker. Figure 6–42 shows some complete and incomplete X plays as well as a sting combination. If a team uses the X series, then any cross-play should be named an X play. However, when the cross of an intended X play is not completed, it becomes a sequence play. Some coaches like to call the incomplete X plays "fake" X's, or "reverse fake" X's.

"Flair" means that two spikers make a fake movement toward each other, and then attack in opposite directions. One spiker makes an in-to-out movement while the other does an out-to-in fake movement. When the spikers attack on both sides of the setter it is called a "split" flair. When they attack on either side of the setter it is either a "front" flair or a "back" flair. The flair-movement pattern can be incorporated into certain plays as an automatic adjustment when the pass pulls the setter into the secondary-target area.

Back-Row Attack

The rules permit a back-row player to attack a set as long as she takes off from behind the 10-foot line without stepping on it. It is permissible and quite common for a back-row spiker to broad-jump on her approach and hit a set that is only about 5 feet off the net.

In recent years the height and ability of the block have improved so much that back-row attack has become an integral part of the men's game. In the 1976 Olympics the Gold Medal Polish men's team introduced back-row attack as a complement to the Polish cross. In 1982 the Brazilian men's team incorporated two back-row attackers into its offensive system and captured second place in the world championships.

The USA women's team started experimenting with back-row attackers in 1978 and found that against teams with an exceptional defense, the back-row attack was not consistently effective. It did, however, have certain value as a surprise weapon and we used it occasionally through 1984. As women's volleyball continues to develop and as the players' physical capabilities increase, back-row attack should become more useful, adding depth and diversity to the attack.

Back-row spikers should be integrated into both serve reception and transition attack. There is not much benefit in having a slow back-row attack, because the blockers have enough time to transfer their attention from the front-row attackers to the back-row spiker. Therefore, a successful back-row attack must be quick and well planned. The quickest back-row attack is from the middle. The next-

quickest and most common back-row attack in today's game is a C2 backset for RB. Back-row attack from the left side is slightly slower than from center or right side, but it is still effective if the attacker possesses great broad-jumping ability. It is not inconceivable that in the near future, particularly for men's teams, a first-tempo attack from back court could be implemented with the setter standing deeper off the net.

In the 5–1 team composition, back-row attack should be used to enhance the offense in the three rotations when the setter is front row with only two front-row attackers. The utility player, opposite the setter in the rotation, should be able to attack from deep court. If the utility player does not have the physical ability to be an effective offensive threat from the back row, then either or both of the ace players or a C quick attacker (C2) may be used for back-row serve-reception attack. Player specialization and serve-reception tactics should guide the choice.

The attack zones for a back-row attacker are the same as for front-row players, but the set must be delivered deeper. The set must still be close enough to the net so that the back-row spiker can hit the ball into the middle of the opponent's court, in the area 18 to 20 feet behind the net. If the back-row spiker can not hit this midcourt angle but instead hits most of her spikes to the base-line area, the opponent's block may ignore her, leaving the back-court floor defenders with responsibility for digging back-court spikes.

Backsets such as the C2 and short front sets such as the 22 appear to be the most effective for back-row attack. Back-row attack in Zone C should come from the RB corner, while attack in the middle usually comes from the LB player. Sometimes the RB player can be used to attack middle sets, especially if she is left-handed.

If the opposing team uses the 5–1 team composition, there is often a tactical advantage in attacking the setter when she is in the back row (at RB). By making the opposing 5–1 setter participate in digging the ball, she is taken out of the opponent's transition attack, forcing the utility player to set and leaving the opponent with only two front-row attackers. In advanced volleyball, when the setter digs the ball and the utility player sets for transition attack, the CB should assume the role of a back-row attacker. If the CF goes for a C attack, the CB should go for a 22, and if the CF approaches for either a 31 or an 11 set, the CB should approach for a C attack (back-row attack).

Ideally, a team should attack with both the utility player and the ace players, and should alternate between the two primary-attack locations,

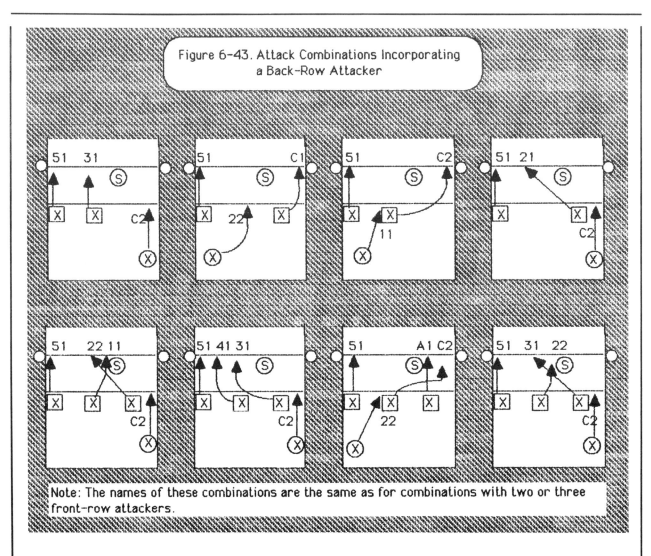

Figure 6-43. Attack Combinations Incorporating a Back-Row Attacker

Note: The names of these combinations are the same as for combinations with two or three front-row attackers.

middle and right side, depending on the opponent's blocking weaknesses or the strength of the back-row attackers in each rotation.

The approach for a back-row attack should start from deep in the court with two or three run-up steps plus a hop. The takeoff should be slow and broad. All the zone designations and set terminology remain the same as for the front-row attack. The only difference is that the setter must realize that the spiker is a back-row player and adjust the depth of the set according to the spiker's ability and preference.

The offensive maneuvers of the front-row spikers must be carefully designed so that they maximize the attack potential for both the front-row and back-row attackers. The main objective is to overload the block, to present more attack options than the blockers can handle.

When there are three front-row attackers and RB is the back-row attacker, the attack formation can be overloaded to the left, leaving an opening for RB to attack down the line. Or the front-row attackers may want to split the block by overload-

ing the right side. In this situation, LF holds the attention of the opponent's RF blocker while CF and RF attack behind the setter, forcing the other two blockers to adjust to their left. This maneuver leaves the center attack zones open for back-row attackers coming from either LB or RB.

Back-row attack must be given careful consideration when designing serve-reception formations, serve-reception attack, and transition attack, especially for men's teams and/or teams using the 5–1 team composition. Figure 6–43 illustrates common back-row attack formations using two and three front-row attackers. Although this figure shows only formations with four attackers, it is possible to have five attackers if desired.

ORGANIZING THE ATTACK

Because of the complexity of attack formations and the vast number of possible combinations, it is very important that a coach use a systematic

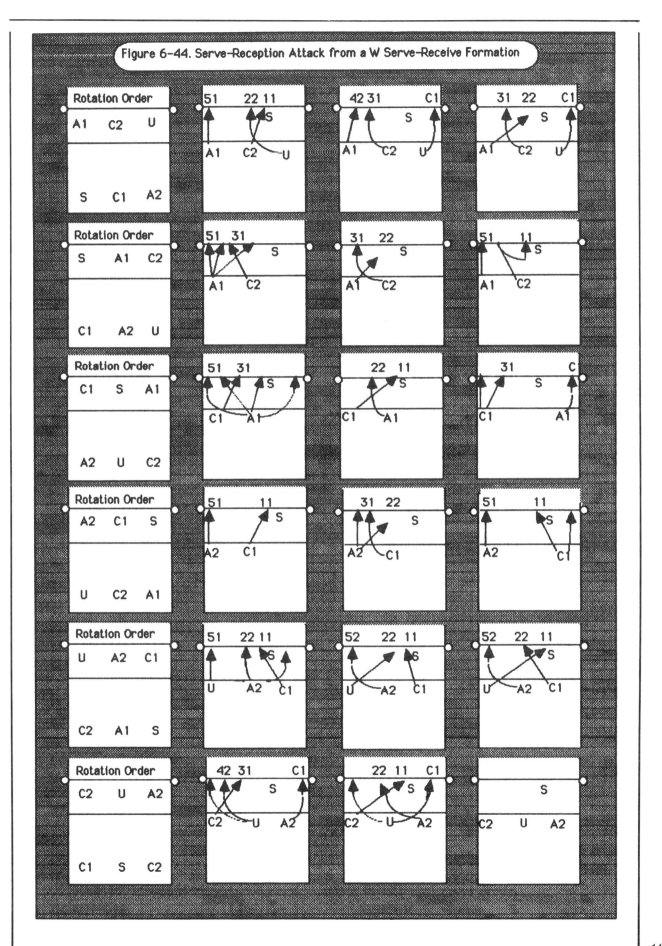

Figure 6-44. Serve-Reception Attack from a W Serve-Receive Formation

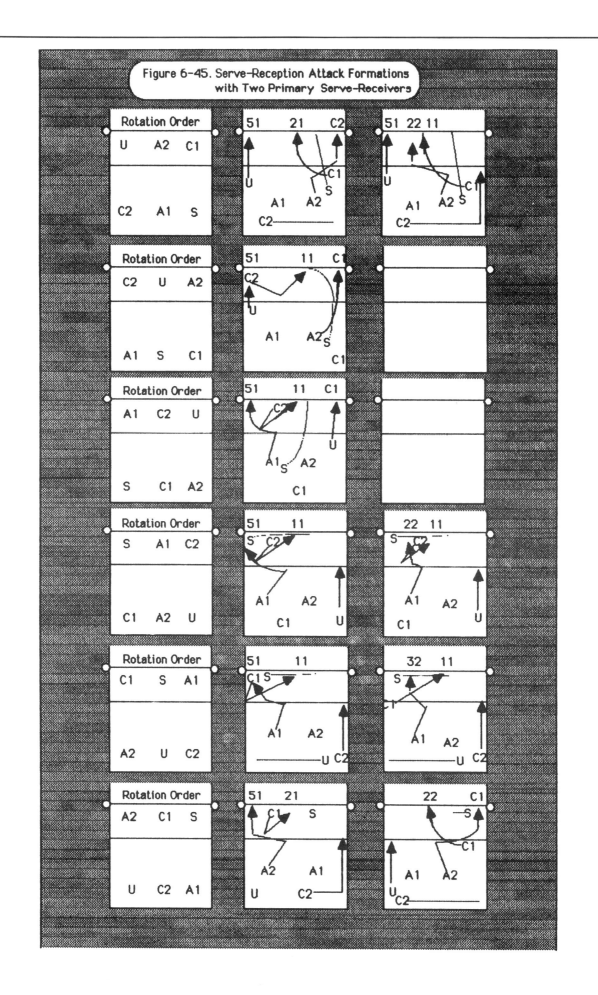

Figure 6-45. Serve-Reception Attack Formations with Two Primary Serve-Receivers

150

approach in organizing the team's attack. In general, attack in volleyball is divided into two distinct phases with little or no bearing on each other: serve-reception attack and transition attack. *Serve-reception attack* is the attack after the pass of the serve. *Transition attack* proceeds or flows from defense, as part of a rally. The serve-reception attack can be preplanned and therefore should be very well organized. Transition attack is more of a response to a situation and is therefore more spontaneous.

Serve-Reception Attack

In designing an attack, the first thing the coach must do is decide whether to adopt a single-tempo attack philosophy in which each spiker masters only one tempo, or a multitempo attack philosophy in which each spiker masters all attack tempos.

In the single-tempo attack concept, only the quick attackers go for the short first-tempo sets; the ace players and the utility player attack outside and act as concealed spikers in sequence combinations. In multitempo-attack systems, all players can attack quick short sets as well as outside sets, and they all operate as concealed spikers in combination attack.

If the multitempo attack concept is adopted, then the *W* formation can be a serve-reception priority formation, and in formations with less than five players the front-line quick attacker may be included in the serve-reception formation. In addition, the parallel-attack formations (straight, sequence, double quick, etc.) can be used in all rotations.

If the single-tempo concept is adopted, the *W* serve-receive formation must be adjusted according to the position of the quick attackers in each rotation. Serve-receive formations with less than five passers should rely mainly on the ace players and utility player. When executing a single-tempo attack from a *W* serve formation, cross-combinations must be incorporated into the attack formations in order to get the various attackers into position to hit the appropriate sets.

Another consideration is whether the serve-reception attack should lead each front-line attacker into her respective specialized position: the ace player to the left side, the center player to the center, and the utility (or in the 6–2 the setter/attacker) to the right side.

These considerations can not be made without taking into account the ability of the players, training time, and level of play.

The USA women's team adopted the multitempo-attack philosophy with much success. However, it is my recommendation that teams with less training time and talent should adapt the single-tempo attack philosophy.

Figures 6–44 and 6–45 illustrate serve-reception attack for a single-tempo attack. The attack formation shown in Figure 6–44 is from the 1976 Gold Medal Japanese Olympic women's team, which used the quick attackers exclusively for first-tempo attack from a *W* serve-receive formation. It is designed so that most of the time the attack formation leads the attackers into their specialized front-line positions. The utility player in these formations has a dual role as both a quick attacker and a second-tempo attacker.

Figure 6–45 demonstrates a single-tempo attack using serve-receive formations with only two primary passers. This formation was used by the 1984 USA Gold Medal men's team and is an example of a very nice solution that satisfies both serve reception and serve-reception attack needs. It used the best passers (A1 and A2) for passing, and maximized the opportunities for both the quick and the back-row attackers. It is interesting to note the complexity of the players' positions in various serve-reception alignments; at times they verge on concealed serve-reception formations. This unique design arranged the players in a way that facilitated the implementation of straight-attack patterns in all rotations with some options for fake movements. USA men's coach Doug Beal created a perfect design that maximized both his players' passing and attack abilities. This is the uppermost consideration in designing serve-reception formations and serve-reception attack.

Organization of Serve-Reception Attack

There are four common methods of organizing and coordinating serve-reception attack:

1. The fixed-attack formation method: just one attack formation is used for all six rotations;
2. The fixed-attack formation by rotation method: a different attack formation is used for each rotation;
3. The number method: each attack formation is given an identification number and one player, usually the setter, calls the formation during play;
4. The varying-attack formation: each spiker calls or signals for the particular set she desires during play.

The coach should select the method best suited to her players' abilities and then progressively advance the team to more advanced methods.

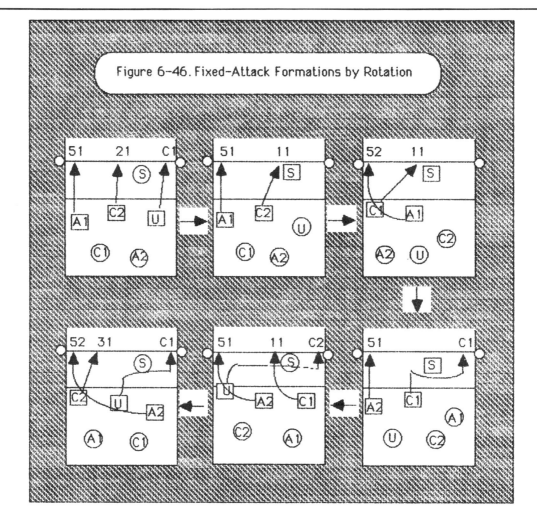

Figure 6-46. Fixed-Attack Formations by Rotation

THE FIXED-FORMATION METHOD This method does not require complex coordination or communication. Usually if a team selects one attack formation to be used for all rotations, the choice will be either a straight attack (Figure 6–33) or a limited X attack on the right side of the court (Figure 6–42).

If a straight-attack system is used from a W serve-reception formation, the spikers will not be led into their specialized front-line positions and each player who passes from the center-court position must assume the role of a quick attacker. This is particularly true for a 6–2 team composition. However, serve-reception formations with less than five players provide the opportunity for a straight attack in all rotations concurrent with the single-tempo attack concept. If the single-tempo attack concept is to be preserved then in certain rotations (more so in a 6-2 than in a 5-1 team composition) the W formation must be modified to at least a four-player serve-receive formation.

A limited right-side X attack is used quite often by men's teams. The most common X plays used are the tight X, the wide X, and the back split wide or the split back tight X. These X plays require only basic communication between the setter and the concealed attacker.

THE FIXED-ATTACK FORMATION BY ROTATION METHOD This method is very simple. It leads the attackers directly into their front-row positions allowing them to perform their specialized roles. If the attack begins from a W formation, then it requires the use of cross-pattern or the incorporation of the slide attack. Figure 6–46 illustrates fixed-attack formation by rotation from a W serve-receive formation.

Figure 6–47 illustrates fixed-attack formation with four and three serve receivers.

THE NUMBER METHOD A coach can designate by number a team's attack formations and have the setter or another assigned player call the selected formation prior to the serve. This concept is quite popular in the USA among college teams. To a certain degree it is a good strategy, because it allows for versatility of attack and for required adjustments in particular situations. It also allows the coach to signal from the bench what formation

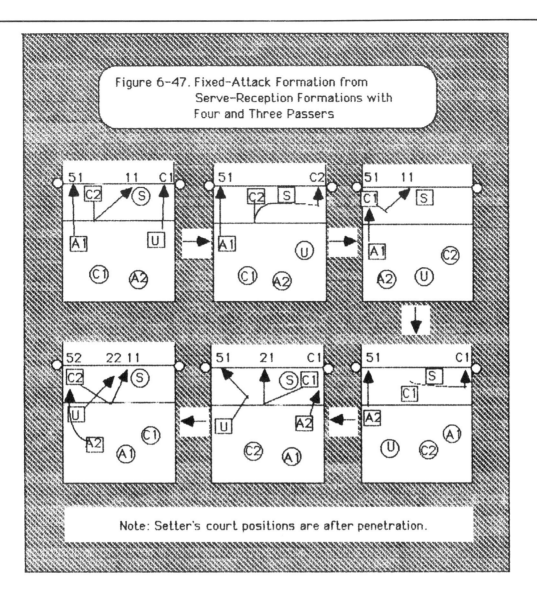

Figure 6-47. Fixed-Attack Formation from Serve-Reception Formations with Four and Three Passers

Note: Setter's court positions are after penetration.

to use, and in timeouts she can be very specific in directing the team's attack. However, a coach should be certain that the list of the attack formations is in accord with her attack philosophy. For the single-tempo attacker concept, the list should include formations allowing each of the attackers to maneuver from every court position according to their designated roles on the team. Ideally, it should allow every player to attack any zone from every court position. The player who calls the plays must learn the limitations of both the attackers and the system and choose the proper formations for each different rotation.

Tables 6-3, 6-4, 6-5, and 6-6 show my method for dividing up, organizing, and naming a variety of attack formations. Table 6-3, the A system, contains attack formations that in principle are wide-out formations laterally spreading the opponent's block. These formations include the straight-

attack formations and formations in which two spikers attack together in adjacent zones, executing sequential or double quick combinations while the third spiker acts independently as a safety.

Table 6-4, the B system, contains attack formations that are centered formations. These attack patterns involve three spikers (if available) in more complex maneuvers often resulting in freezing two blockers at once while the third spiker tries to escape from the third blocker. Instead of attempting to beat the block to a particular net zone, the three spikers often overload one net area in an attempt to deceive and manipulate the timing of the block.

Table 6-6, the C system, contains concealed-attack formations from a W serve-receive pattern. Table 6-5, the X system, contains a few X plays.

I have found these tables to be very useful in getting the players acquainted with the underlying

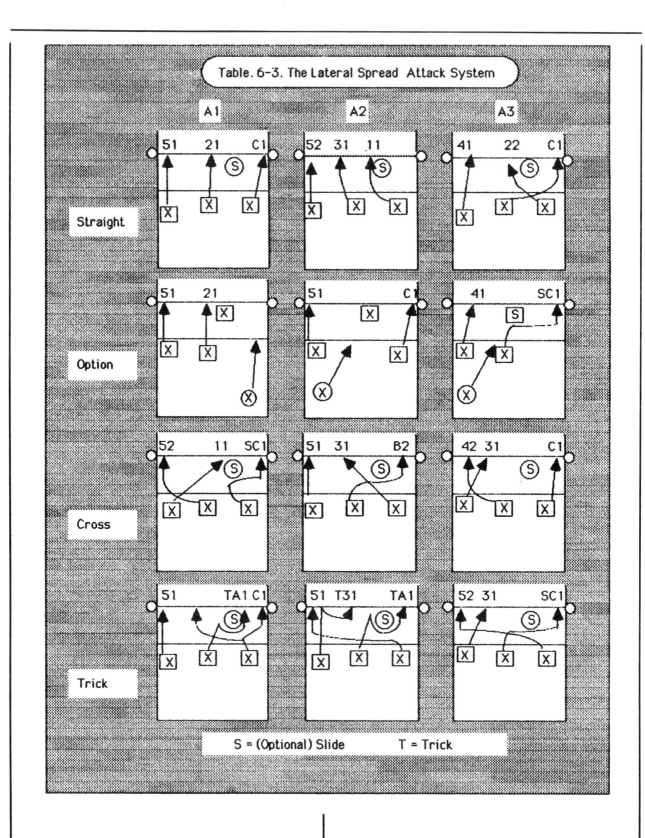

Table. 6-3. The Lateral Spread Attack System

S = (Optional) Slide   T = Trick

concepts of different attack formations, and in helping them to memorize the plays. As a coach, I could direct the team to play the A or the B system depending on the situation or the particular opponent. The A system is effective against tall but slow-blocking teams; the B system is effective against short but quick blockers.

In Table 6–3, system A, the first play on the left-hand side is called A1 straight; the next play below is A1 option, etc. During the game, the setter

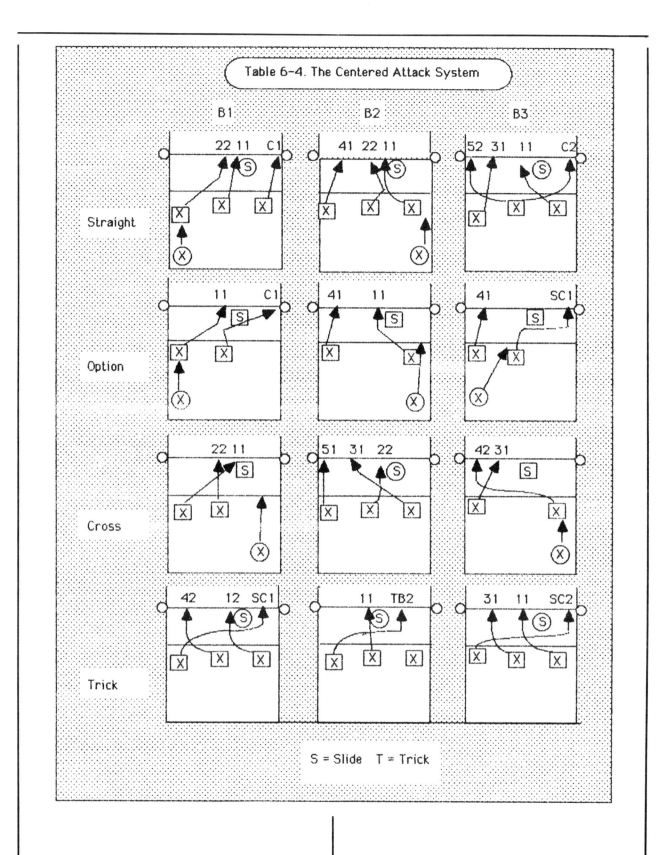

Table 6-4. The Centered Attack System

S = Slide   T = Trick

or the captain of the team calls the desired combination, such as "B1 cross!"

Instead of having a complete play description, one number can be assigned to each play. Some coaches use colors or code names for each play. In situations where a team plays the same opponent several times during the season and the two teams share a common language, play designations should change from time to time to keep the opponent from figuring out which code corresponds to which play.

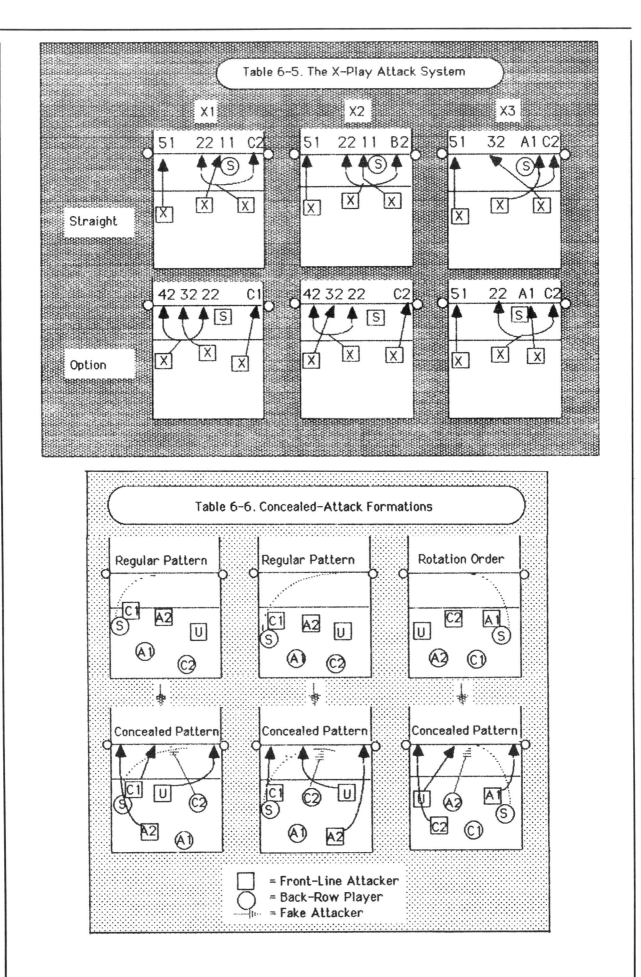

Table 6-5. The X-Play Attack System

Table 6-6. Concealed-Attack Formations

= Front-Line Attacker
= Back-Row Player
= Fake Attacker

In deciding which player should call the offense, a coach has to consider several factors. Ideally, if the setter is highly experienced and capable of implementing the game plan, then she should call the plays. This puts the setter in total charge of the offense, selecting both the play and the hitter who will receive the set. The hitters, meanwhile, are free to concentrate simply on executing their functions in the attack.

The 1984 USA Women's Olympic team used the varying attack formation method for serve reception attack, allowing each attacker to call her own desired set with finger signals.

Laurie Flachmeier signals to Carolyn Becker (top).

Julie Vollertsen and Rose Magers contemplate an attack.

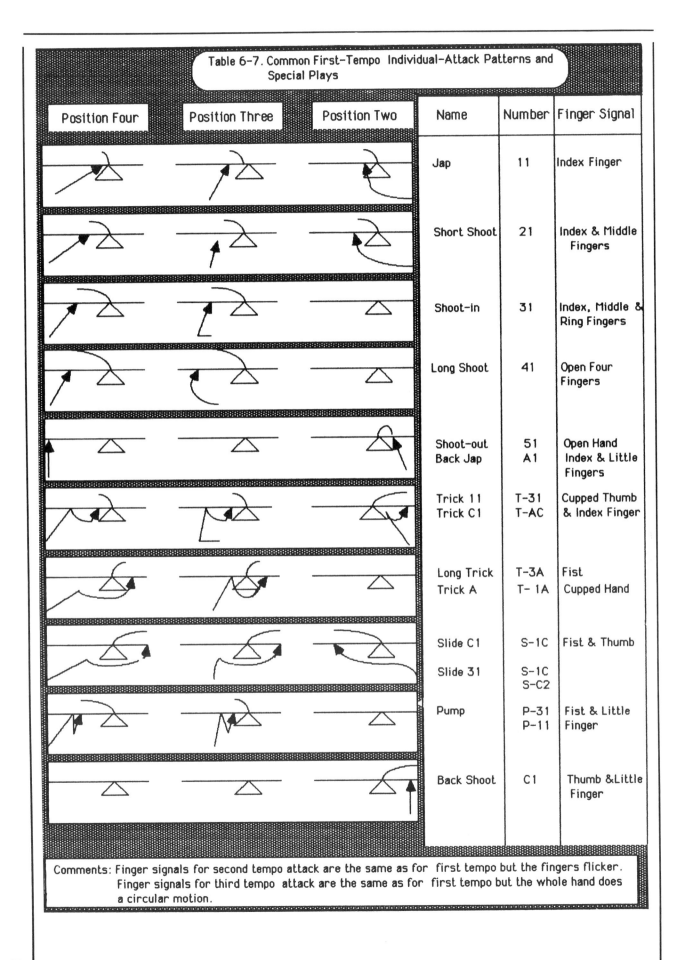

Table 6-7. Common First-Tempo Individual-Attack Patterns and Special Plays

Position Four	Position Three	Position Two	Name	Number	Finger Signal
			Jap	11	Index Finger
			Short Shoot	21	Index & Middle Fingers
			Shoot-in	31	Index, Middle & Ring Fingers
			Long Shoot	41	Open Four Fingers
			Shoot-out	51	Open Hand
			Back Jap	A1	Index & Little Fingers
			Trick 11	T-31	Cupped Thumb
			Trick C1	T-AC	& Index Finger
			Long Trick	T-3A	Fist
			Trick A	T-1A	Cupped Hand
			Slide C1	S-1C	Fist & Thumb
			Slide 31	S-1C S-C2	
			Pump	P-31	Fist & Little
				P-11	Finger
			Back Shoot	C1	Thumb & Little Finger

Comments: Finger signals for second tempo attack are the same as for first tempo but the fingers flicker. Finger signals for third tempo attack are the same as for first tempo but the whole hand does a circular motion.

If the setter lacks competition experience and is not adept at selecting the best play for each situation, the coach should consider having the captain call the plays. Usually the captain has all the qualities a coach looks for in this situation. The captain has experience, leadership ability, and is often the best player, or at least the best hitter, on the team. Having the captain call the plays frees the setter to concentrate on the position of the block and which hitter to set.

In some cases, a setter has both physical tools and game experience, but mentally overloads if she also has to take the responsibility for play calling. Here again, the captain is a good alternate choice.

THE VARYING-ATTACK FORMATION METHOD The varying-attack formation method puts to use the play-set system by allowing each attacker to call her own desired set each time the serve-reception formation is formed. The desired set and tempo can be called audibly or communicated with finger signals (Table 6–7). In order to prevent confusion, in each rotation the C player calls first, the U player calls second and the Ace (A) player calls last. If a back-row attacker is used, she should make the last call. This ordering method is very well suited to the single-tempo attack concept.

It is also possible to use a different order in which the A player calls first followed by center and then the utility player. This concept complements the multitempo attack concept, and the USA women's team used it. Because of the high-noise level that can occur during a game, a finger-signal system is sometimes the best. To avoid letting the opponent see the signals, the spiker simply puts her hand behind her back and makes the proper finger signal while the setter and the rest of the spikers are looking. Because everybody can see the signals, it helps the two back-row players anticipate the oncoming attack and get to their spiker-coverage positions on time.

This method puts the burden of developing the appropriate attack formation on the hitters. Once the attacker calls a play, she assumes the responsibility for success when set. An advantage is that at least three people are involved in calling the plays. If the attack depends on only one person, the success is bound to fluctuate somewhat as that player's concentration fluctuates.

Because the possible number of attack combinations with three or four players is so great, the coach can limit each spiker to only a few options in each rotation. Each rotation is thus limited to only a few possible combinations. The system is fairly simple to learn and execute, because the players do not need to remember formations. All they need to remember are the finger signals that indicate one particular play set only.

Footwork for Front-Line Spikers to Use During the Serve to Maintain Eye Contact with the Ball

In all serve-reception formations, the spikers must use careful footwork to ensure that they maintain eye contact with the ball throughout the flight path of the pass.

When the serve comes on the left-hand side of the center front spiker in a *W* formation, the spiker should turn clockwise toward the ball receiver by stepping backward with the right foot. If the spiker uses an approach with one run-up step plus a hop, she should rock back and lead into the run-up step with the left foot; if she uses two run-up steps and a hop, she should lead with the right foot. If the serve comes to her right side, CF should do the same footwork and body action but with less of a turn; sometimes simply looking back over her shoulder.

When the ball comes on the right side of a left front spiker, the spiker will usually go outside the court slightly when her assignment is a 52. She should then approach the net at about a 45-degree angle. If LF is assigned to go for a first-tempo set, the spiker does not slide out but instead turns clockwise to maintain eye contact with the ball. As soon as the passer contacts the serve, the spiker gauges the speed of the ball and starts moving inside toward her designated attack zone. The number of run-up steps she needs prior to the hop depends on the distance she must travel. If the ball comes on the left side of the LF spiker, the spiker should first open the passing lane by stepping back with the left foot and turning counterclockwise, and then go to the outside. While moving to the outside, the LF must maintain continuous eye contact with the ball. Similar footwork should be used by a CF player (A player) who is assigned to a 52.

When the ball comes on the left side of RF, the spiker should simply turn counterclockwise and step back with the left foot. If the spiker uses a one-step approach, she should step forward with the left foot and follow with a hop. If she uses two run-up steps plus a hop, RF should rock back slightly, take a short step with the right foot, followed by a longer step with the left foot and the hop.

When the ball comes over the right shoulder of

the right front player, she should turn clockwise, pivoting on the left foot. This allows RF to face toward the side line but without interfering with RB's eye contact with the serve as she executes the pass. If RF attacks for an 11, she should rock back on her right foot, make a small step with the left foot forward, and go into the hop. If RF acts as a concealed player in a sequential or an X play, she can use the same technique.

Transition Attack

Many teams fail to recognize the importance of transition attack and practice primarily serve-reception attack. At high levels of volleyball, most points are scored as a result of transition attack, and not by an opponent's errors or by the block. A team should emphasize transition attack almost as much as serve-reception attack, and have some basic rules for organizing the transition offense. Transition attack is harder to plan because it is spontaneous and there are so many variables involved. However, a team can plan certain attack strategies for given situations.

There are four general methods of organizing transition attack: the fixed method; the fixed-by-rotation method; the number system; the varying-attack method.

THE FIXED METHOD In the fixed method, the team employs the same transition-attack pattern in all rotations. The most common attack formation used in this method is the straight attack where CF goes for the 11 or 21, RF for a C1 or C2, and LF for a 51 or 52. With a 5–1 team composition, in the three rotations where there are only two front-row spikers, a back-row attack at right side is incorporated into the attack formation, replacing the front-line attack by the utility player.

THE FIXED-BY-ROTATION METHOD In this method the attack is preplanned according to particular situations. In a 5–1 team composition, there are two situations: the three rotations in which there are three front-line attackers, and the three rotations in which there are two front-line attackers and a setter. Generally, each of these can be divided into three cases according to the location of the block:

Case 1. Right Side: center front and right front block on the right side.
Case 2. Center: center front and left front, or center front and right front, or just center front blocks in the center.
Case 3. Left Side: left front and center front block on the left side.

In order to prevent hesitation in the transition attack it is possible to preplan the attack pattern for each particular situation and case. The following is an example of a simple transition attack after coming off the block (Figure 6–48).

Situation one: three front-line attackers:

Case 1. CF always attacks a 31, RF a C2 (or C1), and LF a 52 (or a 51). If LF attacks for a 51, RF is the safety spiker, attacks a C1.
Case 2. CF always attacks an 11, RF an X option, and LF a 52 or 51.
Case 3. CF always attacks 11, RF an X option, LF for a 52.

Situation two: two front-line attackers:

Case 1. CF blocks together with the setter; the CF should attack behind the setter's back with a slide spike or regular two-foot takeoff. LF should have an option, a 51, or 42, and should audibly call (or signal) the 42 option. RB or LB should go for a back-row 22.
Case 2. Similar to above.
Case 3. CF always attacks a 31. RB attacks a back-row C2.

If a team employs a back-row attack, in situation two, CF should coordinate with the back-row attacker by using the finger-signal method to indicate where she is going to attack on transition. For example, if CF indicates an 11 or a C1, the back-row spiker should attack in the center, probably a 22. If CF signals a 31, then the back-row attacker should hit a C2 set down the line.

In a 6–2 team composition, any one of the previously described cases will apply at all times. If the back-row setter comes to the net to set, then there are three front-row spikers and the first situation applies. If the front-line setter has to set, case two applies. In the 5–1 situation when the setter digs the ball, the utility player becomes the setter. In such cases, the center front should act in the same manner as described for situation two, but LF will only implement a 52. The utility player should learn to set well enough so that when the situation arises, she can catch the opponent off guard with proficient setting. Usually an opponent does not expect a utility player to set a quick attack.

THE NUMBER SYSTEM With the number system, it is often necessary for the play caller (setter or captain) to call two numbers. Prior to receiving serve, the play caller must communicate the number or code for the serve-reception attack forma-

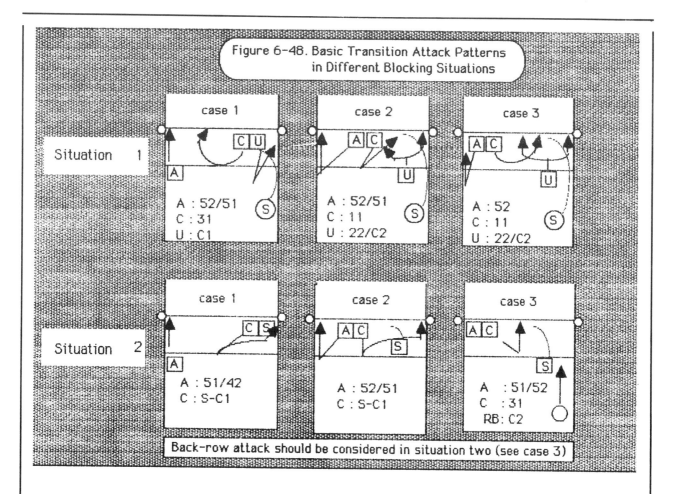

Figure 6-48. Basic Transition Attack Patterns in Different Blocking Situations

Situation 1

case 1
A : 52/51
C : 31
U : C1

case 2
A : 52/51
C : 11
U : 22/C2

case 3
A : 52
C : 11
U : 22/C2

Situation 2

case 1
A : 51/42
C : S-C1

case 2
A : 52/51
C : S-C1

case 3
A : 51/52
C : 31
RB: C2

Back-row attack should be considered in situation two (see case 3)

tion, and a number for transition attack. Prior to serving, the play caller calls one number for transition attack only.

THE VARYING-ATTACK METHOD In this method, the players on the serving team give finger signals to indicate which set they would like to attack on transition.

The USA women's team used a blend of transition-attack systems, depending on our opponent and the situation. One of our systems was the "no-system system" in which none of the transition attackers signaled their requests, but simply attacked wherever they wished. It was up to the setter to recognize their attack patterns and then make the proper set selection. At other times when we were serving, the center front spiker would signal her set request. Then LF and RF would attack without signaling their intentions in advance at appropriate locations. In other situations we would signal for serve-reception attack and then attack on transition, using the fixed-by-rotation method: one transition play for three front-row spikers and another specific play for rotations with only two front-row attackers.

If a coach has experienced high-level players, I feel that the spontaneous no-system system is the best. On the USA women's team we had the luxury of thousands of hours of practice, and one of the finest setters in the world in Debbie Green.

Footwork for Transition Attack

After blocking, each spiker has to get into comfortable attack positions as soon as possible. Figure 6–49 indicates the home positions, which spikers should attempt to get to as quickly as possible after blocking. These positions are similar to the positions in the *W* serve-receive formation, and maximize the player's abilities to hit various types of sets at a wide range of attack zones along the net.

As soon as they come off the block, the spikers must regain eye contact with the ball. Often, the direction players turn in coming off the block is determined by the body's momentum during the takeoff for the block jump.

Generally, spikers should run to their home positions rather than backpedaling. Except when covering very short distances, backpedaling is not advisable because it is too slow.

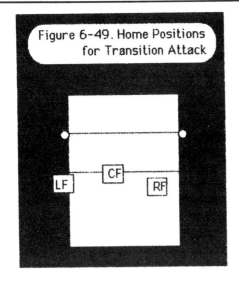

Figure 6-49. Home Positions for Transition Attack

LEFT FRONT If LF lands with her head turning toward the outside, which doesn't happen often, she should continue turning her head and body counterclockwise, make eye contact with the ball, and keep on running to the outside in a circular path that will bring her around facing back toward the court and the set.

If LF turns inside coming off the block, as is usually the case, she might start with a crossover step, pushing away from the net with the left foot, then crossing the left foot over the right. This is followed by a step with the right foot, which should bring the spiker back to approximately the 10-foot line. The hitter can then circle outside, getting into a position about 3 feet behind the 10-foot line and 2 feet outside the court (see Figure 6–49). Throughout this entire movement the hitter should maintain eye contact with the dig, the setter, and the set.

CENTER FRONT Whether CF comes off the block with her head turned to the left or the right, she immediately regains eye contact with the dug ball during its flight to the setter. By keeping eye contact with the ball, she will automatically turn her body in the correct direction.

After blocking on the right side, CF may want to spike a slide C1 behind the setter's back or an 11 in front of the setter. In this case she should run to the home position near the center of the court keeping eye contact with the ball. CF then rocks back slightly and implements a step and a hop when going for an 11. For the slide, CF steps up toward the net and then moves parallel to it, sliding behind the setter.

In some situations, CF needs to go from her blocking position at right side for a 31. The exact path CF travels and the distance she gets back off

the net is largely determined by the trajectory of the dig. A high-trajectory dig gives enough time for CF to run to the home position, then approach for the 31 using two run-up steps (right-left) followed by the hop. On the other hand, with a low-trajectory dig CF may have to use a very shallow circular path from the right-side blocking zone to the attack zone. In this case, CF finishes the approach with only one step (on the left foot) followed by the hop.

When CF blocks on the left side and wants to go for an 11, she can either go in a semicircle, or angle back. The footwork for a semicircular approach from the left side to the center usually will require two run-up steps and a hop. If CF uses the angle-back approach pattern, she should simply run to the home position and then take one run-up step plus a hop.

To go for a C2 slide behind the setter's back, CF should run on a slight arc along the net, take off just behind the setter, and broad-jump parallel to the net toward the C slot.

RIGHT FRONT After coming off the block, RF should retreat to his home position which is about 8 feet from the right sideline and 3 feet behind the 10-foot line. Usually, when she comes off the block, RF will be turned toward the inside of the court. With a right over left crossover step, a step with the left and a clockwise turn, RF should reach home position keeping her right foot in front of her left. The approach is made by stepping forward onto the right foot, then the left foot, and finally the hop. This footwork is very important if RF is involved in a sequential play or an X play in combination with the center front.

During transition the time available for the blockers to get back and prepare to become attackers is very limited (about 1.1 to 1.3 seconds). Therefore, the footwork must be precise. Often the spikers have only enough time to back off a very short distance and must attack using only a hop. At other times they will be able to get back to their home positions and attack using a complete approach with two or three run-up steps and a hop.

In practice, the coach should create all kinds of situations simulating real game situations. These drills will improve the spikers' orientation and increase their ability to implement different transition-attack possibilities.

Fake-Attack Formations

When a team with a 5–1 composition uses the *W* serve-reception formation and there are only two attackers in the front row, the team can shift the hitters to the left, to the right, or split them at

LF and RF. The back-row passer closest to the front line can be used as a fake attacker (Figure 6–50). Figure 6–51 illustrates serve-reception attack from a *U* serve-receive formation with a back-row fake spiker.

Fake-attack formations were popular until the late seventies, but against experienced teams they are not very effective for serve-reception attack; after they're done once, the opponent catches on. However, during transition attack, when the opponent's block responds spontaneously, fake-attack formations can sometimes work because the opposing blockers lose track of the eligible front-row attackers. Most often, the fake is performed by the utility player coming from the right side. The movement has to be carefully synchronized with the two front-line attackers, particularly CF.

Another problem with using fake attackers is that they weaken spiker coverage. Usually, it's more beneficial in these rotations to incorporate a back-row attack.

Concealed-Formation Attack

To confuse an opponent, or to make use of its best passers, a team can utilize various concealed serve-reception formations. Table 6–6 presents some concealed-attack variations of the *W* serve-reception formation.

In concealed-attack formations, back-row players come to the net for fake attacks, while front-row spikers who were hidden deep in the court suddenly appear, confusing the block. In designing and implementing these concealed-attack formations, a coach must take into consideration these factors:

1. If the main purpose of the formation is to provide an additional element of surprise to the attack, then the concealed formations must be used sparingly or the opponent will soon figure them out.
2. If the primary purpose of the formation is to utilize the talents of the best passers, then the formations can be used on a regular basis.
3. Whenever concealed-attacker formations are used, it is better to switch ace players into the back court rather than quick attackers. This is especially true if the formation is used to maximize the passing skills of the ace players, or if the team uses a single-tempo attack concept.
4. Whenever more than three players are involved in the attack (as spikers or fake spikers) spiker coverage is weakened.

Switching Players into Their Specialized Attack Positions

Players can be switched to their specialized front-line positions either during serve-reception attack or immediately after its completion. Usually, attack formations can be designed to lead the

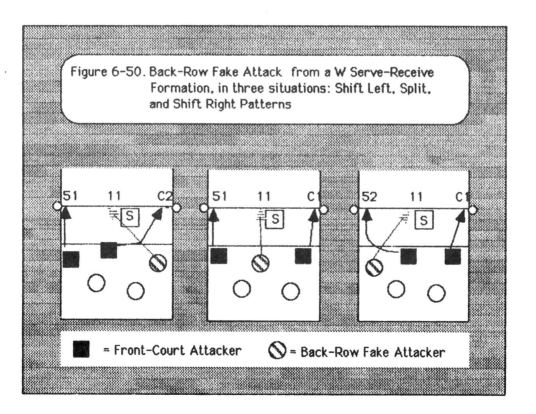

Figure 6–50. Back-Row Fake Attack from a W Serve-Receive Formation, in three situations: Shift Left, Split, and Shift Right Patterns

■ = Front-Court Attacker   ⊘ = Back-Row Fake Attacker

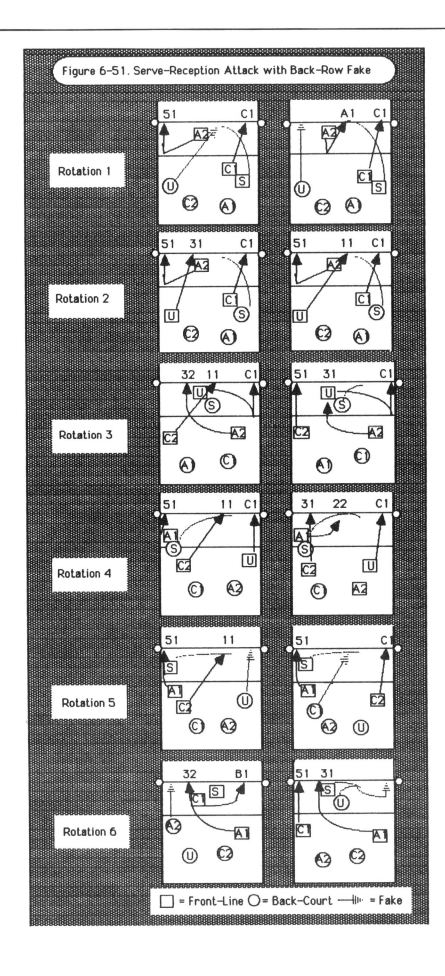

Figure 6-51. Serve-Reception Attack with Back-Row Fake

Rotation 1

Rotation 2

Rotation 3

Rotation 4

Rotation 5

Rotation 6

□ = Front-Line ○ = Back-Court —‖⊪ = Fake

spikers directly into their specialized attack positions. However, sometimes for tactical reasons players do not end up in their positions at the end of the serve-reception or transition attack, and therefore need to switch quickly.

If time allows, the players can make a complete switch in one movement. If time is limited, they might have to make a partial switch on the way to their proper positions and then wait for the next opportunity to complete the switch. Figure 6–52 illustrates basic principles of switching at the end of serve-reception attack. Generally, both the ace and the utility players switch behind the center player's back. The ace player switches in front of the utility player or the setter. The same rules apply in switching positions by the net after serving.

Free Ball

A *free ball* is defined as a ball returned softly by the opponent over the net. Most free balls are bumped or finger-set over the net. Consequently, they have a high arc and relatively little horizontal velocity. They are easy to anticipate by watching the actions of the opponent getting ready to bump or set the ball over the net.

Free-ball transition attack should be executed with extra speed to take full advantage of the opportunity. The pass should be a finger pass with a trajectory that allows the setter to jump-set, tip, or spike the ball. It is also suggested that all players call out "free ball" as soon as they detect that the opponent has decided to play a free ball.

Free-ball situations usually present great opportunities to score points. To capitalize on these opportunities, each team should have specific free-ball plays. A team using the 6–2 composition needs only one play. A 5–1 team should have two free-ball plays, one for three attackers and one for two spikers plus the setter.

The USA women's team successfully used the left cross-sting (Figure 6–38) for three attackers, and the wide-out slide double quick (B3 option; Table 6-4) for two attackers.

Down-Ball Play

A down ball is usually hit by a spiker not in a comfortable position to jump and hit the ball with full force. She usually lobs it, spiking it with medium speed while standing flat on the floor or with a very slight hop for timing. These situations can be anticipated. The blockers should call "down ball" and retreat off the net to their home positions. The team should have two different plays to use when there is a down ball, one play for two

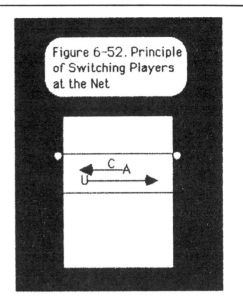

Figure 6–52. Principle of Switching Players at the Net

spikers and another for three. For three spikers, I suggest using a sequential or an X formation on the right-hand side. For two, a quick double split (with or without a slide) can be useful.

Tactical Considerations for Multiple Attack

The success of a team's attack is largely determined by the cumulative effect of the offense. This cumulative effect can only be achieved by continuous and consistent team efforts in execution and strategy. Each player on the team must know and understand her role and her specific contribution to the overall offensive scheme. Players must also realize that in multiple attack, creating the opening in the block is as important as the actual hitting of the ball. The overall effectiveness of a multiple-attack offense can be enhanced if these basic concepts are followed:

1. The attack formations must be consistently initiated from the same court positions and in the same way every time, but alternating between centered attack and a lateral spread attack. The objective is to keep the blockers confused, to keep them moving back and forth, always wondering where the attack will come from. To accomplish this, the attack should shift back and forth from middle to outside. In addition to periodically attacking the middle, the attack formations should incorporate fake maneuvers that create the constant threat of a middle attack.

Inside-out attack patterns are generally more effective than outside-in patterns. Inside-out formations draw the opponent's outside blockers in toward the center of the net. If the ball is set wide, especially to zones 5 and C, these outside blockers have a hard time getting back into position in time. Often they will arrive too late and block with either poor penetration or poor hand position, or both. In addition, because the outside blockers are in motion, rather than prepositioned, the middle blocker is also delayed in getting into position to contribute to the block.

It is important to keep in mind that an inside-out attack will not be effective unless there is a real threat of an attack in the middle. This means that the middle attackers must be capable hitters, and that the offense must utilize these hitters often enough to make the opponent respect the threat.

2. The pass should have a low trajectory but yet should be high enough when it reaches the net for the setter to jump-set. The setter, in turn, must make every possible effort to jump-set every ball.

3. It is the attackers' responsibility to establish the proper positions and timing in relationship to the setter. The setter is responsible for making the proper set selection.

4. Spikers should approach the spaces between the blockers rather than facing the block head-on. Therefore, before starting to attack, the spikers must be aware of all three blockers' initial positions. Are they centered, spread, or shifted to either side? Does the opponent commit with the quick attacker or use see-and-respond blocking tactics? Does the opponent use zone-blocking or one-on-one blocking? Does the opponent attempt to block with one, two, or three players in the middle? (These subjects are covered extensively in Chapter 7, "The Block.")

5. Each spiker must be able to execute a variety of spiking techniques, alternating hard hits, off-speed shots, and tips. The tips and off-speed shots are important weapons the spiker should use to avoid exposing certain tendencies that the opponent's defense can anticipate. Figure 6–53 illustrates some of the most vulnerable areas for tipping when attacking a man-down defense formation. In addition, spikers should not attempt to hit the ball straight down. Hitting straight down slows down the attack and increases the chances of getting blocked even by a short blocker.

6. The attack should be directed into the seams of the floor defense, in particular to the corners and the area midway between the crosscourt defensive players. The floor defense usually assumes a court position higher up against a quick attacker. Quick attackers in particular should be able to hit into the deep corners that are almost always open. Outside sets for a fast attack should be run fairly deep off the net, about 1 to 1.2 meters (3 to 4 ft.). This speeds up the attack, reduces the screening power of the block, and allows the spiker to hit hard to the back court.

7. It is very important to distribute the balls equally among all attack positions. It is worthwhile to remember that attack on the right side is usually quicker and more difficult to defend against than attack from position 4 (LF).

8. A wide-out attack is very effective against tall teams, especially teams with particularly tall middle blockers. A centered attack with sequential and double quick formations is effective against short blockers.

9. Generally, it is an effective strategy to attack

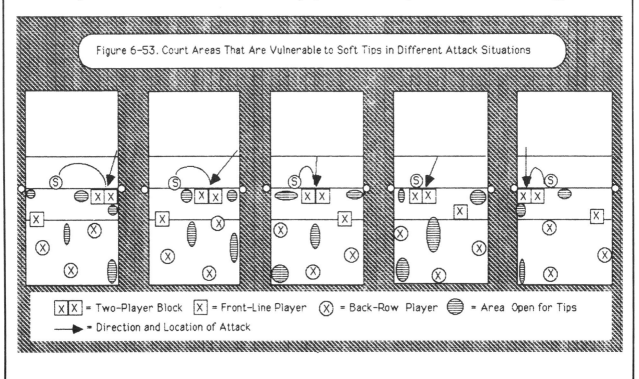

Figure 6–53. Court Areas That Are Vulnerable to Soft Tips in Different Attack Situations

x x = Two-Player Block   X = Front-Line Player   Ⓧ = Back-Row Player   ⊜ = Area Open for Tips

——▶ = Direction and Location of Attack

the opposing setter when she is back row. Forcing the setter to dig the ball will often disrupt the opponent's transition attack. Neutralizing the setter is a particularly important consideration when playing against a team that uses the 5–1 team composition. When the opponent's setter is in the front line, it is advisable to attack on the opposite side. This strategy should be used often when encountering a solid block. Rather than taking a chance on attack, the team should be patient and create an opportunity to score with their own block or on another transition opportunity. If the opponent's front-row setter is short and does not jump well, then it can be advisable to attack over the setter.

10. When attacking on transition with the chance to score a point, the attack should be done with no hesitations or fear of making an error. In these situations, players should be encouraged to take risks, because there is nothing to lose and a lot to gain.

11. Radical adjustments of attack are rarely recommended. The best chance a team has is to execute the attack for which it was trained. Too often, major adjustments in attack create a loss of rhythm and a loss of interest among attackers who are given a secondary role. However, the coach should develop in advance special attack strategies against different teams to take advantage of their weaknesses. These adjustments should be team-oriented adjustments in which the role of every spiker is not diminished, but rather redirected.

12. There are many variables that dictate the nature and direction of the transition attack. However, whenever possible, a team's counterattack should be directed to the opposite side, away from where the opponent attacked. This strategy works well when the transition is very quick and therefore does not allow much recovery time for the opposing spiker attacker to get into her proper defensive position.

SPIKER COVERAGE

Spiker coverage is a transitional phase of the game. Every time a spiker goes up to attack, the rest of the team must go into a coverage pattern, prepared to save a ball that might be deflected off the opponent's block back into the spiker's court.

Effective spiker coverage gives the spiker security, recovers somewhere between four and six blocked balls per game, and provides an opportunity for players to switch smoothly into their specialized defense positions from serve-reception attack. As the attack becomes more complex, so does the spiker coverage. Thus, teams that implement a four-player attack have a harder time maintaining consistent spiker coverage.

A coach has to design a spiker-coverage formation for each particular attack, keeping in mind that spiker-coverage responsibilities are different for serve-reception attack and transition attack. They also vary slightly depending on whether the setter is in the front or back row. Players have to realize that there is not just one assigned spiker-coverage position they always assume; responsibilities change with each attack and court

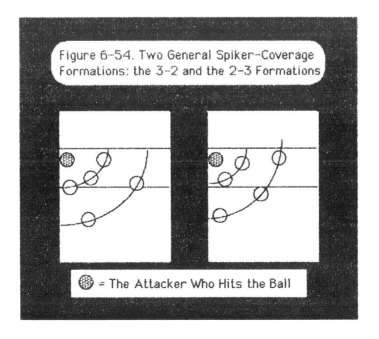

Figure 6–54. Two General Spiker–Coverage Formations: the 3–2 and the 2–3 Formations

⊕ = The Attacker Who Hits the Ball

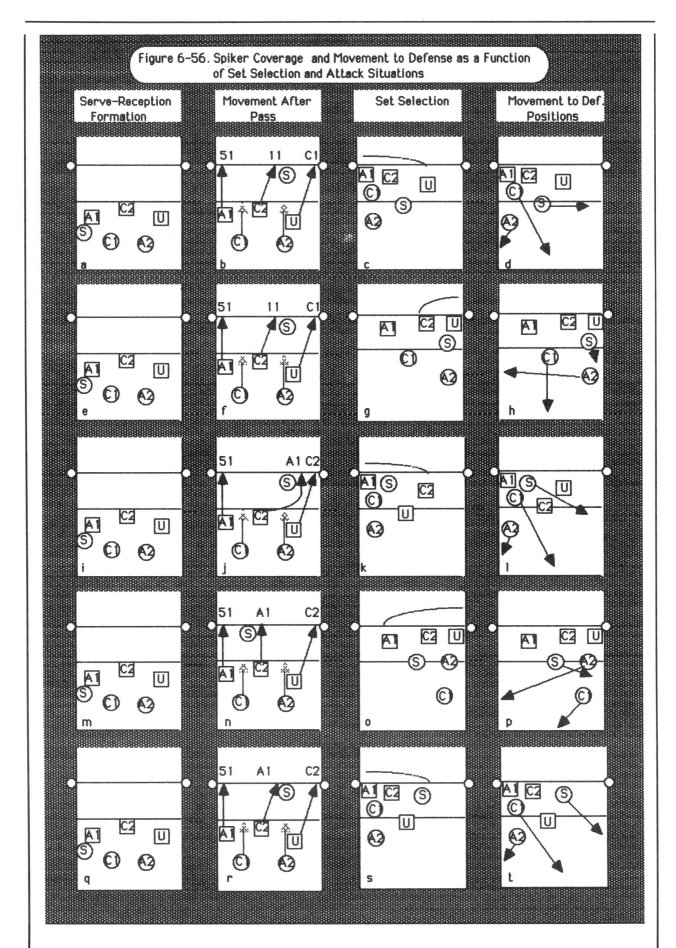

Figure 6-56. Spiker Coverage and Movement to Defense as a Function of Set Selection and Attack Situations

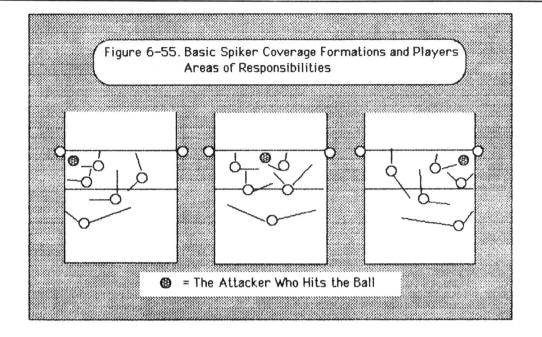

Figure 6-55. Basic Spiker Coverage Formations and Players Areas of Responsibilities

⊕ = The Attacker Who Hits the Ball

positions are filled by different players, depending on who is closest.

There are two basic spiker coverage formations, the 3–2 and the 2–3 (Figure 6–54). In my experience, I have found the 2–3 method to be more effective, and I will limit the following discussion to this method. (Notice that in both formations, the positioning of the coverage creates two arcs, two semicircles of protection around and behind the spiker.)

Figure 6–55 illustrates the desired spiker-coverage formations around left front, center front, or right front players. A team should always attempt to fill these formations, letting whichever player is closest occupy the position.

To cover an outside attacker, the two players closest to the spiker should face the block. The distance of the front two players from the spiker depends on the closeness of the set to the net. The remaining three players should also face the block. They are positioned behind the two outside-coverage players.

Sets that are quick or low are usually deflected at a sharp angle straight down, so spiker coverage for these sets should be tight. Tight sets against tall blockers are also frequently blocked straight down. Since short blockers tend to deflect the ball toward the deeper part of the court, the spiker-coverage formation in this situation should be deeper.

During spiker coverage, all players should keep eye contact with the ball, also observing the arm swing of the spiker and the hand position of the blockers. This will improve their anticipation and timing in response to the deflected ball. As the spiker starts her arm swing, all players must lean forward and assume a fairly low body posture. Each player must have a clearly assigned area of responsibility and a well-defined direction to move in, as illustrated in Figure 6–55. Most of the ball recovery in spiker coverage is a reflex action. Players must be trained to react spontaneously within their areas of responsibility.

Figure 6–56 illustrates spiker-coverage formations during serve-reception attack for a variety of attack patterns. Notice how C2 and S alternate positions (c, k) and how S and U alternate positions (c, s). Since the pass or the dig does not come to the target, the setter may not always have the time to be one of the two players in the tight-coverage arc when the attack is made from the weak side. In such a case, other players must compensate (n, p).

The last column in Figure 6–56 illustrates the movement of the players to their specialized defensive positions after spiker coverage. Occasionally, the switch can be done immediately after the pass. For example, in the first rotation, if C1 passes the ball directly behind C2, the roles in the spiker coverage of C1 and A2 can be switched immediately. After transition attack, the players are already in their specialized defensive positions and therefore do not need to switch after spiker coverage.

7

THE BLOCK

The block is a team's first line of defense. Blocking is a very explosive, dramatic maneuver that serves several functions. The primary function of the block is to intercept an attacked ball, either returning it to the opponent's court for a point or side-out (called a "kill" block) or deflecting the ball upward and back to the court defense (called a "soft" block).

Another important function of the block is to screen certain areas of the court, influencing the direction of the opponent's attack and thus reducing the court area the floor defense must cover. Without the screening the block provides, the floor defense can only guess where the attack will be aimed and will have far less success digging the ball. A consistently effective block can also be a formidable intimidation factor; if blocked repeatedly, some hitters lose confidence and become prone to making errors.

Only front-line players are permitted to block. One, two, or three players jumping together or independently constitutes a block. Players may reach over the net as far as possible but they may not touch the net and they may not contact the ball be-

fore completion of the opponent's attack.

After the 1976 Olympics, the rules concerning blocking were changed. Since then, teams have been allowed to contact the ball three times in addition to touching it while blocking. Therefore, the ball may contact the hands of one or more blockers, and the team still has three contacts remaining to execute its transition offense. Also, a front-row player can make two consecutive contacts with the ball as long as the first contact was part of the block. These changes have added greatly to the game, producing longer rallies and more effective transition attacks.

Blocking is probably the most difficult team skill. Against a quick, well-coordinated multiple attack, the maximum response time for a block is .14 of a second, less than for any other skill in volleyball. Although more points are scored by transition attack than by blocking, without an effective block a team will not be able to dig the ball and counterattack for a point. Blocking demands quick reactions and excellent coordination among players.

It is difficult to assess the qualities that make a good blocker; technique and physical ability alone do not suffice. A player could be an excellent spiker with a good jump, and yet be a weak blocker. Being a strong blocker requires a good sense of timing, the ability to anticipate and pay attention to detail, a tough, resilient spirit, and an innate feel for the game acquired with experience. Obviously, height is also an asset.

Blocking tactics are as important as blocking technique. A good block has to adapt quickly to the opponent's attack, and since the opponent's attack may vary during a match, a team must be able to adjust its blocking tactics accordingly.

BASIC CONCEPTS OF BLOCKING

Here are some fundamental concepts to help acquaint the novice coach with the mechanics of organizing the team for blocking.

Blocker Specialization

Blocking positions should coincide with attacking positions. Generally, the ace players block on the left side, the center players or quick attackers block in the middle, and the utility player or the setter block on the right side. It is possible to switch these blocking assignments for tactical reasons if needed; this topic is discussed later in "Matching Blockers Against Particular Spikers."

One of the first things that blockers should do is observe the opponent's preparations for attack. This is done before the serve (if the blocking team is serving) or immediately after completion of the attack (if the blocking team is receiving serve). During this time it is very important that the blockers communicate with each other regarding the opponent's attack formation, specifically the number and deployment of front-row spikers.

If the opponent has a front-row setter with only two attackers, the blockers should point out the location and call out the numbers of the two spikers. They should also remind themselves and the back-court defense to be ready should the setter decide to tip or "dump" the pass.

If the opponent has three front-row spikers, their numbers should be called out. It is also very impor-

tant to observe whether the opponent is using a concealed-attacker formation for serve-reception attack. Once the opponent's potential front-row attackers have been identified, the blockers can decide upon their specific blocking strategy if it has not already been dictated by the coach.

It is important that in each rotation there be a leader, perhaps the center front or a more experienced player, who leads the block, directing fine adjustments during the game and making occasional eye contact with the coach to get instructions if needed.

In some situations, the players' positions in the rotational order correspond to their specialized front-line positions. But in most cases, the players must switch from their position in the rotation to their assigned blocking position. When their team is serving, blockers should switch as soon as the serve is contacted. Players must also switch after completing the serve-reception attack, but this can be more complicated. Sometimes there is not enough time to make the switch, or only enough time to make a partial switch.

For example, if a spike is deflected up in the air near the net, the spikers may be forced to remain in position and block an immediate attack by opposing front-line players. Another common situation is when a dug ball is passed high and with great velocity to a position near the net. If the attackers are too busy switching to their assigned blocking positions, they may not be ready to respond to a quick tip or attack by the opponent's front-row setter or front-row attackers.

A basic rule often used by coaches is: don't switch if the ball is in the opponent's front court (in front of their 10-foot line). Occasionally, a player may switch positions in stages, as time and the flow of the action permit. For instance, in a situation in which the ace player is at RF, the setter at CF, and the middle blocker at LF, the ace player might first switch with the setter, and then later in the play find time to complete the exchange by switching with the middle blocker. Making this type of two-stage switch is especially important if the setter is short and/or not a very effective center blocker. Of course, if time permits, the players should hurry to their assigned positions immediately. This puts them in position to carry out both their blocking and transition-attack responsibilities with maximum efficiency.

The suggested traffic lanes for switching, whether after attack or after a serve, are the same: the middle blocker always moves to his CF position in a lane closest to the net; the ace player moves to LF behind CF, and the setter or utility player moves to RF behind the left front (See Fig-

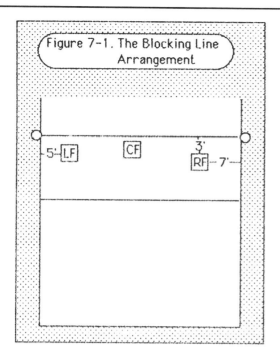

Figure 7-1. The Blocking Line Arrangement

5'—LF   CF   3'
                RF—7'—

In addition, standing off the net allows short blockers or poor jumpers to increase their jump by taking a short forward step. In conjunction with the short forward step, these blockers can use a more exaggerated arm motion to further increase their jump. It is important to understand that these positions off the net are only starting positions. As soon as they have determined the opponent's point of attack, LF and RF blockers must move up and jump close to the net so that the spiker can not drive the ball between the block and the net.

INDIVIDUAL BLOCKER'S TECHNIQUE

This is the basic technique of each individual blocker when blocking independently or together with teammates. The coordination of two or three blockers blocking together as a unit will be discussed later.

Ready Body Posture

This is the optimum posture allowing the blocker to respond quickly to every eventuality presented by the opponent's attack.

In the ready posture, the blocker faces the opponent and studies the developing attack.

ure 6–52). While switching, blockers must keep eye contact with the opponent's spikers and the ball.

The Line Arrangement

The three front-line players may assume one of the two basic blocking arrangements: the line arrangement or the stacked arrangement. The stacked arrangement is less frequent and will be discussed later.

In the basic line arrangement (Figure 7–1), RF should stand about 1m (3') off the net and about 2.13m (7') from the right sideline; LF should stand about 70cm (2') off the net and about 1.5m (5') from the left sideline; the center player should stand evenly spaced from both blockers and about 50cm (20") from the net. There are several reasons why LF and RF (particularly RF) should stand off the net:

• to widen the field of vision. Usually, each blocker is assigned to watch a particular spiker. Being slightly off the net allows the blocker to watch both the setter and his assigned spiker at the same time.
• to allow the outside blockers to retreat to their defensive court positions more quickly. (This is especially true for RF.) If the opponent attacks with quick backsets, japs, or shoot-ins, the LF and RF players may have to abandon any participation in the block and concentrate on digging at their assigned defensive positions.
• to allow more room for the middle blocker to adjust laterally.

In the ready posture, the blocker faces the opponent and watches the attack as it develops. His feet are positioned side-by-side and perpendicular to the net, shoulder-width apart, with the toes pointed very slightly inward. The arms may be held, according to individual preference, in one of two ways: with the hands slightly above shoulder height, forearms perpendicular to the floor and palms facing the net; or with the hands at about waist height and forearms parallel to the floor. Although the first method, with the hands at shoulder height, is more popular, I have found that the quicker blockers often use the second. Keeping the arms down at waist height facilitates faster lateral adjustments and a more explosive jump from a stationary position.

In the ready posture, the blocker's back should be straight, the knees slightly bent, and the feet placed flat on the floor. His body weight should be over the base of support, or just slightly forward. The legs should be bent at the ankles about 50 to 60 degrees so that the knees are brought just forward of the toes and the butt is just forward of the heels. Bending the ankles lowers the body weight further down without any additional bending of the knees, thus preventing undue strain on the knees, yet still enabling the blocker to jump or make lateral adjustment very quickly.

Takeoff and Jump

Occasionally a blocker has to jump from a standstill directly from the ready position. At other times the blocker jumps immediately following a lateral adjustment. The foot work for lateral or forward adjustments, and the takeoff following such adjustments, are discussed in the following section.

To jump from the ready posture, the blocker should first lower his body weight, press his arms down, bend his knees to about a 90-degree angle, and bend at the hips. During these compression movements, the blocker should keep his back straight and his eyes on the ball. He then jumps vertically, exploding for maximum altitude. As the blocker rises, his arms straighten at an angle toward the top of the net. Short blockers may incorporate a small hop into their takeoff in an effort to generate a higher jump.

In certain situations, the blocker will have no time to bend his knees beyond the angle at which they are already bent in the ready posture. In these situations, the blocker should push off with as much thrust as he can, using the quadricep muscles in his thighs and his calf muscles, as well as a swift upward arm motion.

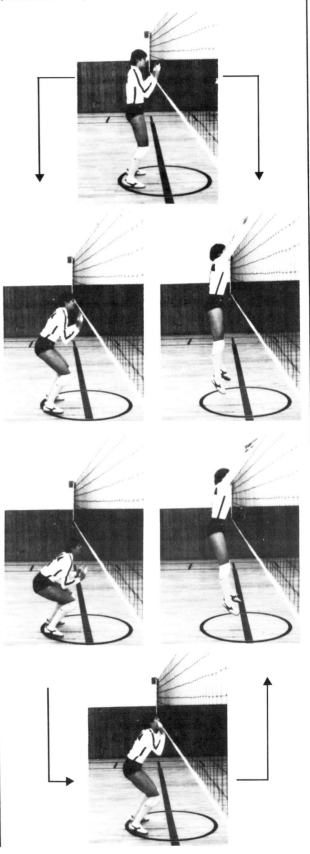

The blocker should be able to jump up directly from the ready blocking body posture. Given enough time, the blocker should bend forward, bending his knees also, and then jump up, shooting his arms forward and upward to penetrate over the top of the net.

Arm and Hand Position

Upon takeoff, the arms should immediately shoot forward and upward at an angle to penetrate over the top of the net. The arms should *not* be extended vertically up over the head and then brought forward with a downward motion. This technique may result in net violations as well as mistimed and ineffective blocks. The arms should be kept straight and parallel to each other with the distance between the arms being less than the width of the ball (8″). This is achieved by shrugging the shoulders inward. The fingers should be spread with the thumbs pointing toward each other and the palms slightly cupped and firm; the distance between the thumbs should be about 2 to 3 inches.

The farther the player is, laterally, from the ball, the more spread apart his hands can be. The blocker nearest the ball should keep his hands and forearms close together, so that the ball can not penetrate between his hands or wedge through between his arms. Players who do not possess great hand strength should keep their hands together, or even have the thumbs slightly overlapped. If the thumbs are overlapped, then the thumb of the outside hand should be over the thumb of the inside hand.

The wrists should be held stiff, ready to repel the ball. The degree to which the wrists are flexed depends upon the particular block. For a kill block, the wrists should be flexed slightly down; for a soft block, the wrists might be flexed slightly back with somewhat less tension in the palm.

Because of the greater jumping ability and "hang time" of both male hitters and blockers, men block slightly differently than women. Male blockers should not fully extend their arms immediately after takeoff. Instead, they should keep the arms

The fingers should be spread with the thumbs pointing toward each other and the palms slightly cupped and firm. Players who do not possess great hand strength can overlap their thumbs slightly.

The arms should be kept straight and parallel to each other, less than a ball's width apart. This is accomplished by shrugging the shoulders inward.

bent slightly at the elbow and make a lateral adjustment (sometimes called a "sweep"), closing the block in the direction of the ball and the spiker's intention. Then they can straighten their arms to complete the block.

Because they will probably be contacting the ball closer to net height than men do, female blockers should extend their arms to the ball immediately after takeoff.

Timing of Takeoff

Generally, against a first-tempo attack, unless dictated by different blocking strategy, the blocker should jump with the spiker. If the sets are close to the net (like an 11 set), the blocker should attempt to "roof" the ball. On higher balls, second or third tempo, the blocker should jump after the spiker just before the spiker reaches the apex of his jump. If the spiker is farther back from the net, then the blocker must delay his jump even more. A blocker should jump later (against a spiker with a slow arm swing) than against one with a quick arm swing. A short blocker (or a blocker with poor jumping ability) should jump later against a tall spiker, or against a spiker with very good jumping ability who is hitting from a high point.

The blocker should not jump too soon and become a target for the spiker. Not only can the spiker see the block and hit past it, but he also can use it to his own advantage by purposely hitting the ball out of bounds by deflecting it off the blocker's arms. The timing of the block should be such that the ball is intercepted while the block is on its way up, just before or at the peak of the block jump. Contacting the ball as the block descends is less desirable, because the block unfolds and loses some control on the way down. In addition, contacting the ball on the way up deflects the ball down in a sharper angle and with a greater speed than a stationary block would.

Penetration Over the Net

The blocker should attempt to reach over the net and place his hands as close as possible to the ball. The closer the hands are to the ball, the more court area is screened away from the spiker by the blocker (Figure 7–2). This helps the floor defense tremendously in reading and anticipating the spiker's intention.

The amount of penetration by the blocker is determined by two factors: the physical ability of the blocker to penetrate, and the blocking situation. Men usually penetrate more than women because they jump higher and can get their arms farther over the net. Women should attempt to get their

A combined block reaches over the net in an attempt to roof a quick attack by the Soviet team.

elbows over the net, making sure that the arms are placed as close to the top of the net as possible so that contact with the ball is made on the other side of the net.

When the ball is low and close to the net, the blocker should attempt to place his hands on top of the ball and roof it. When the ball is farther away from the net, the blocker should make a careful judgment. He should attempt to place his hands as close to the ball as possible, but without lowering the height of the block too much. The greater the penetration over the net, the lower the height of the block becomes. In these situations, the hands of the blocker should be positioned underneath the ball at an angle so that if the ball is hit downward, it will hit the heel of the hands.

Body Posture in the Air

At the apex of his jump and just before contact with the ball, the blocker should firm up his stom-

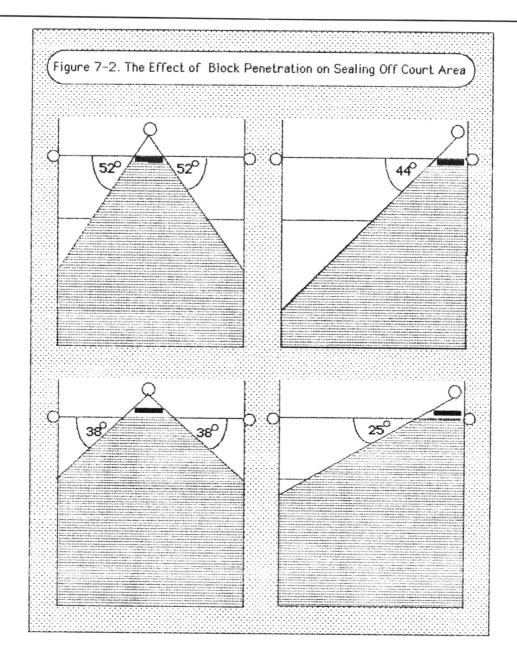

Figure 7-2. The Effect of Block Penetration on Sealing Off Court Area

Contact with the Ball

ach and shoulder muscles. This action unifies the whole body, providing a greater body mass to resist the impact of the spiked ball. The head should be brought down closer to the arms, or placed between the arms with the chin down; placing the head between the arms allows for a greater arm penetration over the net. Eye contact with the ball must be maintained at all times.

The legs should be kept straight at the knees. Bending the knees forward lowers the butt and the shoulders and thus limits the blocker's reach. The greater the arm penetration over the net, the greater the body's spike posture. This is a natural situation in which the legs move forward to counteract the forward lean of the upper body.

The hands should be placed in the proper position and held there, frozen. If the hands are placed correctly, the ball will deflect off them at the desired angle. There is usually no need to use any wrist action against the ball, unless it is hit very slowly. Occasionally, crafty hitters will attempt to hit a soft shot over the block as it comes down. Blockers should be taught to retain body control and at the same time flick such a ball down with a quick but controlled wrist action.

Blockers should not push against the ball with any arm movement; pushing toward the ball often results in net violations. Blocking is a controlled

The greater the arm penetration over the net, the more the body pikes. Thus, the blocker should bring his legs forward to increase his reach.

action in which the blockers attempt to present a barrier that walls off a portion of the court from the opposing spiker. Blockers must learn to simply put their hands up against the direction of the spiked ball and hold them there.

Landing

When a blocker starts descending, he must pull his arms back to avoid touching the net.

The landing should be done softly on the toes, cushioning the impact by bending the knees. If he is completely off balance, the blocker might cushion his fall by dropping all the way down to the floor. If the blocker jumped high, he should land on both feet even when a movement for a successive block is required. Trying to cushion a high jump by landing on only one leg takes too long, and the recovery is often difficult.

Sometimes blockers do not have to jump very high; particularly middle blockers, and sometimes left front ace players who are concerned with relatively low but quick first-tempo sets. If the blocker jumped low with the quick attacker and the setter delivered the ball to another spiker, the blocker may find it advantageous to land on one leg. In this situation, the blocker is trying to recover and get outside fast enough to cooperate with a teammate on a multiple block. By landing on only one leg (the one opposite the direction he must move in) the blocker gains valuable time and can push off as soon as he makes contact with the floor.

During the descent the blocker must turn his head back toward his side of the court to regain eye contact with the ball (unless, of course, it was deflected back into the opponent's court). Immediately upon landing, the blocker should assume the ready position for his next movement as dictated by the situation.

Movement to the Ball

More often than not, the blocker has to make a lateral adjustment, moving to the blocking point. Side-shuffle (sidestepping) movements and running are both used for lateral adjustment. For short distances (6 feet or less), one or two shuffle steps on the toes should be used. The player moves parallel to the net, facing the opponent throughout the movement. Then the blocker either makes a step-close, or a short hop with both feet, into the block point for takeoff. (The hop can help short blockers

to jump a bit higher.) Outside blockers, unless off the net, almost always use the side-shuffle step.

For longer distance the blocker should simply turn, run, and execute a takeoff similar to what a spiker does. This technique is almost always used by center front blockers who must travel more than 10 feet to close a multiple block with a teammate. CF should start his movement to the right with the right foot and to the left with the left foot. The run should always start with a very short step followed by progressively longer steps. At the end of the run the blocker should use a short low hop, or a step-close, to get to the blocking point.

Because the distance that CF blockers must cover varies constantly, it is difficult to always take off into the hop with a preferred foot; therefore, CF blockers should be able to lead into the hop with either foot. In effect, this means that CF blockers must be able to use footwork patterns similar to both right- and left-handed spiking approaches. Personally, I feel that alternating feet at takeoff is preferred over maintaining consistent footwork, which often requires longer running steps and a longer hop. If the CF blocker always takes off toward the right side with a left-right takeoff foot sequence, then he must start his movement to the right with a crossover step (left foot crossing over the right foot). Similarly, a movement to the left should start with the left foot, immediately followed by a hop into a right-left takeoff sequence. In either case, the length of the

Usually the hands should be held still in the proper position. However, quick and well-controlled wrist action can be used to deflect slow balls.

Blockers should regain eye contact with the ball as soon as possible. Because turning the head turns the whole body, blockers should usually attempt to land with their shoulders at an angle to the net rather than parallel to it.

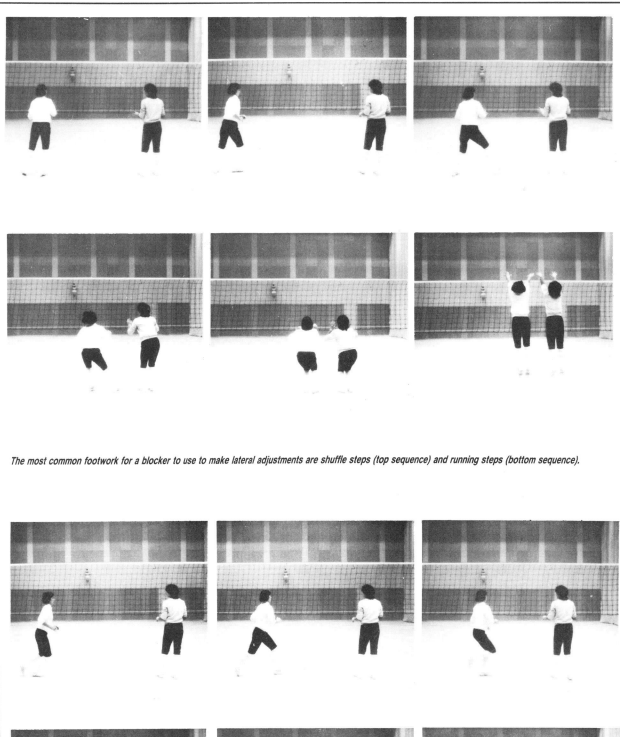

The most common footwork for a blocker to use to make lateral adjustments are shuffle steps (top sequence) and running steps (bottom sequence).

steps and the hop needs to be adjusted to the distance the blocker must travel.

During the hop (or step-close) the blocker should use an arm swing similar to that used by spikers, but in an abbreviated form to avoid net violations. At the end of the hop, the lead foot is placed on the floor with the heel first and then the toes. The trailing foot comes down and is placed flat on the floor. The toes of both feet should point in the direction of the spiker. Thus, after the CF blocker moves to the right, he should be positioned at takeoff with his left foot and left shoulder slightly closer to the net; after moving to the left, his right foot and right shoulder should be closer to the net. *After* taking off, the blocker rotates slightly to square off with the net. Squaring off is very important because if the blocker faces the spiker, he can easily deflect the ball out of bounds. But squaring off with the net at the block point does consume valuable extra time. Squaring off *after* takeoff accomplishes the same goal but with no wasted time. Against simple, slow attacks, blockers have the luxury of squaring off at the block point.

At times the RF blocker may need a straight forward blocking approach to the net. To move toward the net, the RF blocker can use a step-close or a hop. In either case, the right foot should lead. If a hop is used, then it must be short and low, and both feet should contact the floor simultaneously.

Biomechanical measurements have shown that for short distances, shuffle steps prove to be quicker by about 5 percent than turning and running. For long distances, running steps are quicker, and the average jump following running steps is 4.6cm (1¾″) higher than that following shuffle steps.

For optimum timing and positioning, the movement of the blocker should not be faster than the movement of the ball; this allows for better eye

Foot positions of RF (left) and CF (right) at takeoff for blocking the opponent's 51 attack.

contact with the ball and the spiker. The faster a blocker moves, the less he can see. Obviously, when the blocker can anticipate the direction of the set and the point of attack, he should shift into position ahead of the set.

Eye Contact

The following description is very general and may differ for different blocking strategies (as explained later in this chapter).

In the ready position, the blocker should look directly into the eyes of his assigned spiker, searching for cues and attempting to intimidate the spiker. Next, the blocker should focus on the pass, still watching the movement of his spiker in his peripheral vision. Then the blocker should concentrate on the setter and look for cues that may reveal his intention. Once the ball is released from the setter's hands and its direction is known, the blockers should converge on the blocking point. While moving, the CF blocker should first make brief eye contact with his teammate blocker, and then immediately regain eye contact with the ball. As the ball nears the spiker, the blocker should see both the arm swing of the spiker and the ball. When the ball is released by the setter, the RF and LF blockers should focus their attention on their respective spikers. Each blocker must keep his eyes open during blocking and maintain continuous eye contact with the ball after the block.

Anticipating the Setter

Sometimes the particular relationship between the ball and the setter exposes the setter's intention and allows the blocker to anticipate the direction and tempo of the set. When playing against experienced setters artful in disguising their intentions it is more difficult to anticipate. The following is a list of some hints that may help the blocker predict the setter's intentions:

1. When the setter sets balls off the net from a low body posture, he will usually set high and outside.
2. When a setter contacts the ball in front of his body, he will usually set forward.
3. When the ball is very tight and above the top of the net, the setter usually makes a quick one-hand set.
4. When a setter saves a ball that bounced off the net, he will usually deliver a high set in the direction he is facing.
5. When a setter arches back with the ball behind his head, he will usually backset.
6. During the flight of the pass the setter normally

The better blockers manage to keep their eyes open during the blocking action.

makes eye contact with the spiker he wants to set.

7. Some setters consistently set short balls when jump-setting, and others consistently set long balls when jump-setting.

8. A setter who is close to the net and assumes a low body posture will often set to a concealed attacker approaching for a second-tempo set.

9. A setter moving away from the net to accept a low ball will usually set forward.

10. A setter running forward along the net will usually set for quick attack either directly in front or behind him.

11. When backing up along the net, a setter will set quickly behind his back or immediately in front of him, or else high to the opposite side. In these cases, it is advisable for the blocking formation to adjust right or left, moving together with the setter.

Cues for Reading the Spiker

In high-level volleyball it is difficult to anticipate and read a spiker's intention. Spikers are so versatile and experienced that they do not reveal their intention until the very last instant, just prior to ball contact. Nevertheless, the following hints may help to anticipate the spiker's intentions:

1. If the spiker is not properly aligned with the ball, he may have only one direction available for a power hit. If the ball is in front of and outside the spiker's hitting shoulder, his power hit will be crosscourt (See Figure 6–13); this is particularly true for a right-handed player spiking from the right side, and for a left-handed player spiking from the left side. If the ball is past the midline of the spiker's body, closer to his nonhitting shoulder, he will hit across his body.

2. An inexperienced spiker will hit down the line off a straight approach; following an angle approach he will most often hit crosscourt. Such spikers tend to hit in the direction of the line of body momentum in the approach.

3. Low and quick outside sets are almost always hit crosscourt by inexperienced players. More advanced players hit them straight down.

4. Balls off the net are more often hit crosscourt than down the line.

5. When the spiker jumps under the ball or has poor takeoff technique, expect a tip or a ball hit off the block.

6. At times, before the spiker starts his approach, he may reveal his intention by making eye contact with his target.

7. A beginning spiker given a poor set should not be blocked at all. In beginning volleyball, a team should learn to be very selective about when and when not to block. At lower levels it is quite often best not to block at all.

The Kill- and the Soft-Block Techniques

There are two basic blocking techniques, the *kill block* and the *soft block*. In principle, good blockers should always attempt to kill block whenever possible.

The kill block, sometimes called an "attack" block, is a more aggressive blocking technique in which the blocker intercepts the ball before it crosses the net, deflecting it down into the opponent's court for a point or side-out. It is accomplished by reaching over the net and placing the hands as close as possible to the ball. At times, in particular for low sets and balls tight to the net, the blocker may be able to place his hands close to the top of the ball and roof it.

The soft block is a more passive block used when the spiker has a reach advantage over the blocker, and when the blocker is late or delaying his jump on purpose. In executing a soft block, the palms should either be parallel to the net, or flexed slightly backward with the wrists loose. The soft block has three purposes: to shelter part of the court against a sharply angled down attack; to touch the ball and slow its speed; and to deflect the ball back to the blocker's teammates.

When a blocker is too late getting to the block point (often the case with the center blocker), instead of attempting to penetrate for a kill block, he should flex his wrists back slightly and attempt to deflect the ball back to his teammates. If a blocker is late and still attempts to penetrate, he will often end up deflecting the spike downward between his own body and the net.

At times a blocker might delay his jump on purpose, either because he has a reach disadvantage against the spiker, or because he wants to see the release of the ball by the setter first and then jump. This is called "see-and-respond" blocking, and is discussed later in this chapter. In either of these situations, the player should execute a soft block.

Special consideration should be given to soft blocking in organizing the floor defense. Because the blockers do not jump as high for a soft block as for a kill block, they descend and make contact with the floor sooner, allowing them to share responsibility for recovering balls tipped softly over and around the block. This, in turn, allows the floor defense to assume a wider and deeper formation. Such tactics are useful when playing against a team with a fast and powerful attack.

DOUBLE BLOCK

A team usually attempts to create a double block with two players covering one spiker. A dou-ble block can be formed at any given net zone. When the attack comes on either the right or left side, the middle blocker joins one of the outside blockers. In these situations, the outside blocker is responsible for determining the position of the block, and the middle blocker is responsible for closing up to form a solid two-player block. If the block is formed in the center court, the roles are reversed. During fast-paced rallies, the center blocker is sometimes delayed. In these cases, the

When the CF blocker gets to the block point too late, he should attempt to soft block rather than to kill block. Short players should most often use soft blocking tactics.

outside blocker closest to the attack should try to block the best-shot angle of the opposing spiker. In all double-blocking situations, both blockers should jump straight up, with no drifting movement sideways.

Hand Positions

Ideally, the hands should be lined up so that the hit ball approaches the seam of both pairs of hands. This gives the maximum protection against the spiker's attack. The specific positioning of the hands varies according to the location of the block (Figure 7–3). The distance between the inside hands of the blockers should be less than the diameter of the ball (8″).

When the block is positioned on the right side of the court, the outside hand of the RF blocker should be turned inside and penetrate a bit more than the left hand to prevent wipe-offs. The left hand of the right blocker should also be turned in slightly, but not as much as the right hand. Both hands of the center blocker should be parallel to the net, with the left hand slightly lower than the right, to help intercept balls "cut" at a crosscourt angle by the attacker.

Teams at more advanced levels of competition generally have players of reasonably equal size and jumping ability. Even the smaller players on

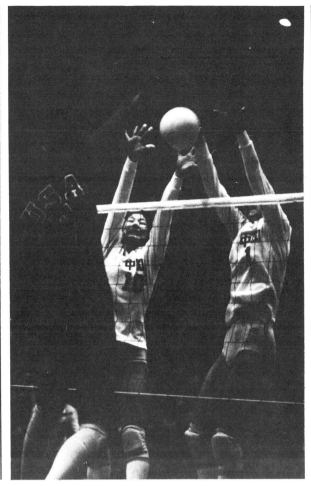

The ball should be lined up against the seam of the two pairs of hands. The outside hand (for RF or LF) should be turned inside and penetrate slightly more than the inside hand. Both hands of the CF blocker (#10) should be placed parallel to the net.

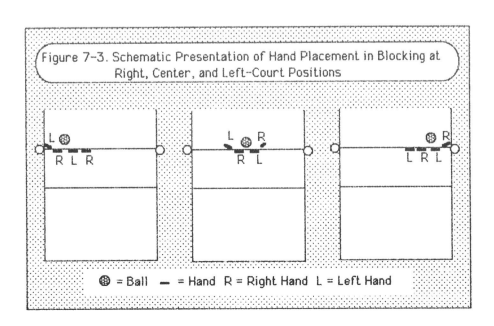

Figure 7–3. Schematic Presentation of Hand Placement in Blocking at Right, Center, and Left-Court Positions

⊕ = Ball — = Hand R = Right Hand L = Left Hand

Sue Woodstra (RF) and Laurie Flachmeier (CF) demonstrate movement from initial blocking positions to block a 52 set. Note Sue's initial body orientation and footwork to the takeoff position. Also note the arm swing of Laurie (CF) during the hop and takeoff.

these teams are capable of blocking effectively. For these teams it is desirable to have the hands of both blockers at the same height, even if it requires that one blocker make a jumping adjustment. The amount of penetration by both blockers should be about equal, with the outside blocker penetrating slightly more with his outside hand.

Uneven penetration by the two blockers can result in a hole in the block, especially if the middle blocker penetrates much more than the outside blocker. Having the blockers' hands at a uniform height is important because many balls are blocked as the result of a cooperative effort; the spiked ball may contact one hand of each blocker simultaneously, or the ball may be deflected twice, first from one blocker into the hands of the other blocker, and then back down into the opponent's court. If the blockers' hands are at different heights, the ball may be hit off only the higher pair of hands. These balls usually ricochet out of bounds or at extreme angles, making them difficult for the back-court players to retrieve.

At lower levels, such as high school, the outside blockers, particularly the setter at right front, are often much shorter than the middle blockers. In this case, it is usually better to sacrifice uniformity in blocking height in order to get maximum effectiveness from the middle blockers. If the outside blockers are weak and can barely reach over the top of the net, it would be foolish to open up most spikers' favorite shot (the crosscourt) by limiting the jump and penetration of the middle blocker. The best strategy is to play good defense behind the short blocker, and hope that the middle block-

ers will have more blocks than ricochets.

When blocking a ball on the left side of the court, the left outside blocker should turn his left hand in to prevent a wipe-off, and his right hand should be turned in slightly. Both hands of the center blocker should be parallel to the net, with the right hand slightly lower.

When blocking in the middle of the court, the outside hands of both blockers should be flexed down slightly at the wrist. Together with the hands of the CF player, they form a semicircle around the ball. The outside hands can penetrate slightly more than the inside hands. The seam of the block should be aligned against the ball.

Situational Blocking

It is very difficult to generalize about blocking because almost every situation requires different considerations and adaptations. The following are some examples of specific blocking situations and their solutions.

BLOCKING A 52 AND 53 ATTACK When blocking relatively high outside sets, the RF blocker should be at the block point before the spiker has jumped. The middle blocker should close in next to RF and both blockers should jump straight up together. RF should be aligned with the midline of a right-handed spiker's body. If the attacker is left-handed, RF should set the block point farther outside so that the seam of the block is aligned against the ball.

If the ball is set outside, near the antenna, the right hand of the outside blocker should be lined

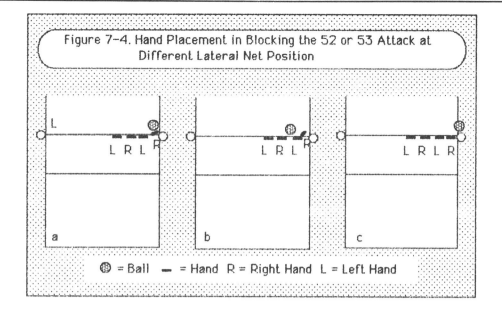

Figure 7–4. Hand Placement in Blocking the 52 or 53 Attack at Different Lateral Net Position

a   b   c

⊕ = Ball   — = Hand   R = Right Hand   L = Left Hand

up against the ball (Figure 7–4a). It is important to leave a gap the width of the ball between the outside hand and the antenna, with both hands parallel to the net. Setting up a ball's width from the antenna allows the blockers to cover the maximum area without taking a chance on blocking a ball that would otherwise hit the antenna. If the set is 1 or 2 feet inside, the blockers should align themselves in such a way that the ball is in the seam of the block (Figure 7–4b).

If the set is wide and slightly outside the antenna, the block should not penetrate. The hands should be placed parallel to the net at a distance from the antenna that would prevent the spiker from hitting into the side part of the right hand of the RF blocker (Figure 7–4c). Generally, the closer the set is to the net, the closer to the antenna the hands should be placed. Obviously, if the ball is very wide and outside the antenna, there is no need to block at all. The spiker will not be able to attack with much power and the floor defense should be able to take care of the situation. Dispensing with the block in this situation increases the preparation time for the transition attack.

If the set is very close to the net, the block should try to surround the ball. Under all circumstances, the blockers must seal off the spiker's hit down the line.

Normally, the block should jump a fraction of a second after the spiker has jumped; at the beginning of the spiker's arm swing. If the spiker outreaches the block, the blockers should use the soft-blocking technique and delay the jump as much as possible, hoping to intercept the ball on their way

To block a slow set, it is the responsibility of the outside blocker (#5) to set up the position of the block. The CF blocker (#12) is responsible for reaching into the seam of the block. Note the hand placement of the RF and CF blockers.

up. The amount of penetration should be minimal, or none at all. At times a short blocker confronting a tall spiker should consider keeping his arms slightly off the net while executing a soft block. Often this allows the blocker to contact the ball on its descent at a lower point and shelter a greater portion of the court. It takes advantage of the spiker's tendency to try to hit straight down over short blockers.

If the ball is more than 5 feet from the net, the block should delay its jump, waiting until the spiker is just about to contact the ball. Basically, the farther the set is from the net, the later the block should jump. If the set is off the net 5 feet or more, the block should screen off the crosscourt shot and let balls hit down the line for the floor defense.

BLOCKING A C2 ATTACK The principles involved in blocking the 52 and 53 attacks also apply to the C2 attack. However, the block should be aware that a right-handed spiker attacking a C2 presents a situation similar to that of a left-handed spiker attacking a 52; thus, the block must be positioned a bit wider to take away the line shot. Because the set travels a shorter distance, LF must move to the block point very quickly. If LF hesi-

To block a quick attack, both blockers should assume responsibility for the seam of the block and reach into it.

Often the blocker must reach toward the outside of the court. In these situations it is critical that the hands be kept parallel to the net.

tates or does not determine the block point promptly, the middle blocker will be delayed and may not have enough time to close up and seal the block.

BLOCKING A 51 ATTACK A 51 is a very fast set that requires a quick-adjustment movement to the outside by both blockers. Usually they have only 1.0 second, or less, to react and execute the block. RF should use one or two shuffle steps; if he has been drawn in close to the center of the court, he may need to turn and run, leading with the right foot. The center blocker should start his run by placing the right foot off the net and behind the RF, then running in a slight curve to avoid being slowed down by RF. RF has to move to position as quickly as possible to avoid being in the way of the moving middle blocker.

Quite often, the middle blocker will not have enough time to get close to the outside blocker. In this case, the blockers will have to jump while farther apart and reach toward each other into the seam. This is sometimes called "sweeping" into the hole or seam, a responsibility of both blockers. The outside blocker will reach into the seam using a slight rotation at the hips. His right hand should be on the side of the ball and penetrate a bit more

In general, the block should screen off the crosscourt angle shot against a quick 51 or C1 set, whether the sets are tight or deep.

The Chinese team attempts to block Flo Hyman's 31 attack. Both blockers reach into the seam with their bodies far apart.

Often the RF (#9) or the CF (#1) have no choice but to reach with only one hand to stop a 31 or a 41 attack.

than the left hand. The center player reaches sideways into the seam with both hands parallel to the net and tilted downward slightly. If the center front is so late that he can not reach into the seam with two hands, he should reach with one hand. Seen from the spiker's perspective, the inside contours of both players reaching sideways toward each other should form an oval shape. If the hands are positioned properly, the ball will deflect toward the center of the court.

When both CF and RF have to make a long lateral adjustment outside to block a quick set, both may need to reach toward the outside, keeping their palms parallel to the net. In general, the block should screen off the crosscourt angle against a low, fast 51 set, whether it is tight or off the net. The block should jump with the spiker when he is close to the net, and slightly after when he is farther away.

BLOCKING THE C1 ATTACK The same blocking technique for the 51 is used to block the C1, only reversed.

BLOCKING THE 31 ATTACK When blocking a 31, RF may need to make one step to the left. The center blocker will need to use a side step and a short hop with both feet to the right. Usually there

Y. Mitsuya (#6; 1984 Japan Olympic team) jumps with the spiker in an attempt to roof a quick 31 attack by the Korean team.

will not be enough time for CF to get his body next to the outside blocker so both blockers must reach into the seam.

Often the 31 will develop so quickly that CF will have only enough time for one side step and a jump. In this case he can reach into the seam with one hand to form a three-hand block with RF. When both CF and RF are delayed, each can reach toward the seam with one hand. Of course, if the other team was successful in occupying CF with another spiker, RF may have to confront the 31 in a one-on-one situation.

When playing against a team that uses the 5–1

composition, a coach can make it easier for his blockers to block the 31 by making lateral adjustments along the net. When the other team has only front-row spikers and both are shifted to the left, the opposing blockers may make a corresponding adjustment to their right. This accomplishes two things: it cuts down the distance between CF and his outside blockers, thus reducing the time needed to create a double block; and it often enables LF to take primary responsibility for blocking quick sets in the zones closest to the setter (11 and A1). This, in turn, allows CF to move toward the right side, into the second or third zones.

Naturally, if the opponent's CF spiker moves to attack in the zones behind the setter (B and C), LF must recognize this and adjust back to his left. In addition, overloading the blockers to the right side can be risky if the opponent has a formidable back-row attack at right side.

If the 31 set is close to the net and if the block is on time, the blockers roof the ball. If the set is off the net, the block should screen the angle shot.

BLOCKING 11, A1, AND 31 ATTACK When the opponent runs a quick multiple attack, blocking these fast sets depends on the team's overall blocking strategy. If the blocking tactics emphasize committing with the first-tempo attack, then the blocker must jump with the spiker, penetrate, raise his hands as close as possible to the ball, and attempt to roof it.

However, if the blocking strategy uses see-and-respond tactics and is geared to blocking the second-tempo sets (especially the concealed attackers), the blockers should jump after they have seen the set released. In this case, blockers confronting first-tempo quick sets should use the soft blocking technique, hoping that the spiker will hit downward into the block and the ball can then be deflected back into the blocker's side. The blockers should make educated adjustments for the above situations, based on pregame scouting information, and on individual tendencies of both the setter and the spikers as observed during the game. The blockers may learn that an individual spiker in a particular situation has a preferred shot; it could be down the line, crosscourt, crossbody, whatever. The block should make the proper adjustments to take away this favorite shot.

TRIPLE BLOCK

In principle, men should use a three-player block as often as possible, while women should use it only as a surprise strategy. A triple block forces the floor defense to cover a much larger area; instead of two blockers and four defenders, the ratio is now three blockers and only three defenders to cover tips, off-speed shots, deflections off the block, and hard-driven spikes. The triple block is more difficult for women because they don't penetrate as much as men and thus leave more of the back court exposed.

Whenever an opposing spiker is capable of consistently hitting the ball over the block, the triple-block strategy should be discarded. Also, the triple block should be used cautiously when the setter of a 5-1 team composition is in the back row. In this situation, the opponent may purposely direct his attack toward the setter, even resorting to tips or off-speed shots in order to take the setter out of the transition attack, forcing the utility player or another player to set, probably high outside.

A triple block can be formed at any given point along the net. If time permits, the actual mechanics of assembling three blockers is simple. Blocks using three players have to be very well coordinated with the floor defense. Otherwise, obvious openings are created behind the block for the opponent to attack. A consistent triple block strategy should be complemented by a floor defense applying the principles of a box defense. (See Chapter 8, "The Box Defense.")

The distance between players is about 1 foot, the same as for a two-player block. When the block is on the outside, either right or left, the three blockers should attempt to surround the ball, with the outermost player turning his hands inside toward the ball and penetrating slightly more. This reduces the likelihood that the spiker can wipe off the block and helps deflect the ball back into the court. The inside blocker closest to the center of the court should keep his hands turned only slightly toward the ball and pointing downward. The middle blocker should keep his hands parallel to the net. When the block is in the middle, the outside players should turn their hands toward the ball and slightly downward; the center player should keep his hands parallel to the net (Figure 7-5).

Against an opponent's serve-reception attack, a triple block is quite difficult to assemble and therefore uncommon. However, when the opponent's pass is poor, or when the opponent has only two front-line attackers both positioned on one side of the court, the triple block may become a useful part of the blocking strategy. Again, overshifting the blockers in this situation can backfire if the opponent can effectively attack from the back row. However, on transition attack, when the dig is off the net and the block can anticipate which hitter will receive the set, a triple block can be a useful

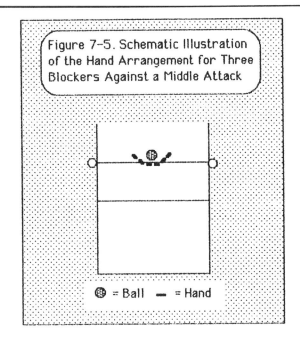

Figure 7-5. Schematic Illustration of the Hand Arrangement for Three Blockers Against a Middle Attack

🔵 = Ball   — = Hand

surprise weapon and a team should train for such opportunities.

The blocking team has to be careful not to ignore front-row setters who at times can be very effective by spiking or tipping. And the blockers must always be careful against teams that can attack from the back row. As a general rule, triple-block formations become exceedingly risky any time the opponent possesses the capacity to attack consistently from the back row.

*B*LOCKING STRATEGY

As the opponent's attack becomes more varied and sophisticated, blocking becomes more complex. A multiple attack imposes significant constraints on the block's reaction time, and the cross- and fake-cross formations present additional problems for clear communication among the blockers. Some of these problems may be resolved by a well-designed blocking strategy. Here is an explanation of some of the more complex and modern blocking strategies.

The two basic blocking arrangements are the *line arrangement* (Figure 7–1) and the *stacked arrangement* (Figure 7–10). Two blocking systems can be implemented from the line arrangement: the *zone-blocking system* and the *man-to-man blocking system*. The stacked arrangement lends itself to the man-to-man blocking system. In addition, two kinds of blocking tactics, *see-and-respond blocking* or *commit blocking* (Figure 7–6), can be applied in each of the blocking systems.

Zone-Blocking System

The zone-blocking system is the most widely used. It was initially designed to stop a straight parallel attack. It is ideally suited to block teams with a slow simple attack and teams that don't use sequential or X formations. However, with some minor adjustments and good coordination among the blockers, it can also be applied effectively against more complex attack formations.

After years of experimenting with the man-to-man system and all its possible tactical variations, I found the zone-blocking system to be the most effective for women, and possibly for men.

Blocker's Zone of Responsibility

In the zone-blocking system, the blockers are arranged along an almost straight line, and each blocker is responsible for protecting his particular zone. The right front player covers zone 2, which extends from the right sideline toward the middle of the court (Figure 7–7). The left front player covers zone 4, extending from the left sideline toward the middle of the court. The middle blocker covers zone 3, which overlaps the other two zones, extending almost from sideline to sideline.

This allocation of area responsibility does not prevent the three blockers from converging at any point along the net and forming a triple block.

In the area where zones 2 and 3 overlap, RF and CF combine to form a double block. Similarly, where zones 3 and 4 overlap, it is CF and LF. In the middle of the court, CF can block by himself, or all three blockers can come together, or a double block can be constructed by CF in combination with either RF or LF. A team can use any one of these possibilities, depending on its overall strategy and on the time available.

When time is very limited, usually CF will be forced to block by himself. When there is more time, as in the case of a high set in the middle, the three blockers might come together. However, the most common blocking strategy is to block with two blockers in the middle. The question is, which two? With a 6–2 team composition, the decision of who is going to help the middle depends on who is the better blocker, LF or RF. If these two blockers have equal ability, then it will depend on the nature of the opponent's attack. If the opponent uses a quick attack to their right side, and sets high to their left, then the right front and center front blockers should block the middle. Conversely, if the opponent uses quick sets to their left side and sets higher safety sets behind the setter, then LF should help CF block high sets in the middle.

For a 5–1 team composition, in the rotations where the setter is in the front line, the setter

The 1984 USA Olympic women's team used a triple block on the outsides as a surprise weapon. The USSR uses a triple block anticipating a 53 attack by the Japanese team. Note the timing of the individual blockers.

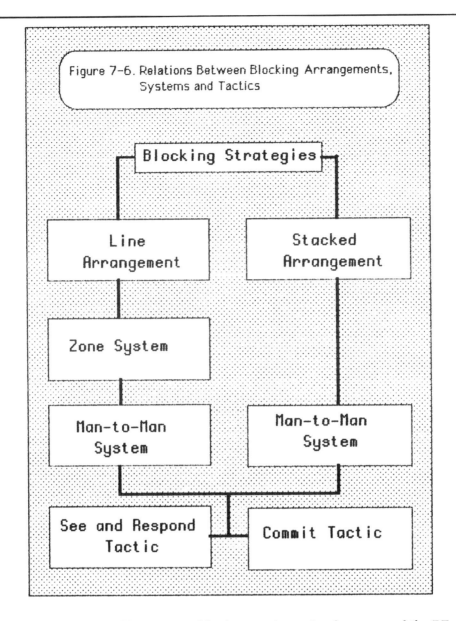

Figure 7-6. Relations Between Blocking Arrangements, Systems and Tactics

Blocking Strategies

Line Arrangement

Stacked Arrangement

Zone System

Man-to-Man System

Man-to-Man System

See and Respond Tactic

Commit Tactic

should help block in the middle if he is a capable blocker. When the setter is back row, LF and CF should block the middle. This will help protect the setter as much as possible from receiving the attack and keep him available to set for the transition attack. Keeping RF out of the middle when the setter is back row makes it easier for RF to set the transition attack if the setter is forced to dig the ball.

As long as the opponent runs a simple attack with relatively high sets, the blockers have no difficulty guarding their zones of responsibility. No matter where the opponent attacks, there will always be two blockers confronting one attacker. However, when the opponent implements even a basic quick attack, the blockers may find themselves unable to fulfill all of their zone responsibilities. For example, if the opponent executes a straight attack with their CF going for an 11 set, the

LF spiker going for a 51, and the RF spiker attacking for a C1, obviously each blocker must guard one attacker. The RF blocker guards the LF attacker, the CF blocker guards the CF spiker, and the LF blocker guards the RF attacker. Thus, if the CF blocker jumps with the quick middle spiker, then a set to either of the outside spikers will find the attacker guarded by only one blocker. Actually, a set to any of the attackers will create a one-on-one situation for the spiker, because the CF blocker who jumped against the middle hitter does not have time to land and then join the outside blocker. Although in a one-on-one situation the spiker will usually be successful, it is not the worst situation for the blocking team. More complex attack combinations, such as cross- and X plays, may free the attacker from the block altogether. To minimize the occurrence of such events, the USA women's team introduced the "see-and-respond"

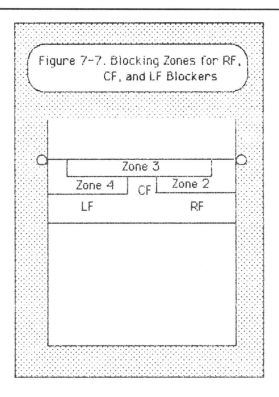

Figure 7-7. Blocking Zones for RF, CF, and LF Blockers

Zone 3

Zone 4   Zone 2

CF

LF   RF

In the commit blocking method, the blocker who stands in front of the quick attacker jumps as soon as the quick attacker does; the other blocker attempts to assist this blocker if the set is delivered to the quick attacker. Here the CF (#5) of China commits against Japan's quick attacker while the LF (#8) blocker attempts to assist in blocking the quick attack.

and the zone "commit" blocking tactics. These tactics were used interchangeably to match each different opponent's attack style, capabilities, and tendencies.

See-and-Respond Blocking Tactic

The principle of the see-and-respond blocking tactic is that the blockers don't move or jump until they have seen the release of the set. Regardless of what attack formation the opponent employs, the blockers don't make any major adjustments. Once the set is released, then the blockers respond quickly by jumping, or first moving laterally and then jumping. The object of see-and-respond blocking is to soft-block the quick attack and double-block the slower sets.

To maximize the success of this blocking tactic, the blockers should study the setter and look for cues. At the same time the blockers must observe the movements of the spikers in their peripheral vision. In response to the spikers' movements, the blockers can make small lateral adjustments to the right or left.

When a quick attacker jumps for a first-tempo set, the blocker who stands in front of him should raise his arms. If the spiker does get set, the blocker takes off into the jump. If the set goes in another direction, the blocker then moves in that direction. Sometimes very tall women blockers can simply get up on their toes when confronting a quick attacker. This extra height is sometimes sufficient to soft-block an opponent's quick attack if it is very low. To block the quick attack, the blockers should use the soft-blocking technique. They should also use the soft block whenever they are late against a second-tempo attack.

See-and-respond blocking tactics should be used against teams that mostly attack from the outside and/or teams implementing a slower type of quick attack in the middle. It should also be used by teams with a tall experienced CF blocker who has a good understanding of the opponent's attack system.

Commit Blocking Tactic

The main purpose of the commit blocking tactic is to stop an opponent's quick attacker by jumping with him before the set is released. The blocker who stands in front of the quick attacker jumps as soon as the quick attacker does, while the other two blockers attempt to assist this blocker if the set is delivered to this attacker. The following four methods help make this blocking tactic less vulnerable to sequential attack and X attacks in particular.

THE OPTION BLOCKING METHOD This system was designed by Jim Coleman and used by the USA men's team during 1979 and 1980 when Coleman was head coach. The following is an excerpt

USA vs. Japan, 1979. The USA team executes a see-and-respond blocking tactic in which all three blockers wait for the concealed player (#2). No blocker jumps with the quick attacker.

from Coleman's article "Option Blocking" (1983):*

In this form of option blocking, the blocking team commits a player to a specific potential quick set. The option blocking used by the USA men's team in 1979 and 1980 were as follows:

A. Option Four Blocking: The defensive left front blocker, position 4, is committed to jump with, to block, the opponent's quick middle attack (11 set). The reason for using this tactic is to defend against a probable X or crossing pattern. With middle hitter stopped by outside blocker, the middle blocker can concentrate on stopping the opponent's second attacker coming into the middle on the crossing pattern. If the play is run into offensive zone B2 or C2 (to the left of the committed blocker) the offense has won the tactical battle. At this point, the defense has two weak hopes. The committed blocker may be able to recover enough to make a blocking attempt. The best chance for defense is for court position five digger (down the line) to be prepared to dig the unblocked shot. For this reason, it is important that the diggers be knowledgeable about the blocking options being employed. . . .

B. Option Three Blocking: The center blocker, position 3, is committed to jump with, to block, the offensive quick hit (sets 11 to 31). For many years this has been the standard defense to stop middle attacks. The primary blocking will be one-on-one and the defense will be vulnerable to crossing patterns. In order to defend against the crossing patterns, the outside blockers may pinch toward the center blocker. With this strategy, the threat of crossing play has virtually assured offensive success to relatively quick outside sets (51 and C1). . . .

C. Option Two Blocking: In option two blocking, the front right blocker (position two) is committed to jump with, to block, the offensive 31 set. The reason for using this defense is to stop a probable 31 set, to defend a left-side X play, or to defend the left inside plays. This option leaves the defensive right side (position 2) vulnerable to quick outside attacks (51 sets). Considerations here are similar to those discussed in option 4 blocking.

The option method is recommended for teams that have carefully studied their opponent's tendencies, and should be used in conjunction with other blocking methods. This method is too complex for inexperienced teams to use.

THE SHIFTING METHOD The primary purpose of the shifting method is to create at least a one-on-one blocking situation on cross- and X-play attacks, while allowing each blocker to keep his own zone-blocking responsibility. This method relies on good communication between blockers.

*James Coleman, "Option Blocking," *The Journal of National Volleyball Coaches Association,* V. 4, No. 2, May 1983.

In the shifting method, each blocker is responsible for observing the movement of one opposing attacker. The LF blocker is responsible for the opponent's RF attacker, the CF blocker for the opponent's CF attacker, and the RF blocker for the opponent's LF spiker. When each of the attackers approaches the attack zones opposite their respective blockers, then there is no problem and the basic commit method can be employed. However, in a cross- or a fake-cross play, the assigned spiker may go to a different attack zone while at the same time another spiker might come into the blocker's zone. The blockers must have a reliable way of communicating among themselves or they may be fooled by the switching of the attackers and a spiker may end up without a blocker.

On the USA women's team, it was the responsibility of each blocker to call out when her assigned spiker moved out of the blocker's zone to somebody else's. The most important information to convey in calling out the opponent's attack is the movement of the concealed attacker. If the concealed spiker moved from left to right (seen from the blocker's point of view) the blocker would call out "cross." If the concealed spiker moved from right to left, the blocker would call out "tandem." If the spiker made only a fake movement, the same blocker who called either "cross" or "tandem" was responsible for immediately calling "no," indicating that the cross or the tandem was incomplete. Most of the time, this communication system was sufficient for the blockers to make adjustments within their zones for the new spiker. Figure 7–8 illustrates the sequence of adjustments made by blockers in response to an opponent's X play.

The shifting method can be applied easily and effectively to the see-and-respond zone-blocking tactic.

THE DOUBLE JUMP Even the best shifting method is not foolproof and at times can leave a spiker unguarded. A blocker in the shifting method who jumps against the quick attacker can use a double jump to further safeguard against this happening. The blocker's jump must be very low and done early, before the quick spiker jumps. If the ball is set to a different spiker, he still may have a chance of getting to the other blocker in time to assist. Because the blocker jumps a bit ahead of the quick attacker and does not jump very high, he should have a good chance to join his teammate in blocking an outside attack or in blocking the concealed spiker on an X play. In addition, the early jump by the blocker could influence the setter to alter his set selection, abandoning the quick attacker in favor of the concealed attacker or the

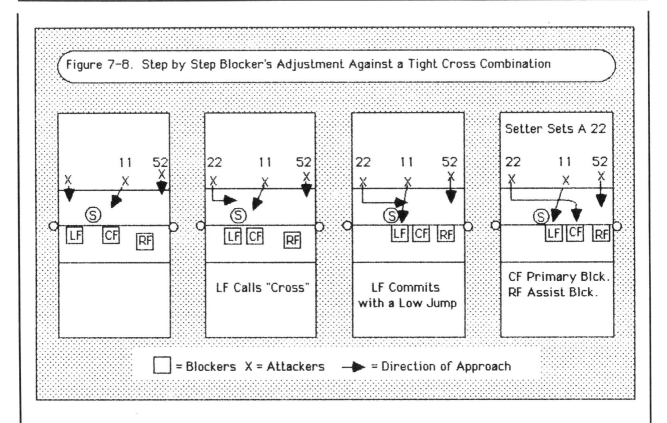

Figure 7-8. Step by Step Blocker's Adjustment Against a Tight Cross Combination

LF Calls "Cross"

LF Commits with a Low Jump

Setter Sets A 22

CF Primary Blck.
RF Assist Blck.

□ = Blockers   X = Attackers   ➔ = Direction of Approach

outside spiker. At times this can be tactically advantageous, especially when anticipated in advance with the other blockers and the floor defense specifically positioned to defend against the outside attacker or concealed spiker.

THE OVERLOAD METHOD As the name implies, the purpose of this method is to overload a particular blocking zone with two blockers guarding one spiker. This method is effective when playing against a team that employs a 5–1 team composition without a back-row attack. When the setter is front row with only two front-line attackers in a split serve-receive formation, then the blocking team may overload to either right or left (Figure 7–9). In these situations, two blockers are guarding one spiker while one blocker guards one spiker. If the opponent uses a shifted serve-reception formation with both hitters to the left or to the right, the blocking team can shift accordingly (Figure 7–9). These overload arrangements can also be employed when implementing the see-and-respond blocking tactics.

It is important that the adjustment of the blocking arrangement be done at the last possible instant, during the opponent's pass or dig, so as not to reveal the blocker's intention to the opposing setter.

Man-to-Man Blocking System

In the man-to-man blocking system, each blocker follows one spiker wherever he goes in an attempt to have at least one blocker on each spiker at all times and to get two blockers in position whenever possible. This means that frequently the blocker who jumps with a quick attacker has to hustle over into position to jump again as part of a multiple block. The man-to-man blocking system is very complex and should only be implemented at high-level volleyball. This system has recently been given a boost by the Russian, Brazilian, and USA men's teams.

The USA women's national team experimented with the system over the years but ultimately rejected it for several reasons. The floor-defense players had to continuously adjust to different blocking combinations. More often than not, the block ended up in a man-to-man blocking situation that placed an added burden on the court defense. I also found this system cumbersome for planning and organizing a smooth transition attack because the spikers frequently wound up out of their specialized positions. After each blocking situation, the spiker could end up in a different position, so even if the defense digs the ball accurately to the setter, the chances of a successful transition attack are reduced.

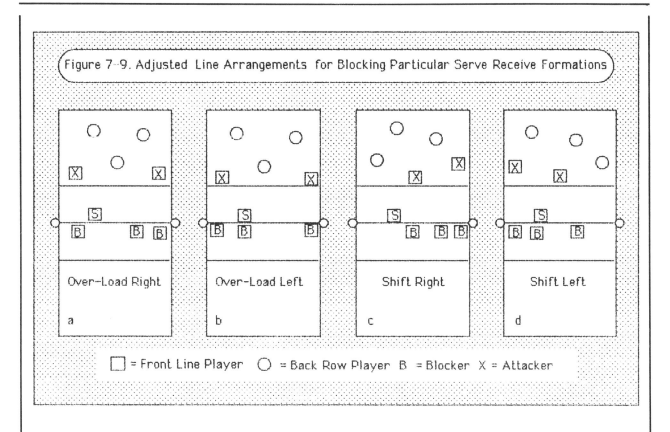

Figure 7–9. Adjusted Line Arrangements for Blocking Particular Serve Receive Formations

Over-Load Right
a

Over-Load Left
b

Shift Right
c

Shift Left
d

☐ = Front Line Player ◯ = Back Row Player B = Blocker X = Attacker

I found that against teams like Japan, China, and Korea—teams that could benefit from such a system—their attack patterns were so quick, unpredictable, and varied that our blockers were out of place most of the time. Generally, in high-level volleyball, women run more complex attack formations than men. In addition, most men hit from so far above the net that they force the blockers to commit most of the time against a quick attacker. On the other hand, women blockers can still get by using the see-and-respond tactic. For all these reasons, I would be more inclined to recommend the man-to-man blocking system for men rather than women.

For the man-to-man blocking system, the blockers can be arranged in the line arrangement and the stacked arrangement.

LINE ARRANGEMENT—COMMIT In the line arrangement of the man-to-man blocking system, commit-blocking tactics designate that each blocker follow and block one particular spiker. No matter where the spiker goes, and no matter the tempo at which the spiker attacks, it is the blocker's responsibility to follow his assigned spiker. Blockers must focus attention on their assigned spiker rather than on the setter. This system is often used to stop a dominant spiker who roams around attacking in various zones. The best

blocker is assigned to track this spiker wherever he goes.

Traffic rules along the net need to be established to prevent blockers from colliding. Two suggested rules are: blockers covering a slower-tempo attack should move behind blockers covering a first-tempo attack; and blockers moving from right to left should move in front of blockers moving from left to right.

A blocker who committed himself against a spiker not set must move quickly after landing from his jump in the direction of the set in an attempt to assist the engaged blocker.

THE STACKED ARRANGEMENT—SEE-AND-RESPOND Figure 7–10 illustrates the basic stacked arrangements in which the stacked blocker stands behind one of the other two. When used with the see-and-respond blocking tactic, these stacked arrangements are designed primarily to stop variations of an X attack. For illustrative purposes, the stacked left formation will be used to demonstrate the basic principles of blocking from stacked arrangements.

The center front blocker keeps eye contact with the RF and CF spikers. (If opponent's LF spiker then attacks for 11, then the CF blocker must watch all three spikers.) The stacked blocker focuses his attention on the setter, with the respon-

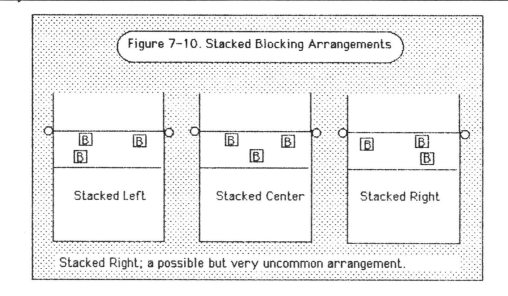

Figure 7–10. Stacked Blocking Arrangements

Stacked Left

Stacked Center

Stacked Right

Stacked Right; a possible but very uncommon arrangement.

sibility of blocking the opponent's concealed spiker and the left front spiker. The right-side blocker must shift his attention between the LF attacker and setter. If the RF blocker sees that the LF does not make any effort for a quick attack, the blocker should concentrate on the setter. The center front blocker will commit against the opponent's middle or right-side attacker, whichever comes to the net first (Figure 7–11a, d, e). The stacked blocker does not move until he sees the direction of the released set. He then moves to block either the concealed player in the X formation (Figure 7–11b, c, d) or the safety left front spiker (Figure 7–11a).

However, if the opponent's LF attacker approaches for a first-tempo attack, such as a 31, he'll be ignored by the center front blocker, and the right front blocker will commit against him (Figure 7–11e). The center front blocker will immediately focus his attention on whichever opposing spiker, CF or RF, comes first (Figure 7–11b, c, d). Again, the stacked blocker will watch the setter and not move until the release of the set.

If the opponent likes to run X formations on the left side, as illustrated in Figure 7–11c, or if it can be identified that in certain rotations the left-side X is run, the formation can be changed to a right-side stack in which the right front blocker becomes the stacked blocker, standing directly behind the center front blocker.

THE STACKED FORMATION—COMMIT The stacked-formation commit-blocking tactic is similar to the stacked-formation see-and-respond blocking tactic, except that the stacked blocker has a different responsibility.

The stacked blocker does not focus on the setter but rather on the opponent's center front and right front spikers. His primary responsibility is to follow the concealed player in the combination. However, if the opponent's center front and right front spikers both attack at first tempo for a double quick (tight, tight split, or wide split), the stacked blocker has the responsibility for blocking the RF spiker. The center front blocker is responsible for the CF spiker (Figure 7–11d).

To increase the probability of success of the stacked formation (for both commit and see-and-respond tactics), the blocking team should have a good knowledge of the opponent's attack tendencies in each rotation. They should know, for example, whether the opponent uses a single-tempo or multiple-tempo attack philosophy, and whether the opponent always attempts to bring the attackers to their specialized front-line positions or only in certain rotations.

BLOCKING ADJUSTMENTS

The key to successful blocking is knowing where, when, and whom to block. It is up to the coach to adjust his team's blocking strategy according to each different situation and opponent. To do this, the coach must have charts based on observation and scouting reports that include the following pieces of information:

- the opposing setter's set-selection tendencies at the beginning, middle, and end of each game;
- changes in the setter's set-selection tendencies as the match progresses;

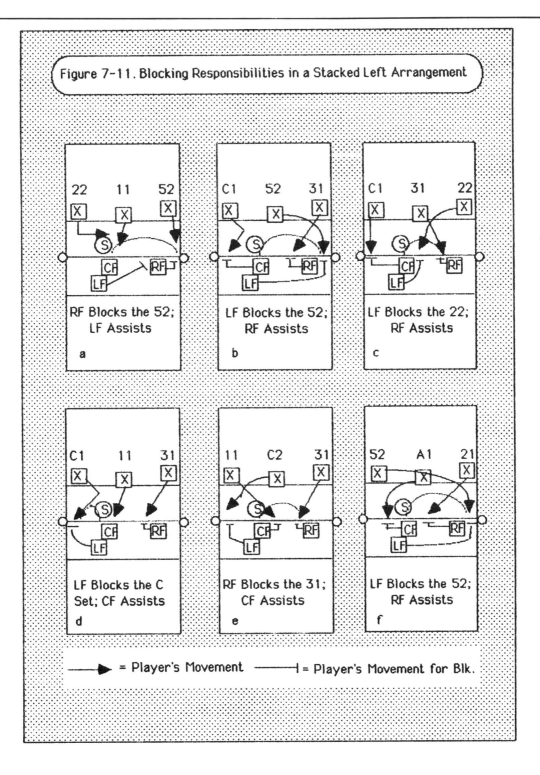

Figure 7-11. Blocking Responsibilities in a Stacked Left Arrangement

RF Blocks the 52; LF Assists — a	LF Blocks the 52; RF Assists — b	LF Blocks the 22; RF Assists — c
LF Blocks the C Set; CF Assists — d	RF Blocks the 31; CF Assists — e	LF Blocks the 52; RF Assists — f

—▶ = Player's Movement ——┤ = Player's Movement for Blk.

- set-selection tendencies by rotation, for both serve reception and transition attack;
- tendency charts on the opposing spikers, showing their preferences for hitting crosscourt, down the line, across the body, etc.; and
- attack combinations by rotation, both serve reception and transition.

The last point is particularly important. Being able to anticipate the combination allows for a more effective organization of the block and makes it easier to decide upon the use of the stacked or line arrangement.

If possible, this information should be gathered through scouting the opponent prior to the match. During the match the coach must have at his disposal statistical data indicating which hitters are receiving the most sets and what the efficiency of each spiker is in both serve reception and transition attack. A team manager, the assistant coach, or even a substitute on the bench can gather these statistics.

The key player to study is the opponent's setter. The coach and player should be well aware of his behavioral and tactical patterns. How does he set under pressure? In tight situations? By rotations? When he's back or front row? When does he or doesn't he jump-set? To better anticipate the attack, coaches and blockers should attempt to determine which of the following common tendencies apply to their opponent:

1. At the beginning of a game, a setter may rely heavily upon quick middle attack, whereas toward the end of the game he might more often use the concealed attackers and the ace players.

2. In serve reception, a setter may often set to middle and back while on transition attack he may concentrate on setting the ace spikers.

3. In tight situations, the setter may avoid taking any risks with the quick attacker and set outside. When he does set outside, he may set very high balls, giving the blockers enough time to adjust. In this case, the blockers should concentrate on the quick attackers just in case they do get set. There will be plenty of time left to redeploy the block against the outside hitter.

4. In the beginning of the game, a setter may tip a lot but toward the end of the game he may avoid tipping. The block and the floor defense should both study the tipping patterns of the setter when he is front row or back court. Some setters actually tend to tip more often when they are back row than when they are front row. This applies especially to short setters who tip up and over the block without violating the rules governing back-row attack.

5. The coach has to look for the ratio of outside sets to middle sets by rotations, by game phases, and for both transition and serve-reception attack. This ratio often varies, particularly between serve reception and transition attack. Teams that play poor floor defense are almost always incapable of running quick-transition attack in the middle; against these teams the middle blockers should always use see-and-respond tactics.

6. In transition attack, quite often the setter will deliver the ball to the opposite side from which the attack came. If this is the case, a coach should consider using plays that lead his blockers into their specialized front-row positions. Otherwise, a middle blocker or utility player

who attacks at left front may not be able to switch to his blocking position fast enough to participate in blocking the opponent's transition attack on the opposite sideline.

In addition to studying the setter, the blockers must be aware of how many spikers there are in the front line and where they are positioned in the serve-reception formation. They must also study the shot preferences and rhythm of each particular spiker.

If the opponent has a very good passing capability and a setter who is very deceptive and unpredictable, the blocking team may elect to use a probability blocking strategy in which the blockers predetermine who and where they are going to block. If their choices are correct better than 50 percent of the time, then they are doing well. Sometimes this strategy is better than trying to stop every possible attack and ending up stopping none.

Here are some suggestions for blocking adjustments in particular situations.

Matching Blockers Against Particular Spikers

Usually blocking positions coincide with attack positions; ace players block on the left side, quick attackers block in the middle, and the setter and utility players block on the right side. For tactical considerations, it is possible to switch a player so that his blocking position is not the same as his attacking position.

For example, suppose that an ace player is both the team's best blocker and its most reliable transition attacker. This player can be switched to the right side to oppose the opponent's best spiker. Such a move can be tactically justified if the blocking efficiency of the team is far better than its floor defense. Before taking such a step, the coach has to take into account the effect of such a change on the transition attack. While the change can increase the efficiency of the block, if the ball penetrates the block there'll be less chance to gain a point by the transition attack. The trade-off needs to be evaluated.

Compensating for a Weak Right-Side Blocker

There are several ways to minimize the vulnerability of a weak right-side blocker:

1. If possible, the rotations should be organized so that the three best servers serve when the weak

blocker is in the front row. They should be instructed to serve very hard so that the opponent's pass will be less effective and the setter will be forced to set high sets to the outside. The weak blocker can then pull off the net and assume a court defensive position, usually behind the block or on the opposite side. In this instance the other two blockers will have enough time to form a double block wherever the point of attack is.

2. Similar tactics can be used during the opponent's transition attack when the setter's set selection can be predicted by his position in relationship to the ball.

3. Continuously switching the weak blocker's position along the net after the opponent's pass is in the air can distract the opposing setter, reducing his concentration and affecting his execution of the game plan. The weak blocker can also fake going to another position and then return to his normal spot.

4. At times, a weak blocker inspires the opponent to continuously set high balls in his direction. But this can backfire and prove to be self-defeating for the opponent, altering their natural rhythm, and possibly even annoying the other spikers who don't get their usual number of sets. In addition, once the opponent adapts to a new rhythm, switching the weak blocker to another position could prove devastating to a team that can not recover its original rhythm.

5. Against opponents who use the 5–1 composition, a weak blocker should be in the front line during those rotations when the opponent has only two front-line spikers.

6. If one of the opponent's ace spikers jumps high enough to hit over both right front players (the utility player and the setter), while the other ace spiker can beat only the weak blocker, it is advisable to match the weak blocker against the stronger ace spiker. This increases the chances that the better blocker will be successful against the weaker ace spiker.

7. It is always better to put a weak right-side blocker against the opponent's slower, though perhaps taller, ace spiker. The slower spiker can quite often be blocked by a weak blocker who uses the soft-blocking technique.

Adjusting Blocking Formations According to Setter's Position

When the blocking team serves, or immediately upon completion of their own attack, the blockers assume initial positions usually relative to the opponent's primary target. Often, however, the opponent's pass or dig is not to the primary target and the opposing setter has to move forward or backward along the net to get to the ball.

In these situations, the blockers should adjust their formation laterally to the left or right following the setter. This is due to the fact that when the setter moves closer to his left sideline, his backset will usually be a little bit higher and slower than it would be from the primary target area. When he moves closer to his right sideline, his forward set to his left front spiker will usually be a little bit slower. Since a setter moving in one direction often has a tendency to set in that same direction, by shifting laterally the blockers are drawn into position. And they can devote more attention to stopping quick attacks near the setter, because if the setter sets high to either sideline, they will still have enough time to react and reposition the block.

Deceptive Blocking

There are a few spikers who always seem to find a way to take advantage of the block, leaving the blockers helpless and hopeless. Two methods can be used to outwit such cunning spikers: the hands-down block and the sweep block.

HANDS-DOWN BLOCK If the opponent's spiker often "wipes" shots off the outside blocker, at times that blocker should pull his hands down just before the spiker hits the ball. Obviously, this will result in a hit out of bounds, and occasionally some embarrassment for the spiker. The hands-down technique can discourage the spiker from continued use of the wipe-off tactic. The success of the hands-down technique is especially sweet if the blocker implements it at critical times. In deciding when to drop his hands, the blocker should study the spiker's eyes and arm swing carefully.

SWEEP BLOCK Spikers who seem to find a way past the block (either down the line or crosscourt) can sometimes be stopped by a preplanned sweeping block action. The block goes up and then suddenly sweeps to the left. Then the block goes up and suddenly sweeps to the right. This becomes a guessing game between the spiker and the blocker; if coordinated well with the floor defense, it can work for the benefit of the blocking team. This technique is used most often by men's teams, or women's teams with tall blockers who are powerful jumpers. It is not recommended for weak blockers who have all they can do just to get over the net. It is important for the blockers to practice maintaining the correct hand position during execution of the sweep movement. They must guard against the tendency of the leading hand, the hand closest to the direction of the sweep, to pull away from the net. Sweep blocking has to be well coordinated or else openings are created in the block, but the technique can be implemented effectively at certain times.

To Block or Not to Block

At a lower level of volleyball, the block has to be very selective in deciding whether to jump or not. It is usually a good policy not to jump at all when the spiker hits 4 to 5 feet back from the net, or is underneath the ball, or in some other awkward situation. In these circumstances the block often becomes more of a liability than a weapon. Many times the block will just tip a softly hit ball into the open areas in front of the floor defense. At these times, a team should rely upon the floor defense and the ensuing transition attack.

When a blocker (particularly the middle blocker) is late, it is sometimes better that he not jump at all; instead he should assume a position closer to the single blocker to pick up tips or deflections. A delayed jump usually results in an opening in the block that the floor defense does not anticipate. Often the ball ricochets between the hands of the two blockers and dribbles down to the floor, or bounces into the net.

At a higher level of volleyball, a team should also be selective about when to block. Each opposing spiker has to be evaluated with regard to his ability to hit the ball from different distances off the net. In women's volleyball, it is quite safe not to block a spiker who hits the ball 6 or 7 feet away from the net without a strong approach. On these occasions the team should call a "down"-ball defensive formation and maximize its transition play.

When it is obvious that a blocker is going to be too late to effectively participate in the block, he should not attempt to jump at all, but should move toward the single blocker and become responsible for tips. This gives the player assigned tip responsibility enough time to move back to a deeper court position where he can assist in digging. (Court positions behind single and multiple blocks are covered in the chapter on floor defense.) On the other hand, when the player assigned to pick up the tips has no time to retreat, it is then much better for the blocker to jump and attempt to reach with at least one hand to help the other blocker. If this is impossible, this blocker should jump straight up and screen part of the net. The floor defense can then concentrate on covering behind the hole in the block. A well-trained team can anticipate these situations fairly well by following the sequence of events taking place by the net.

FLOOR DEFENSE

The first line of defense is the block and the second is the floor defense; the two are deeply interrelated. The block responds to the opponent's attack, while the floor defense responds to both the opponent's attack and the block. Since all players who do not participate in the block take part in the floor defense, the number of players in either line can vary. A front-line player who does not participate in the block is called an "off-blocker."

The primary purpose of the floor defense is to dig an attacked ball that penetrates or passes by the block, and redirect it to the primary target. The most commonly used defensive technique is the two-arm dig, similar to the pass in serve reception, and the angle considerations in redirecting the ball are similar but more complex. The floor-defense players assume different predetermined court formations in response to the opponent's attack and the position of their own block.

The floor-defense players can use a variety of body postures and skills enabling them to effectively dig the opponent's attack. To facilitate a smooth transition attack, the dig should be accurately directed to the primary target where the setter expects the ball. When digs are accurately deflected to the target, the transition attack is more effective and the team is in control.

I often refer to defense as an "attack," as an aggressive act by the player toward the ball. Defense should not be thought of as a passive response wherein the player waits for the ball to come to her. Every player needs to develop the physical skills and mental attitude to actively pursue the ball. The player must learn to isolate each attack as if it were a one-on-one situation. The instant the spiker is up in the air, the defensive player should say to herself, "I'm going to dig you no matter what you do." Often the difference between digging or not digging a ball is simply the desire to get it.

The player must expect and *desire* the opportunity to play the attacked ball. This is an attitude that should be cultivated and fueled through training and inspiration. Defensive skills provide the player with the tools to pursue the ball and keep it alive, but it is the player's attitude that determines just how much she is willing to exert herself and how successful she will be.

A team's performance in defense reflects its state of mind, its tenacity, pride, and desire to win. Defense is probably the best barometer by which to measure a team's fighting spirit, its mental and physical toughness. A great defensive play can often boost a team's morale more than a great play in attack. It's also very difficult for an opposing spiker to cope mentally with the repeated failure of not being able to put the ball away.

Many teams, especially men's teams, shy away from improving their defensive skills because of the difficulty of training involved, lack of time, and perhaps their overall game philosophy. Also, some coaches simply don't understand how defense works. These teams stress serving, serve-reception attack, and the block. Indeed, all of these are important, but to reach a high level of volleyball emphasis must be placed on defense as well.

Statistical analysis shows that on the average, in high-level volleyball competition, only 13 percent of points are made by serving, 30 percent by blocking, and about 10 percent through opponents' errors. The remaining 47 percent of points are scored by transition attack. This shows the value of an effective defense.

Often a coach asks, "Which is more important—defense or offense?" Both are very important, but defense not only helps to score points, it also helps prevent the opponent from scoring. A team that can maximize both offense and defense has a better chance of winning. Given equal ability on serve-reception attack, the team with a better defense has the winning edge.

BASIC CONCEPTS OF DEFENSE

The size of the court is constant, but elements like the height of the block, the speed of the ball, the quickness of the defense players, are variables that must be taken into consideration when designing defensive formations to cover the court.

There are three basic concepts that apply to defensive formations:

1. *Centered formations*—The floor-defense players guard the center of the court, leaving the outside area around the perimeter exposed. The players are fairly stationary in anticipation of the attack, and then they spread out, retreating and reacting as the ball is hit.
2. *Line defense*—The three back-row defenders establish a straight line 5, 6, or 7 feet from the base line, leaving behind them a substantial court area that is unguarded.
3. *Perimeter defense*—The defensive players move from the outside court toward the inside to dig the ball.

Each one of these concepts has some merit, but the best and most challenging defense is the perimeter defense, covering most of the court. It is my belief that challenge causes improvement, and therefore I would not choose the other two methods even when coaching young players, because they might develop improper habits and never reach their full potential. Occasionally the other two methods might be used for tactical reasons.

PERIMETER/SEE-AND-RESPOND DEFENSE

In order to have an effective floor defense, a team's fundamental skills have to be suited to their defensive formations and be in harmony with the total defensive philosophy. The coach must first clarify for herself what defensive tactics she wants to use and then develop the skills to fit those tactics.

The USA women's national team used the *perimeter/see-and-respond defense.* In this defensive philosophy, the players move to the outside of the court immediately after the set, evaluate the block situation, and adjust accordingly. They then *see* the spiked ball and *then respond,* moving forward inside the court. If the block covers a player's area of responsibility, this player is automatically released from her assigned area and assumes responsibility for tips.

The advantages of perimeter/see-and-respond defense are:

1. The player can see the ball better around the block. Maintaining more prolonged eye contact with the ball improves reaction time.
2. Forward movement is quicker than backward movement.
3. More of the court area can be covered.
4. Seeing the ball first and then responding eliminates guesswork. Success in getting to the ball on time depends on the player's ability, rather than on probability or guesswork.

The implications of this defense philosophy on the development of defensive skills are:

1. In her ready posture, the player must be in the least balanced position possible, leaning forward to allow her to move quickly and respond to the ball with no waste of time.
2. The player's feet position must allow her the quickest possible movement, both forward and sideways, into her area of responsibility.
3. Players are trained to attack balls in front of them, or to either side at a 45-degree angle (Figure 8–1) as close to the floor as possible.

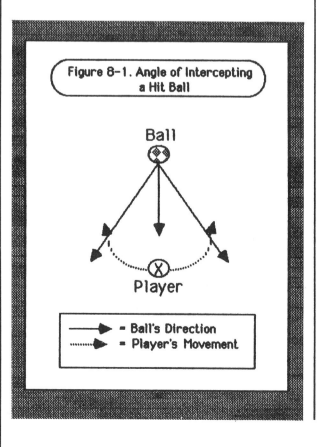

Figure 8-1. Angle of Intercepting a Hit Ball

Ball

Player

———▶ = Ball's Direction
·······▶ = Player's Movement

4. Because the players see the ball first before they respond, training has to emphasize quickness and agility so the player can beat the ball to the floor.
5. Players must learn to extend their body fully to increase their range beyond their base of support.
6. Because players are trained to play the ball in front of them while in motion and in off-balance positions, they must acquire recovery skills.

I see defense as being very dynamic and flexible, capable of adjusting to situations created by the opponent's attack. The time element dictates what players can and can not do. One predetermined formation can not solve all the attack situations the opponent creates. It is the opponent's attack that forces the defensive team into certain positions. Players and the coach must both understand that defense is a reaction to the opponent's action.

The multiple-combination attack attempts to throw the defense out of position by moving the ball very quickly along the net. If the defensive players don't understand how to react to the multiple attack, they can't function. During the sixties and seventies, Eastern European women's teams ignored the tremendous changes in the development of the attack and still continue to employ a more passive and rigid defense geared toward defending against a slow, or predictable, type of offense. In today's volleyball such a defense is impotent.

Ultimately, defense becomes a competition between the player and the ball: the player has to develop the proper skills, speed, and desire to beat the ball at any cost.

A player should have the ability to read the opponent's attack and be in position against hard-hit balls. She must also be able to pursue the ball, to lunge and reach for it, getting her body totally out of balance if necessary. In men's volleyball, balls travel at great speed so the ability to anticipate and be in position plays a significant role. In women's volleyball, balls are not hit as hard but they are placed strategically and unpredictably so the ability to react and pursue them is critical.

Sequence of Events

Although defensive players must respond to every situation created by the attack, most of the movement of the defense actually takes place before the ball is attacked. It's difficult to generalize about defensive movements or to break them down into a specific sequence of events (essentially "freeze-framing" moments that are part of a larger continuum), because there are so many variables involved. These variables include: the time element, location of attack, effectiveness and height of the block, degree of deception in the attack, distance of the spike from the net, and speed and ability of the defense player.

The following sequence is the ideal movement pattern for my defense philosophy in which the players spread out to the perimeters and then move in, squeezing the court like a sponge. This expanding and contracting movement pattern gives the team a better opportunity to see the ball and to cover more court area. It keeps the players in motion just prior to the dig, helping them to play the ball in front of them.

Immediately after the opponent gains possession of the ball, the defenders assume an *initial defensive formation,* prepared to receive a quick attack, standing in the *ready body posture.* If there is no quick attack, the player then adjusts to her *home position* out on the perimeter of the court, evaluates the attack and block situation, makes a *preparatory movement* toward the *pursuit point,* and then *pursues* the ball.

INITIAL DEFENSIVE FORMATIONS The team should assume an initial formation as soon as the opponent gains possession of the ball after either the serve or an attack. This initial formation is designed to counteract the opponent's quick attack, in particular the 11 and 31 sets and second-ball tips by the setter. Each defensive system (man-up or man-down) has its own particular initial formation that will be illustrated and discussed in "Team Formations."

One should realize that a ball dropping in a free fall from a height of 7 feet 4 inches only takes .69 of a second to hit the floor. A player standing still at a distance 10 feet away from the ball can not retrieve it if she responds immediately upon release. Obviously, a ball that is pushed down by the setter will hit the floor in even less time. With a typical 11 set, there is only about .3 to .5 of a second between the release of the ball by the setter and the time it is hit by the spiker. This does not allow for much adjustment or movement by the players.

READY POSTURE The defensive player should assume the ready posture whenever she prepares to dig the ball. The ready posture for floor defense is similar to the ready posture in serve reception. It allows the player to respond quickly to all directions, particularly forward.

The feet should be slightly wider than shoulder-width apart, with the right foot in front of the left.

The exact positioning of the feet varies according to the player's court position and is discussed in detail in "Team Formations." The toes and knees are turned slightly inward. The angle at the ankles should be about 45 degrees and the angle at the knees about 90 degrees.

It's important that the player drive her knees downward to decrease the angle at the ankles as much as possible. This brings the body's center of gravity down and forward and yet allows the knees to maintain only a 90-degree angle, a comfortable stance. The player leans forward so her body weight is distributed over the balls of the feet. The head is lifted slightly and the eyes maintain contact with the opponent's attacker.

The shoulders should be in front of the knees so that the trunk is almost parallel to the floor. The arms hang loosely with the elbows in by the side of the body, shoulder-width apart, and bent at about a 90-degree angle. This arm position allows the player to respond with either a forearm dig or an overhead finger dig.

If the ready posture is correct, the player should be able to place her palms on the floor without changing the angle of her knees by simply bending slightly more at the waist.

ADJUSTMENT MOVEMENT The adjustment movement is the movement made from the initial formation (whether by running, backpedaling, shuffling) to the home position. This adjustment movement occurs during the set phase up until the moment that the spiker jumps. As the defense player moves, she carefully reads the opponent's attack and her team's block and then aligns herself accordingly in her home position. The specific footwork recommended for each player is discussed later in "Team Formations."

The basic ready body posture for floor defense. The degree to which the arms are bent depends on individual preference. Foot positioning may vary slightly depending on the player's court position.

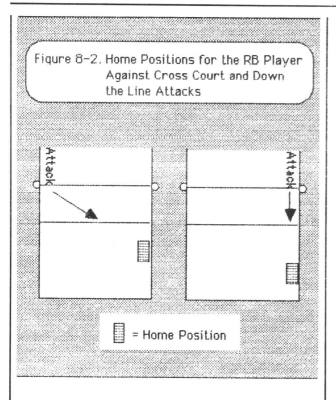

Figure 8-2. Home Positions for the RB Player Against Cross Court and Down the Line Attacks

Attack

Attack

▦ = Home Position

HOME POSITION

HOME POSITION Each defensive player has a different home position near the court perimeter against different attack directions. Figure 8–2 illustrates the home positions for RB against a cross-court attack and against a down-the-line attack. The home position is the best position from which to see and evaluate the attack and adjust to the positioning of the block.

The home position is not a particular spot on the court but rather an area. The choice of the particular spot within the home position area depends on the relationship between the block and the spiker, and on the time available. In her home position, the player assumes a ready body posture, carefully evaluates the options of the opponent's spiker, and begins her preparatory movement toward the pursuit point.

The player gives herself an enormous advantage when she can get to her home position because from the home position she can better evaluate the attack and choose the best pursuit point on the lateral range of the spike; and when she does pursue the ball, she will have generated a forward momentum that will propel her more quickly to the ball.

THE PREPARATORY MOVEMENT Preparatory movement is done from the home position to the pursuit point in line with the arm swing of the opponent. The preparatory movement starts after the opposing team's spiker jumps and ends when she begins her forward arm swing. This prepara-

tory movement is a slow step-close shuffle movement toward the ball. It can begin with either foot, but the right foot should always be kept in front of the left, except for CB who sometimes keeps her left foot forward when the attack comes from the opponent's LF. The steps should be short and slow, simply to get the body in motion as the player stalks the attack.

If timed perfectly, the player will arrive at the pursuit point exactly at the moment the ball is hit. Because the player has slight momentum when arriving at the pursuit point, her center of gravity is in front of the toes, allowing her to respond more quickly then she could from a standstill. The preparatory movement gets the body in motion so that it is ready to execute the lightning-quick response needed to dig fast-moving spikes.

The body posture during the preparatory movement should be the same as in the ready posture, but the player should lower herself as she moves forward, keeping constant eye contact with the spiker's arm swing and the ball.

THE PURSUIT POINT The pursuit point is the point on the court where the defensive player is at the moment the opposing spiker contacts the ball. The pursuit point can be any place along an arc, depending on the position of the block in relationship to the ball. The preparatory movement needs to be timed so that when the player arrives at the pursuit point, her feet are fixed but her upper body is leaning forward. The hips should be low and the player should have eye contact with the ball.

At the pursuit point, the player sees the ball get hit and then moves after its direction is obvious. This see-and-respond tactic differs greatly from anticipation defense in which the player guesses where the ball will be hit and moves there prior to the hit.

When all players are at their pursuit points, they are in the final defensive formation. In general, the pursuit point for the left front defender against an attack from position 4 (the opponent's LF) is about 7½ meters (24'7") from the ball. For LB and CB, the pursuit point is about 8½ meters (27'10") from the ball. It is about 6½ meters (21'4") for RB. If the block effectively covers RB's area of responsibility, she is released to a new pursuit point behind the block to pick up tips.

Figure 8–3 illustrates the lines or arcs along which the pursuit points are most likely to be located in a man-down defensive formation against an attack from position 4. It also shows the preparatory movement of each defender as she adjusts from her home position to the pursuit point.

PURSUIT OF THE BALL The actual pursuit of the

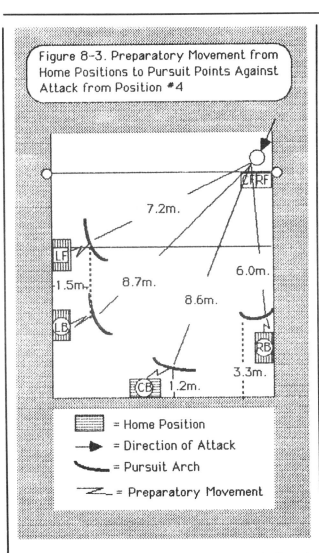

Figure 8-3. Preparatory Movement from Home Positions to Pursuit Points Against Attack from Position #4

7.2m.

LF

1.5m.   8.7m.

6.0m.

LB   8.6m.

RB

CB   1.2m.   3.3m.

▦ = Home Position

➡ = Direction of Attack

⌒ = Pursuit Arch

⌇ = Preparatory Movement

If the hop is used to begin pursuit of the ball, it should be a very low short jump with the feet landing wide apart. Instead of the hop, I recommend a forward-slide footwork, always keeping contact with the floor with at least one foot.

ball begins when the spiker contacts the ball and its direction is obvious. The manner in which the player pursues the ball depends on the distance from the defender to the ball and on the time available, a function of the height and speed of the attacked ball.

Many players start their pursuit with a very short forward hop. My team used the hop until 1979 when I realized that some players had a difficult time synchronizing their hop with the opponent's spike. The hop has other limitations as well. For one thing, it is time consuming. Once the player is airborne, she can't make fine directional adjustments until she contacts the floor again. The hop also elevates the body's center of gravity.

For these reasons I recommend starting pursuit to the ball with a short forward-slide footwork, and then stepping either to the left or right but always maintaining contact with the floor with at least one foot and keeping the hips low. This footwork leads much more easily into the extension dig, the extension roll, the sprawl and the dive because the body's center of gravity is in front of, at least, the back foot. The entire body posture and movement are geared to retrieving fast balls that come in front of the player. Balls that come at the player higher up can be easily played by straightening the knees.

The player should always attempt to dig the ball as close as possible to the floor. This gives her more time to control the ball and also creates more time for the transition attack to get organized. Obviously, if the ball comes at chest height this becomes impossible.

The forward slide or a step toward the ball is the preferred technique to begin ball pursuit, allowing the player to continue easily into the extension dig, the sprawl, the extension roll or the dive. Note how easily the player responds to a tip by a USSR player.

If the ball is in front of the player, she should always attempt to move underneath it, keeping her hips lower than the ball at the moment of contact. By going underneath and through the ball, the player imparts a reverse spin that reduces the ball's chances of being deflected over the net. Going through the ball on its side imparts a side spin deflecting the ball at a sharper angle, also preventing it from going over the net. Reverse or underspin also makes the ball hang in the air for an extra fraction of a second, giving valuable additional time for the setter and the transition attack to get organized. Sometimes it's necessary or desirable to impart both reverse and side spin to the ball simultaneously.

If the ball is low and outside the midline of the body to either side, the player has to try to go underneath it and to the side, imparting a side spin to the ball. If the ball comes waist height or higher, she may have to raise her body by straightening her knees and bringing her arms closer to the body to receive the ball. Similarly, if a high ball comes to her side, she may have to make a step to either side and drop one shoulder down to dig the ball as in passing. The right shoulder drops if the ball comes to the left, and vice versa.

Cushioning the ball is not a conscious action because there is not much time to consciously react to a ball traveling at a speed of 60 to 100 mph, or more. Cushioning is accomplished by keeping the shoulder muscles loose so that the arms give under the impact of the ball. Imparting reverse spin to the ball also creates a cushioning effect.

The choice of which defensive skill to employ in playing the ball depends on the location of the ball and the time available for the player to react.

Range

The moment the spiker makes contact with the ball, the defensive player is, in a sense, at the center of her own range of response. Dividing this range into three concentric circles can be useful for determining what balls a player is capable of digging and what techniques she should use.

Figure 8–4 defines the three circles as short, me-

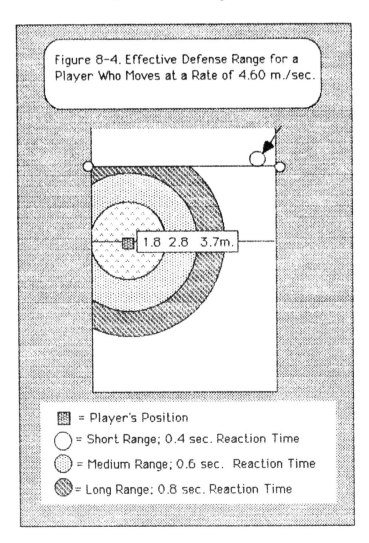

Figure 8–4. Effective Defense Range for a Player Who Moves at a Rate of 4.60 m./sec.

1.8 2.8 3.7m.

▦ = Player's Position
◯ = Short Range; 0.4 sec. Reaction Time
◔ = Medium Range; 0.6 sec. Reaction Time
◉ = Long Range; 0.8 sec. Reaction Time

Table 8-1. Application of Defensive Skills According to Range and
Speed of Ball

Range	Speed of Ball		
	Fast Ball (.4 sec.)	Medium Ball (.6 sec.)	Slow Ball (.8 sec.)
Short	Extension Dig Dig Dive Sprawl (Collapse)	Knee Drop Finger Dig	Knee Drop Finger Dig
Medium	Extension Roll Dive Sprawl	Extension Dig/Roll Dive Sprawl	Knee Drop Lay-out
Long	Extension Roll	Extension Dig/Roll	Run Through
Beyond		Extension Dig/Roll One-Arm Dig	Extension Dig/ Roll

Table 8-2. Expected Percent Success Rate of Retrieving the Ball
at Different Ranges for Given Ball Speed as Expressed by Time

Range	Speed of Ball		
	Fast Ball (.4 sec.)	Medium Ball (.6 sec.)	Slow Ball (.8 sec.)
Short	70%	90%	100%
Medium	45%	70%	90%
Long	5%	45%	70%
Beyond	——	5%	45%

dium, or long range, and balls that come to these ranges are therefore short, medium, or long balls. For women, the radius of the short range is 1.80 meters (about 5'10"); the radius of the medium-range circle is 2.76 meters (about 9'); and the radius of the long-range circle is 3.68 meters (about 12'). These distances are based on measurements taken during women's competition.

An experienced defensive player can move at the rate of 4.60 meters per second. Therefore, hard spikes that hit the floor between .3 to .4 of a second can be reached only in the short range. (It's interesting to note that the radius of the short range coincides with the average height of a woman volleyball player.) Slower spikes that hit the floor between .4 to .6 of a second can be dug in the short and medium range. Balls that travel between .6 and .8 of a second (medium spike, soft tip) can be reached in all three ranges. Balls that take more than .8 of a second to hit the floor can be reached beyond the long range. Balls in this category include soft tips and balls deflected deep off the block.

Table 8–2 shows the success rate for digging balls in different ranges at different ball speeds. Table 8–1 shows which defensive skills to use in each of the three ranges for balls hit at different speeds.

The information presented in Figure 8–4 was based on data compiled from very experienced players. Obviously, expectations for beginners should be lowered.

The extension dig, the sprawl and the dive are the skills to use against fast low balls in the short and medium range (Table 8–1). The sprawl can not cover as wide a range as the extension dig and the dive, but it's useful for short-range balls and forward and sideways one-hand digs. The knee drop should be used for medium fast balls directed toward the player's feet, or for slower balls that give the player plenty of time to position herself underneath the ball. Digging the ball close to the floor maximizes the time for the transition attack. For balls in the long-range zone, the extension roll and the run-through are the primary techniques for fast and slow balls respectively.

INDIVIDUAL DEFENSIVE SKILLS

In women's volleyball, it's crucial that the ball be accurately redirected to the target. Otherwise, a deceptive transition attack can not be successfully executed. Defensive skills have to be finely tuned and developed.

Retrieving a fast spike is less a conscious reaction than a purely reflex reaction. Therefore, proper motor habits must be developed through continuous and specific repetition of training. There is no substitute for quantity training in developing the correct spontaneous reflexes. Even after these skills are mastered, a player must continuously practice them, more so than any other volleyball skill, in order to maintain a high skill level. Defensive skills are the first to degenerate and disappear when training is reduced.

In drills, the coach has to control the time element so the player must respond to a ball within .3 of a second. To achieve this, the coach can hit the ball hard or move closer to the player and hit softer balls. The response time for the player should be reduced progressively as her reflexes and skills improve.

Each defensive situation demands almost a totally new skill. Digging a low ball is different from digging a high ball; rolling forward is different from rolling sideways; digging in a balanced position is different from digging-in motion. Therefore, the coach must create a broad range of gamelike situations in practice. The players should be trained in such a way that skills aren't learned as separate movement in isolated situations but rather as a part of a broader continuous defensive picture.

Many teams limit the bulk of their defensive training to pepper drills. Playing pepper is good for warming up the shoulders and training basic arm technique, but it doesn't help in actual defensive situations. In pepper, the ball always comes from the same point and is returned to the same point. In an actual game, the ball comes from a wide variety of directions and has to be returned to the same target.

The coach must balance her defensive-skill training, making sure that she pushes her players to their maximum ability but still allowing them a certain amount of success. Without this occasional success, the player becomes discouraged.

The Arm-Extension Dig/Extension Roll

The arm-extension dig is a useful technique to dig hard-hit balls that come in the short- and medium-range areas around the player. The player moves from the pursuit point toward the incoming ball with a forward-slide footwork and bends at the waist, lowering the hips and driving the knees forward to decrease the angle at the ankles. The body weight should be forward. As the ball nears the floor, the player extends her arm forward and underneath the ball. One foot is forward and the

Laurie Flachmeier (left and center) and Linda Chisolm (right) demonstrate an extension dig.

Kohji Kojima, coach of Japan's 1972 and 1980 Olympic teams, demonstrates the principles of the arm extension dig with Hirose Miyoko (1984 Japanese Olympic team).

The extension dig can end in a knee drop, sprawl, collapse, extension roll, or dive, depending on the player's speed and reach. Julie Vollertsen (1984 USA Olympic team) demonstrates some of the most common extension digs for fast balls.

215

An extension dig into a back flip is most often used to handle medium speed balls; advanced players can use this technique to retrieve fast balls.

Hirose Miyoko demonstrates an extension dig moving into a barrel roll. This technique is often used to retrieve slow balls in the long range where the player approaches the ball with relatively great speed.

Paula Weishoff moves with her left foot forward into a forward extension roll over her left shoulder. (1) Laurie Flachmeier also leads with her left foot but rolls over her right shoulder. (2) This rolling technique is used to pursue slow balls in the long range.

The dig is executed in a manner similar to the pass in serve reception.

body weight is distributed mainly over this front foot (very similar to a forward knee drop).

If the ball is slightly beyond normal arm reach in front of the player, she should execute an extension roll by pushing off from the back leg, straightening both knees and thrusting forward, extending her arms and body underneath and through the ball. She cushions herself by falling sideways to the floor, first contacting the floor with the hand opposite the side she's falling to. The heel of the other hand slides on the floor and then immediately flips over so the back of the hand is on the floor. The body slides onto the floor on its side from the shoulder blade down to the waist and thigh. Usually the knees don't touch the floor.

If this movement is done very quickly, the body momentum may carry the feet over the head. If the movement is done relatively slowly without too much forward momentum, the player can simply barrel-roll out of this position and right herself as quickly as possible.

The ball is directed to the target by dropping a shoulder and rotating the arm platform at an angle to the floor. If the ball comes to the right or left side of the player, the player reaches for the ball dropping the opposite shoulder; the shoulder closer to the setter during the reach to the ball is the one that should drop. The arms should not swing at the ball. The arms should simply create the proper rebound in the vertical and lateral directions. The shoulder muscles should be loose.

The Dig/Power Dig

The dig is executed in a manner similar to the pass in serve reception. It is used to retrieve fast- or medium-speed balls that come at the player from different heights and angles.

When the ball comes to the player at knee height or higher, the player straightens her knees slightly and receives the ball as in serve reception. Again, the hips should be slightly underneath the ball and the arms fairly close to the body almost vertical to the floor. The player can lean back slightly, if necessary.

When the ball comes on either side of the body's midline, the player reaches for the ball with her arms crossing the body, dropping the shoulder closest to the setter.

The dig can be executed from an enormous variety of postures with the knees bent at different degrees and the arms held out in any direction, depending on the needed angle of deflection. It's imperative that the hips be underneath the ball, but the body weight can shift to either side, over the left or right foot. In principle, it's best to dig the ball when the body leans to one side or the other with the arms slightly across the body rather than in front, just as in passing.

In the LF, LB, and RB court positions these digs are used to retrieve balls directed from the opponent's court position #4. The dig can be executed from an enormous variety of postures, but the player must always attempt to direct the ball to the target.

The power dig is used for fast balls that come toward the feet of the defensive player. When a low fast ball comes toward the player's feet, she should drive her knees toward the floor and at the same time bend at the waist very quickly, getting her arms underneath the ball close to the floor (collapse). The feet are side by side or in a slightly staggered position. The player directs the ball to the target by rotating at the hips and shifting her body weight. The forward-bending action at the waist gets the arms to the ball quicker than a squat, because the contraction of the abdominal muscles creates tremendous forward torque on the

The power dig is used to retrieve very fast balls that come toward the player's feet. The player should drive his knees toward the floor while bending at the waist, getting the arms underneath the ball. Ball control is accomplished by rotating the hips and shoulders and shifting the body weight from side to side.

upper body, bringing the shoulders closer to the floor at a faster rate than the pull of gravity. When the player squats, sitting down and back, her body descends only at the rate of gravity.

The Forward Sprawl

This technique is useful to reach fast spikes a short distance in front of the player. Initially, the player moves as if for an extension dig, extending her arms and her body toward the ball. If the player does not have enough momentum to carry through the ball, she digs it with both arms and then collapses onto the floor. As the player's body drops, she contacts the ball very close to the floor with both arms and then breaks the fall with her hands, collapsing onto her chest. The knees are spread wide apart and, after contact with the ball, the inside of one or both knees usually contacts the floor. Often the player will continue sliding forward a little on her chest as the lower legs flip up slightly.

Since the player is now flat on the floor on her stomach, to make a quick recovery she can roll sideways over either shoulder onto her back. If the player rolls over her left shoulder, she should raise her right knee up toward her chest as she rolls, then cross the right foot over her body and place it on the floor. She can use her hands to help her stand up.

The forward sprawl can be punishing to the body, particularly for women. Too much repetitive training of this technique is very taxing physically.

The Sideways Sprawl

The sideways sprawl is used for a fast ball coming to either side of the defender in the short to medium range. While digging the ball, the player collapses onto her side. Contact with the floor is

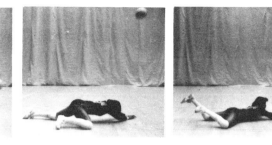

Side and front views of a forward sprawl, an effective technique for digging fast balls at a short to medium range.

made all along the length of the side of the body, beginning with the lower part of the leg, continuing up along the thigh and finally up to the shoulder blade. While falling to the left, the player should raise her right leg to help push the upper body downward. While falling to her right, she should raise her left leg. The collapse can be done directly from the ready posture or after a step to the side.

Contact with the ball should be made very close to the floor with two arms, but if the ball is too far away, the player should reach with one arm and contact it on the inside of her forearm. The player can right herself with a rocking movement, back and up, or by using the same technique described in the forward sprawl.

Lay-Out

The lay-out is used to pick up fairly slow balls, like tips or balls that are soft-blocked and have a change of direction and speed. It can also be used when the defensive player does not have great body momentum going into the dig. The lay-out is used quite often when the opponent tips and the defense player is in a low-body position with his body weight back in anticipation of a hard hit. The defender doesn't have enough push-off from her legs to reach the ball and it is still too far away to reach simply by extending into the sprawl. The defender can execute the lay-out, putting her left hand on the floor (if the player is right-handed), and using it like a lever to pull her body weight forward the extra distance to get to the ball. The ball is contacted with the back of the right hand and flipped up with wrist action.

The sideways sprawl is used for fast balls approaching either side of the player in the short to medium range. Raising the leg helps lower the body to the floor more quickly.

The Dive

The dive is a technique more commonly used by men than women. The player drives her knees toward the ground and with a quick straightening of the legs, she thrusts forward. Players should be able to dive from a ready position or with a step. The defender contacts the ball with two arms and then places both hands on the floor and lowers her body. If the ball is to the side, she might contact it with one hand.

It's important that her hands hit the floor up in front of the player in the direction of the momentum. Otherwise, she might fall and hit her chin on the floor. Using her arm strength, the player lowers herself slowly, chest first, down to the thighs. Her back is arched, her head up and her legs bowed. She then pulls herself through, propelling her body forward. The pull-through creates a sliding movement of the body on the stomach.

The dive has its limitations. When the body is airborne, it moves more slowly than when running. Therefore, the dive should not be used to cover long distances. It's also difficult to have much ball control while diving. At times the body arches too much and the back is prone to injury, in particular at the moment of contact with the floor. When the floor is slippery, the dive becomes increasingly dangerous, and it's very stressful on the shoulders.

Because of its wear and tear on the body, the dive can not be practiced repeatedly and is therefore difficult to perfect. For obvious reasons, it's particularly uncomfortable for women.

At certain times a player has to use the dive. For example, when a tip drops close to the net, the player must move to the ball very quickly without crossing the center line. In this case, she has no choice but to dive for the ball to avoid going over the line.

The Run-Through

Sometimes a player has to cover a long distance to reach a slowly hit ball or one with a high-rebound trajectory off the block. In this case, the player should simply run through the ball and dig it while in motion. When the ball is deflected off the block to the side of the court, the right or left back player has to run through it, imparting side spin to direct the ball to the target. Often CB has to chase balls deflected off the block that go behind the endline. Handling these balls requires practice to develop the proper timing and feel, because body momentum is so great the player can easily lose control of the ball.

To execute the run-through, the player chases the ball, lowering the appropriate shoulder so as to

The dive cushions the body after jumping forward head first to reach for a low ball, contacting the ball with one or both arms. Diving requires great shoulder and arm strength and is difficult to practice repeatedly and perfect. Actually, the better defensive players do not dive. When diving, often the body arches too much and the back becomes prone to injury at the moment of contact with the floor.

accurately redirect the ball to the target. The ball is dug with both forearms. At times the player will have to extend herself substantially at the end of the run to reach the ball. On these occasions her body may be off balance. The player must learn to dig the ball and then let herself fall to the floor and roll whichever way the body momentum carries her. The roll can be done after contacting the ball in any direction, within or beyond the court.

This particular skill requires special practice and training because usually the player is running fast and must go into the roll from a great speed. This maneuver is different from going into a roll after an extension dig. The body is usually more

One hand digs do not offer much ball control and should only be used in emergencies or when the player cannot reach the ball with both arms.

The finger dig is legal but demands a great deal of practice and skill to execute well.

upright at the start of the fall and has to be lowered with control.

Occasionally, the angle of deflection to the target will be so acute that the player will have to bend her elbows during the dig. Beginning players should not be encouraged to bend their elbows.

One-Hand Dig

Beginners should be taught to dig with two arms, because it teaches them better body discipline and coordination. More experienced players must sometimes use the one-arm dig. The one-arm dig is often used in conjunction with the side sprawl. The left or right arm extends sideways, bent slightly at the elbow, and with a scooping action of the wrist, contacts the ball on the side of the arm.

To dig a hard-hit ball with one arm, the player simply extends her arm to the side and digs the ball with the inside of the forearm. The player must make sure that she does not make any rotational movement at the instant of contact. Rotation of the arm during contact will deflect the ball backward. The arm should be held almost straight, firm but not too rigid in order to better absorb the impact of the incoming ball.

Slower balls can be scooped with one arm by bending the elbow and the wrist up at the same time. Contact is made along the upper side of the wrist or hand and the hand should be loosely cupped.

Finger Dig

When a soft off-speed shot or a ball deflected off the block comes to a player at about head or shoulder height, she should use the overhead finger dig, similar to finger passing, or setting. She should approach the ball leading with her legs and hips underneath the ball, and the body leaning back. Contact with the ball is made over the head.

Overhead Dig

When a very fast ball comes toward a player's face or slightly above her head, she should raise both hands palm up and join the hands at an angle, with one on top of the other, intertwining the thumbs. Contact with the ball is made on the outer edges of both hands.

After the 1984 Olympics, the rule governing dou-

The hand grip for the overhead dig.

ble hits was modified. Now, double contacts are permitted as long as they are part of a single attempt to play the ball. Players can now defend against balls at head height by putting up two fists and contacting the ball with the bottom of the hands.

This technique is also used by women on the third contact to get the ball over the net when the ball drops behind their back.

Single Knee Drop

The knee drop is a technique to pick up short- or medium-range balls. It can also serve as an intermediate step, leading the body into an extension dig for hard balls.

The forward knee drop is useful for balls that drop in front of the player. The player makes a relatively long step toward the ball, bending the forward knee as she leans over the thigh to play the ball. The knee of the back leg drops and the back leg is dragged forward with the inner part of the knee on the floor.

The side knee drop is done by stepping to one side and placing the inner part of the opposite knee on the floor. The dropped knee is pulled in somewhat, keeping the butt close to the floor while the body leans forward. If moving to the right, the player should drop the left knee. Moving to the left, she should drop her right knee.

Getting the correct knee down is very important. Many beginning players do it backward, dropping the leading knee. This not only limits their range, but it also puts them in an awkward and unstable semikneeling position. With the lead knee on the

floor and the body off balance, it is very difficult to drop the opposite inside shoulder in order to play the ball correctly. Proper knee-drop form can give the body further extension to reach toward hard-hit balls using the extension dig. Contact with the ball should be made close to the floor and somewhere between the knees.

Double Knee Drop

The double knee drop is commonly used by setters to recover balls from the net, and occasionally by floor-defense players to retrieve a fast ball directed to the player's feet, or medium-range soft balls. The player simply lowers her knees to the floor by leaning slightly backward to reduce the impact. To prevent injuries this must be a controlled kneeling action, using the muscles around the ankles and the quadriceps of the thighs to lower the knees. At times, the two-knee drop can be an intermediate step leading into the forward sprawl.

The Roll

The roll is not a technique for digging. It is a maneuver that allows a player with forward momentum whose body is completely out of balance to fall to the floor, cushion herself, and get back on her feet quickly. It is more commonly used by women, while men tend to use the dive or the sprawl. The roll is often necessary when a player has to chase a ball, or when she has to launch herself with great velocity at a hard-hit ball, especially in the medium and long range. The roll should give a player confidence to increase her range by getting out of balance without fear of injury.

The player extends her arms, contacts the ball, and then allows herself to fall onto the floor and execute a roll. It really doesn't matter how the roll is executed, or in which direction. The player should simply let her body momentum carry her through the roll. It can be a barrel (sideways) roll, a roll with one or both feet going over the head, or

The double knee drop can also be used when bumping the ball backwards over the net.

Forward and side knee drop.

The roll cushions the fall to the floor after a dig. The roll should give a player confidence to reach for distant balls without fear of injury. I feel that rolling is quicker and more controlled than diving.

one of the specially developed rolls that involve kicking over one shoulder. The player should learn to reach out for the ball keeping either foot in front, and then roll left or right from either foot. This will avoid wasting time by switching legs. Often players only know how to roll to the right from the right foot, and to the left from the left foot.

If LB wants to dig a ball that drops to the left middle area of the court and her right foot is forward, to be able to redirect the ball to the target, she should bring her left knee forward and roll to the left. I call this technique "Rita's flip" (reversed roll) because Rita Crockett of the USA national team was the first player I ever knew who became proficient at it, even against hard spikers. This technique is very useful for a setter who has to chase a ball dropping near the 10-foot line between court positions #3 and #4. This right-leg forward roll to the left technique enables the setter to set the left front spiker using the forearm bump setting technique.

A screw under should be used near the net.

"Rita's flip," rolling off the left foot through the right shoulder (top) and vice versa (bottom). Rita Crockett could execute this move even when digging a very hard ball. Timing is critical in redirecting the ball to the setter.

The Screw-Under Roll

To execute the screw-under roll, the player takes a long step to the ball, pivots slightly around the front foot, digs the ball, and then falls backward onto her back. Normally, this technique should not be used except when the ball is near the net or comes off the net and is close to the floor. The screw-under allows the player to play the ball without crossing the court midline.

The One-Hand Bump

In situations where a player is retreating off the net after blocking and has to contact a ball slightly too far behind her head, she can use the one-hand bump. She bumps the ball with the heel of one hand, keeping her hand in a loose fist. The main purpose of the bump is simply to keep the ball in play. Obviously, very little control can be exerted with the bump, but it's preferable to trying to finger pull a ball that is behind the back and getting called for a foul. By bumping the ball high enough in the air on the second contact, the blocker gives the back-row setter and the other transition spikers time to get into position. Sometimes the one-hand bump is useful for back-court players when the ball is deflected off the block and is going out of bounds fairly high over the player's head. The player jumps and hits the ball with the heel of the hand trying to deflect it back into the court toward the setter.

Balls Off or Near the Net

To retrieve balls coming off the net, the player should assume a low body posture with her shoulders at an angle to the net, facing the target. If the setter is trying to rescue the ball, she should try to get into position to bump-set one of the hitters. One foot should be closer to the net than the other, about a foot away from the court midline. This position will allow the player to handle balls that rebound off the net or balls that drop along the net. The player should learn to handle these balls with

Teams should regularly practice retrieving balls that bounce off the net.

one or two arms. The ball should be hit with one arm with a scooping wrist action on the inside of the wrist and it should be contacted below the bottom of the net.

The player has to learn to anticipate the rebound of the ball off the net. The tighter the net, the more the rebound. If the ball hits the top of the net, it will usually drop straight down. If it hits the bottom, it pops out quicker and farther back off the net. A knee drop is often a good technique to use in playing balls out of the net.

It is important that the ball be played with a slight angle back into the court.

TEAM FORMATIONS

The main defensive formations are the man-up and the man-down and variations of both. The function of the defensive formation is to provide a framework for player coordination. It should be flexible enough to accommodate every attack situation. The formation is basically an organizational principle allowing players to adjust cohesively on the court in response to different attacks. If the coach insists upon a rigid formation that doesn't adjust, it might be effective against one opponent's style of play but not against another's.

In organizing a team's defense and assigning areas of responsibility, the coach has to clearly define who is responsible for the seams between players. Within the framework of the formation, the coach can emphasize or deemphasize strengths and weaknesses of certain individuals by allocating to them larger or smaller areas of responsibility. Players must know the traffic rules and areas of responsibility for each formation. Without that knowledge hesitations or collisions inevitably occur.

Each formation has its weakness. In high-level volleyball competition, the efficiency of attack is about 40 to 50 percent or more. So when it comes right down to it, a formation or a system is only as good as the technical ability of the players executing it.

Regardless of the formation, the key to successful floor defense lies in the players' ability to anticipate and evaluate the block's role in a particular attack situation. Instead of trying to predetermine which area is taken by the block and which by the floor defense, the defenders should respond to the block as the blockers respond to the attack. This concept demands extra movement from the defensive players to ensure that a greater court area is covered.

The players must clearly understand that no matter what formation or arrangement they are in, *all* players must play the ball at all times: before the attack, during the attack, and after the ball is dug. A player must continuously be a useful contributor to the team's defensive efforts. Too often, a player isolates herself in a particular court position and if the ball doesn't come to her, she makes no response at all. Such an attitude must be changed by training the team to act as a cohesive unit with all players responding together at all times for every ball.

Unless some front-line players are physically incapable of blocking effectively, there should be at least two blockers up against every attack. The following discussion pertains to defensive formations involving two or more blockers. Defensive formations around one blocker are discussed separately in a later section.

This section covers three topics: man-up defense, man-down defense, and situational defense. The concepts presented in the man-up and man-down defense are geared primarily for defending against high attack. The situational defense discusses adaptations of the man-down formation to counteract quick multiple attack. The coach should know how to adjust the man-down formation to defend against quick-attack offenses.

Terminology

Figure 8–5 defines the names of defensive players in their court positions in relation to the opponent's attack. Figure 8–6 illustrates a subdivision of the court into nine equal squares of 3×3m each. These court divisions may be helpful in specifying court locations for descriptive purposes, or in actual game competition when directing the attack or the defense.

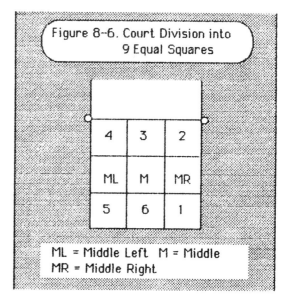

Figure 8–6. Court Division into 9 Equal Squares

4	3	2
ML	M	MR
5	6	1

ML = Middle Left M = Middle
MR = Middle Right

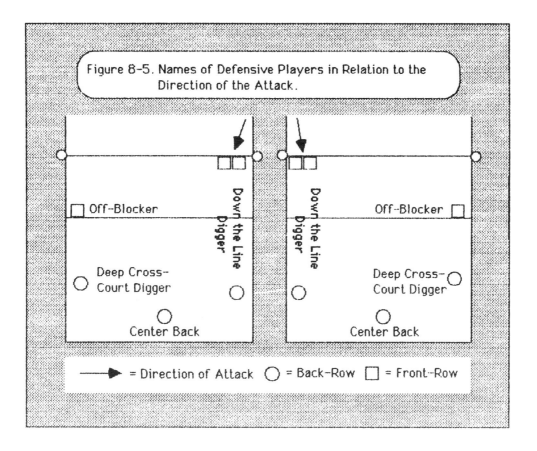

Figure 8–5. Names of Defensive Players in Relation to the Direction of the Attack.

Off-Blocker

Down the Line Digger

Deep Cross-Court Digger

Center Back

= Direction of Attack ○ = Back-Row □ = Front-Row

Feet Position for Defense Players

The feet position in the ready posture (whether in the initial, home, or pursuit position) establishes the player's orientation toward her area of responsibility in the defensive scheme. It also determines in which direction the player can move quickly in response to the ball. When tenths of a second mean the difference between digging and not digging a ball, such tiny details as feet position can make all the difference.

When the feet are placed one in front of the other in a staggered position (Figure 8–7a), the player can respond very quickly forward or backward, but her lateral movement is slowed. Turning the toes and knees slightly in improves lateral mobility somewhat. When the feet are placed side by side in an even line (Figure 8–7b), the player has quick lateral mobility, but her forward movement is hampered. Leaning forward so that the body weight is on the balls of the feet can help facilitate faster forward body movement. Figure 8–7c shows a combined staggered side-by-side foot position in which the feet are wider apart. This compromised position is the best because it allows for both forward and lateral movement.

In designing the defense, the coach should consider that feet position orients the player's body toward her area of responsibility. A player whose area of responsibility is primarily forward should have her feet in a staggered position in the ready posture to maximize forward mobility. However, if her area of responsibility is more lateral, then the feet should be in a side-by-side position. If the area of responsibility is forward and to the sides at the same time, then she should have her feet in a combined staggered and side-by-side position. Having all players properly oriented with the correct foot positions will help prevent them from moving on collision courses and will also minimize hesitation, providing for better coverage of the gray areas between players.

Angle Consideration

As in serve reception, players should be aware of the angles involved in redirecting the spiked ball to the target. At the time of contact with the ball, it's really not important how the feet are positioned. What is important is the geometric relationship between the direction of the incoming ball, the arm platform, and the target.

In both serve reception and floor defense, the ball must be redirected to the same target. But the serve always comes from approximately the same direction, whereas in floor defense, the ball can come from any place along the net in a wide range of directions—crosscourt, down the line, and in between.

When the opponent attacks from their positions #2 or #3, the defensive player, no matter what court position she is in, should attempt to dig the ball from left to right as in passing. She should keep her arms on the left side of her body (Figure 8–8c, d). Figure 8–8a, b illustrate the preferred arm position for receiving a spike from position #4.

When the opponent attacks from their position #4, the off-blocker (LF on the defensive team) should dig the ball with her arms to the left or straight in front. A right-to-left arm action might deliver the ball back to the opponent over the net. When digging a ball in front, the off-blocker must impart a great deal of reverse spin to the ball to prevent it from going back to the spiker. (Reverse spin is created by going through and underneath the ball.) By keeping her arms more parallel to the floor, or perhaps even bending her elbows a little more, she can deflect the ball at a more vertical angle.

The deep crosscourt digger (LB) can dig the ball on her right (Figure 8–8b) or left side, or in front. The distance to the target is quite substantial and therefore there is less chance of deflecting the ball past the target over the net, especially if she keeps her shoulders loose enough to absorb some of the speed. Nonetheless, the preferred manner for digging by LB is to hold her arms to the left side or to contact the ball in front of her body.

If a player stands at CB (position 6) and the opponent attacks from their position #4, the recommended digging action is either in front or to the right side of the body. If the ball is hit down the line, RB should dig the ball with a right-to-left arm action, or straight forward out in front. When digging the ball straight in front, RB must impart a great deal of reverse spin by going under and through the ball to reduce the chance of deflecting it over the net. Figures 8–8c, d illustrate the recommended arm positions for digging balls attacked from opponent's positions #2 and #3.

It should be remembered that, as in passing, cushioning the ball to reduce its speed is accomplished by keeping the shoulder muscles loose. This cushioning is even more important for defensive players because of the high speed of most incoming spikes.

MAN-UP DEFENSE

In the classic man-up defense, one player, called the "man-up," is assigned to always play behind

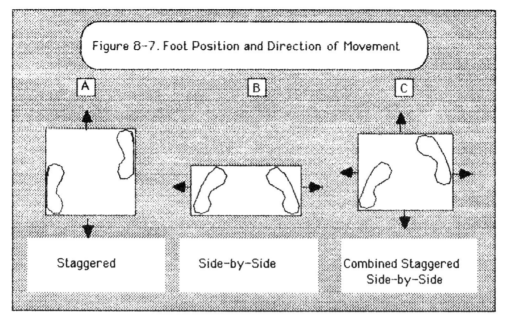

Figure 8-7. Foot Position and Direction of Movement

A

B

C

Staggered

Side-by-Side

Combined Staggered
Side-by-Side

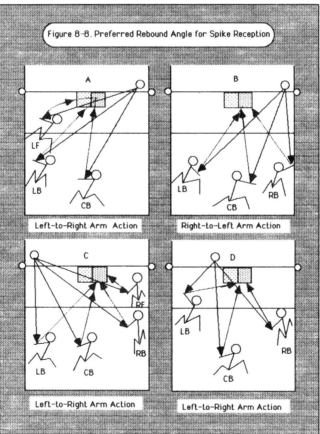

Figure 8-8. Preferred Rebound Angle for Spike Reception

A

LF

LB

CB

Left-to-Right Arm Action

B

LB

CB

RB

Right-to-Left Arm Action

C

RF

LB

CB

RB

Left-to-Right Arm Action

D

LB

CB

RB

Left-to-Right Arm Action

the block (Figure 8–9a, b). This could be any back-row player but for purposes of player specialiation it's desirable that one pair of players positioned diagonally opposite in the alignment share the job.

In a 6–2 team composition, the back-row setter is usually the man-up player. In a 5–1 team composition, when the setter is in the back row she plays behind the block. In the other three rotations, the man-up player is the player who stands behind the setter, usually the utility player or the center player if the 5–1 setter plays CF in the front row. The man-up player moves from side to side behind the block about 10 to 12 feet away from the net. Her main responsibility is to pick up soft tips and deflections over and around the block.

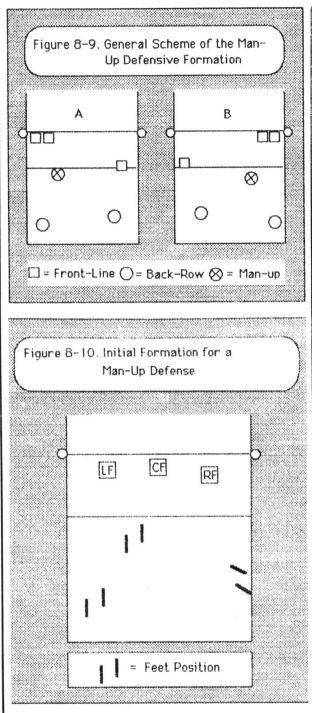

Figure 8-9. General Scheme of the Man-Up Defensive Formation

□ = Front-Line   ○ = Back-Row   ⊗ = Man-up

Figure 8-10. Initial Formation for a Man-Up Defense

LF   CF   RF

▮ ▮ = Feet Position

Initial Formation

As explained earlier, the initial formation is designed to cover a tip from the opponent's setter or a quick middle attack from an 11 set. Figure 8–10 illustrates the initial formation for a man-up defense, showing feet position as well. Note that the man-up player is shifted slightly left of the center of the court. Note, also, that the feet of RB are almost perpendicular to the right sideline; this enables RB to play defense against a quick-attack spike hit toward the right sideline.

In the initial formation the blockers should make a very slight adjustment to the right or the left in response to the opponent's pass.

Adjustment to Home Position

This adjustment is against high sets when there is enough time for the player to get to the home position where she can read and evaluate the opponent's attack. Figure 8–11a, b illustrates the movement to home positions for players in the man-up formation in response to attacks from the opponent's positions #4 and #2.

The man-up player shifts left or right, depending on where the attack comes from, using side-by-side or shuffle steps, and positions herself about 10 to 12 feet from the net on the inside shoulder of the center blocker where she can maintain eye contact with the ball.

The off-blocker retreats from the net to about the 10-foot line and aligns herself with the ball and the arm swing of the spiker. The adjustments of the off-blocker are usually done by running. She turns into the court and runs into position while maintaining eye contact with the ball. Note the difference between the home position of the left front and right front off-blockers. The left front off-blocker usually retreats farther off the net than right front because a 52 set takes longer than the C2 set. These positions also facilitate accurate deflection of the dig to the target by allowing the players to dig more balls on their left sides.

The deep crosscourt digger should adjust from the initial position to the home position by shuffling back (for left back) or shuffling to the side (for right back). The deep crosscourt digger aligns herself with the inside shoulder of the middle blocker so that she can keep eye contact with the ball. Note the difference in positions of the crosscourt diggers. RB is closer to the net than LB for the same reasons that the off-blockers retreat to different depths.

Adjustments by the line diggers (left or right back) are done by backpedaling to their home position. Line diggers should always get to the sideline in their home positions. Note that the home positions for line diggers are closer to the baseline than for the crosscourt diggers (Figure 8–12a, b). The distance of the home position for line diggers varies according to their individual ability. Quicker players should retreat closer to the base line.

Feet position in the home positions is also illustrated in Figure 8–11c, d. Note the feet position of the left front off-blocker; she uses the combined staggered side-by-side (Figure 8–11c) position so

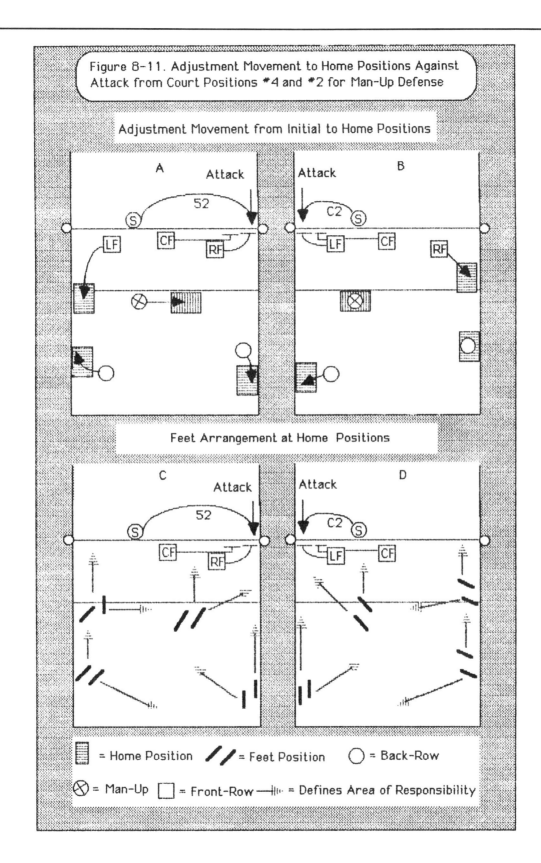

Figure 8-11. Adjustment Movement to Home Positions Against Attack from Court Positions #4 and #2 for Man-Up Defense

Adjustment Movement from Initial to Home Positions

A — Attack — 52 — S — LF — CF — RF

B — Attack — C2 — S — LF — CF — RF

Feet Arrangement at Home Positions

C — Attack — 52 — S — CF — RF

D — Attack — C2 — S — LF — CF

▤ = Home Position   ∥∥ = Feet Position   ◯ = Back-Row

⊗ = Man-Up   ▢ = Front-Row   ⊢∥⊦ = Defines Area of Responsibility

that she can respond quickly both along the 10-foot line *and* toward the net. Also note the feet position of RF and RB against a C2 attack; their feet are almost parallel to the net with the right foot slightly in front of the left. This allows for more lateral mobility. The feet position for the line digger is different from that of the crosscourt digger. It maximizes both forward and lateral movement.

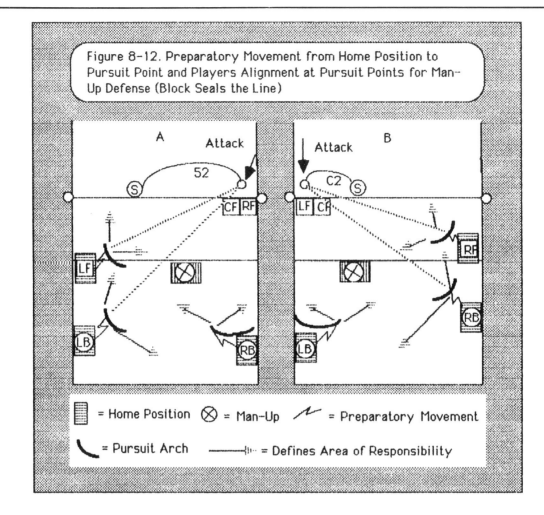

Figure 8-12. Preparatory Movement from Home Position to Pursuit Point and Players Alignment at Pursuit Points for Man-Up Defense (Block Seals the Line)

☐ = Home Position ⊗ = Man-Up ⟋ = Preparatory Movement

❮ = Pursuit Arch ━━━╫┉ = Defines Area of Responsibility

Preparatory Movement/Pursuit Point

From the home position, the player makes a slight preparatory movement toward the inside of the court using shuffle steps and maintaining the same feet position as in the home position. She then moves to the pursuit point. The player should time her preparatory movement carefully so that she arrives at the pursuit point precisely at the moment the spiker contacts the ball. At that time her body should be heavily leaning forward so that when she sees the ball, she can respond to it immediately.

At the pursuit point, the left front off-blocker should align her left shoulder with the ball and the right shoulder of the spiker (Figure 8-12a). This ensures that she can pass from left to right. The deep crosscourt digger (LB) aligns herself with the inside shoulder of the middle front blocker and the opponent's widest possible hitting angle. The pursuit point of LF is slightly more inside the court than that of RF.

At the pursuit point an off-blocker at RF should align her left shoulder with the ball and the right shoulder of the spiker (Figure 8-13b). Right back should align herself slightly inside the shoulder of the middle blocker closer to the net and inside the opponent's widest-possible hitting angle. This ensures that she can dig from left to right, moving toward the base line.

The line diggers at left and right back make their preparatory movement from home position to the pursuit point on a shallow arc. If the line is screened by the block, they move inside (Figure 8-12a, b). If the line is open, they move up slightly with very short steps to the pursuit point on the sideline (Figure 8-13a, b).

Areas of Responsibility

Figure 8-14 illustrates the area of responsibilities and movement path for each of the defensive players in a man-up formation against slow attacks coming from different directions.

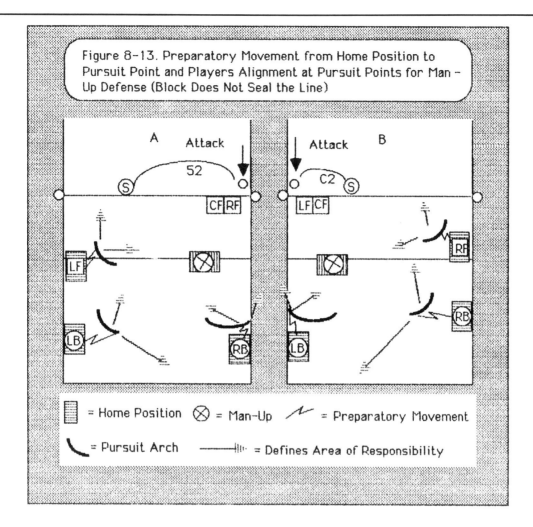

Figure 8-13. Preparatory Movement from Home Position to Pursuit Point and Players Alignment at Pursuit Points for Man – Up Defense (Block Does Not Seal the Line)

= Home Position ⊗ = Man-Up ⌁ = Preparatory Movement

= Pursuit Arch ————⊪ = Defines Area of Responsibility

ATTACK FROM OPPONENT'S LF POSITION #4 (FIGURE 8–14A) The area of responsibility for the left front off-blocker is toward the net and toward the inside of the court parallel to the net. She should not reach to her right, particularly for high balls, because there is a good chance they will be deflected out of bounds. The man-up player is responsible for tips around the block.

The crosscourt digger is responsible for balls between herself and the off-blocker, and for balls that come toward the left sideline behind the off-blocker. She is also responsible for:

• balls that come toward her and toward the left back corner;
• balls that go through the block;
• balls off the block;
• medium-speed balls that go over the block toward the base line to position #6.

The right back line digger is responsible for balls hit down the line or off the block to the outside. She is also responsible for medium-speed balls that go over the head of the man-up player. If the line is well screened by the block, then RB should shift toward the inside of the court to help guard court area #6 (Figure 8–14c).

ATTACK FROM OPPONENT'S RF POSITION #2 (FIGURE 8–14B) The man-up player is again responsible for tips around the block. The right front off-blocker retreats from the net and is responsible for balls that come to her, balls between herself and the net, and for short balls that come to her left.

The right back crosscourt digger is responsible for balls that come toward the sideline from the 10-foot line to the base line, including the back right corner. She is also responsible for guarding position #6 against balls that penetrate or pass over the block.

The left back line digger is responsible for balls that come down the line, and for balls that go over the man-up player toward the middle of the court into position M. If the line shot is screened by the block, LB should slide toward the inside of the court to help guard position #6 (Figure 8–14d).

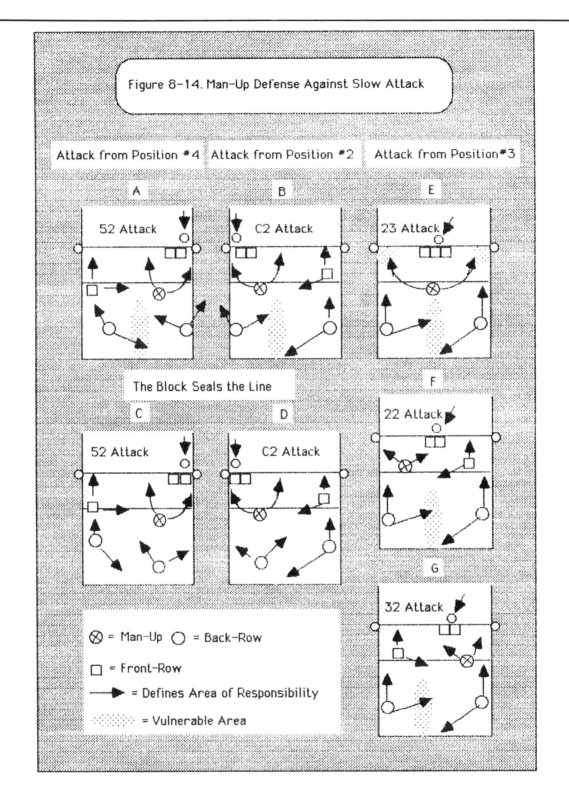

Figure 8-14. Man-Up Defense Against Slow Attack

Attack from Position #4 | Attack from Position #2 | Attack from Position #3

A — 52 Attack

B — C2 Attack

E — 23 Attack

The Block Seals the Line

C — 52 Attack

D — C2 Attack

F — 22 Attack

G — 32 Attack

⊗ = Man-Up   ○ = Back-Row

□ = Front-Row

——➤ = Defines Area of Responsibility

⋯⋯ = Vulnerable Area

Figures 8–14e, f, g illustrate the arrangement of players in the man-up formation against centered attacks. The players' areas of responsibilities are defined by the arrows.

The man-up defense system is relatively simple and clearly defines each player's court responsibilities. Since one person, the man-up player, is responsible for the tips, the other players can focus solely on hard-hit balls and deep deflections. The main weakness of this formation is that it leaves court position #6 quite vulnerable (as illustrated in Figure 8–14). Nevertheless, if the team has a big block and the opponent plays a slow attack, it is difficult for the opponent to take advantage of this weakness.

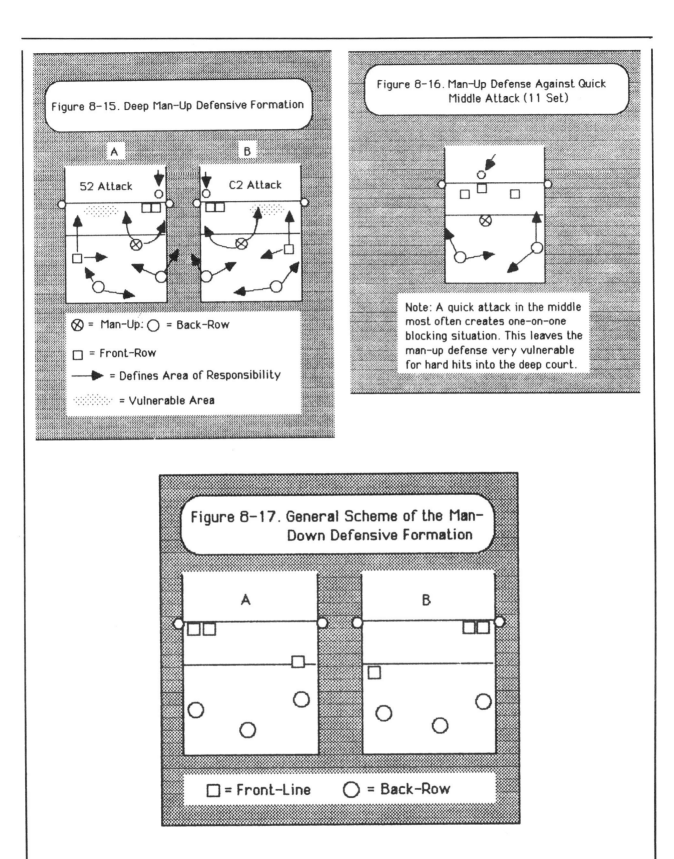

Figure 8-15. Deep Man-Up Defensive Formation

A
52 Attack

B
C2 Attack

⊗ = Man-Up: ○ = Back-Row

□ = Front-Row

→ = Defines Area of Responsibility

:::::: = Vulnerable Area

Figure 8-16. Man-Up Defense Against Quick Middle Attack (11 Set)

Note: A quick attack in the middle most often creates one-on-one blocking situation. This leaves the man-up defense very vulnerable for hard hits into the deep court.

Figure 8-17. General Scheme of the Man-Down Defensive Formation

A

B

□ = Front-Line   ○ = Back-Row

If time allows, the man-up formation can be made even stronger by having the off-blocker retreat to a deeper position behind the 10-foot line. This allows the left and right back players to retreat closer to the base line (Figure 8–15) where they can then effectively cover court position #6. The drawback is that it puts a lot of strain on the off-blocker and at times may eliminate her from transition attack because of this extra defense responsibility.

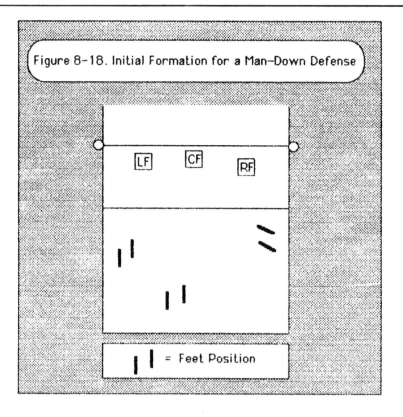

Figure 8-18. Initial Formation for a Man-Down Defense

⫼ ⫼ = Feet Position

Up until the sixties, the man-up defense system was the most commonly used. However, with the introduction of the multiple attack in the sixties, the man-up defense lost some of its attractiveness. This is because a quick attack does not give the off-blockers the time needed to retreat to their assigned defensive positions. The team is then left at times with only two defensive players, left and right back, to guard the deep court.

This is most obvious when an opponent attacks an 11 set. Often only the middle blocker has the time to jump, and the other two off-blockers have no time to retreat off the net. Figure 8–16 illustrates a situation in which the opponent attacks an 11 set and the off-blockers are not able to join the middle blocker. It is obvious that the whole court becomes exposed and vulnerable. Similar situations can occur when the opponent attacks a 31 set or employs an X play that isolates the front-line blockers.

MAN-DOWN DEFENSE

Developed to counteract the quick multiple attack, the man-down defense has become the most popular defensive formation (Figure 8–17). Instead of having the man-up player responsible for all tips behind the block, in the man-down defense that responsibility is divided among left and right back and/or the off-blocker whenever she can't retreat off the net or is released from her area of responsibility.

The man-down defense allows the defense greater flexibility in adjusting to a wide variety of attack patterns. Dividing responsibility for tip coverage allows the team to have a player at CB, in court position #6, strengthening the defense in covering the base line. Also, that player can act as a deep safety, covering behind the other two back-row players.

Initial Formation

Figure 8–18 illustrates the initial defensive formation against quick attack and the correct feet position for each player in the man-down defense. Note that CB assumes a court position left of the center of the court. The right back player stands closer to the 10-foot line than LB and farther inside the court from the sideline. Also note the similarity of the feet positions of the right back player in both the man-up and the man-down initial formations (Figure 8–10).

Adjustment to Home Positions

Figure 8–19a, b, illustrates the movement patterns from the initial formation to home positions for players in the man-down defense against high outside attacks from opponent's position #4 and #2. Each player must retreat to her home position

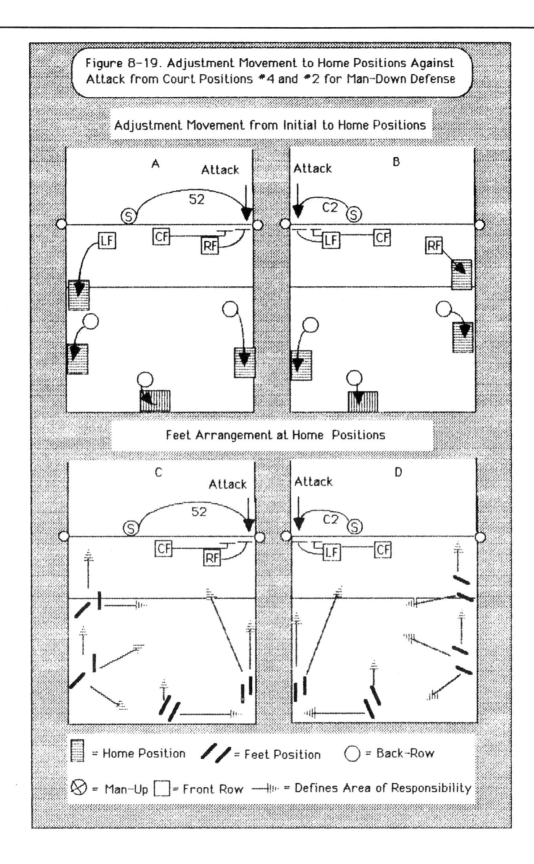

Figure 8-19. Adjustment Movement to Home Positions Against Attack from Court Positions #4 and #2 for Man-Down Defense

Adjustment Movement from Initial to Home Positions

Feet Arrangement at Home Positions

▦ = Home Position ⁄⁄ = Feet Position ◯ = Back-Row

⊗ = Man-Up ☐ = Front Row —ᴵᴵᴵ∙∙ = Defines Area of Responsibility

whether she is a crosscourt digger or the line digger. From her home position, the line digger can see whether the block has effectively sealed off the line shot. If so, she can move up behind the block to pick up tips. When the block covers the ball then she can release forward into the tip zone.

Figure 8–19c, d illustrates the feet position for players in their home positions. Note that the feet

Foot position for the RB, CB, and LB floor defenders at home position against cross-court attack. Compare with Figure 8-18.

of the left front off-blocker and the left back deep crosscourt player are in the combined staggered side-to-side position. Against an attack from position #4, these two players are almost facing the net in their home position. Also note the similarity between the man-up and man-down defense systems with respect to the feet and home positions of the right front and right back players (Figure 8–11).

Preparatory Movement/Pursuit Point

Each player makes a very slow preparatory movement from the home position to the pursuit point, timing it in such a way that when each arrives at her pursuit point the spiker is just contacting the ball. The player then sees the direction and speed of the attack and responds accordingly.

At the pursuit point, the crosscourt digger aligns herself with the block and the opponent's attacker in the same manner as in the man-up defense. The line digger retreats to her home position and, if the line is closed, moves up behind the block. Center back aligns herself with the seam of the block and the ball. If there is a hole in the block, CB must move into position behind this hole to defend balls through it.

Figure 8–20 illustrates the preparatory movement from home position to pursuit point against an attack from position #4. In general, the pursuit point for LF is about 7½ meters (24'7") from the ball, while LB and CB are about 8½ meters (27' 10") from the ball, and RB about 6½ meters (21' 4") from the ball. The right back defender can assume lower or higher positions and pursuit points, depending on her ability. A quicker player should be positioned closer to the base line than a slower one.

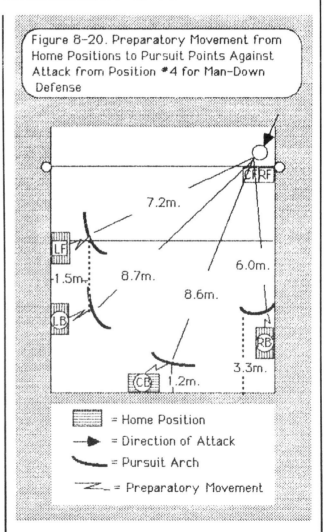

Figure 8-20. Preparatory Movement from Home Positions to Pursuit Points Against Attack from Position #4 for Man-Down Defense

7.2m.

6.0m.

1.5m.

8.7m.

8.6m.

3.3m.

1.2m.

▦ = Home Position

➡ = Direction of Attack

⌒ = Pursuit Arch

〰 = Preparatory Movement

Man-Down Defense Against Slow Outside Attack

The principle of the man-down defense against high attacks from the opponent's right and left sides is that either the line digger or the off-blocker

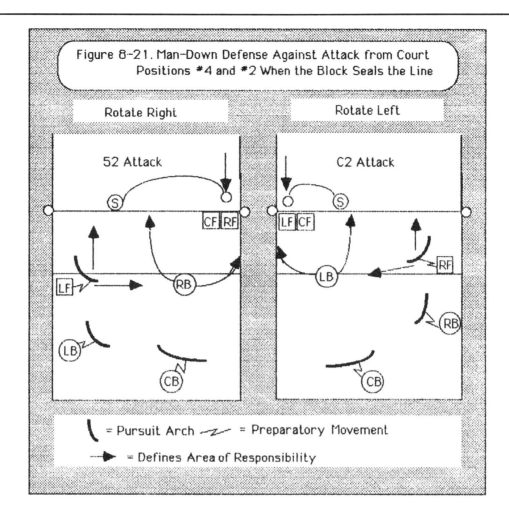

Figure 8-21. Man-Down Defense Against Attack from Court Positions #4 and #2 When the Block Seals the Line

Rotate Right

Rotate Left

52 Attack

C2 Attack

╲ = Pursuit Arch ⤳ = Preparatory Movement

⟶ = Defines Area of Responsibility

will be released to assume responsibility for covering tips behind the block. Generally, if the line shot is left open by the block, then the blockers are far enough inside the court so that the middle blocker is effectively shielding the off-blocker's area of defensive responsibility. Since the block is shielding the off-blocker from direct hits, she can move in to cover tips. Similarly, when the line is sealed off, then the off-blocker has to defend against hard-driven balls but the line digger is free to come up behind the block. Obviously, when the block does not protect either the line or the sharp-angle hit, both the line digger and off-blocker must assume a deep wide-court position against a hard hit. In this case they have to rely upon their quickness and skill to pick up short tips. In these situations, the line digger is responsible for tips behind the block (court positions #2 and #4) whereas the off-blocker is responsible for tips inside the block (court position #3).

When the line digger goes behind the block, the formation is said to rotate, to the right or to the left. When the off-blocker goes behind the block, the formation is called a "box defense."

ROTATIONAL FORMATIONS The rotate right and rotate left defensive formations are common when the opposing attacker can not hit hard down the line. This often happens when the set is wide (past the antenna) and tight to the net, or when the outside blocker is tall and/or a good jumper and the spiker can not hit over the block. Figure 8–21 illustrates the man-down left and right rotational defensive formations.

ROTATE TO THE RIGHT When the opponent sets high to position #4, the line shot should be sealed and the defending team may implement a rotate right defense. The RB line digger first retreats to her home position near the base line (Figure 8–19), then immediately moves up once the block is in position and covers around the block for short tips. Right back's forward movement should be done on a slight angle toward the inside of the court. If RB first moves to the outside, along the sideline, and then to the inside, she may be too late to recover tips in court area #3. At the same time, she may experience difficulties in retrieving balls deflected off the block outside the right side-

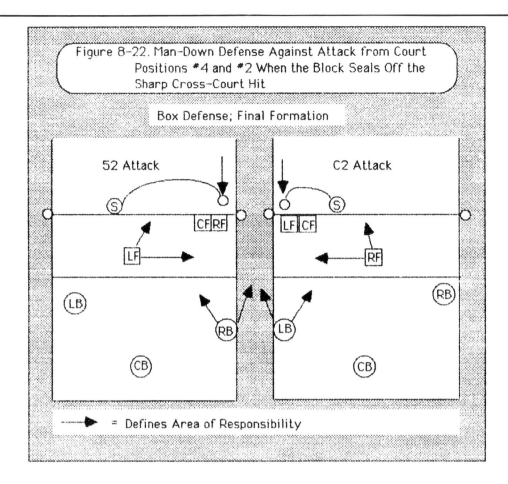

Figure 8-22. Man-Down Defense Against Attack from Court Positions #4 and #2 When the Block Seals Off the Sharp Cross-Court Hit

Box Defense; Final Formation

52 Attack

C2 Attack

------▶ = Defines Area of Responsibility

line. The line digger must carefully evaluate the situation while in the home position before moving up. The line digger's movement up behind the block should start just a fraction of a second before the opposing spiker contacts the ball.

The off-blocker adjusts back off the net to the deepest area of her home position. She is responsible for balls between herself and the net, and for short balls out in front at about the 10-foot line. Her movement is in two directions only: toward the net and into the court parallel to the net. She should not reach to the right, particularly for high balls. The deep crosscourt digger (LB) also retreats into the deep court, and CB shifts to the right to cover behind RB. All four floor-defense players swing from left to right in a circular motion. The various methods of coordinating movement among back-row defensive players is discussed in a later section.

ROTATE TO THE LEFT When the opponent sets a slow ball to court position #2, the LB line digger first retreats to her home position and then moves up to cover for short tips over and around the block (in a manner similar to what RB does when the attack comes from position #4).

The off-blocker and RB retreat away from the net to the bottom part of their home positions. Center back shifts to the left along the base line. However, because the home positions of RF and RB (Figure 8-19) against crosscourt attack are not as deep as those for LF and LB, rotation to the left is not as pronounced as rotation to the right. The right front off-blocker is responsible for balls between herself and the net, and for short balls to her left toward the 10-foot line. Notice that RF digs balls to her left while the LF off-blocker should avoid digging to her right. This is because of angle considerations in relation to the target as explained previously and illustrated in Figure 8-8.

The Box Defense

Figure 8-22 illustrates a box defense formation. The box defense is more common when the set is off the net and the block seals the crosscourt shot, or when the opponent uses a quick attack. (This is covered in detail in the next section on situational defense.) The box defense should also be used when the CF blocker is a tall, effective blocker, but the outside blockers are short or not good jumpers. In addition, when an outside set does not go all the way to the sideline, the block will be positioned a few feet inside the court. This is another situation

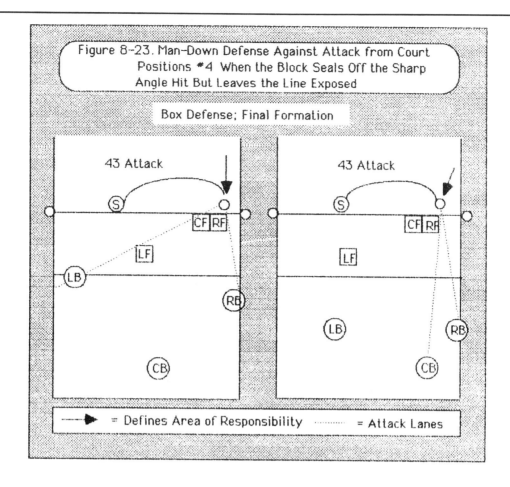

Figure 8–23. Man–Down Defense Against Attack from Court Positions #4 When the Block Seals Off the Sharp Angle Hit But Leaves the Line Exposed

Box Defense; Final Formation

43 Attack

43 Attack

⟶ = Defines Area of Responsibility   ⋯⋯ = Attack Lanes

where the box defense should be used.

Whenever the line is open, the possibility of a sharp crosscourt hit to the off-blocker's area should be sealed off by the middle blocker. The off-blocker first adjusts to her home position and then immediately moves closer to the block to cover tips. The line digger also adjusts to her home position. If the line is completely exposed for a direct hit, the line digger must stay deep. However, if the line is partially vulnerable, the line digger must move up along the sideline until she sees the ball behind the block (Figure 8–23). In the box defense arrangement, the off-blocker and the line digger share the responsibility of covering tips behind and on either side of the block. While the off-blocker is responsible for tips behind and inside the CF blocker, the line digger is responsible for tips near the sideline. She must also pursue balls deflected off the block outside the court.

Occasionally, the off-blocker must assume total responsibility for tip coverage behind the block. This situation may occur when a very short outside blocker is playing against an opposing spiker who can comfortably hit over her. This forces the line digger to stay deep and puts tip-coverage responsibility on the off-blocker. Whenever possi-

ble, it is recommended not to fully commit the off-blockers for tip coverage, especially if they are LF ace players. Retrieving tips may eliminate these ace spikers from the transition attack. The box defense is more common against attack from opponent's court position #2 than from position #4.

Coordinating the Floor Defense/Areas of Responsibility

Whether a rotational or box defense is used, when the opponent attacks from positions #4 or #2, there are three possible methods for coordinating movement and allocating areas of responsibility among the three back-row floor defenders.

THE CROSSCOURT DIGGER OVERLOAD (FIGURE 8–24) This method is probably the most common method of coordinating the defense. The success of the crosscourt overload method depends greatly on the ability of the right and left back players. The off-blocker's responsibility is similar to that described previously (see "Rotate to the Right" and "Rotate to the Left" and "The Box Defense").

When the attack comes from position #4 (Figure 8–24), the crosscourt digger retreats to her home

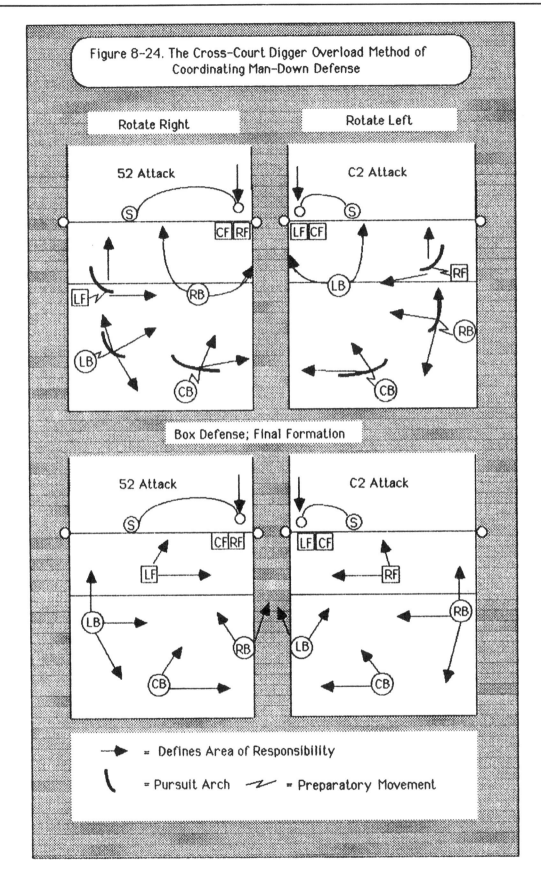

Figure 8-24. The Cross-Court Digger Overload Method of Coordinating Man-Down Defense

Rotate Right

Rotate Left

52 Attack

C2 Attack

Box Defense; Final Formation

52 Attack

C2 Attack

→ = Defines Area of Responsibility

= Pursuit Arch   = Preparatory Movement

position, positioning herself inside the left shoulder of the CF blocker. She is the only player who

moves in three directions. She digs to her left (between herself and the LF off-blocker, and also be-

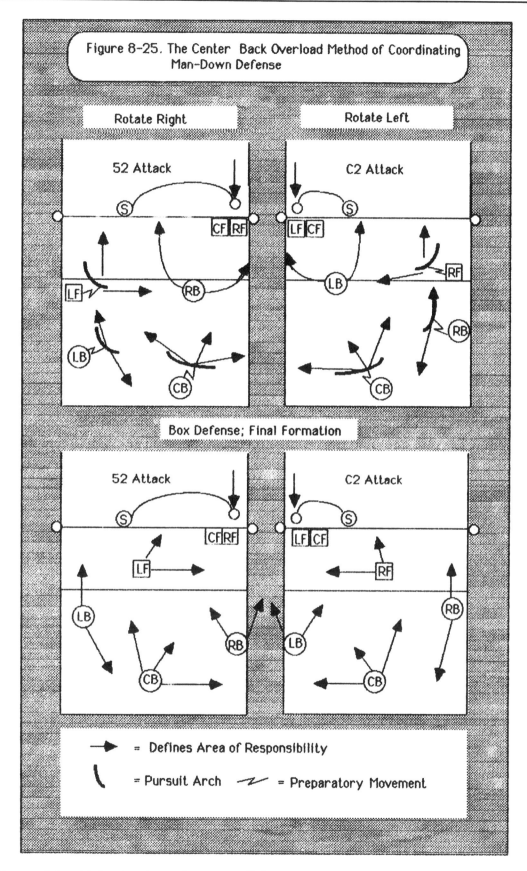

Figure 8-25. The Center Back Overload Method of Coordinating Man-Down Defense

Rotate Right

52 Attack

Rotate Left

C2 Attack

Box Defense; Final Formation

52 Attack

C2 Attack

→ = Defines Area of Responsibility

(= Pursuit Arch   ⌐ = Preparatory Movement

hind LF toward the sideline), to her right (to cut off the corner), and forward toward the middle of the court, court position M (Figure 8–6), for tips and soft shots. If the LF off-blocker moves inside and

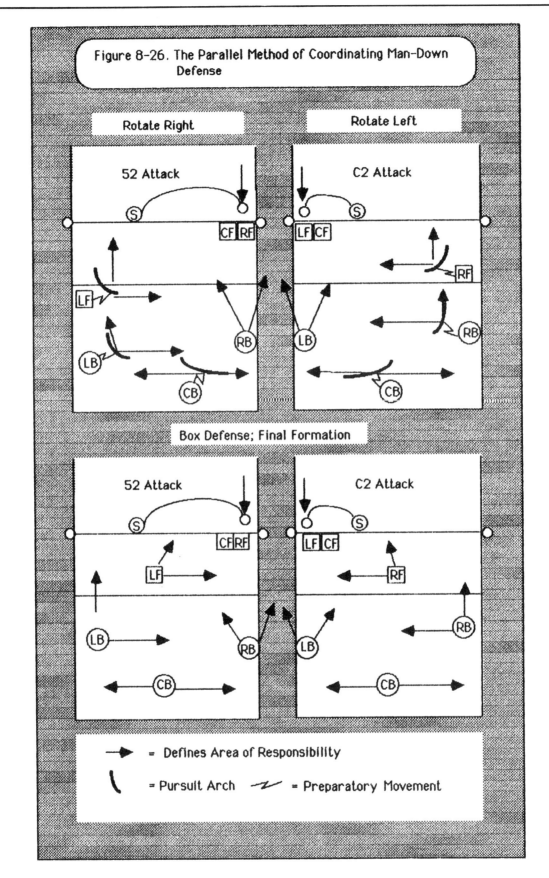

Figure 8-26. The Parallel Method of Coordinating Man-Down Defense

Rotate Right

52 Attack

Rotate Left

C2 Attack

Box Defense; Final Formation

52 Attack

C2 Attack

→ = Defines Area of Responsibility

(= Pursuit Arch   ⤳ = Preparatory Movement

closer to the block (box defense), the LB must also cover LF's area against medium-speed balls and soft shots going toward the left sideline. Center back guards court position #6 behind the seam of

242

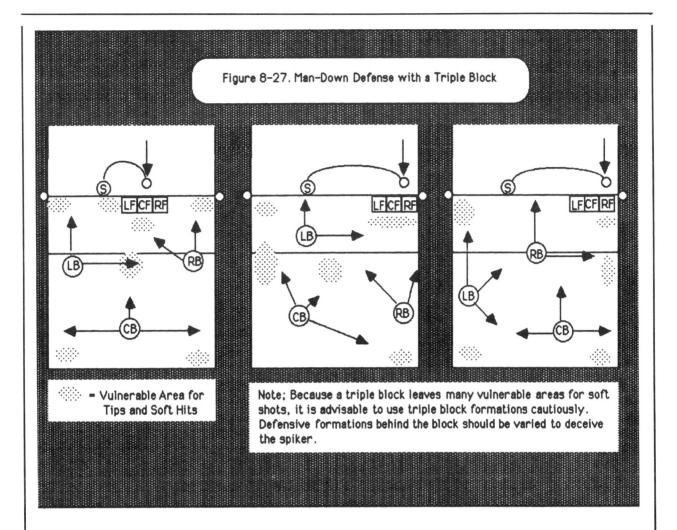

Figure 8-27. Man-Down Defense with a Triple Block

:::: = Vulnerable Area for Tips and Soft Hits

Note; Because a triple block leaves many vulnerable areas for soft shots, it is advisable to use triple block formations cautiously. Defensive formations behind the block should be varied to deceive the spiker.

the block and picks up any ball that goes through, over, or off the block to this position.

Center back is also responsible for guarding court position #1 and court position MR (middle right) behind the right back player when RB moves up behind the block in the rotate-to-the-right defense. The center back player must work in close coordination with the right back player and observe whether the right back is positioned deep or has moved up behind the block. Whichever area is left by the RB should be picked up by the CB. The right back line digger guards the line and covers behind the block for tips. Her position and movement are determined by whether her area is screened off by the block or exposed to a hard down-the-line hit, as explained previously.

When the attack comes from position #2 (Figure 8–24), the deep crosscourt digger (RB) retreats to her home position. The home position of the RB crosscourt digger is a little closer to the net than that of the LB crosscourt digger. The right back digger positions herself inside the right shoulder of

the CF blocker in such a manner that a wide crosscourt hit will come to her left side. Such positioning creates a better angle of deflection for directing the dug ball to the target. Right back is responsible for hard-hit balls to the right sideline, tips to the middle, and hard-hit balls to the right back corner. Center back is responsible for guarding position #6 and also positions #5 and ML behind left back whenever LB moves up behind the block. Left back guards the line and behind the block. If the line is not sealed, she stays deep (box defense) but if the line is screened off, she moves behind the block (rotate to the left).

THE CENTER BACK OVERLOAD (FIGURE 8–25)

When CB is a superior defensive player, the coach can broaden her area of responsibility by having her guard the base line, pick up balls in the middle of the court, and play in front of the left back or right back player. The left and right back players then become responsible only for deep attacks to the sidelines and corners. In this method only center back has the responsibility of moving in three directions.

THE PARALLEL METHOD (FIGURE 8–26) From 1980 to 1984 the USA women's team used this method in certain rotations and we found that it worked very well. It's a very effective method when the middle blocker is strong and tall and the outside blockers are fairly weak. Three players— the off-blocker, the deep crosscourt digger, and center back—move parallel to each other.

The court is divided into lanes of 10 feet each. The hard sharp-angled crosscourt shots hit toward the corner or the sideline should be intercepted by left or right back, while medium-speed shots that are longer and loftier are picked up by CB. Right and left back are responsible for picking up balls in the middle of the court. The line digger plays the hard down-the-line shots and covers short tips over the block near the sideline. The off-blocker picks up tips inside the block toward position #3 and those in the seam between positions #3 and M.

Man/Down Defense Against Slow Attack in the Middle

Figure 8–27 illustrates the basic formation for floor defense against slow attack using three blockers. As the diagram shows, a triple block leaves many court areas vulnerable for soft tips and off-speed shots. To hide these areas, I recommend frequent altering or adjustment of the defensive formation. One time LB and RB may move close to the block; at other times only LB may move up, while RB stays deeper in the court. It is also important that CB stays in her back-court position, sees the ball first, and then responds, instead of playing a guessing game. The center back defender must stay close to the base line and run down the long off-speed shots that come over or off the block. Remember, forward movement is quicker than backward movement. Once CB has moved too far up, the corners are wide open for medium-speed hits.

Situational Defense

I like to refer to most defense as "situational defense" because the defensive players must continually adjust and respond to each individual attack situation presented by the opponent. The man-down defense is a flexible defensive formation that works well for situational defense and should be used by teams at a high level of play.

Actually, certain adjustments of the man-down defense formation create arrangements similar to the man-up formation, especially against high attack. The arrangement used to defend against the attack is the same, but different players assume the various court positions. Against quick attack the arrangement of these two methods should be the same, but the man-up formation is not flexible enough to allow it. The man-down formation should most often be used to defend a quick attack.

Up to now, we have dealt primarily with defensive formations against an outside attack in nonemergency situations, where each player has the time to go through the optimum defensive sequence: from the initial formation to the home position to the pursuit point and finally, the actual pursuit and play of the ball. However, when playing against a quick attack, quite often the players do not have the time to go through this entire sequence. Instead, they must go directly to the pursuit point. Figure 8–28 illustrates two possible adjustment sequences against outside attack: one for nonemergency (slow attack) and one for emergency (quick attack).

In the emergency sequence, the defensive player must make sure that upon arriving at the pursuit point the body is leaning forward. The player doesn't start pursuit until the ball is hit and its direction is clear. The preparatory movement from the initial position to the pursuit point is usually very limited, done by backpedaling or side-shuffle steps. In any case, each player should make her best effort to retreat as close as possible to the home position. Again, the feet position should orient her toward her area of responsibility. Defensive success in emergency situations greatly depends on the ability of the players to retreat fast enough to give more depth to their defensive play and to squeeze the court from the outside in. The see-and-respond concept always applies.

Figure 8–29 illustrates the differences between man-down formations in nonemergency and emergency situations. It also shows the similarities and differences between the final defensive formations in response to attack from different locations— outside attack versus inside attack for both quick and slow sets. Figure 8–29a, d illustrates simple rotations to the left and right against outside attack.

Figure 8–29b, c illustrates the formations against a slow middle attack that does not come in combination, in which case two blockers are up. The players retreat first to their home positions and then adjust to their pursuit points, now slightly different. The off-blocker moves closer to the block because it covers her area of responsibility. Right or left back moves up slightly closer to the net to

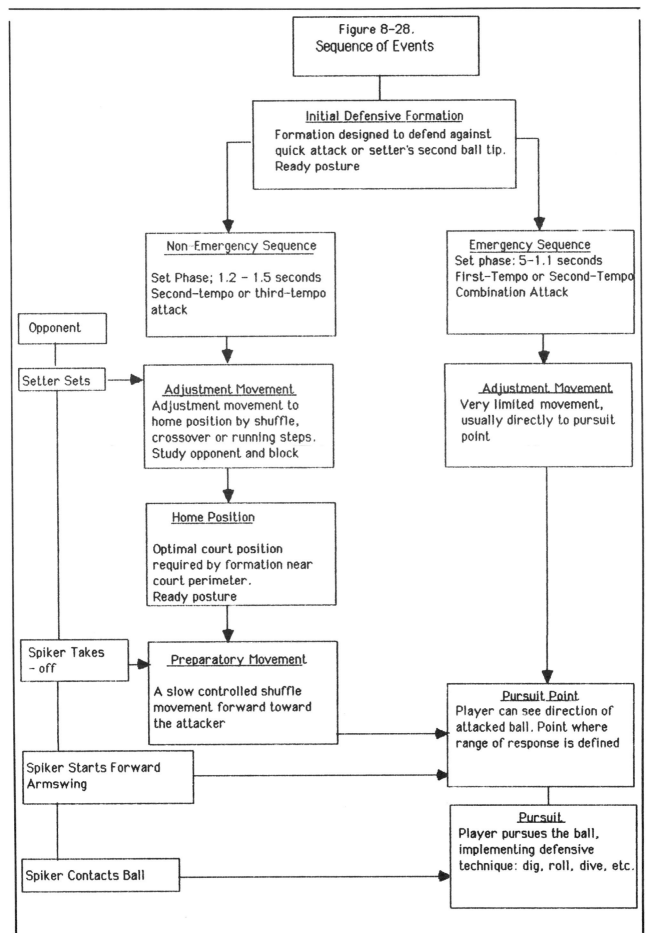

Figure 8-28.
Sequence of Events

Initial Defensive Formation
Formation designed to defend against quick attack or setter's second ball tip.
Ready posture

Non-Emergency Sequence
Set Phase; 1.2 – 1.5 seconds
Second-tempo or third-tempo attack

Emergency Sequence
Set phase: 5–1.1 seconds
First-Tempo or Second-Tempo Combination Attack

Opponent

Setter Sets

Adjustment Movement
Adjustment movement to home position by shuffle, crossover or running steps.
Study opponent and block

Adjustment Movement
Very limited movement, usually directly to pursuit point

Home Position
Optimal court position required by formation near court perimeter.
Ready posture

Spiker Takes – off

Preparatory Movement
A slow controlled shuffle movement forward toward the attacker

Pursuit Point
Player can see direction of attacked ball. Point where range of response is defined

Spiker Starts Forward Armswing

Pursuit
Player pursues the ball, implementing defensive technique: dig, roll, dive, etc.

Spiker Contacts Ball

245

guard against tips to court positions #2 and #4 respectively. Center back stays deep and guards the entire base line. These formations are box formations in which responsibility for short tips is shared between the off-blocker and line digger on the opposite sideline.

In emergency situations, against quick sets and a multiple-combination attack, the defensive players should anticipate holes in the block, or even the likelihood of only a one-player block. The effectiveness of the defense then greatly depends on quick movement of the off-blockers. The quick attack attempts to isolate them and prevent them from participating in the floor defense. The off-blockers must counter by retreating quickly to the pursuit point, or toward the block as in a box defense, to guard against tips. The line diggers must retreat from their initial formation back toward the base line to avoid leaving the floor defense with only two defensive players against hard spikes.

When the opponent attacks a 51 set (Figure 8–29h), RB retreats back as close to the home position as time allows. Center back shifts to the right behind the block. Left back's movement is synchronized with the center front blocker; if CF appears to be able to close the hole in the block, LB should stay wider at the home position. If CF jumps but leaves a hole in the block or does not jump at all, then LB should establish a pursuit point closer to the center of the court.

When the opponent attacks a 31 set (Figure 8–29g), LF retreats off the net in a slight circular movement toward the block. Right back must retreat back at least two steps on an angle to the sideline. Both the off-blocker (LF) and RB guard against tips on either side of and behind the block. Center back shifts to the right and defends behind the seam of the block. Left back moves to her pursuit point, guarding against crosscourt hits to the left sideline and to the deep corner.

When the opponent attacks an 11 set (Figure 8–29f), unless she can get over in time to block, RF is responsible for tips behind the block. (Remember, with a floating numbering system for the attack zones, if the pass pulls the setter toward the center of the court, a quick set directly in front of the setter is still an 11 set, but it is now hit at a point along the net where RF may be able to participate in blocking.) Center back stands in her initial position off to the left of the center of the court and guards the seam behind the block. Left back, in anticipation of an 11 attack, may step back toward the baseline, observing the left front blocker. If the left front blocker jumps, LB is released forward to guard against tips in court position #4. The block is the most important part of the defense for stop-

ping the 11 attack. Soft blocking strategy, in conjunction with the see-and-respond tactic, may improve the chances of the defense to defend against 11 sets.

When the opponent attacks the quick backset (A1 or C1) (Figure 8–29e), it's very difficult to defend against because of its great speed. To defend against the C1 attack, the initial defensive formation can be modified only a little. Center back makes a step toward the center of the court and positions herself with her right foot to face the spiker. Her main responsibility is to guard the middle of the court against tips and hard hits and to dig hard-hit balls coming to her left by moving toward the base line. Left back retreats toward the base line and positions herself about a foot from the sideline. Right front moves toward the block, as in a box defense, to pick up tips, while RB retreats to home position and is responsible for crosscourt hits toward the sideline and deep in the corner. This is a unique formation in which CB plays a major role in digging short balls that come toward the center court, while RB digs the long crosscourt shots.

Situational Defense with a One-Player Block

Occasionally, only one player forms the block. Sometimes it's on purpose for tactical considerations. At other times, in emergency situations only the blocker nearest the set has time to respond. When only an outside blocker jumps, CF should be responsible to fall off the net and cover tips behind the block.

Figure 8–30 illustrates floor-defense formations with only one blocker in a nonemergency situation. Figure 8–31 illustrates floor-defense formations with only one blocker in an emergency situation. The primary difference between the two is that in the nonemergency formation, the off-blocker (either right or left front) can retreat all the way back to the home position. In an emergency situation lack of time keeps the off-blockers fairly close to the net.

A team should not use the man-up defense if it intends to employ primarily a one-player block (for the same reason that a team that plays against a quick-multiple attack should not use the man-up defense). Generally, at beginning levels, it's better to have only one blocker up than two blockers with a hole in the block. However, at a more advanced level, it's better to have two blockers up, even if they can not assemble a solid block. Then it becomes the responsibility of the defensive players to recognize that a hole in the block exists and

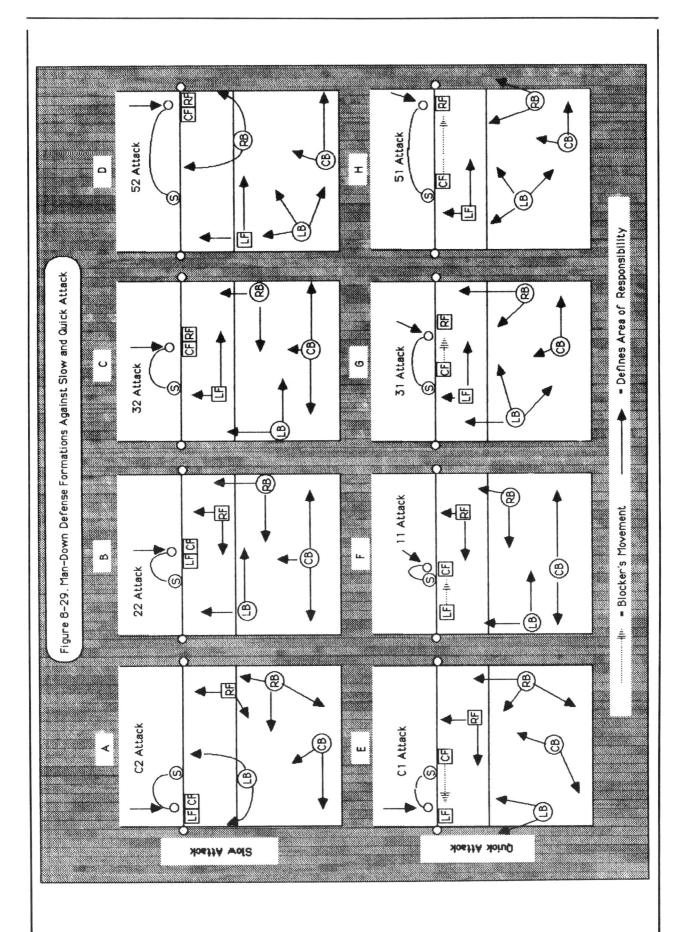

Figure 8-29. Man-Down Defense Formations Against Slow and Quick Attack

247

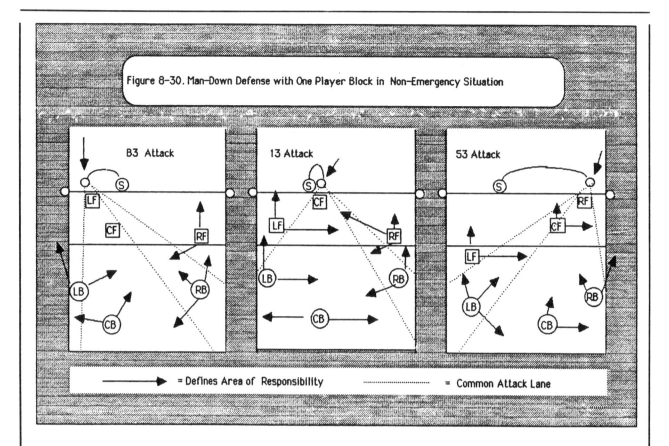

Figure 8-30. Man-Down Defense with One Player Block in Non-Emergency Situation

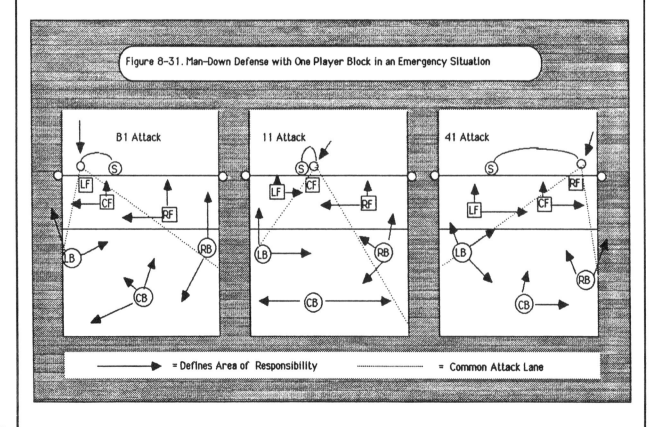

Figure 8-31. Man-Down Defense with One Player Block in an Emergency Situation

create a kind of pocket defense around the hole.

Combined Man-Up and Man-Down Defense Formations

At times, a team can combine the man-up and man-down defense formations.

When the setter is back row in a 5–1 team composition, the team may prefer to play with the setter as a man-up player. Then when the setter is front row, the team can use the man-down formation. Obviously, this is possible only when playing against a slow attack and trying to conceal the vulnerability of the man-up defense.

Another possible way to combine the two systems is to play man-up only when the attack comes from the opponent's position #4, and play man-down when the attack comes from the opponent's position #2. This is quite a good solution when playing against an opponent who runs a straight attack with a quick C1 backset and a fairly slow 51 forward set (or second tempo).

In addition, a team can occasionally consider allowing CB to come up behind the block against high sets (Figure 8–32). Center back penetration behind the block should be considered against high sets from a man-down formation when the center front blocker is very tall and effective while the outside blockers are weak. This often happens when a short setter is front line in a 5–1 team composition.

A team may use a combined man-up and man-down defense formation in different phases of the game. For example, against the opponent's serve-reception attack, the team may implement a man-down defense, while against the opponent's transition attack the team may use a man-up defense. This is an effective strategy against teams that don't have good transition attack, especially if they have only two front-row attackers. It is also effective when the defensive team chooses to have the setter play behind the block in order to speed up their own quick transition attack.

Often a team that uses a 5–1 team composition will find that the opponent tries to attack the setter as often as possible whenever the setter is back row. In this case, the coach should consider alternating between the man-up and man-down defense to make it more difficult for the opponent to locate and attack the setter.

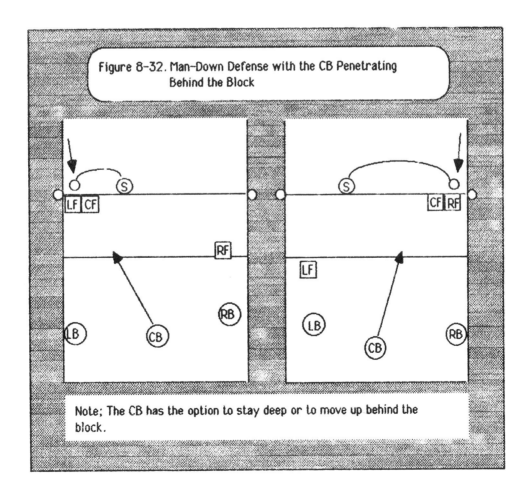

Figure 8-32. Man-Down Defense with the CB Penetrating Behind the Block

Note: The CB has the option to stay deep or to move up behind the block.

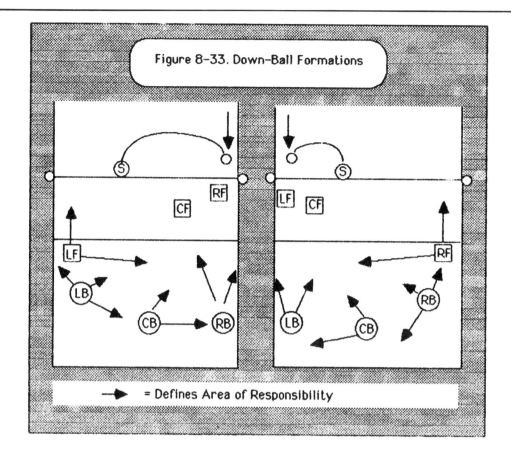

Figure 8-33. Down-Ball Formations

= Defines Area of Responsibility

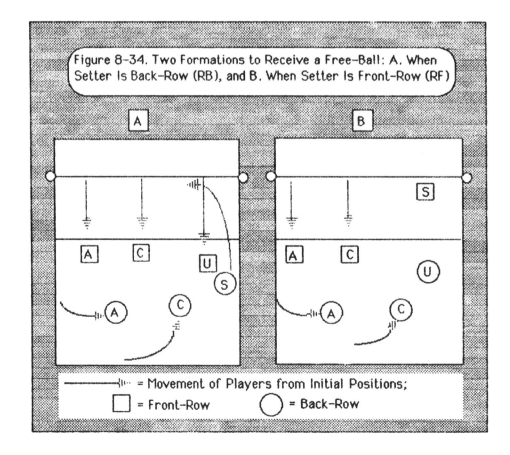

Figure 8-34. Two Formations to Receive a Free-Ball: A. When Setter Is Back-Row (RB), and B. When Setter Is Front-Row (RF)

= Movement of Players from Initial Positions;
☐ = Front-Row   ◯ = Back-Row

Down-Ball Defensive Formations

Sometimes the opponent's spiker is not in position to jump and hit a hard, sharply angled spike; maybe the set was too far off the net, or the spiker was occupied on defense and could not recover in time to make an approach. In this situation, the defense should call "down ball" and immediately move back to cover the court, especially the back 12 to 15 feet. Figure 8–33 illustrates the down-ball defensive formations.

If the setter is back row on a down-ball play, she must first participate in the floor defense and then move to the target for setting after making sure that the ball is not coming to her. The center blocker should quickly retreat toward the 10-foot line in a position approximately in line with where the ball will cross the net. It is her job to watch for soft hits and balls that bounce off the top of the net. The front-row player diagonally opposite to the spiker is responsible for covering the middle of the court.

Free Ball

When the opponent can not attack the ball or play it over the net as a down ball, but must instead save it with a high lob, the defensive team should call "free ball" and immediately assume formations similar to serve-reception formations. Figure 8–34 illustrates two formations to receive a free ball, one when the setter is front row, and one when she is at RB. Generally, a free ball should be passed to the setter with the overhead finger-passing technique. If it is lobbed very deep in the corner, the underhand passing technique may be

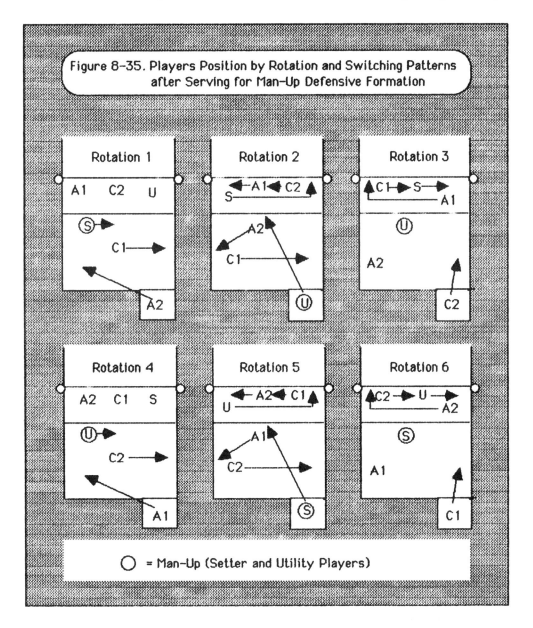

required, especially for young players who lack the strength and control to overhand-pass a long distance. The free-ball pass should have a low trajectory but still be high enough for the setter to attack or jump-set.

A team should practice its free-ball plays until it can score at least a 90 percent success ratio on free-ball opportunities. A free ball is really a gift the team should be able to exploit.

Switching for Player Specialization

In Chapter 6, "The Attack," it was shown how players can switch during the attack or spiker coverage into their specialized front-row and back-row positions—ace players moving to LF, center players moving to CF, and the setter or utility player to RF. It's also been shown and discussed how players switch from the serve-reception attack through spiker coverage into their defensive positions in the back row—ace players to LB, center players to CB, and the setter or utility player to RB.

Figures 8–35 and 8–36 show the players' positions during the serve, and their switching patterns into the initial defensive formation for man-up and man-down formations respectively. Obviously, some adjustments of these switching patterns have to be made, in particular when the ace player serves from a very long distance behind the end-line and can not make it all the way to the left back

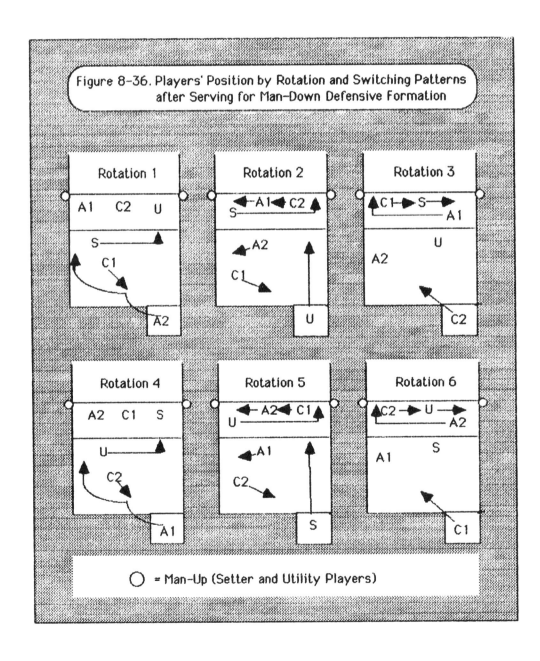

Figure 8–36. Players' Position by Rotation and Switching Patterns after Serving for Man-Down Defensive Formation

Rotation 1

A1　C2　U

S———▲

C1

A2

Rotation 2

S——◄A1◄C2▲

▲A2　▲

C1

U

Rotation 3

▲C1►S►

———A1

U

A2

C2

Rotation 4

A2　C1　S

U———▲

C2

A1

Rotation 5

U◄A2◄C1▲

◄A1　▲

C2

S

Rotation 6

◄C2►U►

———A2

A1　S

C1

O = Man-Up (Setter and Utility Players)

positions quickly. In this case, she can go first to the center in one move and then, during the transition attack, switch through the spiker coverage to her defensive position.

Reading the Opponent's Attack

In reading the opponent's attack, the defensive players should look for the following cues:

1. *The relationship between block and the opposing spiker.* Whatever area is not covered by the block must be compensated for by a defensive player. From the home position or from wherever she happens to be in the court at the time, the defensive player has to evaluate the effectiveness of the block against the attack, and then get into position to cover holes or vulnerable areas.
2. *The distance of the ball from the net.* The farther the ball is from the net, the deeper the defensive formation can be.
3. *The spiker's relationship with the ball.* The defensive player has to carefully analyze the relationship between the ball and the shoulder of the hitting arm. If a shot down the line is impossible, the digger should move up behind the block. If the crosscourt hard hit is impossible,

the crosscourt digger should move over to the middle.
4. *The spiker's approach pattern.* At the beginning level of volleyball, the approach pattern of the spiker may reveal her intention. A straight-down-the-line approach usually means a hit down the line. An out-to-in approach usually means a crosscourt hit. Well-trained spikers can hit line or crosscourt shots from either approach. The defensive player should try to observe the position of the spiker's feet on takeoff. From the opponent's position #4, if the feet are square with the net, a hit down the line should be expected. If the left foot of a right-handed spiker is considerably in front and closer to the center court than the right foot, a crosscourt hit is likely.
5. *The eye direction of the spiker.* Some spikers look at the spiking target before their approach.
6. *The arm swing of the spiker.* The defensive player must key in on both the ball and the arm swing of the spiker to detect its direction and speed.
7. *The jump.* The explosiveness and balance of the spiker during her jump could be a cue for whether the spiker intends to hit a hard or soft shot. Usually when the spiker is in an off-balance position, she will tend to hit a controlled shot, a soft hit, or a tip.

APPENDICES A & B

APPENDIX A: Summary Statistics Sheet

OPPONENT: _____ LOCATION: _____ DATE: _____

FINAL SCORE: _____

TEAM	PLAYER'S NAME	TOTAL ATTACK					SERVE RECEIVE ATTACK				TRANSITION ATTACK						BLOCK		SERVE		OTHER ERRORS	
		%	TA	TPT	TSO	TE	%	A	SO	EPT	%	A	PT	SO	EPT	ESO	PT	SO	PT	E	PT	SO
TEAM 1	1.																					
	2.																					
	3.																					
	4.																					
	5.																					
	6.																					
	7.																					
	8.																					
	9.																					
	10.																					
	11.																					
	12.																					
	TOTAL																					
TEAM 2	1.																					
	2.																					
	3.																					
	4.																					
	5.																					
	6.																					
	7.																					
	8.																					
	9.																					
	10.																					
	11.																					
	12.																					
	TOTAL																					

T = Total ; PT = Point; SO = Side-Out; E = Error; A = Attempt (ball kept in play); Other Errors = Officials' Calls

APPENDIX A: Passing Statistics

OPPONENT: _____ LOCATION: _____ DATE: _____

FINAL SCORE: _____

EXAMPLE: Calculation of Passing Efficiency

Efficiency =

$$\dfrac{\left[(7\times5) + (2\times4) + (1\times3) + (1\times1) + (1\times0)\right]}{5 \times 12} \times 100 = 78\,\%$$

Score $= \dfrac{5 \times 78}{100} = 3.9$

PASS RATINGS

5 = A perfect pass
4 = A low pass to the target
3 = A pass off the target but within the 10' zone
2 = A pass behind the 10' zone, quick combinations are not possible
1 = A pass that goes over the net
0 = An Ace

TEAM	PLAYERS NAME	PASS RATINGS 5	4	3	2	1	0	SUM	SCORE	EFFICIENCY
TEAM 1	1.	#####	||					12	3.9	78%
	2.									
	3.									
	4.									
	5.									
	6.									
	7.									
	8.									
	9.									
	10.									
	11.									
	12.									
	TOTAL									
TEAM 2	1.									
	2.									
	3.									
	4.									
	5.									
	6.									
	7.									
	8.									
	9.									
	10.									
	11.									
	12.									
	TOTAL									

257

APPENDIX A: Equations to Calculate Attack Efficiency

Serve-Receive Attack Efficiency (%) = $\left(\dfrac{SO}{A + SO + EPT} \right) \times 100$

Transition Attack Efficiency (%) = $\left(\dfrac{SO + PT}{A + PT + SO + EPT + ESO} \right) \times 100$

Total Attack Efficiency (%) = $\left(\dfrac{TPT + TSO}{TA + TPT + TSO + TE} \right) \times 100$

APPENDIX B : Statistical Sheet by Rotation

ROTATION		Front Row — Attackers (LF CF RF), %	Front Row — Attackers (LF CF RF), %	Front Row — Attackers (LF CF RF), %	Front Row — Attackers (LF CF RF), %	Front Row — Attackers (LF CF RF), %	Front Row — Attackers (LF CF RF), %	Front Row — Attackers (LF CF RF), %	TOTALS (P, %)
GAME 1	1								
	2								
	3								
	4								
	5								
GAME 2	1								
	2								
	3								
	4								
	5								
TOTAL									

INDEX

A

Ace players, 14, 15, 58, 102, 123, 151, 163, 165
  alignments and arrangements of, 16, 19
Aces, 23
Alignments, 15–22, 35
  considerations for, 17
  defined, 15
  diagonally balanced, 16–17, 19–20
Angle approach in attack, 112
Arm-extension dig, 214–217
Arms
  in blocking, 175–176
  nonhitting, 94–95
  in spiking, 92–95, 97, 102
Arrangements, 15–22
  balanced, 16
  blocking and, 173, 192, 199
  defined, 15–16
  serve-reception formations, 37, 49–62
Attacks, attackers, 2, 5, 8–9, 14, 85–169. *See also*
    specific attacks
  additional techniques for, 125–128
  approach patterns in, 112, 113
  changes in, 8–9
  concealed formation, 156, 163, 172
  defined, 8, 85
  fake approach in, 112, 113, 125–126, 132, 137–140,
    162–163, 164
  individual, 86–102
  organization of, 148–167
  pump in, 126–127
  sequence parallel in, 132, 134
  setter's penetration to target after, 67–68
  slide in, 127–128
  spiker coverage and, 163, 167–169
  sting in, 132, 134, 135, 139

switching players into specialized positions for,
  163–165
tandem play in, 132, 133–134
team formations for. *See* multiple (combination)
  attacks
trick play in, 126, 145, 146

B

Back roll, 76
Back-row attack, 21–22, 97, 103, 115, 147–148
  in multiple attack, 128, 130
  second-tempo sets in, 123, 124
Backsetting, 65, 70, 82, 124, 147
Balls, 3–4, 42, 224. *See also* Serves, serving; Sets,
  setting
  Bernoulli's effect and, 24–25
  calling, 54
  contact with, 27, 29, 30, 45–46, 64, 73, 96, 177–178
  cushioning of, 4, 48–49, 212, 226
  down, 165, 204, 250, 251
  in emergency passing, 48
  free, 117, 165, 250, 251–252
  movement to, in blocking, 178–181
  in nonemergency passing, 46–48
  pursuit of, in defense, 209–212
  rebound, recovery of, 3–4, 48–49, 82
  spin of, 3, 25–26, 27, 30, 31, 48–49, 82, 96, 104–106,
    124, 125, 212, 226
  sweet spot of, 27, 30
Beal, Doug, 151
Bernoulli's effect, 24–25
Blocks, blocking, 5, 6, 9–10, 77, 81, 82, 113, 171–204.
    See also Commit blocking, Double blocking;
    Man-to-man blocking
  adjustments for, 200–204
  arm and hand position in, 175–176

J

Jumps
  biomechanical analysis of two-foot takeoff for, 99–102
  in blocking, 174, 176, 204
Jump set, 78–79, 114, 117, 121, 166
Jump-spike serve, 6, 25, 31–33
  serve reception and, 58, 61–62
Jury, 12

K

Kill (attack) block, 9, 171, 183–184
Knee drop, 222

L

Lay-out, 219
LB (left back) players, 4–5, 16, 20–21, 46, 61, 67, 160
  in back-row attack, 147, 148
  defense and, 209, 223, 226, 230, 234, 238, 242, 243, 244, 246
  in W formation, 52–54
Lead attackers, 132–140
LF (left front) players, 4–5, 15, 16, 20–21, 61, 68, 73, 74, 123, 125, 148
  attack organization and, 159, 160, 161, 162, 166
  attack patterns of, 112
  blocking and, 172, 173, 189, 191–194, 199–200
  defense and, 209, 226, 231, 239–242, 246, 252
  in first-tempo sets, 119, 120
  in sequential combinations, 133
  in W formation, 52–54
Line arrangement, 173, 192, 199
Line defense, 206
Linesmen, 12
Loop approach, in attack, 112

M

Magers, Rose, 120
Man-down defense, 10, 209, 210, 234–253
  adjustment to home positions in, 234–236
  box defense in, 238–239
  center back overload in, 243–244
  coordination/areas of responsibility in, 239–244
  crosscourt digger overload in, 239–243
  down-ball, 250, 251
  free-ball, 250, 251–252

initial formation in, 234
man-up combined with, 249
parallel method in, 244
preparatory movement/pursuit point in, 236
reading the opponent's attack in, 253
rotation in, 237–238
as situational defense, 244–249
against slow middle attack, 244
against slow outside attack, 236–238
switching players and, 251, 252–253
Man-to-man blocking, 192, 198–200
  line arrangement-commit, 199
  stacked arrangement-commit, 200
  stacked arrangement-see-and-respond, 199–200
Man-up defense, 10, 226–234
  adjustment to home position in, 228–230
  areas of responsibility in, 230–234
  initial formation in, 228
  man-down combined with, 249
  preparatory movement/pursuit point in, 230, 231
Mental preparations, 17, 34, 37, 49
Minus-tempo sets, 108, 116, 119, 123
Multiple (combination) attacks, 9, 123, 128–148, 207
  back-row attack in, 128, 130
  deceptive approach patterns in, 130, 142
  double quick combinations, 119, 129–132, 141–142
  sequential combinations. See sequential combination attacks
  slow vs. quick, 128
  tactical considerations for, 165–167
  three-spiker, 140–147
  two-spiker, 130–137

N

Nets, 3, 82, 176, 224
Number method, 151–161
  serve-reception attack and, 151–159
  transition attack and, 160–161

O

Off-blocker, 204, 226, 227, 233, 238
Off-speed shots, 106
Officials, roles of, 12
One-hand bump, 224
One-hand dig, 37, 221
One-hand set, 79
One-leg takeoff, 79, 103–104, 127–128
Option blocking method, 195–197
Option players, 14, 15, 16, 20
Overhand serving techniques, 6, 24, 26–30
  float serve, 26–29

PHOTO CREDITS